Mass Media, Mass Propaganda

Mass Media, Mass Propaganda

Examining American News in the "War on Terror"

ANTHONY R. DIMAGGIO

LEXINGTON BOOKS

A division of
ROWMAN & LITTLEFIELD PUBLISHERS, INC.
Lanham • Boulder • New York • Toronto • Plymouth, UK

LEXINGTON BOOKS

A division of Rowman & Littlefield Publishers, Inc.
A wholly owned subsidiary of The Rowman & Littlefield Publishing Group, Inc.
4501 Forbes Boulevard, Suite 200
Lanham, MD 20706

Estover Road
Plymouth PL6 7PY
United Kingdom

British Library Cataloguing in Publication Information Available
Library of Congress Cataloging-in-Publication Data

Dimaggio, Anthony R., 1980–
  Mass media, mass propaganda: examining American news in the "War on terror" /
Anthony R. Dimaggio.
     p. cm.
  Includes bibliographical references and index.
     1.   War on Terrorism, 2001—Mass media and the war. 2. Iraq War, 2003—Mass
Media and the war. 3. Mass media and war—United States. 4. Terrorism and mass
media—United States. I. Title.
  HV6432.D56 2008
  070.4'49973931—dc22   2008004452
  ISBN-13: 978-0-7391-1902-0 (cloth : alk. paper)
  ISBN-10: 0-7391-1902-8 (cloth. : alk. paper)
  ISBN-13: 978-0-7391-1903-7 (pbk : alk. paper)
  ISBN-10: 0-7391-1903-6 (pbk : alk. paper)
  eISBN-13: 978-0-7391-3390-3 (electronic)
  eISBN-10: 0-7391-3390-X (electronic)
Printed in the United States of America

⊖™ The paper used in this publication meets the minimum requirements of American
National Standard for Information Sciences—Permanence of Paper for Printed Library

To Mary, for all your patience and inspiration throughout this project.

Contents

Introduction

Understanding the News
in the "War on Terror"

At the beginning of the twenty-first century, the media seems more important than at any other time in history. In an era when globalization has accelerated with the emergence of new technologies such as the Internet, media reporting is not just a national issue—it is one with global implications. Papers like the *New York Times* reach beyond an American audience; it is considered one of the most prestigious papers in the world. Grassroots media movements have also grown in strength, influence, and range by making use of new communications technology. This point is driven home in a number of academic studies. In *Global Activism, Global Media*, Wilma De Jong, Martin Shaw, and Neil Stammers argue that "Media appear to be increasingly globalised, as national television, press, etc. are subsumed in gigantic worldwide flows of information and ideas, symbolised by the internet, which offers social and political actors new opportunities for direct communication."[1]

Media can no longer be looked at as the exclusive realm of corporate actors and multinational conglomerates. Increasingly, activist networks are promoting their own definition of what it means to "report the news." Community media activist and scholar Kate Coyer speaks specifically about the proliferation of independent media centers (*Indymedias*) on a national and global scale. Immediately following the mass protests against the World Trade Organization in Seattle, Independent Media Centers began to spring up throughout the country, promoting an increasingly popular slogan of *Indymedia* throughout the world: "don't hate the media, become the media." *Indymedia* is radically different from corporate news reporting in that it represents an open publishing structure in which grassroots activists can, and do, become involved in actively reporting the news around them. Activists and community members are encouraged to report for themselves what is happening in local, national, and international news developments and events, and submit those reports to their own *Indymedia* site.

Indymedia are also used as venues for planning local and national activist events; in this sense, it is a valuable activist tool in organizing demonstrations, marches, and direct action as well. Coyer explains: "*Indymedia* has continued to grow since its inception in 1999, both in size and scope. The philosophy of *Indymedia* informs each aspect of the global network and local collectives, from its anti-authoritarian decision making process, to its open publishing flexibility as an organization, decentralization, and commitment to local autonomy."[2] Coyer argues that its open publishing is vital because "it ensures a place for everyone's voice and participation and is key to what makes *Indymedia* a participatory, and thus inherently democratic medium."[3]

While it is important to understand the emerging systems of reporting which challenge private or capitalist ownership of the press, it is also imperative to understand the extent of corporate power when it comes to dominating this vital medium of communication. Although investors and owners may complain about declining levels of profitability, media corporations today appear more powerful than at any time in world history, and they exercise a tremendous amount of influence and power over public opinion in the markets in which they operate. To underestimate the power of such institutions would be a great disservice to any serious study of media politics and mass communications.

It is vital to systematically analyze the ways in which media corporations in America use their resources to portray a favorable image of the United States in the "War on Terror." At the same time, alternate standards of reporting that exist outside of the mainstream press are examined, so as to demonstrate the chasm between the norms and values that drive each system of reporting. This exercise will show that the current standard of reporting, and current trends toward private ownership in the U.S. mainstream, are not inherently natural, but merely a reflection of one way of going about reporting the news, and one form of media ownership. Other models of reporting and ownership do exist—those characterized by less extreme corporate media consolidation and conglomeration, and others defined by *non-corporate* ownership, both of which will be discussed later in this work.

This work was written so as to reach academic and general audiences alike. The concepts discussed throughout are approached so as to provide easy access for those without extensive knowledge of the technical language often employed in many Political Science and media studies. A rigorous analysis of media framing and propaganda is employed in order to appeal to academic and scholarly audiences looking for a more thorough exploration of the way that media institutions operate in the United States and throughout the world. Major concepts are clearly defined, and readers are given ample evidence within each chapter to reinforce basic themes that run throughout the work. This interdisciplinary approach makes this work relevant for a number of different subfields of scholarly study.

A major question that is addressed throughout these pages concerns the "War on Terror": what is the nature of the relationship between the media and government during times of war? To answer such a question, it is vital to analyze the uses of propaganda by all different types of media in the effort to shape public opinion and reinforce certain themes and ideologies at the expense of others. In dissecting media propaganda, one also seeks to answer the seemingly simple question: what is the role of media institutions in the formation of public opinion, and in restricting or fostering access to critical information? Subsequent chapters herein provide a background of the institutional factors that help explain why the mainstream American media has traditionally reinforced state doctrines during wartime. Although I look at reporting during times of American engagement in foreign conflicts, many of the characterizations of media operating procedures apply during times of peace as well.

In addition to exploring pro-war propaganda, I also examine the anti-war views as seen in Progressive-Left media, often referred to by those involved in it as the "independent media." Through the concept of "framing," which has been extensively explored in many pre-9/11 academic studies, I analyze media portrayals and reactions to numerous developments in the "War on Terror," including the U.S. invasion and occupation of Afghanistan and Iraq, the alleged role of the U.S. as a democratizing agent in the Middle East, the growing Iraqi resistance to occupation, unfolding humanitarian crisis in Iraq, the role of the U.S. in "fighting global terrorism," and the Bush administration's portrayal of Iraq as a threat to American national security.

Finally, the relationship between nationalism and patriotic pressures and the media during the "War on Terror" are explored, specifically in regards to the ways in which nationalism impels media actors and media outlets to conform to government foreign policy agendas and propaganda. Media outlets examined in this book include the major national television and print news outfits, such as *Fox News, CBS, ABC, NBC, CNN*, the *New York Times*, the *Washington Post*, the *Los Angeles Times, USA Today*, the *Chicago Tribune*, and the *New Republic*, among others. Progressive-Left media sources that are dissected include the *Nation*, the *Progressive, Truthout, Common Dreams, Z Magazine, In These Times*, and others.

Chapter Layout

The work is divided into eleven main chapters. Chapter 1 provides a basic introduction to the relationship between media and public opinion. It discusses previous academic studies that assist in answering an important question in media studies—what are the effects of the media on the American public? Citing major research that has established links between media reporting and the formation of public opinion, this chapter shows that the media is clearly important in shaping the ways in which the American public thinks about social events and developments. Also addressed is the question of why American public opinion and world opinion were so drastically different at the onset of the Iraq war. After reading the chapter, part of the answer should be apparent—different media systems assist in creating and reinforcing different viewpoints of the U.S. and its role in global affairs.

Before analyzing the pro-war framing of the American mainstream press, it is necessary to lay out some of the underlying structural factors that account for the convergence between the media and the Bush administration's portrayals of the U.S. "War on Terror." Chapter 2 sets out to achieve this goal. Understanding patterns of media framing is essential when looking at the ideology motivating the reporting of the news. Some of the main elements driving reporting include: media power, as exercised through framing and agenda setting; media omission and censorship of controversial, anti-war views; the uncritical transmission of, and reliance on, official statements and propaganda; the use of excessive fluff, or "junk news," as opposed to news stories that are critical of the war; and finally, corporate ownership of the media as an impediment to more balanced reporting of both pro-war and anti-war opinions.

Chapter 3 examines the role of the major American media in reinforcing the claims of the Bush administration that Iraq possessed weapons of mass destruction (WMD). This chapter starts by looking at the marginalization of the Downing Street Memo, a declassified record of the conversation between British Prime Minister Tony Blair and his cabinet concerning Iraq's lack of weapons of mass destruction. The chapter continues with an in-depth analysis of the reporting of the *New York Times* in the months before the war, and reveals a clear pattern of unbalanced reporting in favor of the Bush administration's WMD claims, at the expense of critical reporting and editorializing.

Chapter 4 provides an extensive background to the media's treatment of the Bush administration's efforts to "democratize" Iraq. The media role in promoting a charitable, humanitarian vision of the U.S. is examined throughout the different periods of the Iraq war, including the pre-invasion stage, the invasion stage, the ongoing occupation stage, and the Iraqi elections. In addition to addressing the media's views of Iraqi "democracy," the chapter also focuses on the nature of the criticisms of the Bush administration that *have* appeared in the mainstream press. As this chapter shows, these criticisms have taken more of a pragmatic, limited tone, as they focus on how better to fight the war, rather than how to oppose it. Such criticisms include faulting the U.S. for not having enough troops in Iraq for the pacification campaign, for mismanaging the occupation, and for the large cost of occupying Iraq. These criticisms differ substantially from those addressed in chapter 9, as alternative media paradigms (anti-war sectors of the British and Australian press, the American independent media, and *Al Jazeera*) have presented foundational, substantive criticisms of the U.S. war in Iraq as illegal under international law, as driven by imperial lust rather than democracy, and as the primary cause of unfolding humanitarian disaster. Chapter 4 pays special attention to the editors, reporters, and columnists of the *New York Times*, who have often been inaccurately classified as anti-war.

Chapter 5 addresses the "other side of the coin" concerning the U.S. role in Iraq. If the U.S. (according to mainstream media coverage) is in Iraq to foster democracy, promote human rights, and stabilize the country, what is the role of Iraq's growing resistance? As this chapter shows, Iraqi resistance to occupation has been characterized in reporting and editorializing as bent on destabilizing Iraq, derailing democracy, terrorizing the country, and hampering progress. This chapter dissects the main categorizations of Iraqi resistance as driven by Saddam Loyalists, foreign fighters, terrorists, and "Shi'a extremists." The chapter allots significant time to exploring an aspect of Iraqi resistance seldom addressed in the American major media, namely the nationalist-driven desire on the part of resistance groups to expel the U.S. and establish Iraqi independence. This chapter also takes an in-depth look at Iraq's unfolding civil war, and what role the U.S. has played regarding the re-emergence of ethnic tensions.

Chapter 6 examines the many ways in which anti-war voices have been punished, downsized, or eliminated in American media coverage. Such penalties range from verbal attacks to the firing of critical anti-war media figures that have posed serious challenges to the statements and promises of the Bush administration during the wars in Iraq and Afghanistan. The chapter directs special attention to the power of nationalism in limiting dissent during times of war. Nationalistic pro-war pressures have found a welcome home in the major American media outlets.

Chapter 7 analyzes the ways in which corporate reporting mirrors George Orwell's "Doublethink" propaganda model. The chapter provides a short background, introducing Doublethink in the context of Orwell's classic work of literature, *1984*. Contradictory statements used within the corporate media to describe the Iraq war are explored in this chapter, including the assertion that military force is the best means of promoting peace. Perhaps the most important piece of Orwellian Doublethink that will be examined is the media's promise of democracy in Iraq, pursued alongside media admissions that the United States is pursuing imperial policies in the Middle East, and that most Iraqis do not want the United States in Iraq. Highlighting such contradictory frames is crucial to understanding Orwellian government and media propaganda.

Chapter 8 deals with the separate poles of reporting on Iraq, which are seen in the Progressive-Left press and the mainstream media in the U.S. Concepts such as "collateral damage," Iraqi reconstruction, casualty counts, and Iraqi and American public opinion are examined in great detail. The image of the U.S. as a humanitarian superpower is thoroughly deconstructed. U.S. responsibility for serious human rights violations are examined at length.

Chapter 9 further explores the gulf between American mainstream reporting and alternative paradigms of reporting as seen in other media institutions throughout the U.S. and the world. This chapter examines three alternative media models to that of the U.S. corporate press. These include the American non-corporate, independent media, *Al Jazeera*, and the anti-war leaning sectors of the British and Australian press. As these media systems challenge the legitimacy of the invasion and occupation of Iraq at every turn, the American mainstream media, in contrast, has sought to reinforce the war effort through the use of embedded reporting.

The arguments of specific anti-war reporters and editorialists in each system will be reviewed, including Robert Fisk and Patrick Cockburn of the *Independent* of London, Tariq Ali and Jonathan Steele of the *Guardian* of London, Paul McGeough of the *Sydney Morning Herald*, and David Enders, Aaron Glantz, Amy Goodman, Dahr Jamail, and Rahul Mahajan of the American independent press, among others. This chapter comes to the conclusion that the British and Australian press have generally been more balanced and presented a wider diversity of opinions than the American media in their portrayals of the Iraq war, and that the American public is at a disadvantage for its general lack of access to such critical media outlets.

Chapter 10 looks at a conflict that has not received much attention when it comes to media coverage—the war in Afghanistan from 2001—2002. The chapter looks at three main points: 1. media evaluations of, and displeasure with, potentially peaceful alternatives to war in Afghanistan; 2. media reactions to the motivations for the 9/11 attacks; 3. media coverage of Afghan reconstruction and "democratization"; and 4. issues of human rights and humanitarian disaster in post 9/11 Afghanistan.

Chapter 11 looks at possible future targets in the "War on Terror." Syria, Iran, and North Korea are discussed, as they are the next three countries after Iraq listed as part of the "Axis of Evil" laid out by the Bush administration. As this chapter shows, the mainstream press, like the Bush administration, has been antagonistic to these countries, viewing them as enemies of state that need to be dealt with in order to protect American national security.

Finally, the conclusion focuses upon emerging discussions over the effects of corporate consolidation of the American media. The effects of the regulatory actions of the Federal Communication Commission are discussed in particular. Discussion of corporate monopoly ownership of the mainstream media is not confined only to activist and academic circles; indeed, the issue has become a major focus of reporting. Analyzing the potential for media reform—whether it is toward limiting monopoly control or toward some alternate trend in ownership (perhaps a combination of public and private ownership)—is vital when looking at the issue of imbalanced reporting in American mainstream media coverage.

Notes

1. Wilma De Jong, Martin Shaw, and Neil Stammers, "Introduction," in *Global Activism, Global Media*, edited by Wilma De Jong, Martin Shaw, and Neil Stammers (Ann Arbor, Mi.: Pluto, 2005), 1.

2. Kate Coyer, "If it Leads, it Bleeds: The Participatory Newsmaking of the Independent Media Centre," in *Global Activism, Global Media*, edited by Wilma De Jong, Martin Shaw, and Neil Stammers (Ann Arbor, Mi.: Pluto, 2005), 166.

3. Coyer, "The Participatory Newsmaking of the Independent Media Centre," 170.

1

Public Trust, Media, and the "War on Terror"

Academics have long speculated about the impact of the news when studying the relationship between the media and public opinion. One relevant question comes to mind: what specifically is the influence that the media has, if any, on the public in terms of influencing, shaping, or manipulating opinion? A failure to demonstrate any clear links between media coverage of important political events and issues on the one hand, and the formation of public opinion on the other, would surely deal a critical blow to projects that are undertaken by academics analyzing societal effects of media.

Many academics analyzing the media have long taken for granted the idea that messages disseminated through the media can, and typically do, have a major effect in shaping American public opinion. The assumption typically operates as follows: if consumer trust in media is strong, then propaganda originating from within that media system will be more effective in influencing the opinions and ideologies of audiences; conversely, if public trust in media is relatively weak, media propaganda may be less accepted or convincing to those who follow the news. In other words, if the public, by and large, does not trust media, then why bother studying the effectiveness of media propaganda in the first place?

This work approaches the study of media propaganda from the understanding that the American press *does* retain significant power in influencing and manipulating public opinion. There are a number of past academic studies that have elaborated upon the relationship between media reporting and public opinion formulation at length. These studies demonstrate that the media remains an instrumental agent in influencing public opinion and in informing, and even misinforming, the American public about the world around them.

While the studies discussed below are far from exhaustive, they do allow an introduction into how media affects public opinion in democratic societies.

Media helps determine what local, national, and international "problems" receive the most attention, and which will be deemphasized or neglected Mainstream media controls in large part what Americans see, when they see it, and
how they see it. What media outlets choose to report and to ignore play a major
role in the formation of viewers' opinions and ideologies.

The Power of News:
Examining the Nexus Between Media and Public Opinion

A number of academic studies spanning back to the late 1960s and early 1970s
sought to examine the effects of media coverage within an experimental, scien-
tifically-oriented research approach, in order to demonstrate the media's ability
to influence public opinion concerning important domestic and foreign policy
plans and initiatives. Among the first were Donald Shaw and Maxwell
McCombs, who gained notoriety after publishing the results of their study of
media coverage of the 1968 presidential election.

In their study, Shaw and McCombs sought to demonstrate media power
over the public's perceptions of political candidates, as well as media influence
over voter behavior. Based upon their interviews and experiments with one-
hundred television viewers, Shaw and McCombs determined that the media
played a vital role, not so much in "telling people what to think, but what to
think about" regarding important campaign issues and other matters.[1] This conclusion has also been reinforced by the earlier work of prominent media scholar
Bernard Cohen, in his much-cited work, *The Press and Foreign Policy*.[2]

Drawing from Cohen, Shaw and McCombs' conclusions "suggest[ed] a
very strong relationship between the emphasis placed on different campaign
issues by the media and the judgments of voters as to the salience and importance of various campaign topics."[3] McCombs specifically concluded that "the
media are the major primary sources of national political information [for the
American public]; for most, mass media provide the best—and only easily
available approximation of ever changing political realities."[4]

Other studies revealed similar results concerning the power of media to determine what issues the public views as important. For example, one Gallup Poll
conducted from 1964—1970, focusing on three prominent weekly news magazines—*Time, Newsweek*, and *U.S. News & World Report*—found that there was
a strong correlation between the most commonly focused upon themes in these
three papers and public perceptions of what issues constituted "the most important problem" for the nation during those same years.[5] Such research shows that,
as institutions with mass appeal, media outlets have traditionally served as a lens
through which Americans view the major challenges facing the country.

The studies above had a major effect on the communications field in the
decades following their release. As James Dearing and Everett Rogers explain,
the 1968 presidential-media study "set off a research paradigm adopted primarily within mass communications studies, although it was also appropriated to
varying degrees by a number of political scientists, sociologists, and other aca-

demics."[6] This new research archetype took the study of the effects of media well beyond Presidential elections, though. In their study of media's influence on television viewers, George Gerbner and Larry Gross discussed the media's power as the "constructors of [the] social reality" of the American people.[7] Gerbner and Gross discovered that "the heaviest viewers of television were the most likely to be 'cultivated' by its patterns of images and accept the television world view as their vision of reality."[8]

Gerbner and Gross went further than previous studies, however, in their assessment that the media's framing of important issues and events goes "beyond setting an agenda," as such coverage "activates some ideas, feelings, and values rather than others" and "can encourage particular trains of thought about political phenomena and lead audiences to arrive at more or less predictable conclusions."[9] Progressive scholar and media critic Michael Parenti refers to the media's power to "invent reality"[10] for its audience, as many consumers of media place tremendous stock in news outlets' reporting as a serious and accurate reflection of events in the world around them.

Conclusions about the "agenda setting" power of the media are also reinforced in more recent studies of the effects of the media. Two prominent political-communications scholars, Shanto Iyengar and Donald R. Kinder, situate media framing within the context of "episodic" and "thematic" news coverage in their work: *Is Anyone Responsible: How Television Frames Political Issues.* As "episodic" framing typically includes the reporting of specific news events, "thematic" framing entails more general news trends, such as reporting on poverty, crime, and other general societal trends.

In their experiments on the effects of these two categories of framing, Iyengar and Kinder concluded that their studies "show specifically that television news powerfully influences which problems viewers regard as the nation's most serious."[11] One of the societal "problems" listed by Iyengar and Kinder was military spending, which is well reflected in the strong rhetorical support of American political leaders, media pundits, and reporters for increased funding directed toward the military.

Iyengar and Kinder were clear in their analysis of the importance of newsframes. The fact that tens of millions of Americans are dependent on television news to inform them about national and international issues "gives the media an enormous capacity to shape public thinking."[12] Aside from influencing Americans' opinions about what constitute major national problems, the mainstream media has also been implicated in fomenting particular cultural values. In their study, "Deep Structures: Polpop Culture on Primetime Television," Allen McBride and Robert K. Toburen argue that T.V. media cultivates certain "attitudes, values, and world views," as "there is an apparent conservative, yet still mainstream effect from television viewing, particularly in network news programming. Heavy viewers with liberal or Left-leaning politics become more likely to show evidence of moderating their political views than those with conservative or right-leaning politics."[13]

McBride and Toburen's study suggests that the media is capable of more than just getting Americans to think about particular issues or problems. In fact, media outlets are often very effective in convincing or even manipulating the public of the desirability of mainstream political, economic, and social values at the expense of alternative paradigms that challenge the status quo.

Understanding Public Trust and Skepticism in Media

CNN did not earn the name "the most trusted name in news" for no reason. A strong degree of trust has long characterized the tie that binds corporate media outlets and the American people. A 1998 Gallup poll found that Americans "have generally high levels of trust in many of the major sources of news and information to which they are exposed." This highest level of trust was seen in sources like *CNN*, as approximately 70 percent of those polled said they were confident in *CNN's* reporting accuracy—an intriguing revelation considering that *CNN* scored higher in trust levels amongst those questioned than even respondents' friends and family, of which 64 percent of those polled said they trusted.[14] More recent polling has revealed a similar pattern, despite a modest decline in public trust in some media outlets, and in media overall. The results of a Gallup poll released in 2005 indicated that, of those Americans questioned, 74 percent reported either "some" or "strong confidence" in national newspapers, although these trust levels have fallen since 2000.[15]

One could conclude from these polls that much of the public views the mainstream media as a competent player in political life—as an institution that is necessary in educating the American people. The polls discussed above suggest that a large segment of the public often are not as skeptical as they could be of potentially harmful ulterior motives that may drive media corporations outside of "educating the public."

Americans have provided a number of reasons to justify their favorable views of corporate media. These justifications include: happiness with access to "the news and information they seek in a timely fashion; the breadth of [news] coverage; and the ability to stay informed about a wide range of news developments, both locally and globally."[16] From these responses, one can discern that many believe the mainstream media provides quite a wide range of views in terms of its reporting of major news stories of the day. In regards to the "War on Terrorism," specifically the invasions of Afghanistan and Iraq, one can also conclude that a sizable percentage of the news-viewing public feels that media outlets have done a decent job in providing them with the information needed to make educated assessments of the government's performance in the foreign policy arena.

Public trust in media has been reinforced in other studies. One *CBS/New York Times* poll released in January 2006 found that 63 percent of respondents held either a "great deal" or a "fair amount" of trust and confidence in TV news, newspapers, and radio. When asked about the honesty of mainstream news, 60 percent of those surveyed felt that news media "tell the truth" either "all of the time" or "most of the time" when it comes to their reporting of current events. The same poll indicated that 69 percent of those surveyed felt that news media reports are generally "accurate" depictions of the stories at hand.[17] A *Pew Research Center* poll released in mid-2005 found high levels of favorability for news outlets, on the local and national level, as represented in the table below. Consumer confidence in media ranged between 75 and 80 percent, depending on the type of news outlet.[18]

Table 1.1

Consumer Confidence in the News

News Mediums	Percent of Respondents Confident in Each Medium
Local Television	79%
Daily Newspaper	80%
Network Television	75%
Cable News	79%

Positive perceptions also persist when the public is asked about flagship network anchors. One study conducted by the *Pew Research Center* released in 2006 found that news anchors such as Katie Couric (*CBS*), Brian Williams (*NBC*) and Charles Gibson (*ABC*) were held in high esteem amongst respondents, with 57, 65, and 71 percent positive perceptions respectively. Common descriptions applied to these anchors included "informed," "fair," "knowledgeable," "interesting" "professional," "competent," and "trustworthy," amongst others.[19]

On the other hand, surveys have also surfaced indicating that many Americans reserve some or even a strong level of skepticism for American media institutions. One poll found that 56 percent of those questioned felt that news stories throughout the mainstream media were "often inaccurate."[20] This pattern of skepticism has continued over a number of years, as the table below demonstrates.[21] Along similar lines, 89 percent of respondents of one *Pew* poll also said that news media either "often" or "sometimes" "let their own political preferences influence the way they report the news," as opposed to only 9 percent who said it "seldom" or "never" happened.[22] Such a response is hardly surprising, considering that a certain degree of editorializing in the news is inevitable, no matter how hard reporters, editors, and anchors try to be objective and balanced. But skepticism goes beyond the limited criticism that individual reporters have a bias one way or another. Another survey, done by the *Zogby* polling firm released in May of 2006 found split feelings directed at media reliability, as 42 percent of those questioned reported high or medium levels of confidence in the media, whereas 58 percent expressed low levels of confidence.[23]

Table 1.2

How Accurate are News Stories?

Month/Year	Percent respondents who feel news reporting is "often inaccurate"
06/2005	56%
07/2003	56%
07/2002	56%
11/2001	45%
09/2001	57%
02/1999	58%
08/1998	63%
02/1998	63%
02/1997	56%

Many Americans lambaste media for not being "pro-American" enough. Only 42 percent of Americans surveyed in 2005 believed that the media generally "stand up for America," whereas as many as 40 percent of respondents thought that the news media had been "too critical of America" in recent years.[24] Such perceptions may very well be part of the reason for the decline in the belief in the neutrality of the corporate press, and are likely an important part of the case made by those who point to a liberal bias or slant within the media today.

However one chooses to interpret the polling data though, it is clear that many do not view the press as completely fair, even-handed, or "objective," as over seven-in-ten Americans questioned said they believed the major media "tend to favor one side, rather than treat all sides fairly" when reporting on critical policy matters.[25] This perceived bias is also reinforced by others who criticize the mainstream media for being too close to the government, and too assimilated into corporate America to fairly report the news without providing a consistent, pro-business slant. Such critiques seek to explain in part why, by more than a three-to-one ratio, Americans feel that the news media is "often influenced by powerful people and organizations," rather than serving as an independent medium for evaluating government policy.[26]

Of course, public opinion of media is not static or monolithic; opinions in terms of increased confidence or skepticism in media do change over time, which may account for some of the variance in public trust and suspicion of media from poll to poll. Also, Americans do not stand united behind, or against corporate media outlets. There will likely always be a sizable number of Americans who are skeptical of media, and a significant figure who are generally supportive of the status quo of reporting, although these numbers clearly vary depending upon the poll one is examining. Aside from such issues, one is always left with the problem of the vastly different wording of different polling questions, which may also result in substantively different results in terms of measuring public trust or skepticism in media.

Public opinion of media may also be influenced by specific events in the news, and how media outlets cover them. The Jason Blair (formerly of the *New York Times*) and Jack Kelley (formerly of the *USA Today*) reporting scandals (both journalists were found to be fabricating news stories), along with other media scandals, may have helped incite higher levels of mistrust for media reporting. In sum, polling does not occur in a vacuum; responses are likely influenced by the way media covers major news stories and developments of the day, and by specific points in time when people are questioned—when media scandals may or may not be a salient issue. Sometimes, the news itself becomes the major focus of a story, as in the case of major reporting scandals.

A final possible explanation for such strong variance in indicators of public trust in media may be explained in part by the theory that individuals polled simultaneously hold *both* trustful and skeptical views of news media. While this may seem paradoxical, it may be perfectly understandable or reasonable. Consumers read newspapers and watch television broadcasts on a regular basis, and use such reports to come up with their *own* understanding of how the world works, independent at least in part from the reporting they view. It may be that, in assessing the information available in the news, viewers and readers pick and choose some parts of newscasts to accept or embrace, and others to question or reject. In other words, one may believe that a paper like the *New York Times*, or a network like *CNN* are biased in one way or another, yet also accept some or much of what those institutions report as reliable information about what is happening in the world.

Media in Comparison with Other Political Institutions

Despite strong levels of public skepticism, the news media has often been viewed in a more positive light than many other high-level American political institutions. This may very well be in part a result of the common expectation amongst many Americans that the media serve as a critic of government corruption, exposing lies and deception, and keeping government institutions in check by reporting important news stories and events which Americans expect to be exposed in order to be informed citizens. Such trust of media stands in marked contrast to the favorability ratings of various political entities revealed in the same *Pew Research Center* poll, as the Democratic and Republican Parties retained only 57 and 52 percent favorability respectively, Congress with 41 percent favorability, and President Bush, whose approval rating in 2005 fell as low as 35 percent, by some estimates.[27] Even at some of the lowest points in public confidence in media, news outlets still scored higher than political institutions such as Congress.[28]

Examining Media Power

Whatever one's ideas are about the bias or slant of the mainstream press, it is clear that its influence and power have been growing in an era of corporate media consolidation, monopoly, and oligopoly. Former assistant managing editor for the *Washington Post* and prominent media critic Ben Bagdikian explains corporate monopolization of the media bluntly:

> A cartel of five media conglomerates now control the media on which a majority of Americans say they most rely. These five are not just large—though they are all among the 325 largest corporations in the world—they are unique among all huge corporations: they are a major factor in changing the politics of the United States and they condition social values of children and adults alike. These five huge corporations own most of the newspapers, magazines, books, radio, and TV stations and movie studios of the United States.

They have "acquired more public communications power—including ownership of the news—than any private businesses have ever before possessed in world history. Nothing in earlier history matches this corporate group's power to penetrate the social landscape."[29]

Bagdikian's concerns over the increasing power of the corporate press seem to be reflected by a significant segment of the public, as 49 percent of Americans recently polled indicate that they believe the influence of the corporate media has increased, rather than decreased in recent years.[30] Television network news in particular has long played an important role in influencing public opinion. An *Associated Press* poll released in 2006 found that 63 percent of those surveyed reported that they watched network evening news programs either "every day" or "several times per week," as opposed to only 23 percent who responded "less than once per week" or "never."[31]

Writing in the *Washington Post*, Tom Rosenstiel explains that, "the rise of network television news (*ABC*, *NBC*, and *CBS*) was arguably the most important development in American politics in the latter half of the twentieth century. The arrival of news divisions in the 1950s and 1960s meant that for the first time citizens could regularly see events for themselves." Rosenstiel recaps that "the networks still air nightly newscasts that are often superb, and nearly thirty million Americans still watch."[32]

Although T.V. network news is still important today, there has been a significant decline in its audience, as well as in the readership of national newspapers in favor of different news mediums such as Internet-based news and cable T.V. news networks like *MSNBC*, *CNN*, and *Fox News*. Many Americans are reliant on a wide variety of news mediums, as recent consumption statistics reveal. According to the *Project for Excellence in Journalism*, over one third of Americans consider themselves "regular consumers" of many different types of news sources, including network and cable news, local newspapers, radio news, magazines, and Internet based news outlets.[33] This does not mean, however, that national newspapers are not still important in influencing public opinion. Despite a reduction in the readership of national papers somewhat in the last few years,[34] an estimated 42 percent of Americans still report that they read daily papers on a regular basis.[35]

The *direct* influence of the nation's major national newspapers, however, has always been limited to a narrow sector of the American public. Out of a total U.S. population of approximately 300 million people, the *New York Times*—the nation's most prestigious paper—maintains a total daily circulation of only about 1.1 million, and only 1.7 million on Sundays.[36] When taken together, the top five national newspapers' total circulation is only slightly over seven million on average per day, not counting Internet subscribers. Even the ten largest national newspapers account for only about ten million readers nationwide. Altogether, these print outlets reach just five percent of the approximately 200 million Americans between fifteen and sixty-four years of age.[37]

Table 1.3

National Newspaper Readership (2005)

1. *USA Today*	2,199,052
2. *Wall Street Journal*	2,070,498
3. *New York Times*	1,136,433
4. *Los Angeles Times*	907,997
5. *Washington Post*	751,871
6. *New York Daily News*	735,536
7. *New York Post*	678,086
8. *Chicago Tribune*	573,744
9. *Detroit News/Free Press*	535,036
10. *Houston Chronicle*	527,744

The small number of Americans reached by these ten newspapers has led many to label them as part of the national "elite media." And yet, the print media's influence must be understood to encompass far more than just the narrow readership statistics of the table above. Ben Bagdikian affirms that "the daily newspaper has become the medium for the upper and middle classes," as just under half of American families reported receiving a daily newspaper in 2003.[38] As of 2005, the *Gannett* Corporation (the largest national newspaper group and owner of *USA Today*) controlled ninety-nine daily newspapers nationwide, as well as twenty-one T.V. stations reaching 17.9 percent of the United States. After taking into account non-daily publications, Gannett's national circulation stood at 22.7 million per week, distributed in over 600 different newspapers throughout the country.[39] Other major newspaper conglomerates retain impressive local audiences as well. The *Knight Ridder* Corporation alone owns thirty-two daily newspapers in fifty-eight different markets,[40] while news services like *Reuters* and the *Associated Press* reach millions more every week. As the self-proclaimed "backbone of the world's information system," the *Associated Press* serves thousands of newspapers, radio stations, and television channels in the United States.[41] These statistics demonstrate that the newspaper is not just a medium for the very rich, although it does cater to more privileged middle and higher income Americans.

The power of the elite national print media is in large part based upon its *indirect* ideological influence over the rest of the national media. The *New York Times* is considered the nation's "paper of record" for good reason. As James Dearing and Everett M. Rogers explain:

> The *New York Times* is generally regarded as the most respected U.S. news medium. When the *Times* indicates that an issue is newsworthy, other U.S. news organizations take note. When producers and editors at television stations, radio stations, newspapers, and to a lesser degree, newsmagazines sit down to decide which stories will receive the most time, the best placement, and the biggest headlines that day, they often have checked first to see what decisions the editors at the *Times* have made about the same issues.[42]

And the *New York Times* is but one member of the elite national media. As scholar and media critic Noam Chomsky states: "the elite media are sort of the agenda-setting media. That means the *New York Times*, the *Washington Post*, the major television channels, and so on. They set the general framework. Local media more or less adapt to their structure." This agenda setting media attempts to reach the most educated, affluent, and economically and politically powerful Americans, although it also produces reporting that is filtered down to the mass public. Chomsky continues:

> There's maybe 20 percent of the population that is relatively educated, more or less articulate, [that] plays some kind of role in [national and local] decision-making. They're supposed to participate in social life—either as managers, or cultural managers like teachers and writers and so on. They're supposed to vote, they're supposed to play some role in the way economic and political and cultural life goes on. Now their consent [to national policies and major political, economic, and social agendas] is crucial.[43]

Americans newspapers—whether at the local, state, or national level—claim privileged middle and upper class individuals and families as their primary market demographic. This group, however, has also become the target for all commercial news mediums, as it represents the largest source of revenues in a media system run by profit-driven corporations.

Media Influence Outside the National Newspaper

High levels of news consumption are evident at many levels where media institutions operate. Forty percent of Americans report that they listen to radio news regularly. Radio call-in talk shows alone reach seventeen percent of the American public, although their demographic mainly consists of middle-aged conservative men.[44] As mentioned earlier, cable and Internet news have benefited from substantial audience growth. By 2004, 39 percent of Americans reported watching cable news channels on a consistent basis.[45] In addition, nearly three out of ten Americans now rely on Internet news sources, an increase of 5 percent since 2002.[46] As recently as 2004, 42 percent of Americans explained that they followed the news online at least some of the time.[47] However, it should also be noted that *regular* consumption of cable news is rather small, typically averaging only between one half of a million to 1.5 million people per day for outlets such as *CNN* and *Fox News*. These outlets have been characterized as "narrowcasting" to focused audiences, at least in terms of their attempts at maintaining small core audiences who follow the respective networks daily.[48]

Whatever news medium one chooses to examine, it is undeniable that, when taken collectively, they play an important part in influencing American public opinion. On any given day, Americans are just as likely to tune-in to television news programs as they are to watch television for general entertainment.[49] But corporate media outlets have not taken advantage of their large number of viewers simply to "educate the public," as is sometimes suggested or implied in highminded journalistic rhetoric. The media's most important objective remains, as with any corporation, the maximization of profit. Without steady and increasing corporate profits, media conglomerates would retain the enormous strength and reach that they do today. Much of the public seems to be well aware of the corporate media's primary concern with profits; when asked "what news organizations care about more," 75 percent of respondents polled answered that corporations consider "attracting [the] biggest audience" to be more important than "keeping the public informed."

The studies cited in this chapter are valuable in that they empirically demonstrate that there is an established association between media coverage and reporting, and the formation of public attitudes and opinions related to various current events and societal trends. And while there is much value that comes along with the quantitative research discussed, there are also a number of limitations to many of these works. For such a tremendous amount of data that has been collected in such scientifically oriented academic studies, many of the academic works on "agenda setting" and media effects on the public have come to rather narrow conclusions about the nature of media coverage, and typically ignore the study of corporate media ownership itself, in their selective focus upon "scientific and objective study" of media.

Despite decades of empirical research, most academic studies typically fail to present many important conclusions concerning the power of the media outside of very general and pedestrian assessments that the media has some vague effects on the populace at large in terms of assisting in "setting the agenda" for what issues are to be discussed or in terms of influencing what national "problems" people think about. These conclusions neglect major institutional factors, analyzed by those who seek to criticize the ideology reinforcing profit motive as the primary goal of media corporations. To better understand institutional analysis, one must look to a different school of media criticism which is less prevalent in many mainstream academic studies—one in which the negative effects of corporate ownership of the mainstream press is the major emphasis of study.

Institutional Analysis of Corporate Media

A number of critics have stepped forward to question corporate ownership of the news in a time of increased media consolidation. These scholars and activists view corporate ownership of the press as a means of ensuring the dominance of pro-business views at the expense of views that are critical of corporations and the American political establishment. Unfortunately, their works have often been ignored, downplayed, or caricatured amongst mainstream communications and political science academics. In their seminal work, *Manufacturing Consent: The Political Economy of the Mass Media*, Noam Chomsky and Edward Herman argue that the corporate "media serve the ends of a dominant elite" in order to "inculcate individuals with the values, beliefs, and codes of behavior that will integrate them into the [capitalist] institutional structures of the larger society. . . The media serve this purpose in many ways: through selection of topics, distribution of concerns, framing of issues, filtering of information, emphasis and tone, and by keeping debate within the bounds of acceptable premises."[50] In his follow-up book, *Necessary Illusions: Thought Control in Democratic Societies*, Chomsky further elaborates on this thesis as he maintains that the media are primarily interested in "'selling' privileged audiences to other businesses."[51]

Michael Parenti describes the process by which media corporations seek to infuse news viewers with pro-capitalist, pro-consumer sentiment: "the obvious purpose of ads and commercials is to sell goods and services, but advertisers do more than that. . . they sell an entire way of life, a way of experiencing social reality that is compatible with the needs of mass-production, mass consumption, and capitalist society."[52]

Corporate advertisers allocate massive resources to "selling" commodity-driven lifestyles to viewers, and they are, to a striking level, very successful in that endeavor. To put these efforts into better perspective, corporate advertising in 2004 neared 250 billion dollars, as companies inundated consumers through the use of television, radio, Internet, and newspaper advertising, among other ad venues.[53] By themselves, Internet ads accounted for between nine and ten billion dollars, or 4.3 percent of the total corporate advertising for the year.[54] Corporations spend hundreds of billions of dollars a year on advertising because it is clearly successful in instilling the public with a consumerist, capitalist orientation, thereby directly reaffirming and reinforcing corporate ownership of media. This fact is often lost in mainstream academic studies that neglect analysis of economic factors (such as corporate ownership) that determine the nature of media coverage.

The study of the political economy of the corporate media should be placed at the forefront of analysis of American media. Within a political economy analysis, one looks to analyze the ways in which media corporations work cooperatively with other major corporations and with political leaders in order to reinforce the "privileged position of business" in society today.[55] Corporate media outlets do not merely "represent" corporate America—they are in fact an integral part of corporate America. As Communications Professor Peter Phillips identifies, "the top eleven media corporations in the U.S. form a solid network of overlapping interests and affiliations. The 155 directors of these eleven media corporations sit on the board of directors of 144 of the Fortune 1000 corporations and interlock with each other through shared directorships in other firms some thirty-six times."[56]

Two of the primary goals behind this system of political economy include: 1. the preoccupation (at least for media corporations) with selling affluent consumer audiences to corporate advertisers; and 2. the commitment to the proliferation of corporate capitalism on a global scale, typically through the use of "soft" and "hard" power, as seen in practices such as the promotion of corporate globalization, support for pro-capitalist governments worldwide (regardless of whether they are democracies or not), and an extensive reliance on military force in imposing the U.S. foreign policy agenda.

From a political economy understanding, corporate and government elites do not represent fundamentally separate interests—rather they work together in reinforcing corporate power and prestige in American society and abroad. This is not to say, however, that there is no conflict within this elite class of political and business leaders. Naturally, there is bound to be disagreement within any country among ruling elites, and the United States is no different, as the narrow range of disagreements and criticisms originating from within corporate media over the Iraq war are a clear sign of ongoing debate and disagreement amongst elites. The study of the "Indexing" effect in mass media—which will be discussed later in this chapter—intends to account for ways in which disagreements amongst elites translate into disagreement throughout mass media reporting and editorializing.

Acknowledging the tendency of elites to disagree, however, does not negate the reality that American political and economic elites are largely in agreement over the importance of censoring Progressive-Left critics of government and corporate America. Any understanding of political economy requires the recognition that major criticisms of big business are generally regarded with discomfort and contempt by advertisers underwriting corporate media programming. As a number of media analysts have noted, corporate executives generally prefer to advertise with news outlets and programs that refrain from focusing on stories critical of big business.[57] Such stories tend to raise serious questions about trust in government and big business—hence journalists, editors, and media owners often consider these stories to be a liability.

In his insightful work, *Uncertain Guardians: The News as a Political Institution*, Bartholomew Sparrow expands upon the power of advertisers in shaping media content: "Advertisers may influence news content in several ways. One way is to withhold, or threaten to withhold, advertisements from undesirable programming." Sparrow cites a number of examples where *ABC* and *NBC* executives terminated programming when their content was perceived to reflect negatively upon the oil, tobacco, and automobile industries.[58] A number of other academics have also warned against the dangers involved with advertisers influencing or controlling the messages within media programs.[59] Dean Alger cites a poll by Marquette University of newspaper editors nationwide, which found that 93 percent of editors surveyed felt pressured at some point by advertisers who were trying to influence news or editorial content. Most explained that management had either supported or tolerated such pressures; "37 percent of the editors polled admitted that they had succumbed" to advertiser coercion in determining news content.[60]

Mainstream media outlets do more than just sell consumer culture and capitalism as vital American and global institutions. Media corporations have long promoted the concept of American exceptionalism in world affairs. They idealize the use of violence as a primary means of international dispute resolution. Media outlets assist in emphasizing the danger (or alleged danger) of designated enemies of state; they also promote the notion that the United States is unconditionally committed to promoting democracy and human rights abroad.

In control of media outlets worth billions of dollars, and spending billions more per year on operating expenditures, media corporations are in a strong position to influence the minds of Americans in their pursuit of profit and a corporate friendly public image. The corporate media is also inclined to lend legitimacy to U.S. foreign policy initiatives in the "War on Terror," as it so often has, and will continue to do in the future. With millions consuming corporate news every day, the ideological biases and political and economic preferences of journalists, reporters, editors, media owners, and corporations themselves are unavoidably transmitted, to a large degree, through the media and to the American public. Understanding the transmission of such attitudes and opinions becomes essential when reviewing different areas of political study, including domestic and foreign policy, as well as the public's reaction to the media's treatment of those policies.

What is Mass Media?

Many Americans retain a vague conception of what specifically constitutes a mass media. Mass media is sometimes considered to encompass primarily the *most* popular of corporate media mediums, such as popular television, film, and book publishing outlets. In this work, however, mass media is defined as including the entire spectrum mainstream media, including not just network news stations like *CBS*, *NBC*, and *ABC*—all of which have been described as the preferred news medium of the American masses. Print media, particularly elite media outlets like the *New York Times*, *Washington Post*, and *Los Angeles Times* are also included, primarily because they set the tone and agenda for reporting coming out of locally-based newspapers, as well as for national and local prime time television news programs, and cable and radio news.

Some might argue that to deal with American media in the singular (the media "is," rather than the media "are") is somewhat misleading in that media are not a homogenized system. Many media outlets allegedly take radically different positions on current events than others do. For example, many citizens prefer to distinguish between papers like the *New York* Times (labeled "liberal"), as opposed to papers like the *Washington Times* or *Fox News* (labeled "conservative"). Distinguishing between such mediums does reveal some important differences between various mass media institutions. What this plural framing of the mass media misses, however, are the substantive points in which "liberal" and "conservative" media outlets agree, such as the legitimacy of the Iraq war (at least in terms of promoting democracy and stability). As this work focuses overwhelmingly on the ways in which mainstream media outlets are similar, it naturally adopts a definition of mass media from a *singular* perspective.

The mainstream American media is contrasted, collectively, with other national media systems, such as those in Britain, Australia, and the Middle East. Aside from the American-non-American distinction in my analysis, I also create a dichotomy between the corporate U.S. media—using a variety of synonyms such as the "mainstream press," and the "establishment press" (or just "the media") used to describe it, and American Progressive-Left media (non-corporate media), or the "independent media." As will become more apparent, American Progressive-Left media (as opposed to Right leaning media outlets) serve as a countervailing force against mainstream media in that they focus most stridently on questioning the legitimacy of U.S. foreign policy.

The Importance of Framing

Aside from mass media, other important concepts in media studies used throughout this book include framing and propaganda. The process by which the ideological viewpoints and narratives in the mass media are presented as "reality" can be explained, in part, as framing. Framing of the news refers to much more than a simple slant or bias of each individual story. Framing is the means by which *an entire social reality* is constructed. The narratives adopted by use of one frame over another inevitably influence how news consumers view important issues. The way a reporter, editor, or media institution chooses to frame the news is representative of their preferred worldview. The manner by which media institutions portray the Iraq war (whether reinforcing or questioning it) reveals much about that organization's stance in regards to the conflict. By rendering the war in Iraq as a struggle against terrorism and a quest to democratize the Middle East, those working within the corporate media are essentially sending the message: "This is what I believe, this is what I stand for," whether they choose to acknowledge it or not.

There should be no illusions about the possibility of pursuing objective, value-free reporting. As corporate media sources create a favorable climate for pro-war attitudes to take shape, so too has the American Progressive-Left media taken great strides in its efforts to contradict officially espoused war aims. The Progressive media is not alone in this campaign either. Accompanied by the anti-war leaning sectors of the British, Australian, and Arab media, the American progressive press seeks to present a serious roadblock to the war effort in Iraq.

In presenting foundational, substantive criticisms of "Operation Iraqi Freedom," Progressive media outlets present a critical "frame" that dissects the official reasons for going to war in their own anti-war propaganda. They want to demonstrate that the arguments for war, at their core, are motivated by a preoccupation with American imperial dominance, of which the "War on Terror" is only the latest incarnation.

American corporate media has overwhelmingly taken the position that the U.S. presence in the Middle East is driven by a noble effort to promote self-determination, human rights, justice, and democracy. Although those Iraqis who resist American occupation are attacked in papers like the *New York Times* for relying on "propaganda that has helped fuel the insurgency throughout Iraq,"[61] the propaganda of the American media and government are ignored. It is not considered propaganda, but rather "conventional wisdom," by mainstream pundits like Fareed Zakaria of *Newsweek* that "that the United States should stay engaged with Iraq for years."[62] Acceptance of this "conventional wisdom" inevitably discredits serious opposition to the long-term occupation of Iraq.

The lesson promoted by Zakaria and others in the media seems clear: only enemies of the U.S. engage in "propaganda," as the intentions of the Bush administration are considered an axiom that is unworthy of substantive challenge. Other conventional wisdoms throughout the corporate press include the portrayal of U.S. as committed to a "democratic and unified Iraq," resisting the "terrorism and insurgent violence" of resistance cells "whose tactics grow steadily more lethal" day by day.[63] While most would surely agree that many Iraqi resistance groups have engaged in terrorist acts that destabilize Iraqi society, such a fact does not automatically confirm that the U.S. is unconditionally concerned with promoting democracy, human rights, and self-determination.

When corporate media outlets do criticize U.S. policy in Iraq, they typically rely on narrow assessments of the Bush administration, intended primarily to increase the efficiency and effectiveness of the war campaign. This commitment to supporting the Iraq war relies on pragmatic, pro-war frames, whereby those within the corporate press focus on the best ways to pursue military conflicts (posing only minor challenges along the way). Jeff Cohen, former producer for *MSNBC News* and founder of media watchdog *Fairness and Accuracy in Reporting (FAIR)* explains this practice in more detail: "Mainstream media allow dissent about war—but usually only on tactics, *not motives*. It's acceptable to critique the Iraq war as ill-planned or ill-executed, but not to suggest that the war was less about freedom and democracy than about politics or empire or military bases or oil."[64]

Media critic Reese Erlich provides further insight into the underlying assumptions of mainstream reporters covering the motivations for, and soundness of, U.S. foreign policy in the "War on Terror." In the months preceding the 2003 Iraq invasion, Erlich spoke with numerous American journalists in Iraq, only to find a consensus on the virtuousness of American foreign policy objectives: "I didn't meet a single foreign reporter in Iraq who disagreed with the notion that the U.S. and Britain have the right to overthrow the Iraqi government by force. They disagreed only about timing, whether the action should be unilateral, and whether a long-term occupation is practical."[65] While American corporate media has reported more and more on calls for withdrawal from Iraq as the occupation continues, its "opposition" to the war still fits within the narrow parameters of debate discussed above in that it does not challenge U.S. "humanitarian" motivations.

What is Propaganda?

Propaganda is an important concept that has often been misunderstood in American politics and culture. Propaganda cannot realistically be defined to include only the rhetoric of America's "enemies" or those who criticize U.S. foreign policy. A standard dictionary definition portrays propaganda as the spread of any facts, ideas, or concepts designed deliberately to further one cause or discount another. Propaganda entails the systematic dissemination of *any* given doctrine or dogma, by *any* party, regardless of their outlook on the Iraq war or other important social issues. In other words, it does not, at its core, require deliberate deception. Propaganda, then, is not necessarily inherently "good" or "bad." This point has been made quite clearly by Edward Bernays, the father of the American public relations industry.

In his classic work, *Propaganda*, Bernays put forth a "neutral denotation" of the term, which has been reinforced in other works in the area of media studies.[66] Bernays situated the use of propaganda within the "vast and continuous effort going on to capture our minds in the interest of some policy or commodity or idea." Bernays contended that, "propaganda carries to many minds an unpleasant connotation. Yet whether, in any instance, propaganda is good or bad depends upon the merits of the causes urged, and the correctness of the information published."[67]

In his work, *Projections of Power: Framing News, Public Opinion, and U.S. Foreign Policy*, Robert Entman defines framing as the "highlighting [of] some facets of events or issues, and making connections among them so as to promote a particular interpretation, evaluation, and/or solution."[68] In this work, I sometimes use the concepts of framing and propaganda interchangeably, in that both concepts refer to a systematic bias in coverage in favor of one perspective or another. I also use the concepts of propaganda and framing in regards to corporate media coverage of the "War on Terror" in order to better convey many of the harmful effects of mainstream media reporting, as they have tended to limit open debate on problems regarding American interventions. Jonathan Mermin, author of *Debating War and Peace: Media Coverage of U.S. Intervention in the Post-Vietnam Era* refers to the narrow range of debate in media through the Indexing effect, which has been explored in works by other media scholars.[69] Mermin summarizes: "if there is debate inside the American government over U.S. policy, critical perspectives appear in the news. If government policy has bipartisan support in Washington, however, critical perspectives expressed outside the government are not well reported."[70]

While mainstream journalists are technically independent of government as a result of private, rather than government ownership of the press, they have, in reality, "turned over to official actors the power to set the news agenda and the spectrum of debate in the news."[71] As a result, the press has generally failed in promoting an open-ended public debate over war that transcends narrow partisan perspectives.

Progressive-Left Propaganda

While corporate media coverage is often classified as propaganda, such propaganda necessarily carries with it a much different connotation than Progressive-Left media propaganda, which is not referred to in negative terms throughout this work. The main reason for this distinction between the two types of propaganda (positive and negative) is clear enough: corporate media institutions maintain a monopoly when it comes to reporting the news, whereas Progressive-Left outlets are far smaller and retain much more limited audiences, and, as a result, less influence with the mass public. Public debate inevitably suffers in light of the monopoly dominance of corporate propaganda, as progressive views and criticisms are blackballed from mainstream reporting and editorializing.

Progressive-Left media outlets, on the other hand, have grown primarily as a response to the lack of open debate throughout the mainstream media. Surely it should be considered a positive thing that they add long-neglected arguments (whether one agrees with them or not is irrelevant) to discussions that are sorely lacking in dissident points of view. The very idea of placing Progressive media propaganda on par with corporate propaganda in terms of negative effects is absurd, given the dramatic differences in audience and reader levels between the two types of media. Corporations have thoroughly dominated the mass media since the rise of the modern American media state, thereby limiting debate to those views accepted within corporate culture. As Ben Bagdikian explains about corporate monopoly power that, "By 2000, of all cities with a daily paper, 99 percent had only one newspaper management"—effectively ensuring that each paper retained monopoly rights within its respective area of operation.[72]

While corporate newspapers reach tens millions of people everyday, the Progressive-Left does not even publish a single daily newspaper, let alone one that can reach millions. Even monthly and weekly progressive magazines cannot come close to corporate weekly magazines in terms of distribution levels. Magazines like the *Nation* and *In These Times* retain small circulations of 173,000 and

16,000 respectively, whereas mainstream weekly magazines, as shown below, are radically higher.[73]

Table 1.4

Corporate Weekly Magazines

Name	Circulation
Time	4,026,000
Newsweek	3,118,000
U.S. News & World Report	2,035,000

The most prominent of Progressive-Left monthly magazines retain far smaller circulations than do corporate weekly newsmagazines, as indicated below:[74]

Table 1.5

Progressive-Left Monthly Magazines

Name	Circulation
The Progressive	65,887
Multinational Monitor	4,753
Z Magazine	18,000
Extra!	21,000
International Socialist Review	7,500

Even when added together, five of the most prominent progressive magazines listed in the table above total just over 100,000 readers a month, which equals only 6 percent of the total *weekly* circulation *U.S. News & World Report*, the smallest of the three major corporate magazines. In short, the preoccupation with the negative effects of corporate media propaganda is well merited, given the extreme lopsidedness between corporate and Progressive-Left media markets in terms of their access to, and influence over, the public.

Media Propaganda in the "War on Terror": American and World Opinion at Crossroads

The invasion of Iraq exposed deep fissures between American and world opinion, particularly in regards to crucial issues such as Iraq's alleged weapons of mass destruction and purported ties to Al Qaeda, and the U.S. role as global liberator. As late as March of 2005, 56 percent of Americans still believed that Iraq possessed weapons of mass destruction before the start of the U.S. invasion, despite strong evidence that Iraq disarmed years earlier. Six in ten Americans polled in 2005 also indicated that they thought Iraq provided support to Al Qaeda, despite the fact that no conclusive evidence of a link was presented by the Bush administration or the media outside of mere conjecture.[75] Perhaps most disturbing of all though was the fallacious assumption amongst 54 percent of those questioned that most Iraqis supported the U.S. occupation of Iraq.[76]

The mainstream media played a vital role in manipulating the American public in favor of going to war with Iraq, especially when considering the effectiveness of media outlets in indoctrinating the public with claims of Iraqi WMD and ties to Al Qaeda. Such justifications for war did not spontaneously materialize from no place, or without reason in the minds of hundreds of millions of Americans; rather, these justifications originated from a few key sources: namely the Bush administration, prominent political figures (Democrats and Republicans) and the mainstream media, among other major political actors.

Without media, the Bush administration had no mass venue through which to spread its pro-war messages, as it needed a receptive, largely uncritical audience amongst the corporate media's owners, editors, and reporters. In effect, the media became the conduit for the transmission of the government's pro-war platform, as it transformed itself into a messenger for the Bush administration's portrayals of an imminent Iraqi threat. Amy Goodman of *Democracy Now!* summarizes the state of media complicity as follows: "When George Bush said there were Weapons of Mass Destruction [in Iraq], he could not have done it alone. . .he needed an international apparatus to launder what he said, or to put the stamp of approval on it, and he had it in the U.S. media. More powerful than any bomb or missile, the Pentagon has deployed the U.S. media."[77]

The power of the American media in fostering pro-war attitudes had drastic consequences when reflecting upon the gulf between American public opinion, which was generally pro-war from 2002-2004, and world opinion, which was often more skeptical of the motives and actions of the Bush administration during that same period. The differences in world opinion and American opinion were pronounced in terms of support for, and opposition to, the Bush administration's foreign policy. While 86 percent of Americans polled at the outset of the Iraq war claimed "disarmament of Iraq" as a main motivation for supporting the invasion,[78] international audiences were often reacting with more suspicion to U.S. WMD claims. By April 2003, 75 percent of Americans were still confident that the U.S. would uncover large stockpiles of weapons of mass destruction in post-Saddam Iraq.[79]

On the other hand, a *Pew Research Center* poll conducted throughout a number of European and Middle Eastern countries found that, contrary to public opinion in the U.S., majorities in most countries surveyed felt that "American and British leaders lied when they claimed, prior to the Iraq war, that Saddam Hussein's regime had weapons of mass destruction."[80] This stands in marked contrast to the American public, of which only three-in-ten polled felt that the Bush administration lied in order to go to war, even after no weapons of mass destruction had been found following the invasion.[81] American trust in the presidency continued long after the Iraq invasion, as polling in early 2005 indicated that 55 percent of Americans questioned thought that "the administration told people what it believed to be true" with reference to the justifications for war.[82]

World opinion was also distrustful of the Bush administration's commitment to "fighting terrorism." Although 80 percent of Americans claimed Iraqi ties to Al Qaeda were a main motivation for supporting the invasion, polling information of populations abroad revealed much different results. For example, one *Pew* poll of eight European and Middle Eastern countries (Russia, France, Germany, Morocco, Turkey, Pakistan, Britain, and Jordan) found that majorities in six of these eight countries thought that, rather than contributing to the fight against Al Qaeda and terrorism, the Iraq war had actually been detrimental to the "War on Terror."[83] Over and over again, people throughout Muslim countries expressed doubt that the "War on Terror" was actually motivated by fighting terror;[84] rather, many were concerned that the United States, as a global aggressor, could pose a serious threat to their own countries' national security and safety.[85]

Scrutiny of the Bush administration's unilateralist policies manifested itself within the United States' European allies as well. A *Forsa* poll found that 57 percent of Germans questioned felt that "the United States is a nation of warmongers," whereas only 6 percent believed the Bush administration is actually concerned with "preserving peace" globally.[86] Extensive studies of American misperceptions of the Iraq war reveal that the mainstream press shares major responsibility for the public's pro-war opinions. A series of seven nationwide polls done in 2003 by the *Program on International Policy Attitudes* (*PIPA*) revealed that the likelihood of individuals holding misperceptions regarding the justifications for war were associated a great deal with their consumption of the news coming out of the American corporate media.[87] *Fox News* viewers in particular were the most susceptible to such misperceptions, as the station's audience was more inclined to believe that the Iraqi government retained ties with Al Qaeda members, that the U.S. had found WMD in Iraq, and that the international community supported the U.S. invasion.

Figure 1.1

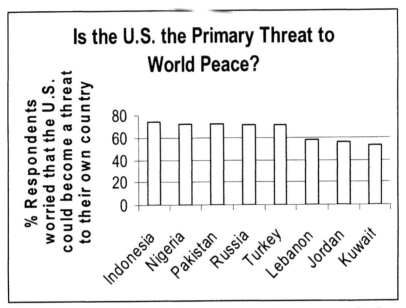

Source: Christopher Marquis, "World's View of U.S. Sours After Iraq War, Poll Finds," 4 June 2004, *New York Times*, 19(A).

Damning in itself was the conclusion reached by *PIPA* that these misperceptions took root more often amongst *Fox* viewers who actually paid *more* attention to the channel's news reports. This trend was not relegated only to *Fox News* though. The *PIPA* polls revealed that the percentage of Americans surveyed who held at least one of three misperceptions (that Iraq had ties to Al Qaeda, that Iraq possessed WMD, and that world opinion supported the U.S. going to war) was rather high for all the mainstream television networks. Seventy-one percent of *CNN* viewers reported at least one misperception, whereas 61 percent of *CBS* viewers, 55 percent of *ABC* viewers, and 55 percent of *NBC* viewers reported holding at least one of these misperceptions between January and September of 2003.

Table 1.6

**Frequency of Viewer Misperceptions
on Iraq in 2003**

Misperceptions:

1. That Iraq Possessed Weapons of Mass Destruction

2. That Iraq had Ties to Al Qaeda

3. That the International Community Supported the U.S. War

Channel's Examined	Percent of Viewers with One or More Misperceptions
Fox	80%
CNN	71%
CBS	61%
ABC	55%
NBC	55%
PBS	23%

Finally, the international community can be contrasted with the American public in that, unlike most Americans, it rejected humanitarian justifications claimed for the occupation of Iraq. At the time of the invasion, 74 percent of Americans surveyed accepted the "liberation of Iraq" as a vital goal in "Operation Iraqi Freedom." Accepting this democratic justification for war, 56 percent of Americans asked in 2005 were still confident that "Iraqi leaders can create a stable government" in occupied Iraq.[88] International opposition to the Iraq war, conversely, was often driven by the assessment that the United States was not adequately concerned with the welfare of the global community. It was accepted throughout much of the Muslim world and Europe that the United States was not seriously concerned with the "interests and needs" of the people of these regions, as "control [of] Mideast oil" was considered to be a major policy goal for American political leaders.[89] On the subject of Iraq, majorities in Jordan, Morocco, Egypt, Lebanon, and Saudi Arabia indicated that they felt the U.S. effort to restore sovereignty to Iraq through elections is "only cosmetic," rather than a full handover of power and sovereignty to the new Iraqi government.[90]

Figure 1.2

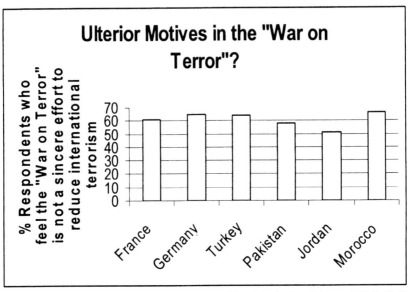

Source: Susan Sachs, "Poll Finds Hostility Hardening Toward U.S. Policies," *New York Times*, 17 March 2004, 3(A).

In general, much of the international community has become less and less trusting of the United States, viewing its "War on Terror" as a means of consolidating American power under the pretext of noble and humanitarian intervention. Positive views of the United States have plummeted in recent years in light of the cavalier foreign policy initiatives of the Bush administration. The issue of Iraq has been the major determining factor in regards to the Arab World. As one 2005 *Zogby* poll shows, sympathy with the United States amongst the citizens of Morocco, Egypt, Saudi Arabia, United Arab Emirates, Lebanon, and Jordan has fallen to near record lows, as between 65 and 90 percent of the public reported unfavorable views of the U.S., depending on the specific country in question.[91] A similar pattern is recognized in Europe and Asia, as confidence levels in the Bush administration have ranged between only 8 and 30 percent in France, Germany, Spain, Russia, Turkey, Pakistan, and Indonesia.[92]

Figure 1.3

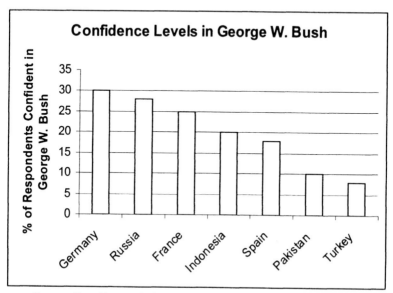

Source: Pew Research Center, "U.S. Image up Slightly, But Still Negative," 24 June 2005, http://pewglobal.org/reports/display.php?PageID=80 (12 September 2005).

While one could persuasively argue that the forces of nationalism have much to do with reinforcing Americans' conceptions of U.S. humanitarianism, this is likely only part of the story. The American mainstream press has also been tremendously effective in convincing Americans of the necessity of war with Iraq. As Americans look to the media with trust and in search of the information necessary to evaluate U.S. policy abroad, they are exposed to a very narrow range of "acceptable" views seeking to reinforce American prestige and power. However, as the Iraq war went on, Americans also became more critical of the U.S. presence in Iraq. Despite consistent calls in the corporate press to "stay the course," and fierce opposition to setting some sort of time table for withdrawal, the majority of Americans began in 2005 to call for a phased withdrawal from Iraq in light of mounting American and Iraqi casualties, as well as the significant economic burden of the occupation. This should be viewed as a major challenge to those within the media and government who promote conventional arguments that require the continued "pacification" of Iraqi resistance and a long-term occupation of Iraq. That public opinion could shift so dramatically away from the official policy agenda of the Bush administration and the mass media, despite the enormous resources allocated to selling the Bush plan, is an important development indeed.

The dramatic shift in public opinion away from the pretexts provided by political leaders and media suggests that the propaganda system is not always effective in inculcating the American public. Charles Lindblom, the author of the classic work *Politics and Markets*, argues "indoctrination of a population by the most favored class is, of course, never a complete success."[93] In the case of Iraq, one can conclude that as the occupation has evolved, the American public has gone from largely supportive in 2003 and 2004, to largely skeptical from 2005 on, despite continued calls from within the media that it was the United States' responsibility, as a humanitarian power, to "stay the course" in Iraq.

The mainstream media's role in promoting pro-war views to the neglect of substantive anti-war claims during the Iraq invasion and occupation should be thoroughly examined. That most Americans uncritically accepted the arguments that Iraq possessed weapons of mass destruction and retained ties to Al Qaeda (thereby lending their consent to the Bush administration based upon false pretenses) speaks volumes about the failure of the mainstream press in its expected task of providing the public with an accurate picture of what is going on in the world today, and providing the public with a better balance between pro-war and anti-war views. In an independent, professional media system, journalists would be expected to treat official claims and propaganda with skepticism, rather than wholeheartedly accepting such claims as incontestable fact. This has not been the case in American reporting.

A Need for More Balanced Debate

While objectivity and complete balance are obviously impossible standards to achieve in journalism, this does not mean that media outlets should not struggle to incorporate the largest number of views possible in regards to the issues they report. In their book, *By Invitation Only: How the Media Limit Political Debate*, David Crouteau and William Hoynes elaborate upon an ideal expected of media organizations: "The role of the news media should be to present the views of diverse groups involved in or affected by any given issue. If citizens in a democracy are to make informed decisions, they must have access to the range of opinions available on potentially controversial matters."[94]

Fair reporting is not about achieving perfect balance, but rather about levels of balance. Media systems as a whole can more or less balanced in their reporting in terms of incorporating a diverse number of views. The British print media, for example, has been far more willing than the American press to incorporate a wider range of ideological views in its reporting of the "War on Terror," as is explained in greater detail later in this book. When American media outlets systematically neglect Progressive-Left perspectives while consistently incorporating mainstream and conservative points of view, what is left is an extreme imbalance in war coverage. As Benjamin Page, author of *Who Deliberates: Mass Media in Modern Democracy* contends: "Public deliberation may be harmed because the media rely heavily upon official sources for news stories." While "it is perfectly reasonable for the media to pay attention to public officials," when "an official point of view is conveyed but other important views are excluded, citizens may be misled." Traditionally, this has been a major problem in media systems like the United States, where "government officials [retain] monopoly control" over media sources.[95]

Notes

1. Elizabeth M. Perse, *Media Effects and Society* (Mahway, NJ: Lawrence Erlbaum, 2001), 27.

2. Bernard C. Cohen, *The Press and Foreign Policy* (Berkley, Ca.: University of California, 1993), 13.

3. Maxwell McCombs and David L. Protess, "The Agenda Setting Function of Mass Media," in *Agenda Setting: Readings on Media, Public Opinion, and Policymaking*, ed. Maxwell McCombs and David L. Protess (Mahway, NJ: Lawrence Erlbaum, 1991), 21-22.

4. McCombs and Protess, *Agenda Setting*, 26.

5. Ray Funkhouser, "The Issues of the Sixties: An Exploratory Study in the Dynamics of Public Opinion," in *Agenda Setting: Readings on Media, Public Opinion, and Policymaking*, ed. Maxwell McCombs and David L. Protess (Mahway, NJ: Lawrence Erlbaum, 1991), 39.

6. James W. Dearing and Everett M. Rogers, *Agenda Setting* (London: Sage, 1996), 12.

7. Perse, *Media Effects*, 98.

8. Perse, *Media Effects*, 26.

9. Perse, *Media Effects*, 106.

10. Michael Parenti, *Inventing Reality: The Politics of News Media* (New York: St. Martins, 1993).

11. Shanto Iyengar and Donald R. Kinder, *News That Matters: Television and American Opinion* (Chicago: University of Chicago, 1987), 17.

12. Iyengar and Kinder, *News That Matters*, 4.

13. Allen McBride and Robert K. Toburen, "Deep Structures: Polpop Culture on Primetime Television," in *Culture and Politics: A Reader*, ed. Lane Crothers and Charles Lockhart (New York: St. Martins), 145.

14. Frank Newport and Lydia Saad, "A Matter of Trust," *American Journalism Review* July/August 1998, http://www.ajr.org/article.asp?id=352 (10 Sep.2005).

15. Editor & Publisher, "Public Confidence in News Media Falls to New Low," 10 June 2005, http://www.independent-media.tv/item.cfm?fmedia_id=11176&fcategory_de-sc=Under%20Reported (10 Sep. 2005).

16. Pew Research Center, "Public More Critical of Press, But Goodwill Persists," 26 June 2005, http://people-press.org/reports/display.php3?ReportID=248 (10 Sep. 2005).

17. *New York Times* and *CBS*, "The *New York Times/CBS* Poll," 20-25 January 2006, http://www.nytimes.com/packages/pdf/politics/20060127_poll_results.pdf (5 Aug. 2005).

18. Pew, "Public More Critical of the Press," 2005.

19. Pew Research Center, "All Three Commercial Evening News Anchors Viewed Positively," 24 August 2006, http://people-press.org/reports/display.php3?ReportID=286 (14 Oct. 2006).

20. Pew, "Public More Critical of the Press," 2005.

21. PollingReport.com, "Journalism," http://www.pollingreport.com/media.htm (8 Oct. 2006).

22. Pew Research Center, "Media Seen as Fair, But Tilting to Gore," 15 October 2000, http://people-press.org/reports/display.php3?ReportID=29 (26 Sep. 2006).

23. Zogby International, "U.S. Public Widely Distrusts its Leaders," 23 May 2006, http://www.zogby.com/News/ReadNews.dbm?ID=1116 (3 Aug. 2006).

24. Pew, "Public More Critical of the Press," 2005.

25. Pew, "Public More Critical of the Press," 2005.

26. Pew, "Public More Critical of the Press," 2005.

27. CBSnews.com, "Bush's Job Approval Hits New Low," 3 November 2005, http://www.cbsnews.com/stories/2005/11/02/eveningnews/main1005982.shtml (3 Aug. 2006).

28. Zogby International, "U.S. Public Widely Distrusts its Leaders," 23 May 2006, http://www.zogby.com/News/ReadNews.dbm?ID=1116 (3 August 2006).; Dan Balz and Jon Cohen, "A Majority in Poll Favor Deadline for Iraq Pullout," *Washington Post*, February 27, 2007, 1(A).

29. Ben H. Bagdikian, "The New Media Monopoly," http://www.benbagdikian.com, (3 Aug. 2005).

30. Pew, "Public More Critical of the Press," 2005.

31. Associated Press and TV Guide, "Katie Couric Heads to Evening News as Poll Shows Viewers Prefer Her in the Morning," 5 April 2006, http://www.ipsos-na.com/news/pressrelease.cfm?id=3040 (15 Apr. 2007).

32. Tom Rosentiel, "The End of 'Network News,'" *Washington Post*, 12 September 2004, 7(B).

33. Project for Excellence in Journalism, "The State of the Media," 2005, http://www.stateofthenewsmedia.com/2005/1 (3 Feb. 2006).

34. Annys Shin, "Newspaper Circulation Continues to Decline," *Washington Post*, 3 May 2005, 3(E).

35. Pew Research Center, "News Audiences Increasingly Politicized," 8 June 2004, http://people-press.org/reports/display.php3?PageID=834 (22 Jul. 2005).

36. Arthur Sulzberger Jr., "The Future of the New York Times," *Business Week*, 17 January 2005, http://www.businessweek.com/magazine/content/05_03/b3916001_mz00-1.htm (2 Dec. 2005).

37. The Chicago Tribune, "Circulation/Audience," 2006, http://classified.tribune.com/-ctadvertiserwebsite/circulation.htm (17 Dec. 2006).

38. Ben H. Bagdikian, *The New Media Monopoly* (Boston, Ma.: Beacon, 2004), 121, 117.

39. Gannett, "Company Profile," 2005, http://www.gannett.com/map/gan007.htm (12 Jun. 2005).

40. Knight Ridder, 2005, http://www.knightridder.com/papers/newspapers.html (12 Jun. 2005).

41. Associated Press, "Facts and Figures," 2005, http://www.ap.org/pages/about/about-.html (7 Jul. 2005).

42. Dearing and Rogers, *Agenda Setting*, 32.

43. Noam Chomsky, "Excerpts from Manufacturing Consent," *Chomsky Info* 1992, http://www.chomsky.info/interviews/1992----02.htm (15 Dec. 2006).

44. Pew Research Center, "News Audiences Increasingly Politicized," 8 June 2004, http://people-press.org/reports/display.php3?PageID=834 (2 Aug. 2005).

45. Pew, "News Audiences Increasingly Politicized," 2004.

46. Pew, "News Audiences Increasingly Politicized," 2004.
47. Project Excellence Journalism, "State of the Media," 2005.
48. Jeff Cohen, *Cable News Confidential: My Misadventures in Corporate Media* (Sausalito, Ca.: PoliPoint, 2006), 166.
49. Pew, "News Audiences Increasingly Politicized," 2004.
50. Edward Herman and Noam Chomsky, *Manufacturing Consent: The Political Economy of the Mass Media* (New York: Pantheon, 1988), 1, 298.
51. Noam Chomsky, *Necessary Illusions: Thought Control in Democratic Societies* (Boston, Ma.: South End, 1989), 8.
52. Parenti, *Inventing Reality*, 71.
53. Lee Drutman and Charlie Cray, "The People's Business," *In These Times*, 18 February 2005, http://www.inthesetimes.com/site/main/article/1971/ (13 Aug. 2005)
54. Business Week, "The Online Ad Surge," 22 November 2004, http://businessweek.com/magazine/content/04_47/b3909401.htm (1 Jul. 2005).
55. Charles Lindblom, *Politics and Markets: The World's Political Economic Systems* (New York: Basic, 1977), 170-88.
56. Peter Phillips, "Ownership and Control of the Media," in *War, Lies, & Videotape: How Media Monopoly Stifles Truth*, ed. Lenora Foerstel (New York: IAC, 2000), 57.
57. Jeff Cohen, "From MacNeil-Lehrer to Nightline," in *Stenographers to Power: Media & Propaganda*, ed. David Barsamian (Monroe, Me.: Common Courage, 1992), 101-12.
58. Bartholomew H. Sparrow, *Uncertain Guardians: The News Media as a Political Institution* (Baltimore, Md.: Johns Hopkins, 1999), 79.
59. James D. Squires, *Read All About It! The Corporate Takeover of America's Newspapers* (New York: Times, 1993); C. Edwin Baker, *Advertising and a Democratic Press* (Princeton, NJ: Princeton, 1994); Lawrence Soley, *Censorship Inc. The Corporate Threat to Free Speech in the United States* (New York: Monthly Review, 2002); John H. McManus, *Market-Driven Journalism: Let the Citizen Beware?* (Thousand Oaks, Ca.: Sage, 1994); William Hoynes, *Public Television for Sale: Media, the Market, and the Public Sphere* (Boulder, Co.: Westview, 1994).
60. Dean Alger, *Megamedia: How Giant Corporations Dominate Mass Media, Distort Competition, and Endanger Democracy* (Lanham, Md.: Rowman & Littlefield, 1998), 163-64.
61. Robert F. Worth, "Sides in Falluja Fight for Hearts and Minds," *New York Times*, 17 November 2004, 13(A).
62. Fareed Zakaria, "Our Last Real Chance," *Newsweek*, 19 April 2004, http://www.fareedzakaria.com/articles/newsweek/041904.html (10 Dec. 2004).
63. Editorial, "The Road Ahead in Iraq," *New York Times*, 26 October 2005, 26(A).
64. Cohen, *Cable News*, 170.
65. Norman Solomon, *War Made Easy: How Presidents and Pundits Keep Spinning us to Death* (Hoboken, NJ: Wiley & Sons, 2005), 116.
66. Edward Bernays, *Propaganda* (Brooklyn, NY: IG, 2005), 11.; Michael Parenti, "Propaganda and Class Structure: Some Working Definitions," in *Stenographers to Power: Media & Propaganda*, ed. David Barsamian (Monroe, Me.: Common Courage, 1992), 43-44.
67. Bernays, *Propaganda*, 39.
68. Robert Entman, *Projections of Power: Framing News, Public Opinion, and U.S. Foreign Policy* (Chicago: University of Chicago, 2004), 6.

69. W. Lance Bennett, "The News About Foreign Policy," in *Taken By Storm: The Media, Public Opinion, and U.S. Foreign Policy in the Gulf War*, ed. W. Lance Bennett and David L. Paletz, (Chicago: University of Chicago, 1994), 25.

70. Jonathon Mermin, *Debating War and Peace: Media Coverage of U.S. Intervention in the Post-Vietnam Era* (Princeton, NJ: Princeton, 1999), 5.

71. Mermin, *Debating War*, 27.

72. Bagdikian, Media Monopoly, 185.

73. Alternative Press Center, "The Alternative Press Center's Online Directory," 2006, http://www.altpress.org/direct.html (17 Dec. 2006).; Project for Excellence in Journalism, "State of the News Media 2006," 2006, http://www.stateofthenewsmedia.org/2006 (17 Dec. 2006).

74. Alternative Press Center, "Online Directory," 2006.

75. Dan Balz and Richard Morin, "2 Years After Invasion, Poll Data Mixed," *Washington Post*, 16 March 2005, 1(A).

76. Balz and Morin, "2 Years After Invasion," 2005.

77. *Red State Road Trip*, DVD, directed by Chris Hume (Truthout/Hit & Run Productions, 2005).

78. Liz Marlantes and Howard LaFranchi, "'Smoking Gun' May Not Affect World's Opinion," *Christian Science Monitor*, 9 April 2003, http://www.csmonitor.com/2003/04-09/p01s03-woiq.html (16 Dec. 2006).

79. Marlantes and LaFranchi, "'Smoking Gun' May Not Affect World's Opinion," 2003.

80. Pew Research Center, "A Year After Iraq War: Mistrust of America in Europe Even Higher, Muslim Anger Persists," 16 March 2004, http://people-press.org/reports/display.-phhp3?ReportID=206 (8 Jun. 2005).

81. Pew, "A Year After Iraq War," 2004.

82. Balz and Morin, "2 Years After Invasion," 2005.

83. Sonni Efron, "U.S. Seen Unfavorably, Poll Shows," *Los Angeles Times*, 17 March 2004, 16(A).

84. Jim Lobe, "Gap Grows Between U.S., World Public Opinion," *Inter Press* Service, 16 March 2004, http://www.globalissues.org/Geopolitics/WarOnTerror/OpinionGap.asp (9 Jul. 2005).

85. Christopher Marquis, "World's View of U.S. Sours after Iraq War, Poll Finds," *New York Times*, 4 June 2003, 19(A).

86. William Horsley, "Poll Finds Europeans Oppose Iraq War," *BBC News*, 11 February 2003, http://news.bbc.co.uk/1/hi/world/europe/2747175.stm (14 Sep. 2005).

87. Steven Kull, "Misperceptions, the Media, and the Iraq War," *Program on International Policy Attitudes*, 2 October 2003, http://www.worldpublicopinion.org/pipa/articles-/international_security_bt/102.php?nid=&id=&pnt=102&lb=brusc (6 Sep. 2005).

88. Balz and Morin, "2 Years After Invasion," 2005.

89. Lobe, "Gap Grows Between U.S.," 2004.

90. Guardian Unlimited, "Polls Apart," *The Guardian*, 26 July 2004, http://www.guardian.co.uk/elsewhere/journalist/story/0,7792,1269523,00.html (10 Sep. 2005).

91. James Zogby, "2005 Arab Attitudes toward U.S.: Good News and Bad News," *Truthout*, 7 November 2005, http://www.truthout.org/docs_2005/printer_110805H.shtml (12 Jan. 2006).

92. Pew Research Center, "U.S. Image up Slightly, But Still Negative," 24 June 2005, http://pewglobal.org/reports/display.php?PageID=801 (17 Jan. 2006).

93. Lindblom, *Politics and Markets*, 212, 229.

94. David Croteau and William Hoynes, *By Invitation Only: How the Media Limit Political Debate* (Monroe, Me.: Common Courage, 1994), 21.
95. Benjamin I. Page, *Who Deliberates? Mass Media in Modern Democracy* (Chicago: University of Chicago, 1996), 9.

2

All the News That's Fit to Omit: A Background to Pro-War Media

Highlighting the power of the mainstream media to influence public opinion in favor of official agendas is not a high priority for many reporters, editors, and owners in the corporate press. When the media's power in shaping public opinion is addressed by journalists and academics, it is often done through the use of stereotypes and romanticism that describe the media as a public watchdog and protector of the common good. The *New York Times*, for example, describes itself as "an independent newspaper, entirely fearless, free of ulterior influence and unselfishly devoted to the public welfare."[1] While the mainstream media is often idealized—as seen in journalistic rhetoric—for its alleged efforts to expose government lies and deception and uncover hidden truths, it is less often described as an institution driven by ulterior motives such as profit.

The view of the American press as committed to muckraking and investigative journalism is not the only description of the mainstream media. The emergence and prominence of "neutral," "value-free" journalism has also played an important role in shaping the behavior of journalists, editors, media analysts, academics, media owners, and many others in the pre and post-9/11 periods. While many journalists speak idealistically about the mass media, they also criticize media outlets in other countries for what they consider biased and unprofessional reporting. The *New York Times* criticizes Arab newspapers for "publish[ing] at the pleasure of their governments,"[2] while the *Washington Post* speaks about "the vicious anti-Americanism that drives the popular media of the Middle East."[3]

Criticisms of Arab media outlets are juxtaposed with support for the American mass media as committed to a "fair and balanced" brand of journalism (the *Fox News* slogan) that mediates between opposing views on important political and social problems, and allowing Americans to choose from a variety of viewpoints by presenting "All the News That's Fit to Print" (the *New York Times* motto). *CBS News* president Andrew Heyward argues that, "There is a long-standing tradition in the mainstream press of middle-of-the-road journalism that is objective and fair."[4] Rupert Murdoch, CEO of *News Corporation* seems to concur, stating that his company, *Fox News*, does not "take any position at all" in favor of the Bush administration or other political leaders.[5] The common feeling amongst mainstream reporters and owners is that mass media institutions are professional in large part because they exist independently of government influence, ownership, and manipulation. It is through this conception of the media that many journalists defend corporate ownership of the press. As corporate conglomerates further consolidate their control over the news, they inevitably mold the opinions and perceptions of the American people regarding crucial matters, such as public confidence in government and the legitimacy of the "War on Terror." The corporate media attempts to influence the public in accordance with the prevailing ideologies that drive the capitalist system. It is under this context that those who consume the news should seek to understand the basic elements comprising corporate media framing.

The corporate press has historically been supportive of American engagement in foreign wars. During the Spanish-American War, William Randolph Hearst's paper, the *New York Journal*, aided in promoting pro-war enthusiasm amongst the American public by printing drawings that showed Spanish agents planting a mine on the USS Maine in Havana Harbor, despite the lack of evidence that Spanish forces had attacked the ship. The lack of conclusive evidence did not stop Hearst, as he encouraged his reporter in Cuba to file reports of Cuban rebellion against the Spanish. Hearst famously promised his Cuban correspondent, "You furnish the pictures, I'll furnish the war."[6] Similarly, support for war took root in the media during World War II and the Vietnam War. In World War II, the U.S. government prohibited the printing of any pictures depicting American casualties until 1943, in order to prevent the public from souring on the war effort.[7]

In the Vietnam War, the mass media went to great lengths to accommodate the Johnson administration's claims that the North Vietnamese had attacked a U.S. destroyer at the Gulf of Tonkin. The *New York Times* reported that "President Johnson has ordered retaliatory action against gunboats and 'certain supporting facilities in North Vietnam' after renewed attacks against American destroyers in the Gulf of Tonkin," despite the fact that journalists at the time had substantial information contradicting the Johnson administration's account of what happened at Tonkin.[8]

As the U.S. escalated the war with Vietnam, newspapers and magazines pronounced government commitment to human rights. In 1966, *U.S. News and World Report* argued that, "What the United States is doing in Vietnam is the most significant example of philanthropy extended by one people to another that we have witnessed in our times," despite estimates that the U.S. was responsible for the deaths of millions of civilians in Vietnam, Cambodia, and Laos.[9] When the media did turn against the war, it was more for pragmatic than moral reasons. After the Tet Offensive, Walter Cronkite claimed the war was "unwinnable," rather than immoral or imperialistic. Such a statement was intended to identify the failure of progress, rather than focus upon American responsibility for the deaths of millions of civilians and the widespread destruction of a country's infrastructure.

In the first Gulf War, the Bush administration and U.S. Central Command undertook a systematic effort to limit reporting coming out of Iraq that did not reinforce the official line. The pool system, used during the invasion of Panama, was resurrected for the 1991 conflict with Iraq. Journalists were not allowed to travel in Baghdad on their own, as they were to be escorted by military personnel at all times, and let into Iraq in profoundly small numbers. In his work, *Second Front: Censorship and Propaganda in the Gulf War*, John MacArthur pointed out that the mainstream press was largely willing to accept official statements regarding "precision weapons" used against Iraqi targets. On *ABC*, Peter Jennings discussed the "astonishing precision" of U.S. smart bombs against Iraq's Defense Ministry, while *Time* magazine claimed, "the pinpoint accuracy of the attacks was spectacular."[10]

There are a variety of factors that need to be addressed in order to better explain the major institutional reasons for the prevalence of pro-war reporting in the American mass media. Some of the main characteristics of mass media reporting include: pro-war framing of the news; the consistent omission and censorship of serious anti-war views and other dissident perspectives; media reliance on official statements and government propaganda in reporting of international events; the dependence on inexpensive fluff, or "junk food" news, as opposed to focusing on reporting stories more critical of U.S. foreign policy; and finally, increasing corporate domination of the media as a structural impediment to more critical, balanced reporting of wartime news.

Dissecting Pro-War Prejudice

Contrary to the denials of many reporters and editors, pro-war framing is a reality that has been well documented by dissident and Progressive media critics. It is desirable to expand upon many of the categories of media framing that have been developed in previous academic and media studies, while also providing relevant recent examples from the "War on Terror." While pro-war framing in the media has always existed, it has become more pronounced in recent years, particularly in the era of hyper-nationalistic reporting that has driven the media establishment since September 11, 2001.

A driving factor that contributes to pro-war framing is seen in the mass media's institutional design. Corporate news outlets are not directly controlled by government interests or run and owned by the government, as in the case of the former Soviet Union, but rather work cooperatively, and to a great degree independently, alongside the government in order to promote the interests of American economic and political elites. This constitutes the core of what has become known as the "political economy of the mass media."[11] Within this political economy, corporate entities (in this case media conglomerates) willingly work with government in support of pro-war frames. Essentially, corporate elites and government elites cooperate in promoting an overwhelmingly uniform view of the world where the United States is seen as the leading force for furthering humanitarianism and democracy.

Agenda-Setting

Although media agenda setting powers were briefly discussed in chapter 1, a more thorough analysis is required. Greg Philo and the members of the *Glasgow University Media Group* believe that the power of television news over the British public is quite substantial, arguing that, "it has a profound effect, because it has the power to tell people the order in which to think about events and issues. It 'sets the agenda,' and decides what is important and what will be featured." Members of *Glasgow* argue that, "television controls the crucial information with which we make up our minds about the world."[12] Much the same argument can be made with regard to attempts in the American press to play an active role in domestic and foreign policy formulation. As the major source of information for millions of Americans, the mainstream press will always be a major player when it comes to influencing the American people.

Attempts to influence or affect public opinion often translate into enormous power when reporting on important events and issues. William Rivers, writing in the early 1980s, argued that, "correspondents who report for the news media possess a power beyond even their own dreams and fears. They are only beginning to become aware that their work now shapes and colors the beliefs of nearly everyone, not only in the United States but throughout most of the world."[13] Twenty-five years later, Rivers' statement seems as relevant as ever, considering the U.S. media's efforts to reach international audiences, as the cases of *CNN International,* the Pentagon-supported *Iraqi Media Network,* and American Internet-based news viewed throughout the world suggest.

Media scholar Shanto Iyengar speaks of a "priming effect" of the media on public opinion, explaining that it represents "the ability of news programs to affect the criteria by which individuals judge their political leaders."[14] Through priming, scholars argue, the public relies on the media to provide information on critical news stories, so that they may play a more pivotal role in policy formulation in a democratic society. By selecting certain stories to highlight at the expense of others, and by stressing certain ideological points of view rather than others, the media assists in setting the terms for acceptable public discourse. "The impact of news coverage on the weight assigned to specific issues in making political judgments"[15] may help determine how the public will react in times of war, as information published in the media that is less critical of the war effort may lead to a lesser degree of skepticism, at least assuming a significant proportion of the population is following some sort of mainstream news source on a regular or semi-regular basis and discussing the news with others.

Past academic studies also reinforce the role of the media in the "framing"[16] and "filtering" of important public policy debates in favor of more conventional ideological positions. In general, the mass media has reported and prioritized international news in ways that conform to the underlying values driving the

"War on Terror." In other words, the subtly, and sometimes not so subtly expressed ideological assumptions that guide reporting, editorial policy, and media positions throughout this war are aimed at confirming the conventional viewpoints laid out in government frames. In their book *News That Matters, Television and American Opinion*, Shanto Iyengar and Donald Kinder reflect upon the reality of television news reporting that is dominated "by official sources and dominant values."[17] The authors view "television news as inherently cautious and conservative medium, much more likely to defend traditional values and institutions than to attack them."[18] These traditional values and institutions often include support for the United States' reliance on force as the primary means of global dispute resolution.

Reporting and editorializing in the mainstream media favors state capitalism over socialist or other non-capitalist frameworks of analysis, particularly in the case of the more openly conservative television and print media such as *Fox News Channel*, the *Weekly Standard*, and the *Washington Times*. "Liberal" media establishments, such as the *New York Times* are also pro-capitalist in orientation.

There are many popular methods by which corporate media framing reinforces pro-war positions. Nationalistic pressure is one such method by which the media establishment can limit dissent in its framing of the news. Presenting a vision of the U.S. as a benevolent superpower in global affairs, many Americans accept, and the major media reinforce, the notion that the U.S. is fighting a war between the "good," "civilized" world and the "evil" terrorists. That the United States is a peaceful superpower—albeit a superpower that sometimes makes modest or serious mistakes and miscalculations—is taken as self-evident. The framing of the Iraq war as driven by noble and humanitarian motivations is typically followed by the assumption that those who support the war are, by definition, patriotic; and as support for war is often deemed patriotic, opposition to war, conversely, is framed (particularly at the beginning of wars) as unpatriotic.

The assumption that patriotism requires support for the Iraq war is an important part of what former *CBS* News Anchor Dan Rather deems "patriotism run amok," for journalists who are reluctant to ask tough questions for fear of being labeled un-American or anti-American.[19] As a result, reporting on the growing U.S. anti-war movement has been relegated to the margins of mainstream reporting. Washington activist Adam Eidinger explains, "I think the media has been completely biased. You don't hear dissenting voices; you see people marching in the streets, but you rarely hear what they have to say in the media. . . The antiwar movement in this country is far bigger than it was during the first few years of the Vietnam War, but you wouldn't know it from the coverage."[20]

Corporate media framing of the U.S. as a benevolent superpower affords the U.S. government the power to act as global enforcer in the "War on Terror." Prominent media critic Robert McChesney calls this the "007 License," under which the U.S. reserves for itself the right to intervene whenever, however, and for whatever reason it sees fit in the affairs of other states.[21] As a result, those in the media establishment who challenge the legitimacy of the 007 License are often punished or disciplined swiftly as to deter future criticisms.

Rupert Murdoch's *Fox News* has become a leading force, although far from the only news source that relies on belligerent nationalism as a means of combating dissent. Murdoch's statement about the "War on Terror," that *Fox News* would "do whatever is our patriotic duty" to further war efforts, is well reflected in the channel's views of the necessity of the Iraq war and the channel's attacks on anti-war activists and other grassroots Leftist groups and individuals who challenge U.S. foreign policy.[22] That the owner of *Fox News* considers it a duty to do "whatever" is deemed by the Bush administration as necessary in fighting terror reveals the level to which mainstream media outlets defer to the authority of political leaders.

Along the same lines, mass media framing of the "War on Terror" relies heavily on positive and negative labeling[23] of specific developments and ideas—labeling that is often determined by the degree of support for, or opposition to the Bush administration and the Iraq war. As the Murdoch example demonstrates, simplistic language and labeling can be useful in reinforcing pro-war stances and attacking anti-war ones. In an ardent pro-war climate, reporters and editors strongly defend the reasons given by the Bush administration for war. In the pre-war climate, reporting lent serious credibility to the administration's claims that Iraq possessed large stockpiles of weapons of mass destruction. Pre-war framing strongly reflected a trust that had developed between the administration and the establishment media, as the administration's claims that Iraq retained ties with Al Qaeda, and that the United States was committed to democratizing the Middle East were accepted as unworthy of substantive challenge.

A similar trust was accorded to pro-war media analysts, pundits, and activists who were allotted significant time and attention throughout the media. On the other side of the fence, anti-war media analysts, pundits, and activists in the independent press presenting foundational criticisms of the validity of the "War on Terror" were often ignored or attacked. To name just a few examples, Brit Hume of *Fox News* argued that anti-war protestors "don't have a credible argument" and are "intellectually and morally confused,"[24] while Jack Dunphy of the *National Review* maintained that those who resist the Iraq war are pacifists.[25]

Another important method of framing is the use of artificial balancing[26] in creating a perception that the corporate press has presented a wide variety of viewpoints in the debate over war, when in fact it consistently relies on a very narrow range of opinion. Balanced reporting requires an inclusion of many different ideological viewpoints, meaning that media is expected to incorporate substantive anti-war views in addition to pro-war attitudes in order to achieve more balanced coverage. Establishment "liberals" such as Alan Colmes of *Fox News'* Hannity and Colmes, and Paul Begala and James Carville of *CNN*'s Crossfire are promoted as the "liberal" answer to Right-Wing conservatives such as Bill O'Reilly, Sean Hannity, and Robert Novak. Contrary to this conventional portrayal, progressives presenting structural and institutional criticisms of western-led neoliberalism and the Iraq war, such as Amy Goodman, Barbara Ehrenreich, Edward Herman, Noam Chomsky, Howard Zinn, Michael Parenti, Norman Solomon, Ralph Nader, and numerous others, are regularly ignored, attacked, or discredited.

One could accurately draw comparisons between the "liberals" and "conservatives" who dominate the mainstream press in that both groups subscribe to the traditional doctrine that the U.S. is, by nature, committed to democratizing the world through the promotion of military force and neoliberalization, and that the current version of the "War on Terror" is the desirable means of combating the international terrorist threat, although one may disagree on some of the methods employed within this war. Of course, blunt news headlines and editorials such as "How the War on Terror Made the World a More Terrifying Place," "Iraq: A Country Drenched in Blood," "Only Negotiations with Iraq's Resistance can Bring Peace," and "Only a True End to the Occupation can Bring Peace,"[27]—common enough in the reporting of mainstream media outlets like the *Independent* and *Guardian* of London—would be unfathomable to print in the United States, where editors and reporters take pride in "objectivity" and "fair-minded" commentary.

Omission and Censorship

The omission and censorship of unconventional views has generally had a detrimental effect on the quality of mass media reporting. Omission and censorship take many forms, including omission of much of the evidence that contradicted the Bush administration's weapons charges and alleged connections between Iraq and Al Qaeda. For the most part, the mainstream media refused to critique the invasion of Iraq as illegal under international and national law. David Barsamian, founder of *Alternative Radio* argues that this is an important example of censorship by omission: "The *New York Times*, this great liberal newspaper, had seventy editorials between September 11, 2001 and the attack on Iraq, March 20, 2003. In not one of those editorials was the UN Charter, the Nuremberg Tribunal, or any aspect of international law ever mentioned. . . . And so if you were reading the *New York Times* over that period, during the buildup to the war, you would not have had the sense that the United States was planning on doing something that was a gross violation of international law, and national law for that matter."[28]

Media censorship, however, is not so simple that it works only from the top-down, with editors and owners rejecting "inappropriate" news stories and firing those reporters, analysts and pundits who do not accept government propaganda as legitimate news sources. What is provided here is an *institutional* analysis, not a conspiracy theory. For censorship to be truly effective, it requires that journalists not only tolerate, but embrace the legitimacy and validity of conventional doctrines that thrive within the media establishment and American elite culture. Journalists are rewarded by either self-censoring or conforming to mainstream political, economic, and social values. Most importantly, they are allowed to keep their jobs, earn promotions, and climb the corporate ladder.

Former *CBS News* anchor Dan Rather explains about the post-9/11 media atmosphere: "What we are talking about here—whether one wants to recognize it or not, or call it by its proper name or not—is a form of self-censorship...in some ways the fear is that you will be necklaced here, you will have a flaming tire of lack of patriotism put around your neck. Now it is that fear that keeps journalists from asking the toughest of the tough questions, and to continue to bore in on the tough questions so often."[29] Rather's comments are all the more revealing in that his revelation was not publicized on mainstream American television, where Rather reported five times a week for *CBS News*, but in the British press, where more critical assessments of the dangers of unchecked American nationalism are often more welcome.

Despite Rather's insights, most journalists and pundits working within the system have not publicly made an effort to critique the nationalistic leanings of the American press, or the effects those leanings have on the possibility for critical news coverage. As those working within the mass media promote pro-war views and pragmatic criticisms of the war, they demonstrate their acceptance of such ideologies.

Most reporters do not need to be disciplined through punishment; they already accept the basic workings of corporate journalism—most importantly the comfortable relationship between reporters and political officials. Such commitment to the veracity of government statements and promises, and to the belief that the U.S. is a liberating force throughout the globe can make condemnations of dissent from within the system seem all the more believable to viewers, as even conservative commentators such as Bill O'Reilly and Anne Coulter exude a certain sincerity in their opinions that is difficult to prove as deliberately deceptive. But it is not just conservative-leaning pundits who subscribe to the official tenets of American foreign policy. Acceptance of official statements *must* run across the board in mainstream journalism for it to be effective.

Journalists will often claim that censorship does not exist in the media, and that they are free to report any stories they wish in a "free" press. Ted Koppel, veteran reporter and former host of *ABC's Nightline,* exemplifies this view well. Koppel explains: "Throughout my entire career, I have never been censored. I've been at *ABC News* for forty-one years, and throughout that time I have never been censored. I have always been allowed to do whatever program I want to do."

Many journalists argue that censorship does not exist because they have not personally experienced it. But their failure to endure overt government censorship does not necessarily mean that censorship does not exist. Koppel himself has admitted the tendency to self-censor in the press. Speaking about deference to the administration's reasons for war, Koppel explains: "when they [the Bush administration] tell me why they're going to war, I certainly have to give proper deference to. . . if the president says I'm going to war for reasons A, B, and C, I can't very well stand there and say, 'The president is not telling you the truth, the actual reason that he's going to war is some reason he hasn't even mentioned.'"[30] Such an admission is extremely revealing when considering that Koppel himself admits that he feels the Bush administration's main motive for occupying Iraq has to do with oil, as opposed to the official pretexts offered. And yet such concerns about America's desire to control Iraqi oil do not arise in Koppel's reports, which he himself admits have generally looked favorably upon the official reasons for war. Had Koppel, amongst other journalists, wanted to focus on U.S. interest in securing access to, and control over, Middle Eastern (and other regions') natural resources, they could have easily cited from the declassified government record; this record has consistently expressed the view that Middle Eastern oil is a major source of strategic power for the United States—one in which American leaders remain committed to gaining control over through the use of military force.[31] As for those reporters and editors in the American media who claim that to focus on the United States' use of force to secure control over Middle Eastern oil is tantamount to a conspiracy theory, it should be pointed out that a very rich analysis of U.S. interest in Iraqi oil is the norm in other media systems, such as the British mainstream press.[32]

Contrary to foreign standards of reporting U.S. interest in Iraqi oil, Koppel is clear on the meaning of "objective" reporting: professional reporters cannot, and do not place their own observations into reporting; they only report official statements, even if they believe that the official reasons for war are intended to deceive or manipulate the public. None of this constitutes "self censorship" to Koppel, who argues that, "I think you have to be very careful when you use the word censorship. Censorship has a very clear meaning to me. Censorship has the force of law. Censorship involves the government saying, 'You cannot report what you want to report. You have to show us everything that you intend to put on the air and we will then decide whether you can or whether you can't.' That's censorship."[33] This limited definition of censorship as only arising from government, and not from within the corporate media system, should be reevaluated in order to gain a clearer understanding of how reporters and editors are subtly pressured to self-censor and conform to official dogmas in the absence of government punishment and coercion.

Transmission of Official Statements and Propaganda

A report from the *New York Times* in March of 2005 revealed that the Bush administration had coordinated efforts with at least twenty different federal agencies in order to create government sponsored—or as the *New York Times* referred to them—"prepackaged news" segments to be run on local television stations throughout the nation.[34] These segments, which cost the American taxpayers over 250 million dollars, were aired without the acknowledgement that they were made by the government with the intent of reinforcing initiatives such as the wars in Afghanistan and Iraq. Such "covert propaganda," as Congress's General Accounting Office classified it, represents only one example of the reliance of the corporate media on official statements in their framing of the news.[35] With the airing of propaganda, viewers are left to wonder, how can one accurately discern official statements and government misinformation from real news reporting? Is there really a difference between media reporting and government propaganda in the "War on Terror"?

In December of 2005, it was also revealed that the U.S. government had spent millions of dollars to print over a thousand pro-U.S. ads and news stories in a number of Iraqi newspapers.[36] In coordination with the Lincoln Group, the Bush administration published stories covering issues such as the Iraqi economy, the growth of Iraqi resistance groups, and the general Iraqi security situation. The *Boston Globe* attacked the administration, as it "trashes the principles of a free press,"[37] although some newspapers were a bit easier on the president. The *New York Times*, for one, situated the paid news articles within the context of the Bush administration's efforts "to build democracies overseas and support a free press."[38]

The planting of pro-government, pro-occupation stories in American and Iraqi newspapers is only the most blatant infringement on independent journalism. More often overlooked are the voluntary efforts of American reporters and editors to uncritically repeat official statements. As indirect agents and disseminators of pro-war views, reporters claim "objectivity" by uncritically transmitting the pro-war statements of American political leaders who have consistently advocate continued war in Iraq.

The close relationship between the corporate media establishment and American political leaders translates into an extensive reliance on the part of the mass media on government points of view. The bond between the government and media is characterized by a high degree of trust, as members of the media establishment are more likely to take official statements and assertions at face value than to seriously question them. In short, reporters and editors fear insulting the official sources upon which they rely to report the news. A study by media watchdog *Fairness and Accuracy in Reporting* conducted during the first three weeks of the Iraq war revealed that, out of all the guests interviewed by the major television networks, including *ABC, NBC, CBS, CNN, Fox*, and *PBS News*, 68 percent were either current or previous government officials, while two-thirds of them were from the U.S. military.[39]

Media critic Edward Herman refers to media acceptance of official propaganda as the "media gullibility quotient," explaining that the "symbiotic relationship between dominant sources and the media makes the latter more reluctant to transmit dissident claims."[40] Media gullibility in accepting pro-war claims is reflected in the statements released from media outlets themselves, as *CNN* announced at the beginning of the "War on Terror": "in deciding what to air," the channel would "consider guidance from appropriate authorities."[41] That *CNN*'s decision characterized the government as an "appropriate" source of guidance in its reporting reveals how the media reinforces a cooperative, rather than adversarial relationship with the government in the post-9/11 period. Such a position makes it more difficult to question government statements during times of war.

Over-reliance on government statements and official press briefings, however, has its benefits, at least from a profit perspective. Constructing news stories based predominantly around official statements allows media corporations to reduce operating and reporting costs considerably by cutting down on expensive investigative journalism. While this practice may be beneficial from cost-analysis perspective, it leads to an extreme imbalance in reporting in favor of administration claims.

Excessive Fluff

Fluff stories are those that have little to no significance from the perspective of educating the public on important domestic and global issues. Sometimes referred to as "junk food news,"[42] fluff is advantageous from a marketing and profit perspective because it reduces reliance on investigative journalism. But fluff is detrimental to professional reporting in the sense that it allows television viewers to technically "follow the news" without learning much of significance about national and international affairs. Emphasis on junk food stories can direct attention away from expectations that news outlets pursue critical, hard-hitting stories related to the invasion and occupation of Iraq, and the American "pacification" campaign conducted against Iraq's resistance groups.

The stations most reliant on fluff news are the twenty-four hour news networks such as *MSNBC*, *CNN*, and *Fox News*, as they increasingly promote "news" stories to fill up their large time slots, despite the fact that they have little importance in the grand scheme of more relevant political, economic, and social issues affecting Americans. Gary Kamiya of *Salon* reprimanded the twenty-four hour networks for peddling fluff news at the expense of more relevant reporting—for relying on "lurid, sexually charged murder cases and shark attacks" as not only "the most important stories, but often "the only stories" that are covered. "The contrast between *Fox's* resolute avoidance of showing bloody images from the war in Iraq and its nearly pornographic immersion in shark bites and unsolved murders," in the summer of 2005, was "glaring. Only death or bloodshed with high entertainment value gets on *Fox*."[43] Similarly, Robert McChesney critiques television networks for concentrating "upon stories that are inexpensive and easy to cover, like lifestyle pieces, court cases, plane crashes, crime stories, and shoot outs."[44]

Some fluff stories ran over the last few years include: the Kobe Bryant sexual assault trial; Martha Stewart's trial, conviction, sentencing, and release; Britney Spear's multiple marriages; Brad Pitt and Jennifer Anniston's divorce; Bennifer: the breakup of Ben Affleck and Jennifer Lopez; the continuing adventures of the Bush twins; the Laci Peterson murder trial and Scott Peterson's conviction and sentencing; the search for the missing jogger, Lori Hacking; the story of Private Jessica Lynch; Michael Jackson's child molestation trial; the Runaway Bride; the Robert Blake murder trial; and the baseball steroids scandal, to name just a few. That the majority of television news channels spent more time covering the Michael Jackson child molestation trial and Scott Peterson murder trial than covering the question of whether the Bush administration's manipulated pre-war intelligence about Iraqi WMD is cause for concern when reflecting upon expectations that television stations provide critical reporting, rather than entertainment news.

Fluff news, however, encompasses much more than just a few high profile stories such as those mentioned above. Rather, fluff is used on a daily basis, and applied to a slew of less sensational "news" stories. In one example, Rudi Bakhtiar, reporting for *CNN Headline News*, asked who would win in a battle between the Hulk and the Terminator? Bahktiar assured viewers that, of course, the Hulk would win.[45] This example, although only one of many, reveals a growing trend in the corporate media—namely the use of fluff stories as a guise for advertising company products under the facade of "reporting the news." That *AOL Time Warner*, the media conglomerate that released *Terminator 3*, did not see their efforts to advertise summer films as a blatant violation of journalistic standards and ethics shows the extent to which fluff "news" has taken hold of television media, as media corporations resort advertising their own products to fill "news" space. As Jason Miller argues in *Z Magazine*, this drive for profit translates into a "need to maximize the number in their [network] audiences to satisfy their advertisers." Gossip and sensational news, simply put, "draw viewers," and "the higher the shock value, the bigger the draw."[46]

While serving the needs of advertising and trivializing important news stories, fluff news also plays an important part in strengthening notions of consumer-driven citizenry. Emphasis is placed on consuming news, not for the sake of learning about important social events. Rather, news is focused on the "lifestyles of the rich and famous," as celebrity news sells the virtuousness of high levels of fashionable consumption. As a result, Americans who consume a large amount of fluff news may be less adequately informed about other stories that have more direct relevance to their lives, such as the tremendous cost of the Iraq war, escalating American and Iraqi casualties, corporate corruption, lax government regulation of business and the cost to the public, and the increasing danger of groups like Al Qaeda. An inverse relationship develops between "news" consumption and public knowledge of crucial national and international events, issues, and developments, at least according to what limited studies are available.[47]

A History of Corporate Media Consolidation

The modern conception of objective journalism is only about one-hundred years old, as it parallels the rise of the modern corporation, which took its latest form during the mid-to-late 1800s. During this time period, states began to rewrite corporate charters so as to relieve many of the restrictions that had limited the corporation's size and power. Charters were reworked so as to promote further corporate conglomeration and monopolization, as state laws were revised to allow the lifting of restrictions preventing corporations from owning other corporations, essentially relaxing regulations on mergers and acquisitions. Laws were also rewritten to eliminate restrictions on how long a corporation could exist. In 1886, the Supreme Court ruled that the corporation was considered a legal person, meaning that it could now exist indefinitely without fear of the state revoking its charter or infringing upon its property rights in other ways.

Along with this transformation of the corporate form came the rise of professional, "objective" reporting. Before this period, newspapers were free to pursue partisan reporting without fear of being labeled biased or unprofessional, in large part because newspaper markets in major cities often contained over a dozen papers, owned by many different companies. If one did not like the views of a newspaper, they had many others from which to choose. Corporate consolidation changed all of this, as major cities like Chicago saw their number of daily newspapers shrink drastically during this period. The *Chicago American* newspaper, for example, swallowed up fourteen papers between the late 1800s and early 1900s, as it consolidated its control over the city's news through corporate mergers and buyouts. Today, the city of Chicago no longer has a large number of competing dailies, but two: the *Chicago Tribune* and the *Chicago Sun Times*—and the *Tribune* has traditionally been the more dominant of the two.

David Cromwell and David Edwards, authors of *Guardians of Power: The Myth of the Liberal Media* maintain that: "by promoting education in formal 'schools of journalism,' which did not exist before 1900 in the United States, wealthy owners could claim that trained editors and reporters were granted autonomy to make editorial decisions based on their professional judgment, rather than on the needs of owners and advertisers."[48] With partisan reporting and journalism out of the way, corporate newspapers were free to engage in the merger mania that was sweeping the country. This necessarily contributed to a reduction in diversity of viewpoints throughout American cities and towns, as the corporate interest in ever-increasing profits through growing advertising revenue became the major factor driving the reporting of the news. This meant that partisan reporting became a liability, as monopolization meant that the openly expressed biases of fewer and fewer papers were harder to accept when there no longer existed serious competition between a large number of papers and a wider variety of views.

In short, the reduction in the number of newspapers throughout each market meant that partisan journalism seemed all the more inappropriate in the modern era of media controlled by fewer and fewer corporations. The motivation for increased corporate profits drove the reporting of media companies, which now controlled a radically larger portion of individual markets. This promoted more, rather than less, uniformity of views by omitting radical or institutional critiques and analysis by those who were opposed to corporate ownership of media. Today, such views are seen only in Progressive-Left press, and are left out of mainstream media coverage almost completely, as they are largely considered unworthy of attention or rebuttal.

The effects of corporate monopoly dominance of media are still relevant today. This is evident when contrasting the major media markets in Britain and the United States. In Britain, corporate consolidation has taken hold at a slower pace than in the U.S. Take, for instance, two comparable cities: New York and London, which both retain similar populations at eight million people for the former and 7.4 million for the latter. Both are international cities, yet London has four times the number of major dailies as New York. London-based papers include (not accounting for financial papers or tabloids): the *Telegraph*, the *Times (UK)*, the *Guardian*, and the *Independent*, as compared to the city of New York, which has only the *New York Times* (not counting financial papers and tabloids).

Table 2.1

British Newspapers: Daily Circulation for 2005

Telegraph	909,058
Times (UK)	683,417
Guardian	361,494
Independent	259,566

Sunday Telegraph, "Circulation of Quality Newspapers," 2005, http://www.telegraph.co.uk/pressoffice/graphics/research/circaug05.pd (13 Sep. 2005).

Total consumption levels for the London-based papers amounts to just over 2.2 million, as opposed to the *New York Times* with a national circulation of only 1.1 million on average. The dramatic difference between these two cities and their media systems (in terms of corporate consolidation and concentration of ownership) translates in part into significantly different political climates. This is evident after reflecting upon the wider range of opinions presented throughout the British media (from the more conservative leaning *Telegraph* and *Times* to the anti-war leaning *Guardian* and *Independent*), versus the smaller range of "acceptable" opinions seen in major American newspapers nationwide (from the *New York Times*, *Los Angeles Times*, *Washington Post*, and *USA Today*, among others).

American papers have traditionally been far more alike than different in their reinforcement of pro-war arguments, and their questioning of anti-war perspectives. The uniformity in terms of promoting pro-war views (and pragmatic criticisms of the war) as seen in the four American papers listed above is the subject of most of the rest of this book, although the wider range of public debate as seen in the British media is discussed in chapter 9.

Drawing distinctions between the British and the American media is not meant to insinuate that there is something inherently "better" about British corporations than American ones, but to highlight rather that there is more room for expression of a diversity of views within the British press than the American mainstream press, partly as a result of less media consolidation. A number of media critics have persuasively argued that the British corporate media has also promoted pro-war views. David Edwards and David Cromwell critique corporate media in both the U.S. and U.K. as part of the "propaganda system for elite interests"[49]; they fear that mergers and acquisitions, corporate monopolization, and stronger ties between the U.S. and Britain throughout the Iraq war is leading to a convergence in the British media "towards a similarly closed and intolerant, U.S. style media system."[50] While such criticisms are well taken, to assume that the British mainstream media is on par with the American media in terms of relying on pro-war propaganda would be a mistake.

The Illusion of Journalistic Neutrality

Although highly touted, journalistic neutrality exists only in the minds of reporters, rather than in actual practice. The structural factors characterizing corporate media framing discussed above confirm this. Historian and activist Howard Zinn states, "It is impossible to be neutral. In a world already moving in certain directions, where wealth and power are already distributed in certain ways, neutrality means accepting the way things are now. It seems both impossible and undesirable to be neutral in those conflicts."[51] As the co-founder of the *New Republic* and a member of the U.S. Committee on Public Information, Walter Lippmann understood this reality well. Working as a pro-war propagandist for the U.S. government, Lippmann played an instrumental role in shaping public opinion in order to convince a once hesitant American public to support U.S. entrance into World War I. Concerning the myth of journalistic neutrality, Lippmann states: "Were reporting the simple recovery of obvious facts, the press agent would be little more than a clerk. . . . Every newspaper when it reaches the reader is the result of a whole series of selections as to what items shall be printed, how much space each shall occupy, what emphasis each shall have. There are no objective standards here."[52]

In a society where there are winners and losers in implementing public policy, and where the mass media reinforces ideologies that benefit corporate interests in profit, media reporting on important events can never realistically be objective. But a lack of objectivity is not limited only to corporate ownership of media. Progressive-Left media outlets, of course, are just as biased in their reports, although they make no such claims to objectivity or neutrality. In this sense, one can conclude that, regardless of the form of ownership (corporate or non-corporate), media outlets are incapable of achieving objectivity.

What is *not* reported determines a reporter or paper's bias just as much as what *is* reported. What is focused upon and what is ignored, the way a story is written, and how much time is spent, or *not* spent on it, all play a major part in ensuring each reporter's and each media organization's subjectivity. Nonetheless, it is possible to draw a distinction between objective reporting (which has never realistically existed), and the importance of achieving a greater level of balance in reporting. As chapter 9 shows, the British mainstream press has tended to be more balanced in its reporting, in that it is comprised of *both* pro-war and anti-war leaning papers.

Notes

1. Edward Herman, *The Myth of the Liberal Media: An Edward Herman Reader* (New York, NY: Peter Lang, 1999), 71.
2. Susan Sachs, "Arab Media Portray War as Killing Field," *New York Times*, 4 April 2003, 1(B).
3. Jackson Diehl, "Fallujah's Fallout," *Washington Post*, 22 November 2004, 19(A).
4. Jim Rutenberg, "Cable's War Coverage Suggests a New 'Fox Effect' on Television Journalism," *New York Times*, 16 April 2003, 19(A).
5. Claire Cozens, "Murdoch: Fox News Does Not Favour Bush," *Guardian*, 26 October 2004, http://media.guardian.co.uk/site/story/0,14173,1336212,00.html (4 Jul. 2005).
6. Chalmers Johnson, *The Sorrows of Empire: Militarism, Secrecy, and the End of the Republic* (New York, NY: Henry Holt, 2004), 40.
7. Johnson, *Sorrows*, 52.
8. Norman Solomon, "30 Year Anniversary: Tonkin Gulf Lie Launched Vietnam War," *Fairness and Accuracy in Reporting*, 27 July 1994, http://www.fair.org/index.php?-page=2261 (7 Jul. 2005).
9. Mickey Z, *The Seven Deadly Spins: Exposing the Lies Behind War Propaganda* (Monroe, Me.: Common Courage, 2004), 57.
10. John R. Macarthur, *Second Front: Censorship and Propaganda in the Gulf War* (Berkley, Ca.: University of California, 1993), 162.
11. Edward Herman and Noam Chomsky, *Manufacturing Consent: The Political Economy of the Mass Media* (New York, NY: Pantheon, 1988).
12. Glasgow Media Group, *Really Bad News* (New York: Writers and Readers, 1982), 1.
13. William L. Rivers, "The Media as Shadow Government," in *Agenda Setting: Readings on Media, Public Opinion, and Policymaking*, ed. Maxwell McCombs and David L. Protess (Mahway, NJ: Lawrence Erlbaum, 1991), 154.
14. Shanto Iyengar, *Is Anyone Responsible? How Television Frames Political Issues* (Chicago: University of Chicago, 1991), 133.
15. Iyengar, *Is Anyone Responsible?*, 133.
16. Iyengar, *Is Anyone Responsible?*, 11.; See Also Chomsky and Herman, *Manufacturing Consent*, 2.
17. Shanto Iyengar and Donald R. Kinder, *News That Matters: Television and American Opinion* (Chicago: University of Chicago, 1987), 133.
18. Iyengar and Kinder, *News that Matters*, 133.
19. Matthew Engel, "U.S. Media Cowed by Patriotic Fever, Says CBS Star," *Guardian*, 17 May 2002, http://www.guardian.co.uk/bush/story/0,7369,717097,00.html (15 Jun. 2005).
20. Paul Farhi, "For Broadcast Media, Patriotism Pays," *Common Dreams*, 28 March 2003, http://www.commondreams.org/headlines03/0328-05.htm (4 Jun. 2005).
21. Anthony DiMaggio, "Interview: Media Critic Robert McChesney," *Indy* 25, no. 2 (16 April 2003): 8.
22. CNN.com. "T.V. Stations to Air Bin Laden Video," 11 October 2001, http://archives.cnn.com/2001/US/10/11/ret.media.video/ (25 Aug. 2003).
23. Michael Parenti, *America Besieged* (San Francisco: City Lights, 1998), 155.
24. Joe Hagan, "Neworks Consider (Marginal) Protest Coverage at RNC," *Reclaim the Media*, 25 August 2004, http://www.reclaimthemedia.org/print.php?story=04/08/25/053-

911 11 (15 Jul. 2005).

25. Jack Dunphy, "The Sacred Right to Be Stupid," *National Review*, 25 March 2003, http://www.nationalreview.com/dunphy/dunphy032503.asp (2 Jul. 2005).

26. Parenti, *America Besieged*, 155.

27. Kim Sengupta and Patrick Cockburn, "How on the War on Terror Made the World a More Terrifying Place," *Independent*, 28 February 2007, http://news.independent.co.uk/world/middle_east/article2311307.ece (15 Apr. 2007); Patrick Cockburn, "Iraq: A Country Drenched in Blood," *Independent*, 20 March 2007, http://news.independent.co.uk/world/middle_east/article2374380.ece (15 Apr. 2007); Jonathan Steele, "Only Negotiation with Iraq's Resistance can Bring Peace," *Guardian*, 16 December 2005, http://www.guardian.co.uk/comment/story/0,3604,1668520,00.html (15 Apr. 2007); Salim Lone, "Only a True End to the Occupation Can Bring Peace," *Guardian*, 20 November 2003, http://www.guardian.co.uk/comment/story/0,3604,1088935,00.html (15 Apr. 2007).

28. Omar Khan, "Media Censorship: Interview with David Barsamian," *Z Magazine*, 24 February 2005, http://www.zmag.org/content/showarticle.cfm?SectionID=21&ItemID=7307 (19 Jul. 2005).

29. BBC Newsnight "Veteran CBS News Anchor Dan Rather Speaks Out on BBC," *BBC News*, 16 May 2002, http://www.bbc.co.uk/pressoffice/pressreleases/stories/ (7 Jun. 2005).

30. Ted Koppel, "Crisis Coverage and the Candy Bar Imperative," in *Feet to the Fire: The Media After 9/11*, ed. Kristina Borjesson (New York: Prometheus, 2005), 31-33.

31. For a brief review, see the following documents: National Security Directive 26 (1989), National Security Directive 54 (1991), The National Security Strategy (1991), the Defense Policy Guidance draft (1992), and Policy Planning Study 23 (1948).

32. Editorial, "Blood and Oil: How the West will Profit from Iraq's Most Precious Commodity," *Independent*, 7 January 2007, http://news.independent.co.uk/world/middle_east/article2132574.ece (15 Apr. 2007); Michael Meacher, "The Rape of Iraq's Oil: The Baghdad Government has Caved in to a Damaging Plan that will Enrich Western Companies," *Guardian*, 22 March 2007, http://commentisfree.guardian.co.uk/michael_meacher/2007/03/the_recent_cabinet_agreement_i.html (15 Apr. 2007); Heather Stewart, "Iraq Poised to Hand over Control of Oil Fields to Foreign Firms," *Observer*, 25 February 2007, http://observer.guardian.co.uk/business/story/0,,2020560,00.html (15 Apr. 2007); Simon English, "Cheney had Iraq in Sights Two Years Ago," *Telegraph*, 22 July 2003, http://www.telegraph.co.uk/news/main.jhtml?xml=/news/2003/07/22/wcheny2 2.xml&sSheet=/news/2003/07/22/ixnewstop.html (15 Apr. 2007); Kamil Mahdi, "Iraqis will Never Accept this Sellout to the Oil Corporations," *Guardian*, 16 January 2007, http://www.guardian.co.uk/Iraq/Story/0,,1991321,00.html (15 Apr. 2007); Philip Thornton, "Iraq's Oil: The Spoils of War," *Independent*, 22 November 2005, http://news.independent.co.uk/world/middle_east/article328526.ece (15 Apr. 2007).

33. Koppel, *Feet to the Fire*, 34.

34. David Barstow and Robin Stein, "How the Government Makes News: Under Bush, a New Age of Prepackaged News," *New York Times*, 13 March 2005, 1(A).

35. Alternet, "White House Report: The White House Fakes It," 14 March 2005, http://alternet.org/story/21485 (2 Aug. 2005).

36. Jeff Gerth and Scott Shane, "U.S. is Said to Pay to Plant Articles in Iraq Papers," *New York Times*, 1 December 2005, 2(A).

37. Editorial, "Bad News," *Boston Globe*, 2 December 2005), 18(A).

38. Jeff Gerth, "Military's Information War is Vast and Often Secretive," *New York Times*, 11 December 2005, 1(A).

39. Steve Rendall and Tara Broughel, "Amplifying Officials, Squelching Dissent," *Extra!*, May-June 2003, http://www.fair.org/index.php?page=1145 (12 Jun. 2005).

40. Herman, *The Myth of the Liberal Media*, 15, 63.

41. CNN.com, "T.V. Stations to Air Bin Laden Video," 2001

42. Carl Jensen, "Junk Food News 1877-2000," in *Censored 2001: 25th Anniversary Edition*, ed. Peter Phillips, (New York, NY: Seven Stories, 2001), 251-64.

43. Gary Kamiya, "War, What War?" *Salon.com*, 29 June 2005, http://www.salon.com-/news/feature/2005/06/29/aruba/index_np.html (18 Jul. 2005).

44. Robert McChesney, *Rich Media, Poor Democracy: Communication Politics in Dubious Times* (New York: New Press, 1999), 54.

45. Rudi Bakhtiar, *CNN Headline News*, CNN, 20 June 2003.

46. Jason Miller, "Liberating the 'Liberal Media,'" *Z Magazine*, 4 May 2005, http://www.zmag.org/content/print_article.cfm?itemID=7780&sectionID=21 (15 Jul. 2005).

47. *Outfoxed: Rupert Murdoch's War on Journalism*, DVD, directed by Robert Greenwald (The Disinformation Company, 13 July 2004).

48. David Cromwell and David Edwards, *Guardians of Power: The Myth of the Liberal Media* (London: Pluto, 2006), 11.

49. Cromwell and Edwards, *Guardians of Power*, 2.

50. Cromwell and Edwards, *Guardians of Power*, 192.

51. Howard Zinn, *Declarations of Independence: Cross-Examining American Ideology* (New York: Harper Perennial, 1990), 7.

52. Walter Lippmann, *Public Opinion* (New York: Free Press, 1997), 218, 223.

3

Weapons of Mass Diversion

Anthony DiMaggio and Paul Fasse

On May 1, 2005, the *Times* of London put forth a major challenge to the Bush administration by questioning the official justifications for going to war with Iraq. By reporting on the "Downing Street Memo," the *Times* provided intimate details on the Bush administration's one-sided use of pre-war intelligence and manipulation of public opinion concerning Iraq's alleged weapons of mass destruction.[1] There was only one problem—the American media's attention was directed elsewhere. The media's lack of emphasis on the memos meant that the American public was largely prevented from accessing vital information about the Bush administration's pre-war motives.

Marked "extremely sensitive," the first declassified Downing Street Memo (in a series of them) was never intended to be viewed by the British or American public. The memo was only meant to be seen by those in the British government with a "genuine need to know its contents." The memo revealed at least three points in relation to the Iraq war: 1. Despite public statements announcing the opposite, British Prime Minister Tony Blair and U.S. President George W. Bush both decided on "regime change" in Iraq long before the invasion in March of 2003; 2. The Blair government and the Bush administration framed pre-war intelligence in a one-sided manner so as to discount information that was critical of the claim that Iraq possessed WMD. This was apparent when the Blair administration admitted that "the [WMD] intelligence and facts were being fit around the policy of regime change"; and 3. Blair pursued the Iraq war knowing that it was a violation of international law, and instead of tailoring their actions to fit within the standards of such laws, he attempted to use the United Nations and WMD disarmament as a pretext for going to war.

The division between Tony Blair and George W. Bush's public pronouncements about the uncertainty of war, and their actual commitment to war, was significant. Blair's promise that he had made "no decisions" over invading Iraq and that he had "not got to the stage of military action"—that "we have not yet reached the point of decision"—were largely invalidated by his behind the scenes commitment to war with Iraq, with or without international legal support. Similarly, the Downing Street Memos reveal that Bush's statement in early March 2003 that the administration had "not made up" its mind about military action was also false.[2]

Downing Street at the Periphery

As with Tony Blair and his senior ministers and advisers, the American mass media de-emphasized the importance of the memos. The media's coverage, or more accurately the lack of coverage of the memos, is indicative of the comfortable relations between the Bush administration and the mainstream media. Many anti-war critics felt the memos represented a potentially massive scandal for the Bush administration, although the mass media did not seem to agree.

The memos *were* covered in mainstream news reporting, although not typically on the front pages of major newspapers. This led many critics to attack the press for downplaying or ignoring the memos because of their potentially explosive content. The original memo, which was printed on May 1, 2005 in the *Sunday Times* of London did not make an appearance in the *Chicago Tribune* until May 17, 2005, over two weeks later. At that time, the *Chicago Tribune* reported that, "the potentially explosive revelation has proven to be something of a dud in the United States. The White House has denied the premise of the memo, [and] the American media have reacted slowly to it."[3] The *Chicago Tribune* story was important in that it acknowledged that the memos were not receiving the attention many critics thought they deserved in the mainstream press. Subsequent attention was to be directed toward the memos, however, after numerous media activists attacked the press for a lack of coverage.

The *New York Times* printed a story addressing the original memo on May 2, 2005 titled, "For Blair, Iraq Issue Just Won't Go Away—Integrity and Credibility Questions Arise as British Voting Nears." This article, printed on page A9, did mention the memo, but failed to even provide its name. The memo's first reference, which appeared in the 10th paragraph, stated that it was a document "recording a meeting. . . in which [Blair] seemed to swing behind American arguments for 'regime change.'" The contents of the memo included an admission from former British Foreign Secretary Jack Straw, who "described the case for war as 'thin,'" because Saddam Hussein represented less of a threat "than that of Libya, North Korea, or Iran." Later the article stated that Blair denied "that Britain had committed itself irrevocably to war by July 2002," as it failed to hammer home the fact that the memos seemed to indicate the opposite.[4]

The *New York Times* reported on the Downing Street memo a total of eight times in the month and a half period between May first and June seventeenth, 2005. The stories in the *New York Times* and other mainstream papers, by and large, did not appear as features, but rather on the back pages. Sometimes editorials within the press were quite critical of the memos and the Bush administration. Such was the case with a number of *New York Times* editorials. Paul Krugman, an Op-Ed columnist for the paper, discussed the memo in an editorial May 16, 2005, citing some of its key aspects. Krugman discussed how the memo "demonstrated the limits of American power" and "emboldened our potential enemies" as Iraq was "perceived as a soft target," rather than an imminent threat to the United States.[5] On June 2, another Op-Ed writer for the *New York Times*, Bob Herbert, claimed that the memo, "offered further confirmation that the American public. . . [was] spoon-fed bogus information. . . in the run-up to the invasion of Iraq," and "President Bush, as we know, wanted to remove Saddam Hussein through military action. . . . Mr. Bush wanted war, and he got it. Many thousands have died as a result."[6] Herbert and Krugman's columns, however, were but a few examples of critical coverage of Downing Street, and they did not outweigh the lack of coverage seen throughout much of the corporate press.

USA Today did not cover the story until thirty-eight days after it originally broke in the *Times* of London. When the paper did address the memo, it was on page eight, rather than on the cover. The story, printed on June 8, 2005, titled "'Downing Street memo' gets fresh attention," stated that the media's coverage in June represented "the most attention paid by the media in the USA so far."[7] Even though the *USA Today* article went through the details of memo and commented on the mostly silent mood of the mass media, it did not frame the memo's contents as if they constituted a major political scandal. This likely had much to do with the lack of a negative reaction amongst most American political leaders, who did not perceive the memo as a major problem for the administration. If political leaders did not view the issue as a major scandal, how could "objective" reporters do so themselves when they are not supposed to overtly place their own views into reports? This long-standing pattern is standard in press systems that interpret objectivity as prohibiting reporters and editors from actively denouncing or questioning American political leaders within their news reports.

Between May 1, 2005 and July 31, 2005, the *Washington Post* mentioned the original Downing Street Memo, references to it, and its actual contents, a total of twenty-four times. The first mention of the memo was on May 6, in a headline story called, "Blair Wins Historic Third Term; British Labor Party's Victory Is Diminished by Fallout From War in Iraq."[8] According to the *New York Times*, the memo's contents, mentioned in the twelfth paragraph, "raised serious doubts about the legality of the war...suggesting Blair had agreed to support the Bush administration's efforts to oust Hussein." In another story the *Washington Post* printed on June 8 entitled "Seldom-Discussed Elephant Moves into Public's View," also included a quote from Prime Minister Tony Blair claiming that, "the facts were not being fixed, in any shape or form at all."[9] Such official statements were considered necessary in "balancing" out news stories on the Downing Street Memos, even if the statements of those in power were clearly false.

At certain points, editors and reporters did admit media complicity in downplaying the memos, although it was often accompanied by attempts to blame anti-war activists for making too big of a fuss over the issue. Michael Getler, an editorial writer for the *Washington Post*, quoted segments of the memo after he was "inundated" with emails from "self-described media watchdog organizations" that were "on the liberal side of things," and critical of the paper's lack of attention toward the memos. Getler responded to the complaints by acknowledging that, "the reaction to the failure to cover it…is understandable."[10] Another contributor to the *Washington Post*, Michael Kinsley, was harsher than Getler on the critics of the *Washington Post*'s reporting. Kinsley, addressing the memo after "about the 200th e-mail. . . demanding that I cease my personal cover-up," argued that, "fixing intelligence and facts to fit a desired policy is the Bush II governing style."[11] From this admission, one could conclude that editors at the *Washington Post* felt the Downing Street Memos offered little to nothing new to the discussion on pre-war deliberations of the Bush administration.

American television networks also reported the memos, but were reluctant to frame them as evidence that the Bush and Blair governments deliberately deceived the public. To do so may well have led many Americans to fault the media as well for its failure to expose systematic deceptions that took place before the 2003 invasion. *Salon* reported, through an overall analysis of television coverage, that, "between May 1 and June 6, [2005] the story received twenty mentions on *CNN, Fox News, MSNBC, ABC, CBS, NBC,* and *PBS* combined."[12] According to the media watchdog *Fairness and Accuracy in Reporting (FAIR)*, the first major mention of the memo by the T.V. networks, on May 15, 2005, was on *ABC's* Sunday Morning show *This Week*, where Republican Senator John McCain was asked about it. He replied that he did not "agree with it" and then the host George Stephanopoulos promptly dropped the issue.[13]

Some British news outlets joined watchdog groups in the U.S. and criticized the American mass media for its failure to extensively report its contents or make it into a serious political issue. The *Independent* of London noted on June 9 that Americans were turning against Bush and the Iraq war, according to polls. However, the paper concluded that the Downing Street Memo "is unlikely to have played much role as it has been given little prominence in mainstream US reporting."[14] Michael Smith of the *Sunday Times* of London stated concerning the memo: "It is one thing for the *New York Times* or the *Washington Post* to say that we were being told that the intelligence was being fixed by sources inside the CIA or Pentagon or the NSC and quite another to have documentary confirmation in the form of the minutes of a key meeting with the Prime Minister's office."[15]

When No News is Old News

The *Chicago Tribune* reported that, "the public generally seems indifferent to the issue [of the memos] or unwilling to rehash the bitter prewar debate over the reasons for the war."[16] This, however, left open a crucial question which was rarely asked: was the public indifferent because it did not care about the memos' contents, or because much of the public never saw their contents? Most of the American public did not have extensive, if any, exposure to the memos, primarily as a result of the lack of attention paid to the issue throughout the media and amongst political leaders. It was only *after* extensive coverage of the memos in the independent media that a small segment of the public complained to mass media outlets about their concerns over the lack of public exposure. This, in turn, elicited more extensive coverage of the memos throughout the press, as seen in many of the stories described above, although the issue, disturbingly, received less attention then celebrity news stories such as the Laci Peterson murder trial, which became a much larger issue in terms of round-the-clock media coverage. Media critics complained that the mainstream press was neglecting the story because it threatened to undermine the Bush administration during a time of war. *FAIR* condemned the "profound defensiveness" of reporters who de-emphasized the memo. According to *FAIR*, the common argument that "the memo wasn't news because it contained no 'new' information—only raises troubling questions about what journalists were doing when they should have been reporting on the gulf between official White House pronouncements and actual White House intentions."[17]

In reality, mainstream media outlets did not ignore or downplay the memos in 2002 and early 2003 because they were "old news." There was no systematic effort during the run-up to the Iraq war to highlight the fact that the Bush and Blair governments had decided well before March 2003 to invade Iraq, regardless of whether weapons of mass destruction were found. To have placed such an emphasis on government deception at the time would likely have encouraged a larger number of Americans to question what potential ulterior motives the Bush administration possessed for wanting to invade Iraq. In the end, no alternative explanations were provided in the vast majority of mass media reporting.

The WMD Debacle Begins:
A Brief History

On September 12, 2002, President Bush formally announced to the international community that Saddam Hussein possessed weapons of mass destruction and had to be disarmed. "[Iraq] possesses and produces chemical and biological weapons. It is seeking nuclear weapons" and "Members of the Congress" and "the United Nations Security Council, agree that Saddam Hussein is a threat to peace and must disarm."[18] Throughout the next six months, the White House initiated and pursued a long and arduous campaign to convince the American people of the "threat" Iraq posed to the United States and its allies. Vice President Dick Cheney argued that, "there is *no doubt* [emphasis added] that Saddam Hussein now has weapons of mass destruction."[19]

Throughout the accusations and build up to war, Iraq claimed that it did not possess any WMD. In a letter to the United Nations in September 2002, Saddam Hussein stated, "[President Bush] presented utmost distortions on the nuclear, biological, and chemical threats" possessed by Iraq.[20] Predictably, few Americans paid any attention to Saddam Hussein's warnings.

As discussed earlier, the White House worked to create the impression that war was a "last resort" if Iraq did not "rid itself of WMD." On September 24, 2002, President Bush stated, "We love peace. Military is not our first choice."[21] Bush urged the United Nations to draft and pass a new Security Council resolution condemning Saddam for possessing WMD and supporting the introduction of a weapons inspection team into Iraq. The team was to enter the country soon after, although they were unable to find any evidence of hidden weapons of mass destruction.

Despite Bush's warnings of the threat posed by Iraq, there were many skeptical individuals, agencies, and reports suggesting that the assertion that Iraq possessed WMD was tenuous at best. The Defense Intelligence Agency (DIA) issued a report in September 2002 stating that there is "no reliable information on whether Iraq is producing and stockpiling chemical weapons or whether Iraq has or will establish its chemical warfare agent production facilities."[22] Scott Ritter, former U.N. weapons inspector in Iraq throughout the 1990s, reiterated this point stating: "Since 1998, Iraq has been fundamentally disarmed: 90—95 percent of Iraq's weapons of mass destruction capability has been verifiably eliminated. This includes all of the factories used to produce chemical, biological, and nuclear weapons, and long-range ballistic missiles; the associated equipment of these factories; and the vast majority of the products coming out of these factories."[23]

Many throughout the American media and political system had argued, in contradiction to Ritter's assessment, that Saddam either produced WMD after the inspectors left in 1998, or were able to hide them from inspectors during the mid-1990s. Ritter countered such charges, prevalent in mainstream media reporting, arguing that:

> As with the nuclear weapons program, they'd [the Iraqi government] have to start from scratch, having been deprived of all equipment, facilities, and research. They'd have to procure the complicated tools and technology required through front companies. This would be detected. The manufacture of chemical weapons emits vented gases that would have been detected by now if they existed.[24]

Periodically, the Bush administration made concessions that claims about Iraq's possession of WMD were based, at least in part, on speculation. Dick Cheney acquiesced to the fact that, as the *New York Times* reported, "the administration could never know with precision the extent and type of weapons of mass destruction."[25]

After months of continuous political pressure from the U.S., a Security Council resolution was passed to implement a new weapons inspection program in Iraq. On November 25, 2002, the U.N. weapons inspection team led by Hans Blix entered Iraq to search for chemical, biological, and nuclear weapons. After weapons inspectors entered and found no evidence of WMD, the Bush administration continued to argue that Iraq posed a threat, and that the failure to find weapons was an indication that Saddam Hussein was effective in deceiving the inspectors. At the time of the invasion, establishment media sources were still reporting claims that Iraq posed a national security threat to the U.S., despite the failure to find any weapons.

In the 2003 State of the Union Address, the Iraqi "threat" became more perilous as the President testified based on intelligence from Britain's MI6 that Iraq had sought to purchase "significant quantities of uranium from Africa."[26] The uranium charge was compounded with the Iraqi government's alleged attempt to purchase aluminum tubes for use in developing the enriched uranium needed for nuclear weapons.[27] Allied forces found no traces of any reconstituted nuclear weapons program before or after the invasion, and no indication of an Iraqi long-range ballistic program. The International Atomic Energy Agency (IAEA), along with numerous British and American newspapers exposed the Niger-uranium charges as fraudulent soon after its declaration. Most newspapers described the Niger documents as forgeries, signed by a minister that had been out of office for over ten years. The most ostensible of the forgeries was the second dossier supplied by MI6 British Intelligence, which was based off of a twelve year-old PhD thesis.[28]

Continuing to question the claims that Iraq possessed WMD, Hans Blix reported (in February 2003) to the U.N. Security Council: "Since we arrived in Iraq, we have conducted more than 400 inspections covering more than 300 sites. All inspections were performed without notice, and access was almost always provided promptly. In no case have we seen convincing evidence that the Iraqi side knew in advance that the inspectors were coming." Regarding Iraq's supposed possession of WMD, Blix stated that, "UNMOVIC [United Nations Monitoring, Verification and Inspection Commission] had not found any such weapons.[29]

The President and mass media characterizations of Iraq as a security threat to the U.S were questioned by a number of critics throughout the progressive press who felt that the plan to attack Iraq was motivated by reasons other than the threat of WMD. In an interview in December of 2002, media critic and scholar Noam Chomsky argued that the administration was fully aware that Iraq had disarmed and did not pose a threat. This, according to Chomsky, was the main reason why the administration chose to target Iraq: "It was known in advance that Iraq was virtually defenseless"; the Bush administration, Chomsky argued, was "desperately eager to win an easy victory over a defenseless enemy, so they can strut around as heroes and liberators, to the rousing cheers of the educated classes."[30] This view, while reflected in the independent media, was absent from mainstream reporting before the war, as reporters and editors viewed such charges as unfounded, fanciful, or too controversial to be worthy of discussion.

Scott Ritter was less interested in distinguishing between whether the case for war was an "intelligence failure" or a conscious deception on the part of the Bush administration. Ritter argued in his 2003 book *Frontier Justice: Weapons of Mass Destruction & the Bushwhacking of America*, "the intelligence cited by the President has turned out to be either egregiously erroneous or simply pulled from thin air. The details so precisely set forth have turned out to be void of any substance. Did the President lie, or was the intelligence fundamentally flawed? Either case is disturbing. Either case is damning."[31]

Ritter was long known as a proponent of Iraqi disarmament, as his time with the UN disarmament regime in Iraq demonstrated. Although his criticisms of the administration's war claims did garner some attention in the mainstream media before the 2003 invasion (he appeared nineteen times on *ABC*, *NBC*, and *CBS* in the year before the war), he only made one appearance in the post-invasion period on these networks, at a time when his claims about Iraq's lack of WMD had been vindicated.[32] This did not mean, however, that Ritter's arguments were immune from attack during the pre-war period. Ritter was been labeled a "flip flopper" by the *Chicago Tribune*, which portrayed him as inconsistent due to his earlier assessments that Iraq was in possession of WMD.[33] In an interview on *CNN*, Paula Zahn informed Ritter that, "People out there are accusing you of drinking Saddam's Kool Aid."[34] In the pre-war period, most reporters and editors discarded Ritter's suggestion that the Bush administration lied about Iraqi WMD, as the content analysis below suggests.

As has been acknowledged since the 2003 invasion, the Bush administration did not conduct a "pre-emptive strike" to stop an imminent Iraqi attack on the U.S. On the contrary, it utilized the practice of "preventive war," meaning that American leaders invaded Iraq under the assumption that Iraq, at some unknown point in the future, *could* constitute a threat to the U.S. While projections of an Iraqi threat to the U.S. were considered enough reason for the Bush administration to go to war, they did not meet the UN Charter requirements, which outlaws force with two exceptions: UN Security Council authorization, or self-defense against imminent attack. Iraq did not meet either of these standards, in light of evidence available before and after the invasion that Iraq was not in material breach of U.N. disarmament. Media reporting typically repeated inaccurate claims that the U.S. was making a "pre-emptive" strike on Iraq, rather than a preventive one. The difference was crucial, as pre-emptive strikes are conducted in order to deter imminent threats, and preventive strikes are made against countries not deemed an immediate security threat.

Weapons of Mass Distraction:
Media Mouthpiece to War

Despite consistent and adamant claims from the Bush Administration and the media that Saddam Hussein possessed weapons of mass destruction (WMD), the United States could not find any such weapons after months of searching subsequent to the invasion of Iraq. Iraq's supposed possession of WMD was the main reason provided by the White House and the media for the necessity of the invasion, even though there were a number of reputable individuals and agencies that spoke up and criticized such claims. As these figures (Mohammad ElBaradei, Hans Blix, and Scott Ritter, to name a few) continually reiterated that they had found no imminent Iraqi threat to the U.S. or any other country, the Bush administration continued to gain popular support for its invasion and occupation, aided by sympathetic media coverage.

Not all mainstream media organizations accepted the Iraqi "threat," however. Michael Massing of the *New York Review of Books* criticized what he saw as a case of media groupthink over the issue of WMD: "One of the most entrenched and disturbing features of American journalism [is] its pack mentality. Editors and journalists don't like to diverge too sharply from what everyone else is writing."[35]

Not all reporters uncritically subscribed to group think concerning the WMD "threat." The *Knight Ridder* news service, for one, reacted quite skeptically to the WMD claims, suggesting that Iraq was not a security threat to the U.S. Prominent reporters for the paper, including Jonathan Landay and Warren Strobel, ran critical stories regarding the alleged Iraqi menace. Part of the reason for *Knight Ridder*'s distrust for the administration's claims was because the news outfit was more reliant on lower-level intelligence, rather than on sources at the highest levels of government and the intelligence community. Warren Strobel explains that

we had a lot of sources in the bowels of government, and they were telling us a different story, and we chose to believe them rather than the administration's public statements. They were, in many cases, skilled people who either knew the Middle East region, or knew intelligence, or knew WMD issues, and they were saying that the case the administration was making was not true or that they had real problems with the intelligence that they were seeing, and that it didn't add up to the case for war that the administration was making. They were credible people.[36]

These credible witnesses, however, were not considered enough for most mainstream reporters or news organizations, which were more content to take the Bush administration and high-level official claims at face value, rather than engaging in critical, investigative reporting based upon a wide variety of sources.

Strobel's acknowledgement that there were credible experts who disputed the WMD threat is important because it shows that there were other ways in which mainstream media outfits could have reported the issue, should they have chosen to do so. The dramatic difference in coverage between *Knight Ridder* and other corporate sources, then, reflected a conscious choice to emphasize and favor certain intelligence sources over others. This conscious choice, however, should not be overemphasized to the point of neglecting institutional factors. Elite newspapers like the *New York Times*, *Washington Post*, and *Los Angeles Times*—all closer to centers of American political and economic power than news services catering to secondary newspaper markets—were clearly under more pressure to comply with WMD related government propaganda. As Landay himself admitted, "I don't think people really cared [about his critical reporting of WMD] as long as it wasn't having an impact here politically, then we could write what we wanted. If it had been in the *New York Times* or the *Washington Post*, then you would have seen a whole different reaction."[37]

Media critics increasingly blamed the press for perceived failures when it came to preventing the invasion of Iraq, or simply in educating the American public over the possible drawbacks of going to war. One study released in mid 2004 by the Center for International Security Studies and the University of Maryland found that "many stories [before the war] stenographically reported the incumbent administration's perspectives on WMD, giving too little critical examination of the way officials framed the events, issues, threats, and policy options" leading up to war. The study concluded that there were three major faults in pre-war coverage: 1. there was a shortage of stories questioning the "official line" regarding Iraqi WMD; 2. journalists overwhelmingly accepted the attempts to link Iraq to Al Qaeda when it came to the WMD "threat"; and 3. the mainstream media too often portrayed Iraq's alleged WMD as a "monolithic menace," failing to distinguish between different types of weapons and the dangers (or lack thereof) that each weapon posed to the U.S. John Steinbruner, the author of the report's foreword, argued concerning media coverage that, "The American media did not play the role of checking and balancing the exercise of power that the standard theory of democracy requires."[38]

Judith Miller:
An Isolated Case, or a Role Model for a Generation?

For the *New York Times*, a newspaper that continuously proclaims its journalistic integrity by reporting "All the news that's fit to print," Judith Miller was the type of journalist that got the stories they wanted—despite what often amounted to a lack of range in sources when covering the WMD issue. Judith Miller covered extensively and in most cases exclusively on the WMD charges for the *New York Times* during the Bush administration's push for war. However, there was one major problem—her sources for information.

Judith Miller started writing for the *New York Times* in 1977 when the paper wanted "a new breed of hungry young hires" in part due to "losing" the main coverage of the Watergate Scandal to Bob Woodward and the *Washington Post*.[39] In an attempt to separate themselves from the CIA-Valerie Plame scandal surrounding Judith Miller, many at the *New York Times* attacked her personally.

Supposedly, she was "shit to the people she work[ed] with"[40]—her zealous pursuit of stories affording her a reputation as a bit obsessive and difficult to work with.

In the paper's pre-war reporting, Miller provided the *New York Times* with a consistent string of information regarding WMD from Ahmad Chalabi, an Iraqi defector associated with the Iraqi National Congress who was determined to rid Iraq of Saddam and help implement a government representing Western, as well as his own personal interests. Judith Miller herself admitted that Chalabi "provided most of the front page exclusives on WMD to our paper" in the pre-war period.[41] In late 2001 and 2002, Miller ran a number of stories in the *New York Times* that shed light upon Iraq's supposed efforts to produce WMD. These reports originated largely from information provided by Chalabi and his associates, although the stories seem to have been driven largely by his personal interest in toppling Saddam Hussein so as to make room in the new government for Iraqi exiles. The *Washington Post* reported that, "Miller['s] prewar stories about whether Iraq harbored weapons of mass destruction were later disavowed by the *New York Times* as inaccurate."[42] In addition to relying on Chalabi, Miller drew many of her stories from the Pentagon, more specifically, with Richard Perle and Paul Wolfowitz.

Miller indicated in regards to her reporting on Iraqi that the job of a journalist is to uncritically repeat the charges of political officials in power. Miller explained: "My job isn't to assess the government's information and be an independent intelligence analyst myself. . . . My job is to tell readers of the *New York Times* what the government thought about Iraq's arsenal."[43] But Miller omitted an important point, namely that she also considered it part of her job *not* to cite independent intelligence analysts who disagreed with the Bush administration on the WMD issue. Apparently, these figures were not considered a legitimate part of the relevant government opinion in which Miller spoke of.

As a result of her comfortable ties with high-ranking Pentagon and Bush administration officials, Miller was rewarded substantially during the early stages of the Iraq war; taking a position as an "embedded" journalist with the Mobile Exploitation Team (MET), she was allowed to follow American forces that were ordered to search Iraq for weapons of mass destruction.

Miller no longer works for the *New York Times*, primarily as a result of a falling out with the paper's editors after her refusal to reveal her sources for the government leak that led to an uncovering of an undercover CIA agent. Some critics have singled out Miller for unprofessional reporting. Jack Shafer of *Slate* argues that:

The most important question to unravel about Judith Miller's reporting is this: Has she grown too close to her sources to be trusted to get it right or to recant her findings when it's proved that she got it wrong? Because the *Times* sets the news agenda for the press and the nation, Miller's reporting had a great impact on the national debate over the wisdom of the Iraq invasion. If she was reliably wrong about Iraq's WMD, she might have played a major role in encouraging the United States to attack a nation that posed it little threat.[44]

Miller's reporting on the issue of WMD, however, is far from an isolated incident, as it is symbolic of a long-standing practice within the mainstream media of respecting, rather than attacking official sources, especially during times of war. Although Judith Miller is now considered on the "fringe" of mainstream journalism, her reporting is not out of the ordinary—in fact it was the standard in a press that collectively failed to scrutinize its sources regarding Iraqi WMD.

Miller's over-reliance on high-level government sources is actually the norm in covering foreign conflicts and other important issues. Recall that on September 12, 2002, President Bush formally announced to the international community the threat that Saddam Hussein posed to the world in front of the United Nations General Assembly. At this point, the Bush administration had already initiated a serious public campaign against Saddam Hussein and Iraq. However, this speech, delivered in front of the world community, can certainly be seen as the official beginning of the U.S.'s pursuit of an invasion of Iraq. Over the next six months, the *New York Times* consistently and overwhelmingly quoted and reiterated the White House's position on Iraq, while treating opposing views with skepticism, or ignoring them altogether.

From September 12, 2002 to September 18, 2002—the first week of reporting after Bush's speech to the U.N.—the issue of Saddam's supposed possession of WMD was covered on the front page and the international pages (section A) in twenty different articles. Within those articles, thirteen classified Iraqi possession of WMD as either certain or probable. This assumption obviously originated from the statements of Bush and Blair administration officials, although often through statements made by the reporter of each piece themselves. Take one example, as seen in a September 18, 2002 story by the *New York Times*, which reported that President Bush stated: "Iraq must give up...its weapons of mass destruction...or face the consequences."[45] Another example is seen in a September 18 piece reported that, "The Bush Administration had little faith. . . [that] inspections. . . ensure Iraq's disarmament."[46] Within those twenty articles mentioned above, only 5 articles contained statements that were *both* supportive of, and critical of, the administration's WMD charges.

Within one of the few balanced pieces that came out of this time period, the *New York Times* did report that, "Scott Ritter. . . doubted Iraq was still hiding chemical, biological, and nuclear or radiological weapons."[47] This, however, was the only time from September up until late November when the paper reported anything within the international news section on Scott Ritter's statements and claims, although Ritter was previously considered one of the foremost experts on Iraq's weapons capabilities. Most of the skepticism or denunciations of official claims that Iraq possessed WMD came from Iraqi officials. Just two of the twenty articles within this time frame reported only skeptical or negative comments regarding Bush's claims originating from Iraqi political figures, such as Iraq's Deputy Prime Minister Tariq Aziz, and Naji Sabri, Iraq's minister of foreign affairs.

An Analysis of the *New York Times'* WMD Coverage

Throughout this analysis, one sees a consistent pattern of a heavy reliance on pro-war, pro-WMD charges, alongside a systematic neglect of views that Iraq disarmed and did not pose a serious danger to the West. The chart below represents data collected from a content analysis studying the coverage of the *New York Times* from the period of September 12, 2002 to November 30, 2002. This time frame was chosen for analysis because it was within the run-up to the Iraq war, meaning that the *New York Times* coverage was likely having a significant effect on public opinion in terms of the issue of WMD during this period. The period from September 12 to November 30 represents the first month and a half after Bush's landmark speech to the U.N. As a result, media coverage of the WMD issue in the *New York Times* and other major national newspapers was extensive. The data collected is representative of all the articles related to Iraq on the front pages and in the international sections of the paper collected from day-to-day, and from week-to-week.

This analysis was conducted by looking at all of the articles with *any* references, quotes, or reporting concerning Iraq WMD. The categories were determined based upon references within the *New York Times* to any U.S, U.N., British, Iraqi or any other state or international leaders/officials, along with any state agencies (CIA, MI6, etc) who spoke of the issue of Iraqi WMD. As an important side note, any Iraqi, American, or other citizen (who was not either currently or previously holding political office) were not considered in this analysis, primarily because statements from such individuals made up such a miniscule portion of the paper's reporting.

- The "WMD" frame category refers only to stories containing a specific statement that is in favor of the WMD charges. "WMD" also signifies that no negative or critical claim was made or seen within each piece in question. This category is predominantly made up of direct quotes from Western officials claiming Iraq possessed WMD.
- The "No WMD" frame category refers only to articles that included one or more statements that were skeptical of, or refuted the WMD charges. This category includes only newspaper articles that contained critical statements without any reference suggesting or indicating that the WMD charges may have been true.
- The "Balanced" frame category includes stories that contained both "positive" and "negative" references regarding the likelihood that Iraq possessed WMD. In a more balanced media in which reporters and media organizations widely report multiple sides of issues, one would expect that this category would include the largest number of references.
- The "Ambiguous" frame category refers to news article that contained only "neutral" language regarding the WMD charge (this includes pieces that used terminology such as Iraqi "potential" for possessing WMD, the possibility that Iraq "may have" WMD, or that it is "suspected" of possessing WMD). Such conjecture was typically

made by reporters who were discussing WMD charges without relying
on official statements.
* The "*" category refers only to news pieces that discuss the
possibility of a violent Iraqi counter-response using WMD in the event
of a U.S. attack.

Table 3.1

New York Times Stories Analyzed From September 12—November 30 2002: (Total = 205)					
Frame Categories	WMD	No WMD	Balanced	Ambiguous	*
# of *New York Times* news stories that fit within each category	151/205	19/205	29/205	3/205	3/205
% of times this type of article was seen in *New York Times* coverage	73.6%	9.3%	14.1%	1.5%	1.5%

As the data suggest, the *New York Times* overwhelmingly emphasized
reporting of "positive" charges against Saddam and Iraq in the pre-war period.
At a time when media neutrality is vehemently promoted, this analysis undercuts
the media's proclamation that they are an unbiased reporting institution. Rather,
the data suggests a bias toward the positions of the Bush administration. A small
number of government and official sources originating from the Pentagon and
other political leaders were promoted consistently, while other government
officials (weapons inspectors primarily) who were critical of the WMD charges
were given much less time to make the case that Iraq did not possess WMD or
constitute a serious threat to the U.S. Although this content analysis deals
specifically with the *New York Times* articles and not other corporate news

outlets, it is generally representative of the dissemination of the news throughout the corporate press. The extensive use of official sources, considered the main pre-requisite for professional reporting, is evident throughout all establishment sources, rather than in merely a few.

When a "positive" reference to the WMD claims was documented in this analysis, it was primarily from the Bush administration or British officials. Conversely, the "negative" statements that were reported within the time frame were predominantly from Saddam Hussein or other unreputable Iraqi officials, rather than from weapons experts such as Scott Ritter, Hans Blix, Mohammed ElBaradei, Rolf Ekeus, or other critical inspectors and intelligence officials who were calling into question the WMD-related evidence for war. This likely had a stigmatizing effect in regards to those arguing that Iraq no longer posed a threat, as Iraqi government leaders (the primary source for challenges to the Bush administration's WMD claims) were hardly considered legitimate sources for disproving any Iraqi WMD danger by most Americans.

One of the few articles that contained a neutral reference to WMD claims came specifically from a CIA report that posed a question which received very little attention in most pre-war media coverage: "If [Saddam] didn't feel threatened...is it likely that he would initiate an attack using WMD?"[48] Such a line of thought was only reported within three news pieces in the time period above. Furthermore, in one of the articles, Donald Rumsfeld refuted the claim, stating that he "view(s) Hussein. . . [as a threat]. . . and [is] not willing to leave him in power."

The *New York Times* has long been a major "agenda setter," given its overwhelming influence over discourse within the mainstream political framework of discussion and thought. The New York Times' positive framing of the Bush administration's claims very likely persuaded other mainstream outlets to report in a similar fashion. Here is a small sample of headlines taken from an assortment of mainstream newspapers demonstrating a similar framing of WMD claims in the build up to war: The *Los Angeles Times* reported the unfolding WMD story under such banners as "Showdown with Iraq," which implied war was inevitable, rather than avoidable. Headlines included: "Iraq Defies U.N., Powell Says"; "Iraq Seems Unwilling to Give Up Weapons, U.N. Inspector Says"; "Secretary Presses Case that Iraq Moves and Hides Materials and Continues Procurement"; "U.S. Says Baghdad Hiding, Not Dismantling Weapons"; and "Hussein was going to launch missiles armed with toxic warheads if Baghdad was hit with nuclear weapons, U.N. inspectors' report says."[49] One headline from the Wall Street Journal read: "Bush Says Iraq is Short on Time for Disarmament," the assumption being that Iraq possessed WMD in the first place.[50]

The slanted reporting on the WMD issue likely limited public debate regarding the necessity of a war with Iraq. When media sources frame the debate over war in accordance with administration claims, it consequently discounts counterarguments challenging official reasons for war. While more balanced reporting seeks to create a sort of equilibrium between different sides of a debate, devotion to high level intelligence sources (at the expense of dissident claims) ensures tilted reporting and prevents the widespread incorporation of anti-war views in favor of pro-war ones.

From Imminent Threat to Intelligence Error

After the invasion of Iraq and the subsequent laborious and time-consuming search for weapons of mass destruction, the U.S did not come any closer to finding the mystery weapons of mass destruction. The Duelfer Report (a congressional commissioned study) concluded, according to the *New York Times*, that, "Iraq had no factories to produce illicit weapons," and that "its ability to resume production was growing more feeble each year."[51] With the administration's credibility on the line, it attempted, alongside the major media, to portray the WMD charges as part of a broader "intelligence error," rather than based upon outright deception. The establishment press increasingly blamed "bad intelligence," while offering occasional criticisms of their own reporting. Critiques offered throughout papers like the *New York Times* and *Washington Post* revealed that the papers' editors felt they had generally done a decent job in reporting on the WMD issue before the war, although there were some serious mistakes. As mentioned above, the emphasis became one of examining "misguided" intelligence rather than systematic manipulation and misinformation regarding WMD.

The emphasis on "bad intelligence" was a mainstay of post-invasion coverage. In the view of many editors, reporters, and owners, the administration had made a mistake in making the case for war based upon an imminent Iraqi threat, rather than knowingly lied to the public. On May 26, 2004, the *New York Times* editors printed an analysis of their own coverage of the buildup to the war in Iraq. They stated that there had been a general "failing of American and allied intelligence."[52] The *Los Angeles Times* offered similar remarks in October of 2004, when evidence surfaced of a CIA document revealing that Saddam's supposed purchase of uranium from Africa was falsified. The *Los Angeles Times* reported that these sources from the CIA show "fresh evidence of misjudgments" by intelligence agencies—rather than outright manipulation,[53] and that the Bush administration had relied on "misconceptions," rather than fabrications regarding Iraqi weapons.[54]

The *New York Time*'s apology that ran in March of 2004 appeared at times to represent a defense of pre-war reporting, rather than a moment of critical introspection. The paper's editors reflected that:

> Reviewing hundreds of articles written during the prelude to war and into the early stages of the occupation—we found an enormous amount of journalism that we are proud of. In most cases, what we reported was an accurate reflection of the state of our knowledge at the time, much of it painstakingly extracted from intelligence agencies that were themselves dependent on sketchy information.[55]

The paper's editors continued: "But we have found a number of instances of coverage that was not as rigorous as it should have been...Looking back, we wish we had been more aggressive in re-examining the claims as new evidence emerged."[56]

The *Washington Post*'s account of its pre-war reporting on Iraqi WMDs was a bit more critical than that of the *New York Times*. The *Washington Post*'s report on pre-war WMD framing, run in August of 2004, concluded that a systematic bias in favor of the Bush administration was at play:

> The *Post* published a number of pieces challenging the White House, but rarely on the front page. Some reporters who were lobbying for greater prominence for stories that questioned the administration's evidence complained to senior editors who, in the view of those reporters, were unenthusiastic about such pieces. The result was coverage that, despite flashes of groundbreaking reporting, in hindsight looks strikingly one-sided at times.[57]

Pentagon correspondent Thomas Ricks summarized: "Administration assertions were on the front page. Things that challenged the administration were on A18 or A24."[58] Former *Washington Post* assistant managing editor Karen Deyoung informed the paper's readers that: "We are inevitably the mouthpiece for whatever administration is in power. . . If the president stands up and says something, we report what the president said." Deyoung explained that, when statements contradicting official statements are printed, they often appear "in the eighth paragraph, where they're not on the front page, a lot of people don't read that far."[59]

In April of 2005, *Washington Post* staff writers admitted that U.S. intelligence was "dead wrong" regarding Iraq's WMD capabilities.[60] Nonetheless, this type of critical reporting was largely absent before the war, when it would have mattered the most. One editor for the *Washington Post* conceded that more critical pre-war news coverage would have been desirable. "We could have done better," Bob Woodward argued: "We did our job but we didn't do enough, and I blame myself mightily for not pushing harder. . . . We should have warned readers we had information that the basis for [war] was shakier."[61] And yet, the strong self-criticism apparent throughout the *Washington Post* report was also accompanied by the assessments of reporters and editors who highlighted what they felt were strong points in pre-war coverage. Much of the *Washington Post*'s apology was dedicated to deflecting criticisms that the paper over-valued official sources while downplaying or ignoring challenges to the Bush administration's war claims. Woodward defended his paper by arguing that "We had no alternative sources of information," as reporters "couldn't go to Iraq without getting killed."[62] Liz Spayd, another assistant managing editor justified the paper's pre-war coverage by claiming: "I believe we pushed as hard or harder than anyone to question the administration's assertions on all kinds of subjects related to the war. . . . Do I wish we would have had more and pushed harder and deeper into questions of whether they possessed weapons of mass destruction? Absolutely. Do I feel we owe our readers an apology? I don't think so."[63]

The *Washington Post*'s accounts of the failings of pre-war reporting continued past the paper's initial apology. In November of 2005, the paper again defended their pre-war reporting by maintaining that "Bush and his aides had access to much more voluminous intelligence information," than the rest of Washington, and intelligence analysts "were not authorized to determine whether the administration exaggerated or distorted" conclusions regarding Saddam's possession of WMD.[64] But as *Knight Ridder*'s reporting demonstrated, there *were* alternative paradigms through which the administration's WMD claims were reported, and could have been reported.

Contrary to the *Washington Post* and *New York Times*, *Knight Ridder* chose to cite primarily from intelligence officials who were skeptical that Iraq was a danger to the U.S. The lack of critical coverage from most mainstream papers, then, was a product of ideology rather than pragmatism or necessity. Most reporters and editors saw what they wanted to see when it came to the Iraqi "threat." They envisioned a horrifyingly imminent threat—a threat that was supported more by the speculation of political leaders and high-level intelligence officials than by the evidence to the contrary, presented by weapons inspectors and lower-level intelligence analysts.

Notes

1. David Manning, "The Secret Downing Street Memo," *Sunday Times*, 1 May 2005, http://www.timesonline.co.uk/article/0,,2087-1593607,00.html (3 Oct. 2005).

2. George W. Bush. "President George Bush Discusses Iraq in National Press Conference," *White House Website*, 6 March 2003, http://www.whitehouse.gov/news/rele ases/2003/03/20030306-8.html (15 Oct. 2005).

3. Stephen J. Hedges and Mark Silva, "British Memo Reopens War Claim," *Chicago Tribune*, sec. 1, 17 May 2005, 1.

4. Alan Cowell, "For Blair, Iraq Issue Just Won't Go Away," New York Times, 2 May 2005, 9(A).

5. Paul Krugman, "Staying What Course?" *New York Times*, 16 May 2005, 21(A).

6. Bob Herbert, "Truth and Deceit," *New York Times*, 2 June 2005, 25(A).

7. Mark Memmott, "'Downing Street Memo' Gets Fresh Attention, *USA Today*, sec. 1, 8 June 2005, 8.

8. Glenn Frankel, "Blair Wins Historic Third Term," *Washington Post*, 6 May 2005, 1(A).

9. Dana Milbank, "Seldom-Discussed Elephant Moves into Public's View," *Washington Post* 8 June 2005, 14(A).

10. Michael Getler, "News Over There, but Not Here," *Washington Post*, 15 May 2005, 6(B).

11. Michael Kinsley, "No Smoking Gun," *Washington Post*, 12 June 2005, 9(B).

12. Eric Boehlert, "Bush Lied About War? Nope, No News There!" *Salon.com*, 9 June 2005, http://www.truthout.org/cgi-bin/artman/exec/view.cgi/38/11727/printer (25 Oct. 2005).

13. Julie Hollar and Peter Hart, "When 'Old News' Has Never Been Told," *Fairness and Accuracy in Reporting*, July/August 2005, http://www.fair.org/index.php?page=2612 (3 Nov. 2005).

14. Andrew Gumbel, "Americans Turn Against Bush and a War in Iraq that is Getting Nowhere," *Independent*, sec. 1, 8 June 2005, 32.

15. Michael Smith, "The Downing Street Memo," *Washington Post*, 16 June 2005, http://www.washingtonpost.com/wpdyn/content/discussion/2005/06/14/DI200506140126 1_pf.html (17 Jan. 2006).

16. Matthew Clark, "Why has 'Downing Street Memo' Story been a 'Dud' in U.S.?" 17 May 2005, http://www.csmonitor.com/2005/0517/dailyUpdate.html (2 Nov. 2005).

17. Fairness and Accuracy in Reporting, "Justifying the Silence on Downing Street Memos," 17 June 2005, http://www.fair.org/index.php?page=2556 (4 Oct. 2005).

18. George W. Bush, "President Bush Outlines Iraqi Threat," *White House Website*, 7 October 2002, http://www.whitehouse.gov/news/releases/2002/10/20021007-8.html (4 Oct. 2005).

19. Elisabeth Bumiller and James Dao, "Cheney Says Peril of a Nuclear Iraq Justifies Attack," *New York Times*, 27 August 2002, 1(A).

20. New York Times. "In Saddam Hussein's worlds: It's for oil," *New York Times*, 20 September 2002, 16(A).

21. George W. Bush, "Remarks by the President at John Thune for Senate Reception," *White House Website*, 22 September 2002, http://www.whitehouse.gov/news/releases/200 2/09/20020924-16.html (4 Oct. 2005).

22. Stephen J. Hedges, "Pentagon Report Found 'No Reliable' Arms Proof," *Chicago Tribune*, sec. 1, 7 June 2003, 1.

23. William Rivers Pitt and Scott Ritter, *War on Iraq: What Team Bush Doesn't Want You to Know* (New York: Context, 2002), 28.

24. Pitt and Ritter, *War on Iraq*, 37.

25. Bumiller and Dao, "Cheney Says Peril of Nuclear Iraq Justifies Attack," 2002.

26. George W. Bush, "State of the Union Address," *White House Website*, 28 January 2003, http://www.whitehouse.gov/news/releases/2003/01/20030128-19.html (4 Oct. 2005).

27. CNN.com, "Transcript of Powell's U.N. Presentation," 6 February 2003, http://ww w.cnn.com/2003/US/02/05/sprj.irq.powell.transcript.07 (4 Oct. 2005).

28. Nick Fielding and Nicholas Rufford, "No. 10 'Doctored' Iraq Dossier," *Sunday Times*, 11 June 2003, http://www.timesonline.co.uk/article/0,,2087-698571_1,00.html (4 Oct. 2005).

29. CNN.com, "Transcript of Weapons Inspector's U.N. Presentation," 17 February 2003, http://www.cnn.com/2003/US/02/14/sprj.irq.un.transcript.1/ (7 Oct. 2005).

30. Anthony DiMaggio, "Noam Chomsky Analyzes the Bushies," *Alternet*, 6 December 2002, http://www.alternet.org/story/14701/ (14 Oct. 2005).

31. Scott Ritter, *Frontier Justice: Weapons of Mass Destruction and the Bushwhacking of America* (New York: Context, 2003), 50.

32. Steve Rendall, "Wrong on Iraq? Not Everyone," *Extra!* March/April 2006, http://www.fair.org/index.php?page=2847 (5 Oct. 2005).

33. Rendall, "Wrong on Iraq?" 2006

34. Paula Zahn, *CNN America Morning*, CNN, 13 September 2002.

35. Antony Loewenstein, "The New York Times' Role in Promoting War on Iraq," *Sydney Morning Herald*, 23 March 2004, http://www.smh.com.au/articles/2004/03/23/10 79939624187.html (23 Oct. 2006).

36. Warren P. Strobel and Jonathan S. Landay, "The Vice President is Lying," in *Feet to the Fire: The Media After 9/11*, ed. Kristina Borjesson (Amherst, NY: Prometheus, 2005), 369.

37. Strobel and Landay, "The Vice President is Lying," 373.

38. Editor and Publisher, "Study Faults Media Coverage of WMD," 9 March 2004, http://www.globalexchange.org/countries/mideast/iraq/1635.html (10 Oct. 2005).

39. Franklin Foer, "The Source of the Trouble," *New York Magazine*, 7 June 2004, http://newyorkmetro.com/nymetro/news/media/features/9226/ (17 Jan. 2006).

40. Foer, "The Source of the Trouble," 2004.

41. Loewenstein, "The New York Times' Role in Promoting War on Iraq," 2004.

42. Howard Kurtz, "Miller and the Times Agree to Part Company," *Washington Post*, 10 November 2005, 8(C).

43. Loewenstein, "The New York Times' Role in Promoting War on Iraq," 2004.

44. Jack Shafer, "The Times Scoops that Melted," *Slate*, 25 July 2003, http://www.slate.com/id/2086110 (22 Feb. 2006).

45. Todd S. Purdum, "U.S. Hurries; World Awaits—Bush Left Scrambling to Press Case on Iraq," *New York Times*, 18 September 2002, 1(A).

46. Julia Preston, "Rift Seen at UN over Next Steps to Deal with Iraq," *New York Times*, 18 September 2002, 1(A).

47. Judith Miller, "Verification is Difficult at Best, Say the Experts, and Maybe Impossible," *New York Times*, 18 September 2002, 18(A).

48. The New York Times, "CIA Letter to Senate on Baghdad's Intentions," 9 October 2002, 12(A).

49. Robin Wright, "Iraq Defies U.N., Powell Says," *Los Angeles Times*, 6 February 2003, 1(A); Maggie Farley, "Iraq Seems Unwilling to Give Up Weapons, U.N. Inspector Says," *Los Angeles Times*, 28 January 2003, 1(A); Bob Drogin, "Secretary Presses Case that Iraq Moves and Hides Materials and Continues Procurement," *Los Angeles Times*, 6 February 2003, 1(A); Maggie Farley, "U.S. Says Baghdad Hiding, Not Dismantling Weapons," *Los Angeles Times*, 24 January 2003, 13(A); Bob Drogin, "Hussein was Going to Launch Missiles Armed with Toxic Warheads if Baghdad was Hit with Nuclear Weapons, U.N. Inspectors' Report says," *Los Angeles Times*, 1(A).

50. David S. Cloud, Jeanne Cummings, and Michael M. Phillips, "Bush Says Iraq is Short on Time for Disarmament," *Wall Street Journal*, 15 January 2003, 8(A).

51. Editorial, "The Verdict is in," *New York Times*, 7 October 2004, 30(A).

52. Editorial, "The Times and Iraq," *New York Times*, 26 May 2004, 10(A).

53. Bob Drogin and Greg Miller, "Iraq's Illicit Weapons Gone Since Early '90s, CIA Says," *Los Angeles Times*, 7 October 2004, 1(A).

54. Bob Drogin, "Through Hussein's Looking Glass," *Los Angeles Times*, 12 October 2004, 1(A).

55. "The Times and Iraq," 2004.

56. "The Times and Iraq," 2004

57. Howard Kurtz, "The Post on WMDs: An Inside Story," *Washington Post*, 12 August 2004, 1(A).

58. Kurtz, "The Post on WMDs," 2004.

59. Kurtz, "The Post on WMDs," 2004.

60. Walter Pincus, and Peter Baker, "Data on Iraqi Arms Flawed, Panel Says," *Washington Post*, 1 April 2005, 1(A).

61. Kurtz, "The Post on WMDs," 2004.

62. Kurtz, "The Post on WMDs," 2004.

63. Kurtz, "The Post on WMDs," 2004.

64. Dana Milbank and Walter Pincus, "Asterisks Dot White House's Iraq Argument," *Washington Post*, 12 November 2005, 1(A).

4

The Media's War

In Iraq, a dictator is building and hiding weapons that could enable him to dominate the Middle East and intimidate the civilized world, and we will not allow it. . . . The danger posed by Saddam Hussein and his weapons cannot be ignored or wished away. The danger must be confronted. . . the current Iraqi regime has shown the power of tyranny to spread discord and violence in the Middle East. A liberated Iraq can show the power of freedom to transform that vital region, by bringing hope and progress into the lives of millions.
—President George W. Bush
February 26, 2003

Saddam Hussein has threatened his neighbors and the U.S. with war and weapons of mass destruction for two decades. . . the war that has now begun stands to end the single greatest threat to peace in the Middle East; it will help establish that rogue states will not be allowed to stockpile chemical, biological, or nuclear weapons in defiance of the international community. It will also free the long-suffering Iraqi people, who have endured one of the cruelest and most murderous dictatorships in the past half-century.
—*Washington Post* Editorial
March 20, 2003

Rather than playing a critical role in questioning American engagement in foreign wars, the mass media has traditionally promoted an image of the U.S. as committed to promoting democracy and human rights. While the promotion of pro-war views is not a problem in-and-of-itself, the systematic denial of alternative interpretations for American motives does constitute a serious impediment to efforts at achieving more balanced reporting and informed public debate. Chris Hedges, veteran war reporter for the *New York Times*, maintains that, "In wartime the press is always part of the problem. . . when the nation goes to war, the press goes to war with it. The blather on *CNN* or *Fox* or *MSNBC* is part of a long and sad tradition."[1] Nearly indistinguishable in their message, the excerpts from the *Washington Post*'s editorial and President Bush's speech above reveal a great deal about the comfortable relationship between the American media and the Bush administration at the onset of the invasion of Iraq. For those who critically followed media reporting of the Iraq war, the similarity between government statements and news editorials is of no surprise. Rather than serving as hostile medium, challenging government statements about the war, reporters interpreted their commitment to "objectivity" as excluding or limiting critical approaches to evaluating the Iraq war.

This chapter provides a comprehensive background to the mainstream media's framing of the Iraq war, before the 2003 invasion, and throughout the initial and extended phases of the occupation. The efforts to assist in furthering the war's progress are covered at length. Reporting of the war is well characterized by the media's pragmatic efforts to reinforce wartime objectives at the expense of questioning official government statements. As a result, objections to the war's validity and legality are discounted in favor of pro-war coverage.

This chapter refers to the media's commitment strengthening the war effort as "pro-war pragmatism." Along the same lines, the vast majority of the media's criticisms of the war effort are deemed here as "pragmatic criticisms," since these challenges are designed to strengthen, rather than question, the U.S.-led occupation's legitimacy.

Constructing a Democratic Iraq

The mass media became increasingly blunt in its support for the U.S. presence in Iraq at the beginning of the war. Perspectives in favor of the Bush administration and the occupation were not limited to editorial pages, but permeated many levels of reporting. Pro-occupation headlines and reports were the mainstay of American media coverage. A review of some of the most prestigious corporate papers and news networks provides a better portrait of these assessments of the Iraq war.

Over the last few years it has become popular to refer to the establishment of self-rule and self-determination in Iraq as a guiding principle motivating U.S. foreign policy,[2] particularly after the creation of the interim Iraqi government in June 2004 and the "democratic" election in 2005. This positive framing is intended to create the impression that the Iraqi government is a sovereign body and a legitimate representative of the Iraqi people. The *New York Times*, for example, accepted at face value the Bush administration's promise of installing democracy in Iraq, defending what it claims were "democratic elections" in January 2005.[3] In its reporting, the *New York Times* characterized "the American experiment in Iraq"[4] as an attempt to bring "self-rule,"[5] and "[promote] democracy by giving Iraqis practice in the give and take of local government."[6] The paper's editors also spoke of "post-election democratic maneuvering," among other developments in Iraq, claiming "the Bush administration is entitled to claim a health share of credit for many of these advances."[7]

The *New York Times* is far from the only paper that subscribed to the "democratic reforms the U.S. is trying to install" in the Middle East.[8] The *New Republic* commended American leaders who "took up the sword against Arab-Muslim troubles and dared to think that tyranny was not fated and inevitable for the Arabs."[9] The *Washington Post* highlighted U.S. "grand strategy for the Middle East," specifically the attempt "to launch a bold initiative for democratic reform across the region."[10] The paper predicted in 2004 the emergence of "a new transitional government with real executive powers," despite the fact that the interim government lacked independence under the American occupation and the Coalition Provisional Authority headed by Paul Bremer.[11]

The reporting of the *Los Angeles Times* lauded the U.S. effort to "build a future for the country [Iraq] on lofty concepts of constitutional democracy."[12] Portrayals of Iraqi sovereignty and democracy were plentiful throughout the mainstream, as headlines like "Iraqis Quietly Take Power after Bremer's Early Exit" and "Transfer of Power to Iraqis is said to be Well Under Way" were common in newspapers during the alleged transfer of power from the occupation authority of L. Paul Bremer III to the interim government of Prime Minister Ayad Allawi.[13] The assumptions that the Bush administration had transferred full power to the interim regime, and that Iraq was becoming a sovereign nation, were taken as fact, while the U.S. exercise of defacto rule over the country was generally omitted from discussion.

Many stories in the media have been subtler in implying U.S. commitment to democracy and goodwill in Iraq. In one example, *CNN News Night*'s Anderson Cooper explained the "bad news" and "positive news" in a report broadcast in June of 2004—the bad being that four Marines had died in battle, and the good that Iraqi "oil was again flowing" throughout the country after sabotaged oil pipelines had been repaired.[14] Cooper did not elaborate on why it was good news that the oil was flowing again, although his statement seemed to suggest that the flow of oil is a necessary part of reconstruction and the transition from dictatorship to elected government. Nowhere in Cooper's report, however, did he consider the opposite view, taken by many American dissidents that American control of Iraqi oil was detrimental to Iraqi sovereignty and independence in that such resources might be used for selfish purposes, rather than humanitarian reconstruction.

That the U.S. might have invaded Iraq in significant part to gain control of this valuable resource is a perspective that is left continually unaddressed, outside of a few rare exceptions. Indeed statements reinforcing American humanitarianism have been the norm. Nonetheless, increased U.S. reliance on foreign oil will remain an important issue in the future, regardless of whether the mass media acknowledges this fact. As prominent anti-war critic Michael Klare maintains: "the wars of the future will largely be fought over the possession and control of vital economic goods—especially resources needed for the functioning of modern industrial societies."[15]

Another example of subtle pro-war framing is seen in the mass media's handling of Iraq's resistance to occupation. Reporting Iraqi frustration with the occupation nearly a month after the invasion of Iraq, The *New York Times* ran a headline, "Free to Protest, Iraqis Complain About the U.S."[16] In the piece, the paper discussed fierce hostility toward U.S. "liberation" of Iraq as a "paradox"—that is, it was considered unbelievable, but true, that Iraqis would protest coalition forces after the U.S. selflessly "liberated" Iraq.

Most throughout the mass media did not take seriously the notion that a country committed to "restoring essential services, developing economic pluralism and promoting democratic government" could be driven malicious intentions in occupying Iraq, although this same assumption was not held in many other countries. This is most apparent in the systematic refusal to consider such an argument regularly in reporting and editorializing.[17] Progressive-Left media sources, conversely, often suggested that Iraqi nationalism was fueling resistance to occupation; although this interpretation was hard for many mainstream media pundits to fathom, considering the role of the U.S. as a "democratic superpower."[18] The reporting seen in these examples represents a dominant practice in media: newspapers and television news programs allude to U.S. plans and actions in Iraq as efforts to promote "interim rule" and U.S. coordinated elections as vital steps toward creating Iraqi democracy; other critical perspectives are not overtly criticized outright, they are just disregarded through omission.

Noble in Principle:
The Buildup to War

Pro-war framing is discernable throughout the pre-war, invasion, and occupation periods. Pre-war framing centered on the "threat" of Iraq's weapons of mass destruction and, secondly, on the significance of America's "democratic aspirations" in the Middle East. In anticipation of the beginning of the war, *MSNBC* ran a countdown based on the forty-eight hour deadline President Bush had set for Saddam to leave Iraq before he would invade. A *Washington Post* editorial praised the United States' "ambitious military campaign" intended to "eliminate Saddam Hussein's illegal arsenal of weapons,"[19] as the assumption that Iraq possessed a variety of weapons of mass destruction was deemed an axiom unworthy of serious question.

The *New York Times* and *Wall Street Journal* anxiously awaited the invasion, running headlines such as: "How Bush Decided that Iraq's Hussein Must Be Ousted"; "U.S. Exploring Baghdad Strike as Iraq Option"; "U.S. Taking Steps to Lay Foundation for Action in Iraq"; and "U.S. Picks Targets for Baghdad Push."[20] Thomas Ricks, the Pentagon correspondent for the *Washington Post*, described the media prior to the invasion as follows: "There was an attitude among editors: 'Look, we're going to war, why do we even worry about all this contrary stuff?'" Rick's admission highlights the transformation in thinking for many reporters, as the consensus amongst reporters and editors shifted from wondering *if* the U.S. should go to war to predicting *when* the U.S. would go to war.[21] The pro-war atmosphere intensified throughout the early weeks of the invasion, as television and print sources ran headlines such as "How Baghdad Will Fall"; "Creeping Closer to Baghdad"; "Moving In and Taking Over"; "U.S.

Still Has Long To-Do List Before War Ends"; "Television Producers are Struggling to Keep Track of War's Progress, or the Lack of it"; and "Bush and 2 Allies Seem Set for War to Depose Hussein."[22]

Most mainstream pundits sprang into action in defending the drive for war.
William Safire, former columnist for the *New York Times*, promoted the U.S.
agenda as driven "not by any lust for global domination," but by a desire to
"make the Middle East safe for democracy."[23] In the *Washington Post*, David
Riven and Lee Casey announced that the U.S. was obligated to initiate "the swift
collapse of his [Saddam's] regime" in order "to minimize the war's human and
material costs, and to ease Iraq's economic and political reconstruction."[24] In a
Los Angeles Times editorial titled "Peace Isn't Possible in Evil's Face," prominent author and Nobel Prize Winner Elie Wiesel demonized Saddam Hussein,
arguing: "no other option remains," as Saddam must "be disarmed by whatever
means necessary."[25]

So It Begins:
Framing the Invasion

The invasion and initial occupation of Iraq did little to change the mainstream
media's commitment to war. The tactical approach to evaluating American progress persevered unabated. *USA Today* news reports judged the war effort "dar-
ing,"[26] while the *New York Times* applauded the U.S. for having "liberated
Iraq."[27] Within the first month of fighting, Evan Thomas of *Newsweek* wondered: "Did we start the war with enough force?,"[28] while reporters Eric Schmitt
and Barnard Weinraub of the *New York Times* asked "How hard will the remaining forces fight?" and "How quickly will the coordinated allied air-ground attack destroy the Iraqi forces?"[29] In one Op-Ed column in the *New York Times*,
Nicholas Kristof asked similar questions to those of Schmitt and Weinraub,
pondering: "how much should we involve the U.N.?," "Whom should we hand
over power to in Iraq?," and "How long do we stay?"[30] The common assumption
seen here was that the U.S. had a right and obligation to determine how long to
continue the occupation, and who to "hand over power to," despite arguments
made by allies that the invasion was ill-timed, illegitimate, and illegal under
international law and the U.N. Charter.

Headlines from major newspapers did little to nothing in terms of challenging official justifications for war and more to update readers on the war's "progress."[31] As the nation's most prestigious paper, the *New York Times* was a
prominent leader in assessing war progress, as these sample headlines taken at
the time of the invasion indicate: "Bush Defends Progress of War and is
Cheered"; "U.S. Forces Enter Zone to Confront Republican Guard"; "Key Section of City Is Taken In a Street-by-Street Fight"; "U.S. Troops Poised to Oust
Loyalists In Northern City of Tikrit"; "For Allies, the Next Target is Hussein's
Hometown"; "U.S. Picks Targets for Baghdad Push"; "Little Resistance Encountered as Troops Reach Baghdad"; "Marines Cruising to Baghdad"; "U.S.
Tanks Make Quick Strike Into Baghdad"; "U.S. Forces Take Control in Bagh-

dad; Bush Elated; Some Resistance Remains"; "Push to Finish the Job"; "Bush Says Hussein is Out, But War is Not Yet Over"; and, "Pentagon Asserts The Main Fighting Is Finished In Iraq."[32]

The importance of an American victory was repeated in corporate television news as well. Dan Rather, former head anchor for *CBS News*, exemplified the apprehension toward questioning U.S. war objectives quite well, explaining: "Look, I'm an American. . . . And when my country is at war, I want my country to win, whatever the definition of 'win' may be."[33] Rather added about the Bush administration's charges of weapons of mass destruction: "Look, when a president of the United States, any president, Republican or Democrat, says these are the facts, there is heavy prejudice, including my own, to give him the benefit of any doubt, and for that I do not apologize."[34] Rather's comments—specifically his reluctance to set any concrete criteria for what "winning may be" outside of the Bush administration's own standards—revealed a strong, yet blind commitment to the Presidency during times of war. Rather's deference to authority in the case of the Bush administration's WMD claims is representative of most of the reporting in the corporate press before the war. Reporters and media outlets were hesitant to suggest that the Bush administration might retain ulterior motives or be lying about its weapons charges, although this was suggested in much of the anti-war propaganda in the British press, Arab press, and in the American Independent-Left media. This position of deference makes short work of the contention that there is an adversarial relationship between a "sovereign" media system and American political leaders.

Extended Occupation and Evolving Resistance

In the months following the invasion, and as a result of mounting American casualties and increasingly hostile American public opinion, mainstream media coverage drew attention to the importance of promoting Iraqi "stability," the necessity of the "pacification" campaign against resistance groups, and the importance of conducting a prolonged occupation. As most news outlets correctly understood, the war effort had transitioned from a swift invasion period with relatively little resistance (in comparison to previous American wars), into a campaign against guerilla forces that seem to be growing in strength. Under these circumstances, the "humanitarian" role of the United States was highlighted extensively, considering that the WMD justification had been discredited. Thomas Friedman of the *New York Times* argued that, due to increasing instability, "Iraq is a country still on life support, and U.S. troops are the artificial lungs and heart."[35] The *New Republic* editorialized: "whether we like it or not, the future of Iraq is now an American responsibility."[36]

As American casualties increased, and the search for WMD ended unsuccessfully, the mainstream press altered its primary justification for continuing the war from weapons of mass destruction to supporting the "democratic" intentions of the Bush administration. One *Washington Post* editorial congratulated Bush for "his commitment to a long-term struggle to promote freedom in the

Arab world."[37] *CBS Evening News* ran the headline "Fallen Heroes," in honor of American servicemen and women killed in Iraq, reinforcing the perception that those who serve are committed to furthering democracy and fighting tyranny.[38] Fareed Zakaria of *Newsweek* reminded readers who might have started to question the worth of the war of the long-term goal of "establish[ing] democracy in Iraq as a way of breaking the tyrannical status quo in the Middle East that has bred repression and terror."[39]

Iraqi resistance to the U.S., conversely, was marginalized in order to assist American forces in retaining legitimacy in the eyes of the American public. Nationalistic pressures in general were also likely to have played a large part in explaining why many Americans supported the U.S. occupation. The practice of falling in line in support of government does not apply only to media outlets; it applies to the American people as well.

Pro-war framing in early and later stages of the occupation focused on the necessity of crushing resistance cells and organizations so as to enhance the efficiency of the military occupation. On *CNN*, Lou Dobbs criticized the lack of success in destroying guerilla forces, asserting: "This insurgency is growing. Therefore it's successful. What in the world can this country do now, and what is it going to do to deal with that?. . . at what point does the U.S. get tough?"[40] Dobbs added: "We should, it seems to me, as the dominant world military power, prevail in any contest, particularly against a Third World insurgency."[41] The media preoccupation with military superiority and "pacification" neglected many of the underlying reasons for the growth of the "insurgency"—most importantly increasing Iraqi anger at the U.S. presence in Iraq. This anger, while reported occasionally in public opinion polls, was not presented coherently so as to explain why the U.S. was beginning to face greater resistance in Iraq. As a result, the question was not asked: is it the escalation of the "pacification" campaign that may be responsible for the increase in attacks and the growing popularity of resistance groups opposing the U.S.?

The primary emphasis of news reporting focused on how to gauge the "progress against the insurgency," as the *New York Times* accurately depicted the mass media's and military's objectives.[42] Progress—or the lack of progress—was increasingly measured by the number of attacks on American troops, the number of Americans dead, the success in imposing an interim government and in facilitating elections, the cost of the war, and in terms of victories in gaining military control over key regions of the country such as Falluja and Samarra, where major coalition attacks against guerilla groups took place. On the contrary, progress was not typically defined by attempts to end the war and promote withdrawal prior to the 2007 Congressional turn against the war. The *Washington Post* instead editorialized: Bush is "right not to be stampeded by losses or the growing unpopularity of the war into aborting the Iraqi mission or setting an arbitrary timetable for withdrawal."[43] More important, according to the *Los Angeles Times*, was the psychological campaign aimed at the people of Iraq focused on "maintaining moral superiority" on the part of the U.S. "by stressing that the fighting was the insurgents' fault," rather than coalition forces.[44] It is under this mindset that the psyche of the Bush administration and the mainstream media becomes clearer, as their attacks on Iraqi resistance groups created a sort of "black and white" polarization between the occupiers, interested in democracy and human rights, and an "insurgency" intent on derailing progress, stability, elections, and Iraqi self-determination.

The Virtues of Stability

The importance of Iraqi "stability" is a prime focus of mass media reporting, even as the occupation became increasingly violent. Thomas Ricks, reporting for the *Washington Post*, discussed the "bigger challenge" in Iraq, of "creating an Iraqi government presence to prevent key areas from reverting into chaos."[45] The *Washington Post* reported that such "stability" might be won by creating "homegrown military and law enforcement forces" needed to quell unrest and resistance.[46] The general picture presented was one where the Bush administration "hope[d] to show progress toward stability."[47]

According to the model presented in the mass media, the United States is gracious and compassionate in its motivations for the Iraq war—humanitarian in its concern with furthering freedom in the realm of international relations. As social critic and scholar Michael Parenti states, "It is taken as a given that unjust aggression is something this country resists but never practices. That conflicts arising with other nations are the fault of those nations," rather than of American political leaders.[48] Chalmers Johnson, author of *Sorrows of Empire: Militarism, Secrecy, and the End of the Republic* argued, "Our imperialists like to assert that they are merely bringing a measure of 'stability' to the world. For them, the dirty hands belong to older empires, not our own."[49]

Electoral Exaltation

The post-2005 election period witnessed some of the most pronounced euphoria regarding Iraqi "democratization," compared with most any other time period in Operation Iraqi Freedom. The *New York Times* and CNN celebrated "Iraq's first free election in 50 years,"[50] as a "milestone" breakthrough in democratization.[51] Bridget Quinn of *Fox News Live* cheered, "for the first time in years Iraqis will be able to cast their votes freely."[52] Shepard Smith of *Fox News' Studio B* praised Iraqis for "coming out to brave the terror threat," as Iraq's guerilla forces were denigrated for hampering Iraqi progress.[53] American troops were praised by countless reporters, anchors, and pundits, among them Martha MacCallum of *Fox News Live* – for "trying to make Iraq safe for voters."[54]

According to mainstream media sources, the "pacification" campaign was intended mainly to benefit the Iraqi people. Taking media reports and editorials at face value, the American public was told in the media that the "short term" goal of military planners had always been the establishment of a government that would "make most Iraqis feel they have regained their sovereignty"; contrary evidence exposing the Bush administration's opposition to democratic elections was systematically repressed in most reports.[55] This reality is focused upon more thoroughly in chapter 8, specifically in regards to *Guardian* reporter Jonathon Steele's reporting on the United States' strong opposition to elections in Iraq. Other predictions of a newly established Iraqi sovereignty were made by David Brooks of the *New York Times*, who promised, "the arrival of a new government would also mean the end of the American-dominated authority."[56] While Brooks was correct in that the election meant the official end of the U.S. appointed and imposed interim government and the dissolution of the U.S. Coalition Provisional Authority, he neglected to discuss the implications of an indefinite occupation on Iraqi "sovereignty." Likewise, Peter Jennings of *ABC News* made Orwellian remarks concerning post-election conditions: "It is now an Iraqi government having to deal with largely Iraqi violence against *what was the occupation* [emphasis added]. It is no longer in that sense an occupation, even though the military stays here as the guardian of peace and to some extent the guardian of the sovereignty."[57]

The favorable portrayal of the American oversight of "democratic" elections and the continued occupation—although deemed illegal by the U.N. Secretary General Kofi Annan—were necessary in constructing an image of the U.S. as committed to Iraqi self-determination and independence. Media pundits interpreted the election as a vindication of their commitment to the liberalization and democratization of Iraq. Brian Williams, reporting for *NBC Nightly News* explained that "lately, even the harshest critics of President Bush have been forced to admit that maybe he's right about freedom's march around the globe. . . . What if we are watching an example of presidential leadership that will be taught in American schools for generations to come? It's an idea gaining more currency."[58] The *Wall Street Journal* also joined in, in the support for the Bush administration's "vision of spreading democracy—of getting to the 'tipping point' where tyrannies start to crumble"—a campaign that "seems not only to be working but also winning some unexpected converts."[59] *Time* awarded George W. Bush their "Person of the Year" during the 2004 holiday for leading "America's efforts to plant the seeds of liberty in Iraq and the rest of the Middle East."[60]

Election euphoria was not simply a result of Christmas goodwill on the part of the news media; it represented a long-standing campaign on the part of the establishment media to convince the American public of the good intentions of the U.S. in Iraq. Pro-war framing in the media closely paralleled official justifications for war. Most of the observations above do not only somewhat resemble the Bush administration's guidelines for acceptable discourse over the Iraq war, but take it a step further by mirroring government statements. To take one example: the Coalition Provisional Authority's promise to "help Iraq recover from decades of dictatorship, to help the people of Iraq gain elections, democracy, and freedom desired by the overwhelming majority of the Iraqi people"[61] could just as easily have been delivered by the editors of the *New York Times*, the *Washington Post*, or the *Los Angeles Times* (or any other major corporate paper), or by television pundits such as Bill O'Reilly or Lou Dobbs of *Fox News* and *CNN*.

Whether it was print and television outlets as conservative as the *Wall Street Journal* and *Fox News*, or more liberal sources like the *New York Times* and *CNN*, the mainstream media transmitted government promises of democracy, as well as rose-colored assessments of U.S. military progress in Iraq, with only pragmatic interjection. But the transmission of propaganda and official statements did not represent the only trend in the media's reporting of the events in Iraq. As will be discussed below, the crux of the media's criticisms of the Bush administration and "Operation Iraqi Freedom" fall within the parameters of acceptable discourse over the war as determined by the Democratic and Republican parties. Such dialogue over the Iraq war ranges from the least critical perspectives—portrayed in detail in the first half of this chapter—to the most critical perspectives which do not typically venture further than tactical, pragmatic evaluations of how to better pursue the pacification, stabilization, and Westernization of Iraq. These criticisms have not historically included attacks on the U.S. as imperialist or repressive in its foreign policy, although there are rare exceptions.

"Anti-War" Criticisms in the Mass Media

A common stereotype in the corporate press frames the media as liberally biased and vigilantly opposed to the war in Iraq. Some pundits complain about the "overwhelming liberal dominance of the media."[62] *Fox News* talk show host Sean Hannity discusses the "pervasive liberal slant of the dominant news organizations" including "left" corporate news channels such as *CBS*, *ABC*, *NBC*, and *CNN*, and newspapers such as the *New York Times*, the *Los Angeles Times*, and the *Washington Post*.[63] Brent Bozell, founder and president of the *Media Research Center* and author of *Weapons of Mass Distortion: The Coming Meltdown of the Liberal Media*, takes a slightly more nuanced approach to what he sees as liberal control and conservative submission and marginalization throughout the media. While admitting that conservatives are well represented in television commentary, Bozell maintains that liberals overwhelmingly dominate corporate news reporting—and as a result, unfairly dominate the mass media in general.[64]

As the leading liberal establishment newspaper in the nation, the *New York Times* has been the focus of many conservative attacks. Bill O'Reilly lambasted the paper for its allegedly anti-Bush, left-leaning bias, assailing it for "not working in the best interest of the American people."[65] Bernard Goldberg, formerly a reporter for *CBS News*, chastised the *New York Times* because he felt it "went out of its way to attack and undermine the [Bush] administration at every turn" throughout the Iraq war.[66]

For such an extraordinary amount of debate over the prevalence of liberal media, there has often been inadequate effort made by pundits to define precisely what they mean by liberal bias. General attacks on "the liberal media" seem to be more commonplace than in depth conversations over what *exactly* constitutes a liberal bias. The question remains, however: what does it really mean to argue that the mass media is liberally biased or anti-war? Despite the attacks of many of those mentioned above, media viewers are often left with at least some idea of what pundits mean when they complain of liberal or anti-war bias. Many media commentators equate being liberal with being unpatriotic, and threatening American democracy and prosperity. Some of the usual suspects who fit this profile include notable media polemicists such as Anne Coulter, Michael Savage, Bill O'Reilly, and Rush Limbaugh, among many others.

In spreading "anti-American" views, liberals are thought to be guilty of threatening the American government by undermining public confidence in the American political system and in the Bush administration. The argument has even been made that liberals enable terrorism by supporting "Islamic fanatics," leading to an undermining of the Bush administration and the "War on Terror."[67] Despite many attacks made against the liberal media, Americans would do well to better understand what separates liberal, allegedly anti-war media establishments like the *New York Times*, and conservative pro-war media outlets.

A closer look at the *New York Times*—the most prestigious liberal and allegedly anti-war newspaper in the nation—reveals a great deal about the nature of its framing of Iraq, and even more insight into the methods employed in order to create what are largely exaggerated distinctions between establishment liberal and conservative media institutions. To be sure, there are some substantial differences between establishment liberal papers such as the *New York Times* and the *Washington Post* as opposed to more conservative papers like the *Wall Street Journal* and the *Washington Times*, as well as between liberal networks like *CNN* and conservative channels like *Fox News*. Conservative elite media outlets are much less likely to tolerate *any* type of dissent against government and the military, except perhaps those critiques faulting the Bush administration for inadequately escalating the occupation and pacification campaign in Iraq. Conversely, liberal establishment outlets like the *New York Times* and *Washington Post* allow more room for criticism of government, although within narrow limits.

Although the *New York Times* and the *Washington Post* have been willing to challenge the Bush administration on at least some issues in the Iraq war, the papers typically refuse to put up challenges to the occupation on a bedrock level by questioning the legality of the war, or the government's commitment to democracy in Iraq. What is apparent after an extensive review of media wartime criticisms is that more radical to liberal-progressive critiques of the war are either totally un-represented or largely omitted from liberal establishment sources.

The *New York Times* and the Anti-War Myth

The *New York Times* stands at the forefront of the "liberal" establishment news, as seen in the paper's reporting, editorials, and columnist commentaries (Op-Eds). An exploration of the paper's views, particularly in relation to the Iraq war, is a valuable endeavor if one is to understand the range of opinion in the paper, as well as in the rest of the liberal mainstream press. By investigating the paper's "anti-war stances," a picture emerges of what it means to be critical of the war, according to the standards set out within the mass media. By starting with a review of the paper's Op-Ed page—one of the most openly biased sections of the paper—one begins to see that its writers retain many similarities with conservative and "centrist" commentators and pundits.

The *New York Times'* Op-Ed columnists provide criticisms of style (how to better fight wars) rather than substantive challenges (whether U.S. wars are fundamentally imperial or immoral). Out of all the *Times'* liberal columnists, Thomas Friedman has been the most passionately pro-war, although he has taken issue with what he considers the real problem: that "Iraq has still not been fully liberated."[68] His analysis of the occupation fits well within the neoliberal paradigm, which claims that capitalism and corporate globalization, complimented by U.S. military force, are necessary means of spreading democracy, human rights, and justice throughout the globe. Friedman's analysis reflects a logic that seeks to reconcile what many critics consider contradictory principles and developments. While admitting that the U.S. is guilty of having overthrown democratic governments in the past, and that the U.S. "support [s] repressive Arab dictators so they will sell us cheap oil," Friedman still views the U.S. as "the greatest beacon of freedom, charity, opportunity, and affection in history."[69] In his portrayals of a liberal American empire, Friedman believes that the Bush administration selflessly dedicated the U.S. to "the first democracy-building project ever in the Arab world" by committing to a long-term occupation of Iraq.[70]

Friedman's method of pro-war propaganda is incredibly effective, as it seeks to include in public discourse evidence that largely contradicts his own ideological stance. Friedman has reframed conscious American support for repressive Arab dictatorships as a commitment to global democracy. This approach is very different from other propaganda approaches in conservative mainstream media institutions that seek to *totally* ignore and discount evidence that challenges America's global dominance. While conservative pro-war propagandists such as Bill O'Reilly and Robert Novak rarely, if ever, admit to flaws or mistakes in American foreign policy (except that maybe the U.S. is not tough enough in its war efforts), the liberal propaganda approach seeks to lend at least some legitimacy to criticisms of American foreign policy, while ultimately attempting to reconcile, downplay, or discount substantive criticisms in order to reaffirm American hegemony.

In further elaborating on his "democratic-imperialist" paradigm, Friedman explains that the capitalist system relies on military force in order to successfully dominate the globe. Friedman declares: "the hidden hand of market capitalism will never work without the hidden fist. McDonald's cannot flourish without McDonnell Douglas. . . and the hidden fist that keeps the world safe for Silicon Valley's technologies to flourish is called the U.S. Army, Air Force, Navy, and Marine Corps."[71] Critics have argued that it is difficult to divorce Friedman from advocacy of war crimes, considering that he has consistently advocated the destruction of Iraqi infrastructure on a massive scale[72] in order to "democratize" Iraq. In a piece titled "Tom Friedman: The Imperial Chronicler," Mike Whitney speaks with contempt of Friedman's view, "commonplace among American elites that the world should be grateful for the hellfire unleashed by the U.S. military...Friedman postulates a fairytale world where American foreign policy is always governed by principle and genuine humanitarian concern. His role as establishment-scribe is to perpetuate the illusion that the American Goliath may stumble, but the policy is always driven by good intentions."[73]

A Pattern of Reversals

The *New York Times* columnists who have been the most critical of the Bush administration also fall within the mainstream liberal archetype in that they either refuse to condemn, or inconsistently condemn American policy in Iraq. These Op-Ed writers concurrently argue that the U.S. is a repressive imperial power, but also that the problem with the war is that the U.S. cannot find ways to effectively fight and win it. These columnists reaffirm, to varying degrees, the liberal propaganda model as illustrated by Thomas Friedman. The antagonism between the two conflicting positions—between pragmatic pro-war criticisms on the one hand, and radical condemnations of imperial war on the other—makes it difficult to discern a consistent pattern of criticism on the part of these Op-Ed writers.

Bob Herbert, while sometimes presenting progressive condemnations of the war—including condemnations of the loss of American and Iraqi life—has often relied upon a very limited framework for critiquing the war. Herbert's framework centers on what he feels is a major problem behind the war—that it has been "mismanaged," "misguided," and "not sustainable."[74] In one of his editorials, "How Many Deaths Will it Take," Herbert argues that that the problem with the war is that it is "unwinnable," and that, "we've put our troops in Iraq in an impossible situation. If you are not permitted to win a war, eventually you will lose it."[75] Herbert attacks the Bush administration for having "foolishly started" a war that they "can't figure out how to win," as the main problem seems to be that "Mr. Bush had no coherent strategy for defeating the insurgency."[76] Herbert's criticisms are for the most part conventional: "we haven't given them [the troops] a clear mission," "we can't identify the enemy," the war is costing "staggering amounts of money," and the U.S. has failed "to send enough troops to effectively wage the war that we started."[77]

As is the case with other pundits at the *New York Times*, "anti-war" criticisms are limited to tactical critiques of the Bush administration based predominantly upon highlighting military errors that, if corrected, might contribute to a more smoothly functioning occupation and war effort. Throughout the war, though, Herbert began to change his tone a bit by offering anti-war claims with more substance. By July of 2005, Herbert was condemning war planners for their intent "to establish a long-term military presence in Iraq to ensure American domination of the Middle East and its precious oil reserves."[78] Subsequent columns ridiculed Washington for its reliance on the "toxic fog of fantasy, propaganda, and deliberate misrepresentation that [have] been such a hallmark of the George W. Bush administration."[79] While Herbert's attacks should certainly be welcome in any media system that considers the intellectual exchange of many different perspectives on U.S. goals in Iraq, they also seem a bit incoherent, at least in that it is difficult to distinguish a consistent pattern of criticism of the war. If the war is imperial and immoral, designed to secure control over oil rather than promote democracy, then why attack the administration for not effectively fighting it? Why complain that the war is "unwinnable' or "mismanaged" when Americans should not be trying to "win" or "manage" a repressive imperial war in the first place?

Although Paul Krugman has also distinguished himself from other mainstream editorialists by presenting American and Iraqi casualties as unacceptable and by rendering Bush's "imperial officials" and "imperial administration,"[80] his columns also rely on narrow criticisms of the Bush administration for "botching the enlisting of allies" in the Iraq war and for its failure in "training and equipping local forces, and preparing for [Iraqi] elections."[81] Krugman believes that "the truth, of course, is that there aren't nearly enough troops" in Iraq, and that "staying there would require a much bigger army" in order for the occupation to succeed.[82] In a piece titled "A No-Win Situation," Krugman explores the possibility that "a democratic, pro-American Iraq has receded out of reach," the assumption being that democracy is possible under American occupation and coerced neoliberal reforms.[83] By and large, Krugman's "criticisms" of the U.S. conform to the vision of a just and noble war in Iraq.

The *New York Times'* remaining liberal commentators fall within the same category. Nicholas Kristof, while admitting that Iraqis have paid a "horrendous price" as a result of the U.S. invasion, reconciles this by establishing the "good intentions of well-meaning conservatives who wanted to liberate them [the Iraqi people]." Kristof discounts the efforts of Americans "seeking a troop withdrawal that would make matters even worse," concluding that the U.S. must "stay the course" in Iraq and continue the campaign to pacify the country in the campaign to implant democracy.[84]

Also presenting a sometimes progressive-radical criticism of the war is Maureen Dowd, who initially assessed that the invasion was driven by imperial motivations. However, this initial prescription was later compromised in favor of mainstream interpretations of the conflict portraying the U.S. as a force for good in Iraq.[85] In what amounted to a reversal of her original condemnation of the invasion, Dowd complained that, in Iraq, there is "no visible enemy, no coherent plan, and no exit timetable."[86] Equally revealing is Dowd's belief that a major problem with the war effort is the inability of American troops to locate the "bad guys" in Iraq—presumably meaning Iraqi nationalist resistance groups. Equally revealing is Dowd's more recent reversal back to a more radical, Orwellian style of critique of the war, seen when she suggested that the administration's "grand schemes always end up as the opposite. Officials say they're promoting national security when they're hurting it; they say they're squelching terrorists when they're breeding them; they say they're bringing stability to Iraq when the country's imploding."[87]

The point of this analysis is not to take an individual, personality-based approach to studying the *New York Times'* Op-Ed and editorial biases. This exercise is designed for one clear purpose: to demonstrate that, again and again, what passes for liberal "anti-war" criticisms, in what is considered the most liberal, "anti-war" paper in the U.S., are really merely conventional pro-war criticisms, peppered with either minor or contradictory objections. In this sense, by looking at each individual *New York Times* writer, one sees a reemerging pattern that is institutionalized in the mainstream liberal media. As news reports, editorials, and Op-Eds in liberal elite papers begin to call for withdrawal from Iraq, they can be expected to continue disseminating administration propaganda assuring Americans of the noble intentions of the U.S. in Iraq. By late 2006, the *New York Times'* editors had done just this. Although condemning "President Bush's gross mismanagement of the war" and advocating "one last push to stabilize Baghdad," in order to "mediate [Iraqi] sectarian divisions," the paper's editors situated their limited support for U.S. escalation alongside expectations that Democratic leaders present "good ideas for how to get out of Iraq without creating even wider chaos and terrorism."[88]

Falling in Line

Along with other mainstream liberal critics of the war, the *New York Times'* liberal columnists reveal themselves as participants in a corporate establishment that is hesitant to critique the U.S. as imperialist. The *New York Times* is not the only media outlet pushing liberal "anti-war" views. Countless outlets and programs have taken up this approach as the Iraq war continues. The self-described liberal halves of bipartisan programs such as *CNN's Crossfire* and *Fox New's Hannity and Colmes* repeat similar arguments that lend credibility to the American presence in Iraq. Paul Begala, former host and self-portrayed leftist of *Crossfire* argues that the Bush administration "didn't have enough troops" in Iraq "because Bush doesn't want to deal with reality"—reality being determined by the need to more effectively destroy Iraqi resistance.[89] Alan Colmes, described by the *Fox News* website as "a hard-hitting liberal known for his electric commentary,"[90] prefers unwavering support for the Bush administration during the initial stages of war. In an interview with Bill O'Reilly on *Fox News'* The O'Reilly Factor, Colmes admits that, during the Iraq invasion, "I've kept quiet. My choice has been—I have not criticized the administration or this war effort while there are men and women in harms way."[91]

Rather than criticizing the war as aggressive, illegal or imperialist in orientation, the preferred attacks against the Bush administration are far more parochial and pedestrian, certainly not worthy of being labeled a fierce opposition. In his appraisal of the "wretched problem of Iraq," David Ignatius of the *Washington Post* wonders "How do we win this thing, and if we can't, how do we get out?"[92] The *Los Angeles Times* editors concurred, identifying what they feel is a "terribly botched occupation"[93]—a declaration that complimented the critiques of military officials on *CNN*, such as former General Wesley Clark, of a war that "strategically was a mistake."[94] In a column labeled "Time to Quit Iraq (Sort of)," Edward Luttwak urged caution toward an immediate withdrawal, while also granting that, "The United States is depleting its military strength" by fighting against "Ba'ath regime loyalists, Sunni revanchists, local and foreign Islamist extremists and the ever-more numerous Shi'ite militias."[95]

As the leader of the mainstream-Left critics, the *New York Time*'s editors found fault with the ways in which the Bush administration "mismanaged the war," implying that, if the war effort was running more smoothly the paper would lend more support.[96] *New York Times* reporting suggested that "stabilizing Iraq could be more difficult than originally planned,"[97] while the *New Republic*'s Peter Beinart commented that the occupation was "proving harder and uglier than expected" throughout the mass media.[98]

The strength of resistance to the occupation—violent and nonviolent—was unanticipated as a result of what *New York Times* reporter David E. Sanger deemed the "administration's failure to anticipate the violence in Iraq and the obstacles to reconstruction."[99] The question of why such resistance was unexpected in light of decades of fierce Iraqi resistance to foreign occupation going back to the time of the European imperial powers was not discussed in the pre-war period throughout most reporting, although critical scholars did raise the question.[100] Those who felt the war would be a "cakewalk" cast aside the likelihood that resistance against the U.S. would be substantial. In the end, most mainstream reporters and editors did little to challenge the "cakewalk" assumption before the war began, but made such revelations only after the increase in attacks on U.S. troops.

In post invasion reporting, papers like the *Washington Post* conceded that the occupation has been "unexpectedly difficult."[101] Reporters generally interpreted objectivity as prohibiting them from predicting resistance to the U.S. in the pre-invasion period. To do so, they claimed, would mean that they were putting their own opinions into reporting, rather than simply "reporting the news" in terms of covering official statements. The nation's most prestigious papers initially cast aside reservations of potential problems in Iraq before the war began, while acknowledging, "the overly optimistic visions that Washington proclaimed soon after the initial military success."[102] And yet, in the early days of the war effort, the same media outlets expected the "prospective war with Iraq...to be short, with many predicting that combat operations will last two to three weeks,"[103] as they speculated over the "Quick collapse of [the] Iraqi military" as a "very real likelihood."[104]

Many media outlets criticizing the war were not willing to go as far as to argue that it was a strategic blunder though. In a 2005 column in the *Washington Post*, William Raspberry identified what he considered a central problem in leaving Iraq—namely that it "would require a concession. . . that the whole thing was a mistake."[105] *Washington Post* editors seemed to consent to this perspective, arguing that "Regardless of whether the war was right, the situation it produced offers few if any responsible options other than those endorsed by both candidates [Kerry and Bush]."[106] The message was clear: responsible politicians did not advocate a withdrawal from Iraq. Such was the prescription in prominent newspapers like the *Chicago Tribune*, which contended that "The eventual withdrawal of U.S. forces from Iraq threatens to be disastrous," although "evidence is mounting that invading that beleaguered country was a grandiose misadventure."[107] O'Hanlon and James Steinberg added in a *Washington Post* column that, "there is no guarantee that indefinite continuation of the current mission will produce victory," although they rationalized the democratic arguments made in favor of U.S. intervention by denouncing critiques of American imperialism: "The perception of coalition forces as latter-day imperialists is, of course, fundamentally unfair and wrong...we should not plan to withdraw our forces entirely by any set date. . . admittedly, foreign military forces are still a necessary part of the solution in Iraq. Without them the country would probably wind up in civil war."[108] Such appraisals seem intended to create an impression of the U.S. as an unwilling participant in violent conflict, as a power that is dragged into a prolonged occupation, without which Iraq would fall into civil war. Such framing is intended to convince Americans that the U.S. has no choice but to remain in Iraq indefinitely, despite the fact that withdrawal has been promoted by majorities in the U.S., and is supported by the Iraqi public and much of the world.[109] The assumption that there is no alternative to occupation is false, as continued presence in Iraq is only *one* of a number of policy choices available to U.S. planners.

The Indexing Effect:
Support for U.S. Regime Change

By the 2004 Presidential election, elite opinion throughout the mainstream media—short of some significant exceptions like *Fox News*—had largely turned against the Bush administration, but for reasons other than those given in the Independent-Left press. As the election neared, criticisms of the Bush administration's mismanagement of the war steadily increased, often endorsing a regime change in favor of a new Presidential candidate, the Democratic hopeful John Kerry, who it was felt could better conduct the war effort.

Justifications for a change in American political leadership at the time of the election derived much of their strength from pragmatic criticisms of the Bush administration; numerous news outlets sought to abandon what many saw as the Bush administration's sinking ship. The *Washington Post* helped lead the way in terms of its opposition to Bush's reelection. The paper's editors supported "a change in management" of the war, endorsing Presidential hopeful John Kerry.[110] In an opinion piece labeled "Kerry for President," the paper attacked Bush for his administration's failure "to better prepare for post-war reconstruction" and because the administration "repeatedly rebuffed advice to commit sufficient troops" to Iraq.[111] Rajiv Chandrasekaran reported for the *Washington Post* on the "intensifying campaign of insurgent violence that contrasts sharply with assessments by Bush administration officials...that the instability is contained to small pockets of the country."[112] The *Washington Post* often framed the growth of Iraqi guerillas as a result of the administration's failure to get tough. Sebastian Mallaby remarked that the central problem lied in "the hesitation in rooting out insurgent bases in the Sunni heartland."[113] Aside from the problem of not committing enough troops to adequately "pacify" Iraq, the *Washington Post* used the standard criticism about the danger of the Bush administration's distrust of multilateralism, as "the administration developed its policies about preemption and Iraq without readjusting its ideas about allies or coming up with a new strategy for dealing with them."[114] The problem was not that the U.S. went to war, but that it should have done so more effectively by securing support from its allies. This "textbook lesson" of Iraq was referred to in the *New York Times* as proof of "the dangers of going it alone in the world" of global conflict and dispute resolution.[115] At the margins of the mainstream media, alternative news sources like *Salon* postulated that, "if the Bush administration had been prepared to wait for U.N. support before launching its invasion, things could have turned out very differently in Iraq."[116]

Some mainstream editorials and news reports did not target the Bush administration specifically for regime change, but reinforced a general media climate where readers could blame the Bush administration for the lack of progress in Iraq. The *New York Times* gave "reason to wonder whether that vision" of democratizing Iraq "was unrealistically optimistic."[117] *Time* Magazine reasoned that, "the longer the U.S. waits, the more time it gives the insurgency to spread."[118] *ABC News* Military Analyst Anthony Cordesman stated that the Coalition Provisional Authority "got the first year of the coalition occupation in Iraq fundamentally wrong...The effort to rush money into the Iraqi military and security forces recognizes the United States failed to make a serious effort to train Iraqi military and security forces to fight insurgents in any strength during the year following the fall of Saddam Hussein."[119]

The lesson of this chapter is that American mainstream media has been profoundly dogmatic and narrow in its "criticisms" of the President during wartime. An outlook incorporating a wider spectrum of criticisms would need to incorporate more than just comments concerning the lack of sufficient troops in Iraq, the slow pace of "pacification," speculation over Iraq's ability to commit to democracy (rather than the U.S.'s), and the problems of unilateralism as contrasted with multilateralism. To present a more balanced view of the situation in Iraq, the media would surely need to encompass more progressively oriented denunciations of America as an imperial power, in order to allow Americans to decide for themselves whether the U.S. is engaged in democracy promotion in Iraq, or in repression. Typical "critical" views in the mainstream press that assess the cost of the occupation and the war in terms of American lives and perhaps most important, the likelihood of successfully destroying nationalist guerilla resistance, need to be acknowledged as "solutions" that necessarily marginalize institutional critiques of American aggression and empire, as well as support for withdrawal based upon such critiques.

Notes

1. Chris Hedges, "The Press and the Myths of War," *Nation*, 21 April 2003, 16.

2. Elisabeth Bumiller, "Bush Lays Out Goals for Iraq: Stability and Self-Rule," *New York Times*, 25 May 2004, 1(A).

3. Filkins, D. (2004, May 25). Failing to Disband Militias, U.S. Moves to Accept Them.*The New York Times*, A1.

4. David E. Sanger, "Fresh Starts: One for Iraq, One for Bush," *New York Times*, 29 June 2004, 1(A).

5. Christine, Hauser, "Self Rule is Test of Nerves on Local Iraqi Councils," *New York Times*, 30 May 2004, 1(A).

6. Dexter Filkins, "Iraqi Militias Said to Approve Deal to Disband," *New York Times*, 8 June 2004, 1(A).

7. Editorial, "Mideast Climate Change," *New York Times*, 1 March 2005, 22(A).

8. Dexter Filkins, "9 Iraqi Militias Said to Approve Deal to Disband," New York Times, 8 June 2004, 1(A).

9. Fouad Ajami, "Best Intentions: Why We Went, What We've Found," *New Republic*, 22 June 2004, 17.

10. Kessler, G., & Wright, R. (2004, April 21). U.S. Goals for Middle East Falter. *The Washington Post*, A16.

11. Robin Wright, "In Iraq, Daunting Tasks Await," *Washington Post*, 7 July 2004, 14(A).

12. Paul Richter, "U.S. Tries to Adapt as Options Dwindle," *Los Angeles Times*, 15 May 2004, 1(A).

13. Carol J. Williams and Alissa J. Rubin, 20 June 2004, "Iraqis Quietly Take Power after Bremer's Early Exit," *Los Angeles Times*, 1(A); Jeffrey Gettleman, "Transfer of Power to Iraqis is said to be well under way," *New York Times*, 13 June 2004, 1(A).

14. Anderson Cooper, *CNN Newsnight*, CNN, 21 June 2004.

15. Carl Boggs, "Empire and Globalization," in *Masters of War: Militarism and Blowback in the Era of American Empire*, ed. Carl Boggs (New York, NY: Routledge, 2003), 9.

16. Ian Fisher, "Free to Protest: Iraqis Complain About the U.S.," *New York Times*, 16 April 2003, 1(A).

17. Bradley Graham, "A Sharp Shift from Killing to Kindness," *Washington Post*, 4 December 2004, 14(A).

18. Evan Thomas, "Operation Hearts and Minds," *Newsweek*, 29 December 2003, 25.

19. Editorial, "A Question of Will," *Washington Post*, 18 March 2003, 28(A).

20. Jeanne Cummings, J, & Carla Anne Robbins, "How Bush Decided that Iraq's Hussein Must Be Ousted," *Wall Street Journal*, sec. 1, 14 June 2002, 1; David E. Sanger and Thom Shanker, "U.S. Exploring Baghdad Strike as First Option," *New York Times*, 29 July 2002, 1(A); James Dao and Eric Schmitt, "U.S. Taking Steps to Lay Foundation for Action in Iraq," *New York Times*, 18 November 2002, 1(A); Michael R. Gordon, "U.S. Picks Targets for Baghdad Push," *New York Times*, 7 March 2003, 1(A).

21. Amy Goodman and David Goodman, "The Corporate Media in Wartime," *International Socialist Review*, May-June 2005, 52.

22. Perry Smith, "Creeping Closer to Baghdad," *CBSnews.com*, 29 March 2003, http://www.cbsnews.com/stories/2003/03/29/iraq/printable546769.shtml (5 Apr. 2005); CBSnews.com, "Moving in and Taking Over," 7 April 2003, http://www.cbsnews.com/stories/2003/04/07/iraq/printable548217.shtml (5 April 2005); Christopher Cooper, "U.S. Still has Long To-Do List Before War Ends," *Wall Street Journal*, 10 April 2003, 8(A); Bill Carter and Jim Rutenberg, "Television Producers are Struggling to Keep Track of

War's Progress, or the Lack of it," *New York Times*, 25 March 2003, 14(B); David E. Sanger, "Bush and 2 Allies Seem Set for War to Depose Hussein," *New York Times*, 17 March 2003, 1(A).

23. William Safire, "Of Turks and Kurds," *New York Times*, 26 August 2002, *New York Times*, 15(A).

24. Lee A. Casey and David B. Rivkin Jr. "That's Why They Call it War," *Washington Post*, 16 March 2003, 4(B).

25. Elie Wiesel, "Peace Isn't Possible in Evil's Face," *Los Angeles Times*, 11 March 2003, 13(B).

26. James Cox, "U.S. War Machine Under Pressure to Produce Peace and Security," *USA Today*, 11 April 2003, 1(A).

27. Michael R. Gordon, "The Strategy to Secure Iraq Did Not Foresee a 2nd War," *New York Times*, 19 October 2004, 1(A).

28. Evan Thomas, "Operation Hearts and Minds," *Newsweek*, 29 December 2003, 25.

29. Eric Schmitt and Bernard Weinraub, "Battle for Baghdad like War Plan: Kill Enemy, Limit Damage, Provide Aid," *New York Times*, 3 April 2003, 1(B).

30. Nicholas Kristof, "Handing Over the Keys to Iraq," *New York Times*, 15 April 2003, 23(A).

31. Carter and Rutenberg, "Television Producers Struggling," 2003.

32. Adam Nagourney and David E. Sanger, "Bush Defends Progress of War and is Cheered," *New York Times*, 1 April 2003, 1(B); Michael R. Gordon, "U.S. Forces Enter Zone to Confront Republican Guard," *New York Times*, 2 April 2003, 1(A); John F. Burns, "Key Section of City is Taken in a Street-By-Street Fight," *New York Times*, 9 April 2003, 1(A); Dexter Filkins, "U.S. Troops Poised to Oust Loyalists in Northern City," *New York Times*, 14 April 2003, 1(A); Bernard Weinraub, "For Allies, the Next Target is Hussein's Hometown," *New York Times*, 13 April 2003, 6(B); Michael R. Gordon, "U.S. Picks Targets for Baghdad Push," *New York Times*, 7 March 2003, 1(A); Dexter Filkins, "Little Resistance Encountered as Troops Reach Baghdad," *New York Times*, *New York Times*, 5 April 2003, 3(B); Dexter Filkins, "Marines Cruising to Baghdad," *New York Times*, 4 April 2003, 1(B); Steven Lee Meyers, "U.S. Tanks Make Quick Strike Into Baghdad," *New York Times*, 6 April 2003, 1(A); Patrick E. Tyler, "U.S. Forces Take Control in Baghdad: Bush Elated; Some Resistance Remains," *New York Times*, 10 April 2003, 1(A); Michael R. Gordon, "Push to Finish the Job," *New York Times*, 9 April 2003, 1(A); Douglas Jehl and Richard W. Stevenson, "Bush Says Hussein is Out, But War is Not Yet Over," *New York Times*, 10 April 2003, 9(B); Eric Schmitt and Bernard Weinraub, "Pentagon Asserts the Main Fighting is Finished in Iraq," *New York Times*, 15 April 2003, 1(A).

33. Larry King, *Larry King Live*, CNN, 14 April 2003.

34. Common Dreams, "Media Advisory: Rather's Retirement and 'Liberal Bias,'" 2 March 2005 http://www.commondreams.org/news2005/0302-10.htm (16 Oct. 2005).

35. Thomas L. Friedman, "Iraq at the Tipping Point," *New York Times*, 18 November 2004, 31(A).

36. Editorial, "Mission Incomplete," *New Republic*, 26 May 2003, http://ssl.tnr.com/p/-docsub.mhtml?i=20030526&s=editorial052603 (16 Oct. 2005).

37. Editorial, "Kerry for President," *Washington Post*, 24 October 2004, 6(B).

38. Dan Rather, *CBS Evening News*, CBS, 9 November 2004.

39. Fareed Zakaria, "How to Pick a War President," *Newsweek*, 4 October 2004, 24.

40. Lou Dobbs, *Lou Dobbs Tonight*, CNN, 22 October 2004.

41. Lou Dobbs, *Lou Dobbs Tonight*, CNN, 21 September 2004.

42. Thom Shanker, "Rumsfeld on the Ground in Iraq, Gets a Report of Progress Against Insurgency," *New York Times*, 7 December 2003, 13(A).

43. Editorial, "Day of Loss," *Washington Post*, 27 January 2005, 18(A).

44. Tony Perry, "After Leveling City, U.S. Tries to Build Trust," *Los Angeles Times*, 7 January 2005, 3(A).

45. Thomas E. Ricks and Robin Wright, "U.S., Iraq Prepare Offensive to Pave Way for Election," *Washington Post*, 26 September 2004, 1(A).

46. Bradley Graham, "U.S. Says Police in Iraq Need Bolstering, More Arms, Trainers, Backup Units Sought," *Washington Post*, 25 November 2004, 1(A).

47. Richard W. Stevenson, "The White House: Bush's New Problem," *New York Times*, 22 December 2004, 6(A).

48. Michael Parenti, *Against Empire* (San Francisco, Ca.: City Light, 1995), 72.

49. Chalmers Johnson, *The Sorrows of Empire: Militarism, Secrecy, and the End of the Republic* (New York: Henry Holt, 2004), 70.

50. Anderson Cooper, *360 Degrees*, CNN, 30 January 2005.

51. John F. Burns, "Iraqis Begin Tabulating Results of Milestone Election," *New York Times*, 1 February 2005, 8(A).

52. Brigitte Quinn, *Fox News Live*, Fox News, 24 November 2004.

53. Shepard Smith, *Studio B*, Fox News, 27 January 2005.

54. Martha MacCallum, *Fox News Live*, Fox News, 27 January 2005.

55. Editorial, "No Delay for Iraqi Elections," *Los Angeles Times*, 4 January 2005, 12(B).

56. David Brooks, "Can We Save Iraq? No, But the Iraqis Can," *New York Times*, 11 January 2005, 27(A).

57. Peter Jennings, *ABC Evening News*, ABC, 28 June 2004.

58. Brian Williams, *NBC Nightly News*, NBC, 8 March 2005.

59. Editorial, "In Reagan's Footsteps," *Wall Street Journal*, 25 February 2005, http://www.opinionjournal.com/editorial/feature.html?id=110006342 (3 Dec. 2005).

60. Nancy Gibbs, "Person of the Year," *Time*, 27 December 2004, 30-49.

61. Aaron Glantz, *How America Lost Iraq* (New York: Penguin, 2005), 169.

62. Anne Coulter, *Slander: Liberal Lies About the American Right* (New York: Crown, 2002), 60.

63. Sean Hannity, *Let Freedom Ring: Winning the War of Liberty Over Liberalism* (New York: Regan, 2002), 255-56, 260.

64. Brent L. Bozell, *Weapons of Mass Distortion: The Coming Meltdown of the Liberal Media* (New York: Crown, 2004), 57.

65. Bill O'Reilly, *The O'Reilly Factor*, Fox News, 15 December 2004.

66. Bernard Goldberg, *Arrogance: Rescuing America from the Media Elite* (New York: Warner, 2003), 66.

67. Anne Coulter, *Treason: Liberal Treachery from the Cold War to the War on Terrorism* (New York: Crown, 2003), 292.

68. Thomas L. Friedman, "'Groundhog Day' in Iraq," *New York Times*, 11 November 2004, 33(A).

69. Thomas L. Friedman, "9/11 Lesson Plan," *New York Times*, 4 September 2002, 31(A).

70. Thomas L. Friedman, "Are There Any Iraqis in Iraq?" *New York Times*, 8 April 2004, 27(A).

71. Thomas L. Friedman, *The Lexus and the Olive Tree: Understanding Globalization* (New York: Ferrar, Straus, and Giroux, 1999), 373.

72. Thomas L. Friedman, "America's Multiple Choice Quiz," *New York Times*, 31 January 1998, 15(A); Thomas L. Friedman, "Rattling the Rattler," *New York Times*, 19 January 1999, 19(A).

73. Mike Whitney, "Tom Friedman: The Imperial Chronicler," *Z Net*, 15 May 2005, http://www.zmag.org/content/print_article.cfm?itemID=7863&sectionID=1   (3   Nov. 2005).

74. Bob Herbert, "Letting Down the Troops," *New York Times*, 29 October 2004, 25(A); Bob Herbert, "Cut Our Losses," *New York Times*, 28 November 2005, 19(A).

75. Bob Herbert, "How Many Deaths Will it Take," *New York Times*, 10 September 2004, 27(A).

76. Bob Herbert, "Dangerous Incompetence," *New York Times*, 30 June 2005, 25(A).

77. Bob Herbert, "How Many Deaths Will it Take?" *New York Times*, 10 September 2004, 27(A); Bob Herbert, "A War Without Reason," *New York Times*, 18 October 2004, 17(A).

78. Bob Herbert, "Oil and Blood," *New York Times*, 28 July 2005, 25(A).

79. Bob Herbert, "Voters' Remorse on Bush," *New York Times*, 22 September 2005, 31(A).

80. Paul Krugman, "Defending Imperial Nudity," *New York Times*, 4 November 2005, 27(A).

81. Paul Krugman, "The Last Deception," *New York Times*, 21 September 2004, 35(A).

82. Paul Krugman, "Too Few, Yet Too Many," *New York Times*, 30 May 2005, 15(A).

83. Paul Krugman, "A No-Win Situation," *New York Times*, 31 August 2004, 21(A).

84. Nicholas Kristof, "Saving the Iraqi Children," *New York Times*, 27 November 2004, 15(A).

85. Maureen Dowd, "Hypocrisy and Apple Pie," *New York Times*, 30 April 2003, 27(A).

86. Maureen Dowd, "A Moveable Feast of Terrorism," *New York Times*, 11 November 2004, 31(A).

87. Maureen Dowd, "Who's on First," *New York Times*, 29, October 2005, 19(A).

88. Editorial, "Democrats and Iraq," *New York Times*, 12 November 2006, 11(D).

89. Paul Begala, *Crossfire*, CNN, 19 October 2004.

90. Foxnews.com, "Alan Colme's Bio," 2005, http://www.foxnews.com/story/0,2933-130214,00.html (3 Dec. 2005).

91. Bill O'Reilly, *The O'Reilly Factor*, Fox News, 11 April 2003.

92. David Ignatius, "What Bush Can Do to Salvage Iraq," *Washington Post*, 5 November 2004, 25(A).

93. Editorial, "A Failed Presidency," *Los Angeles Times*, 1 November 2004, 10(B).

94. Wolf Blitzer, *Wolf Blitzer Reports*, CNN, 1 October 2004.

95. Edward Luttwak, "Time to Quit Iraq (Sort of)," *New York Times*, 18 August 2004, 21(A).

96. Editorial, "Talking Sense at Last on Iraq," *New York Times*, 21 September 2004, 34(A).

97. Eric Schmitt, "Army is Planning for 100,000 GIs in Iraq till 2006," *New York Times*, 22 November 2003, 1(A).

98. Peter Beinart, "Media Bias," *New Republic*, 14 April 2003, 6.

99. David E. Sanger, "White House to Overhaul Iraq and Afghan Missions," *New York Times*, 6 October 2003, 1(A).

100. Rashid Khalidi, *Resurrecting Empire: Western Footprints and America's Perilous Path in the Middle East* (Boston: Beacon, 2005), 1-36.

101. Thomas E. Ricks, "U.S. Army Changed by Iraq, But for Better or Worse?" *Washington Post*, 6 July 2004, 10(A).

102. Editorial, "Hard Work, Indeed," *Los Angeles Times*, 4 October 2004, 10(B).

103. Thomas E. Ricks, "Duration of War Key to U.S. Victory," *Washington Post*, 19 March 2003, 19(A).

104. Vernon Loeb and Jonathon Weisman, "Quick Collapse of Iraqi Military is 'Very Real' Likelihood," *Washington Post*, 19 March 2003, 18(A).

105. William Raspberry, "A Way Out of Iraq," *Washington Post*, 3 January 2005, 13(A).

106. Editorial, "The Choice on Iraq," *Washington Post*, 22 October 2004, 24(A).

107. Leon Daniel, "Saving America's Face will Exact an Unacceptable Loss of Life," *Chicago Tribune*, sec. 1, 25 September 2005, 1.

108. Michael O'Hanlon and James Steinberg, "Time to Announce a Timetable," *Washington Post*, 2 February 2005, 23(A).

109. Cesar G. Soriano and Steven Komarow, "Poll: Iraqis Out of Patience," *USA Today*, 28 April 2004, www.usatoday.com/news/world/iraq/2004-04-28-pollcover_x.htm?POE=click-refer (15 Nov. 2005).; CNN.com, "Poll: Support for Bush, Iraq War Dropping," 22 May 2004, http://www.cnn.com/2004/ALLPOLITICS/05/14/bush.kerry/ (18 Nov. 2005).

110. Editorial, "The Choice on Iraq," 2004.

111. Editorial, "Kerry for President," *Washington Post*, 24, October 2004, 6(B).

112. Rajiv Chandrasekaran, "Violence in Iraq Belies Claims of Calm, Data Show," *Washington Post*, 26 September 2004, 1(A).

113. Sebastian Mallaby, "A Reason to Back the President," *Washington Post*, 11 October 2004, 23(A).

114. James Mann, "Bush Wanted His Doctrine and the Allies Too," *Washington Post*, 16 March 2003, 1(B).

115. Editorial, "Indispensible Allies on Iran," *New York Times*, 14 August 2004, 14(A).

116. Mitchell Prothero, "Afghanistan: Mission Not Yet Accomplished," *Salon.com*, 21 September 2005, http://www.truthout.org/docs_2005/printer_092105N.shtml (22 Oct. 2005).

117. David E. Sanger, "Bush's Task: to Prepare Americans for Long Fight," *New York Times*, 28 September 2003, 11(A).

118. Romesh Ratnesar, "Can This War be Won?" *Time*, 4 October 2004, 33.

119. Anthony Cordesman, *ABC News International*, ABC, 14 September 2004.

5

Railing Iraqi Resistance: "Insurgency," Militias, and the Unfolding Civil War

If there was ever a question about the mainstream media's displeasure with Iraq's resistance to occupation, it was put it to rest after the March 31, 2004 attack on four American contractors in Falluja. In this attack, the contractors were burned to death in their SUV, as a local mob dragged their dead bodies through the town, and hung them from a bridge over the Euphrates River for onlookers to see. At the forefront of the reporting fiasco, the *New York Times* printed a picture of the charred and dismembered contractors on its April 1 front cover, followed by a close-up on page A12 of one of the burned bodies, surrounded by over a dozen Iraqis.[1] The American media was often quick to imply that the contractors were humanitarian actors who had little to nothing to do with questionable activities in Iraq, and who had unjustly come under attack from fanatical anti-American forces. The *San Francisco Chronicle* reported that the contractors were taking part in "food deliveries around Falluja," while the *New York Times* described their presence as part of the effort to provide "security for food delivery in the Falluja area."[2] Mainstream media sources went one step further by claiming that the contractors were civilians, as the *San Francisco Chronicle, Chicago Tribune, Los Angeles Times, Washington Post,* and *New York Times* collectively repeated this claim over 80 times in the first few days following the attack.[3]

Despite the portrayal of the contractors as "innocent victims," Progressive-Left media sources presented contractors working throughout the country, not as civilians, but armed mercenaries, employed by private security companies assisting U.S. armed forces in Iraq. These critics pointed to the fact that many contractors wore dog tags to reinforce their military-style rankings as conferred upon them by security firms such as Blackwater Security Consulting. The portrayal of the contractors as civilians is one of the many examples of the gulf between the American Progressive-Left and mass media's perceptions of the

U.S. role in Iraq, as the two poles have constructed vastly different identities for the private military forces and contractors working throughout the country. While mass media outfits openly labeled those killed as civilian contractors, independent media sources often portrayed them as private soldiers of fortune, taking part in the violent pacification of the Iraqi people. Russell Mokhiber and Robert Weissman of *Counter Punch* magazine referred to the thousands of military contractors working alongside the American military in Iraq as an "informal army of occupation."[4] Mokhiber and Weissman made reference to the fact that Blackwater Security Consulting, one of the many private military contractors working in Iraq, partook in "full-scale" military battles in Najaf, "with the company flying its own helicopters amidst an intense firefight to re-supply its own commandos" only a few days after the death of its four mercenaries in Falluja. In *Alternet* magazine, Bill Berkowitz characterized them as "soldiers-for-hire"— "veterans of some of the most repressive military forces in the world, including that of the former Chilean dictator Augusto Pinochet and South Africa's apartheid regime."[5] The *Telegraph* of London reported stories of mercenaries, working for Aegis Defence Services, who randomly fired at Iraqi civilians as they drove through the streets of Baghdad—promoting a "trophy" video of their attacks.[6] These depictions stand in great disparity to those of mass media outlets such as *CNN*, which represented private military forces and contractors more positively as providing "everything from security to catering to engineering to consulting in Iraq," and as instrumental in "the protection of personnel working for private companies and non-government organizations in Iraq."[7]

At a time when the U.S. began out-sourcing responsibility for military operations, the private contractors were typically portrayed as a necessary part of the war effort. The deaths of contractors in Falluja in March of 2004 evoked rage and denunciation, since these forces were seen as providing much needed help to an overstretched American occupation army. The *New York Times* described the incident as a "gruesome" and "grisly" attack,[8] explaining that the "enraged mob" of Iraqis "jubilantly dragged the burned bodies" through town.[9] The paper censured the attackers for "one of the most brutal outbursts of anti-American rage since the war in Iraq began more than a year ago," as a "group of boys yanked a smoldering body into the street and ripped it apart."[10] The paper explained that the boys tore the corpses from the vehicle, and pulled the "blackened bodies" as the "frenzied crowd" began "mutilating" them.[11]

The characterization of the attackers was much the same in other mainstream news sources. The *Chicago Tribune* reported the killings as a "celebration" of "cheering" and "dancing," while the *Washington Times* described "cheering crowds" that "reveled in a barbaric orgy."[12] The *San Francisco Chronicle* rebuked this "act of savagery shocking even by the blood-stained standards of Iraq's worst trouble spot."[13] In perhaps the ultimate denigration of anti-occupation resistance, the *New York Times* portrayed the people of Falluja as fiercely anti-American: "Hatred laces the conversations. It hangs from the walls. It burns in the minds of children. As nowhere else in Iraq, Falluja bristles with a desire to confront the American soldiers, to kill them, and to celebrate when they fall."[14] In general, the *New York Times'* portrayal of the people of

Falluja created a picture of resistance fighters as raving lunatics, as opposed to one of nationalists fighting an illegal or illegitimate occupation. It is difficult to argue that the reporting about the Falluja attack was not intended to evoke passionate condemnations of the Iraqi actions in the eyes of the American people. But while media's condemnations of the attacks as acts of murder may have been justified, the demonization of those attacking U.S. forces in Iraq also lacked an understanding of the nature of Iraq's anti-occupation resistance. By reducing all attacks against American forces in Iraq to little more than the acts of murderers, thugs, foreign and domestic terrorists, Saddam-Loyalists, and irrational resisters to democratization (however accurate those labels may be depending on which group is in question), the media ignored, and continues to neglect the nationalist underpinnings evident in attempts to expel American invaders from Iraq. The nationalist character driving the violent factions has been more of a focus, however, of framing in the Independent-Left American press.

Erasing Resistance to Occupation

Over the last few years of the occupation, the mainstream media consistently reported the war in Iraq in a way that represented the American presence as a democratizing, humanitarian agent, and framed resistance fighters as foreign, malicious, fanatical, and repressive. Under this archetype, those who attack U.S. occupying forces are viewed as "one of the biggest thorns in the side of the Americans," as the *New York Times* aptly puts it.[15] The goal of such framing is obvious: the American media has sided with the Bush administration in attempting to convince the American people that the "pacification" campaign is necessary in order to assist Iraq in a transition to democracy, or at least to prevent civil war. Nationalistic pressures arising in the media, amongst the public, and from the Bush administration portray those standing against American occupation as enemies of the state. At the same time, U.S. complicity and culpability in supporting Iraqi paramilitary groups that have escalated ethnic tensions in Iraq has been neglected in most reporting on Iraq's emerging civil war. Rather, such portrayals have been left to other news media outside the establishment press. The growth of these paramilitaries, as well as the corporate media's limited reaction to them, is addressed throughout this chapter.

The American mass media views the significance of Iraq's violent resistance factions to be limited to a very specific range. At best, they are standing in the way of the country's "progress"; at worst, "they," often inaccurately lumped together in the singular, represent a cruel and conniving campaign to destroy American lives for the sake of irrationality, greed, power, and various other self-interested motives. Media condemnations of anti-occupation groups take many forms, some implied, and others more overt. Some of the main negative and condescending labels used to refer to resistance fighters include: "rebels," "militants," "terrorists," "insurgents," "militiamen," "anti-American insurgents," "foreign fighters," "Islamic extremists," "foreign rebels" "extremist Shiites," "rebel militias," "radical Shiite clerics," "foreign guerillas," "anti-American insurgents," "radical insurgents," and "Saddam Loyalists," to name a few. The term "resistance" is almost never used, as it carries with it an assumption that large numbers of Iraqis are opposed to, rather than supportive of the occupation. The media has even gone as far as labeling entire cities, as seen in the case of Falluja, as "virulently anti-American,"[16] as the "epicenter of Anti-American hatred"[17] and "anti-American insurgency."[18]

Attempting to compete with *Fox's* fiercely nationalistic pro-war coverage, other establishment media outlets fault the "insurgency" for causing the Iraqi people "great anxiety."[19] The *Associated Press* condemns resistance attacks on Iraqi oil pipelines as attempts to "undermine the nations' interim government" and "undermine reconstruction efforts."[20] The *Washington Post* has been equally critical of resistance attacks against U.S. soldiers, which it frames as "a relentless campaign of bombings and ambushes by the insurgents."[21] The *Los Angeles Times* berates resistance factions for having "stymied U.S. led reconstruction efforts," arguing further that "insurgent" attacks are designed to "destabilize the government's authority."[22] The *Los Angeles Times* went further to agree with the *Washington Post*, that the groups' "sabotage" hurts "the nation's fragile infrastructure" and is responsible for "thwarting economic progress."[23] Depicting the depravity of these guerillas, *Time* magazine explained: "all the troops in the world may not do any good against an enemy that's firing on you from inside ambulances and using children as human shields."[24]

While it is easy enough to demonize violent Iraqi resistance resulting in the deaths of civilians and the destruction of infrastructure, such one-sided attacks obscure U.S. responsibility for mass death and destruction. Attacks that place all the blame for death and destruction at the feet of "insurgent" groups do little to accurately portray the cycle of violence in Iraq. American forces are inaccurately portrayed as benevolent and peaceful, while only "other" groups—namely the "insurgents"—are guilty of aggression, destabilization, or violence. Any violent actions taken on the part of the U.S. are, by definition, "defensive" and "peaceful" efforts to bring democracy and security to the Iraqi people; any violent efforts undertaken by enemies of the U.S. military are deemed the opposite. Even if U.S. bombings lead to the deaths of thousands of civilians and result in widespread damage to Iraqi infrastructure, such potentially explosive details are downplayed or de-emphasized in favor of lambasting Iraqi terrorists. This is hardly an example of reporting independently from pro-war government propaganda.

All or Nothing

Media portrayals of those resisting occupation have followed an all-or-nothing approach that typically classifies the U.S. armed forces, outside of some isolated deviations, as heroic, and those opposing them as utterly treacherous. Critical news outlets in the Progressive-Left press argue that this reductionism omits from responsibility the force guiltiest of destabilizing Iraq: the United States. Mass media outlets largely exempt the U.S. from responsibility in escalating violent conflicts in Iraq. In the *Washington Post*, Jackie Spinner argued that, in 2004, "Life became worse for large numbers of Iraqis. . . . Suicide car bombings, gun battles, kidnappings, beheadings and assassinations killed thousands of people, sometimes more than a hundred in a single day."[25] Notice Iraqi hardship increases *only* as a result of the actions of those resisting the U.S., *not* the U.S. itself. The *New York Times* purveys one of the more subtle expressions of frustration with the attacks on the U.S.; in one example, reporter Robert Worth addresses the American attempt to fight for the "Hearts and Minds" of Fallujans in opposition to the "propaganda that has helped fuel the insurgency throughout Iraq."[26] Under such an assumption, propaganda is only deemed something in which American enemies partake.

An image of American troops as a friend to the Iraqi people has generally been constructed in the mainstream press. American soldiers are reported "passing out candy to children," engaging in productive reconstruction efforts, and fighting a harmful "insurgency."[27] The United States is not labeled as a hegemonic or repressive power, but rather as a vital tool in promoting Iraqi prosperity. It is here that one sees the most blatant convergence between government propaganda and media propaganda. For example, former head of Iraq's Coalition Provisional Authority, L. Paul Bremer III denounced resistance groups for attempting "to shoot their way to power." Bremer explained: "they must be dealt with, and they will be dealt with."[28] The United States, conversely, is not considered a malicious force which is intent on "shooting its way to power" in Iraq, as American leaders are framed as committed to establishing Iraqi sovereignty and self-rule, despite plans for an indefinite occupation and a radical escalation of violence on the part of the U.S. military.

Prominent media personalities have promoted many of the more blunt stereotypes against Iraqi resistance groups. The late Peter Jennings, former head anchor for *ABC Nightly News*, faulted "the violent men" in Iraq who have tried to disrupt the election and the U.S. occupation.[29] Such a label problematically implies that the U.S., by definition, is not violent—or at least that its actions should not be characterized as so—even in the midst a pacification campaign often failing to distinguish between violent opposition and civilians. Parallel to the sharp criticism of Jennings is that of Charles Krauthammer, a neoconservative columnist for the *Washington Post*, who defends the war by claiming that, "The United States is trying to win hearts and minds; the insurgents are trying to destroy hearts and minds, along with the bodies that house them. They have no program. They have no ideology."[30] Krauthammer's prognosis—or complete lack thereof—of the goals of Iraqi resistance groups, is symbolic of other reports in the mass media that frame guerilla groups as lacking any coherent ideology or master plan. This type of analysis, however, displays a certain naiveté in that it does not delve into the motivations for attacks on the U.S. A probe of such motivations, however, is crucial in order to better understand what type of opposition the U.S. faces in Iraq.

As is discussed later in this chapter, the various resistance in Iraq—violent and non-violent—have often enunciated their own coherent sets of principles espousing national independence in opposition to the foreign occupation. Even

Islamist forces that do not promote Iraqi secular national independence have been very clear about their efforts to foster civil war in Iraq and return Iraq to a more Islamist-oriented government. Such goals hardly represent a failure to enunciate an ideology.

Resistance as Anti-American

Blanket statements equating resistance to occupation with "anti-Americanism" are common enough in mainstream reporting. *MSNBC News* reports that "anti-American voices" are "growing louder" in many parts of Iraq.[31] *CBS News* highlights strong "anti-American sentiments" throughout the country.[32] As the most prominent American newspaper, the *New York Times* repeats the mantra pertaining to "overwhelming anti-Americanism" that is building up throughout Iraq.[33] Local media has followed a similar track, as the *Associated Press* distributes stories throughout the U.S. equating an "increase in calls for the U.S. to leave" Iraq with "anti-American protest[s]."[34]

Mainstream news outlets systematically refuse to ask one simple question: if most Iraqis are in opposition to the occupation, and many are increasingly taking up arms in the name of Iraqi independence, does that really make them anti-American or anti-occupation? While there are surely a great number of forces in Iraq that are "anti-American," is this an accurate label for all those who resist American occupation? As many of those who have contemplated this question understand, there is a critical difference in the way the issue is framed. If one is to believe American media outfits when they argue that those against the occupation are "anti-American," it may have the effect of garnering further support in the United States for the war, as many Americans may view those who are against the occupation as being against Americans' entire way of life. If Americans understand that many throughout Iraq may oppose the occupation, while also admiring American freedoms, then they might be more inclined support a withdrawal of American troops, or at least become more susceptible to criticisms of the war.

The anti-American label validates the occupation by creating the impression that Iraqis who attack the U.S., or oppose occupation, are against the United States as a whole, rather than against U.S. government policies. A blanket focus on "anti-Americanism" has the effect of obscuring legitimate factors that fuel the resentment of U.S. foreign policy. A more appropriate question than "why do they hate us?" may be, why do so many throughout the world hate American foreign policy? This approach reframes the problem in Iraq to be one of anti-occupation sentiment rather than one foundationally based on "anti-Americanism." Rethinking the question is also important in order to distinguish between terrorist forces in Iraq, such as the al-Zarqawi network and other Islamic networks, which *are* in fact driven by fanatical anti-Americanism, and anti-occupation movements (particularly non-violent Iraqi resistance) which is opposed to the U.S. long-term military presence in Iraq.

Distinguishing between the various factions that are violently resisting occupation is also essential if one is to gain a better understanding of the complexities of the Iraq war that are often ignored in the American media. While it is somewhat accurate to refer to a singular "resistance" or "insurgency" to the U.S. in that many Iraqi resistance cells are loosely affiliated in working against the occupation, it is also an inaccurate reference in that it assumes that there exists a single tight-knit group of fighters who work together and share common goals.

After reviewing some of the various factions that make up Iraq's violent resistance, it becomes obvious that different groups retain radically different, often contradictory goals. This means that any framing of a united "resistance" or "insurgency" is flawed at its foundation. Baathist remnants in Iraq have little, if anything in common with foreign Islamist terrorist cells in terms of their ideologies. Likewise, many Iraqis who have taken up violent opposition to the U.S. may not necessarily agree with the basic tenets and principles that guided the Baath Party, Saddam Hussein, or foreign Islamists. Many who commit to violent attacks against the U.S. may just want to see the U.S. withdraw from Iraqi soil, rather than see a return of Saddam Hussein or an Islamist takeover of Iraq. While loosely or temporarily allying with one another, competing factions may progress toward the goal of forcing a U.S. withdrawal; and yet, such associations may also stand in direct opposition to the political, economic, social, and religious agendas that various groups would like to see implemented in Iraq in the long-term.

Iraqi discontent with the occupation, rather than with "American freedoms," is reinforced by the Pentagon Defense Science Board, which released a 2004 report explaining hostility toward U.S. foreign policy in the Middle East. The report concluded: "Muslims do not hate our freedom; but rather they hate our policies."[35] The study cited U.S. support for Israel and its occupation of the West Bank and Gaza, support for repressive regimes such as Egypt, Saudi Arabia, Jordan, and Pakistan, as well as the U.S. invasions of Afghanistan and Iraq. The report went on to state: "In the eyes of Muslims, American occupation of Afghanistan and Iraq has not led to democracy there, but only more chaos and suffering." The study was not heavily emphasized in the American mainstream press, as its contents contradicted the simplistic notion that any hostility directed against American foreign policy translates into blanket "anti-Americanism." The report also questioned the simplistic media-promoted myth that only "insurgents" are to blame for violence, destruction, and terror in Iraq. Still, the report's conclusions should be an integral part of any debate on the Iraq war, at least if the goal of public dialogue is to consider a wide range of views on the reasons for widespread opposition to the occupation.

Fighting Democracy and Prosperity

A common method of discounting resistance groups is to portray them as enemies of civilization, prosperity, and democracy. Will Dunham of *ABC World News Tonight* speaks of the need to "guard against violence intended to derail Iraq's parliamentary elections."[36] The *New York Times* worried about the possibility that this "tenacious insurgency"[37] could "intimidate prospective voters," and "derail" or disrupt the Iraqi elections that took place in January of 2005.[38] The *Washington Post*'s editors sought to portray an inverse relationship between an increase in rebel attacks and a decrease in the possibility of democracy. Citing bombings by the Islamist group, The Army of al-Sunna, the paper's editors argued that the group's escalation of violence reinforces "a stark choice between those who seek to build a new political order based on tolerance and democracy and those who would seek to replace Saddam Hussein with another totalitarian regime."[39] While the *Washington Post*'s portrayal of the group is clearly accurate on one level, it also speaks to the failure of media to distinguish between Islamist resistance dedicated to destroying secular democracy, and resistance groups interested in establishing an independent government outside of not only U.S. domination, but that of Saddam Hussein's Baath party as well. The failure to portray such a nuanced understanding of Iraqi resistance is reinforced by the *Los Angeles Times*, which views election ballots as "the Insurgent's Enemy."[40] The paper's editors believe that "Elections would hurt the guerillas' cause by depriving them of the claim that the nation's rulers were imposed by invaders and thus have no legitimacy."[41] However, the *Los Angeles Times*' editors neglect to explain the differences between various resistance groups, referring to a single "insurgency."

Aside from limiting democracy, resistance groups are also said to stand in the way of humanitarian reconstruction efforts. The *Los Angeles Times* claims that the Iraqi people have "suffered widespread violence" as local resistance fighters have "festered and overtaken local police."[42] Guerilla "sabotage" of "the nation's fragile infrastructure" is seen as "thwarting economic progress" in the post-Saddam era.[43] Victor Davis Hanson of the *New Republic* criticizes resistance forces by arguing: "the promise of consensual government, gender equality, and the rule of law may indeed save the Iraqi people and improve their own security—but only when those who wish none of it learn that trying to stop it will get them killed."[44]

While condemnations of guerilla sabotage of Iraqi infrastructure are also well taken, they also draw attention away from American war crimes and terrorism, as seen in the heavy bombing of civilian areas and the United States' extensive record of destroying Iraqi infrastructure spanning back to the first Gulf War. Thoroughly examining the effects of this bombing on Iraq's infrastructure is not considered a high priority in most media coverage of the war, although such a focus has been the emphasis of reporting outside the mainstream. In his article in the *Progressive* magazine: "The Secret Behind the Sanctions, How the U.S. Intentionally Destroyed Iraq's Water Supply," Thomas Nagy summarizes Defense Intelligence Agency documents showing that, by bombing Iraqi water purification plants, "the United States knew the cost that civilian Iraqis, mostly children, would pay, and it went ahead anyway." The documents describe in great detail the predicted effects of the bombing on Iraq's water quality, and the anticipated increase in "incidences, if not epidemics of disease" such as "cholera, hepatitis, and typhoid." Nagy's attempt to counter the "humanitarian frame" created in the American mass media is perhaps most evident when he states:

> As these documents illustrate, the United States knew sanctions had the capacity to devastate the water treatment system of Iraq. It knew what the consequences would be: increased outbreaks of disease and high rates of child mortality. And it was more concerned about the public relations nightmare for Washington than the actual nightmare that the sanctions created for innocent Iraqis. The Geneva Convention is absolutely clear. In a 1979 protocol relating to the "protection of victims of international armed conflicts," Article fifty-four, it states: "It is prohibited to attack, destroy, remove, or render useless objects indispensable to the survival of the civilian population, such as foodstuffs, crops, livestock, drinking water installations and supplies, and irrigation works, for the specific purpose of denying them for their sustenance value to the civilian population or to the adverse Party, whatever the motive, whether in order to starve out civilians, to cause them to move away, or for any other motive."[45]

Resistance or Insurgency in Iraq?

Shortly after the end of the Iraq invasion, the U.S. government and the media began referring to growing resistance against the U.S. as an "insurgency." Just as it did in the Vietnam War era, the word carries with it negative implications for anti-occupation fighters. An "insurgency" has traditionally been defined as a group of rebels who revolt against a civil authority or already-existing government, usually a national government. In this sense, the Iraqi "insurgency" is considered to be rebelling against the Iraqi government and the U.S. occupying forces. The use of the word insurgency to describe the rebellion goes back to well before the 2005 election and before the alleged handover of sovereignty in June of 2004, as the term was used to describe those attacking the occupation forces during and before the period of the interim Iraqi government. Throughout this work I refer to Iraqi guerillas primarily as "resistance" groups, because the term does not carry with it the conditioned negative implications that come along with the term "insurgency." Honest and open intellectual discussion and analysis of the motives of Iraq's resistance forces (and their legitimacy, or lack there of) require the shedding of loaded terms like "insurgency," in favor of more accurate descriptions. In this sense, the resistance classification seems more appropriate in that it more accurately describes the motives of those involved in attacks on the U.S.

In its descriptions of the Iraq war, the establishment press has laid out a few overarching characteristics intended to define the nature of Iraqi resistance. The standard practice within mass media is to discount resistance groups as Saddam loyalists, "Shia extremists," "terrorists" and "foreign Jihadists."

Saddam Loyalists and "Shia Extremists"

Time and time again, it is argued that Iraqi resistance groups are driven over-whelmingly by those loyal to the Baath Party, and more importantly, Saddam Hussein. Wolf Blitzer drove this point home as he questioned one guest con-cerning the "bulk of the insurgency," wondering: "is this homegrown Iraqis themselves, Saddam Loyalists?"[46] The claim has been repeated extensively in other media sources. The *Chicago Tribune* characterized the battle against anti-occupation forces as one of coalition forces pursuing "insurgents loyal to top-pled President Saddam Hussein"—"insurgents" "who are intent on undermining the U.S.-led effort to democratize Iraq."[47]   The *New York Times* and the *Washington Post* ran various headlines associating resistance groups with Saddam Hussein, such as, "Hussein's Agents Behind Attacks, Pentagon Finds," "U.S. Officials See Hussein's Hand in Attacks on Americans in Iraq," and "Hunt for Hussein led to Insurgent Hub," in order to frame those forces as little more than an embodiment of tyrannical nostalgia for a return to Baath party rule.[48] In the last article, the *Washington Post* took at face value the military's claims in 2003 that there were "five families running the Iraqi insurgency"—that "the upper and middle ranks of the resistance were filled by members of five extended families from a few villages within a 12-mile radius of the volatile city of Tikrit along the Tigris River." Such an appraisal has been discounted in light of growing resistance that is largely decentralized, including supporters from many different walks of Iraqi life. Even the government's own assessments contradicted the media's centralized resistance claim, as former CPA head Paul Bremer III ad-mitted that there was "no evidence...of any centralized command and control" of Iraqi resistance.[49]

The use of Saddam Hussein to discount resistance is no subtle characteriza-tion, since it frames such forces as fundamentally repressive and fanatical, and conveys the idea that Iraqis who oppose occupation lack any independent moti-vations outside of following the wishes of the Baath Party and Saddam Hussein. As the Progressive-Left *Covert Action Quarterly* magazine argues: the media have attempted to convince Americans that "the peoples of Iraq. . . do not have any feelings about their respective motherlands," that "all they have is love for their kidnapped President."[50] This assumption has been increasingly challenged after Saddam Hussein was captured, tried, and executed, and as resistance at-tacks continue to grow. Reinforcing the "resistance equals Saddam loyalty" mindset, Fareed Zakaria of *Newsweek* believes the appeal of Iraq's resistance cells "has clear limits," and that, "While it has drawn support from all Iraqis because of its anti-American character, it is essentially a Sunni movement fueled by the anger of Iraq's once dominant authority."[51] Jim Hoagland of the *Washington Post* seems to agree, lambasting "former Baathists and foreign Sunni extremists who turned Fallujah into Terrorism Central."[52]

Mainstream media sources have also attempted to invalidate resistance in-spired by Moqtada al Sadr as driven and supported by "Shia extremists."[53] Sadr was singled out as a "violent Shia theocrat" working against the interests of

Iraq,[54] and as an "illegitimate religious leader"—his followers nothing more than "a bunch of thugs."[55] Some writers tried to separate Sadr from the majority of Shiites. Fareed Zakaria claimed that "the 'weightier elements' within the Shia community, like Grand Ayatollah Ali Sistani do not support the firebrand cleric . . . nor does Al-Sadr have a large following."[56] Some, however, have resorted to racist stereotypes against the entire Shia community. Steven Vincent of the *National Review* denounces Sadr for "lead[ing] his nation off a cliff" by resisting the U.S., explaining, "there is something unstable and ungovernable at the heart of Shiism—something that is not specific to Sadr's intifada, but which in fact runs through the entire religious sect: a deep attachment to lost causes, alienation, failure, and death."[57] The *Chicago Tribune* deemed Sadr a "troublesome cleric," with the "potential to thwart U.S. hopes for a resolution" of re-emerging Iraqi sectarian tensions, questioning whether he "can be tamed, disarmed, prodded back into the political process or perhaps military crushed."[58]

Largely exempt from mainstream reporting and framing of the conflict is the argument made outside the mainstream press that resistance groups, although decentralized and diverse, represent a nationalist rebellion against the American occupying authority. In light of his research into, and hands-on experience interviewing members of various resistance cells, Zaki Chebab explains in his book *Inside the Resistance*, that guerilla cells often seem to be comprised of between 5 and 8 people: "small cells ensure the continuation of the resistance in case the American forces arrest them," as the capture or death of the members of one small cell has little effect on other resistance cells.[59] In *Tom Dispatch*, a progressive news source and Left blog, Michael Shwartz also repeats claims of decentralized resistance. Schwartz addresses the "assumption that [Iraqi resistance] is organized into a familiar hierarchical form in which the leadership exercises strategic and day-to-day control over a pyramid shaped organization." This type of structure, "described by both military strategists and organizational sociologists as a 'Command and Control' structure, " is problematic, according to Schwartz, as it may "apply well to a large bureaucracy or a conventional army, but invariably provides a poor picture of a guerilla army, which helps explain American military failures in Iraq." In light of this decentralized nationalist rebellion, military "progress" in the suppression of various groups seems to have been limited, as critical reporting suggests. Patrick Cockburn of the *Independent* of London reports from Iraq that, "military progress claimed by Bush is largely illusory. . . [the U.S.] is confronting the five million-strong Sunni Arab community which can carry on the fight as long as it wants. . . . The Sunni community has also learnt that its armed resistance is very effective in achieving its aims."[60]

The mainstream media has occasionally admitted that attacks on the U.S. are driven by nationalist aspirations for a sovereign Iraq. The *New York Times*, for example, acquiesced that Al Sadr's anti-occupation Mahdi Army is "less a discrete military organization than a populist movement that includes everyone from doctors to policemen to tribal sheiks."[61] *USA Today* reported that "the insurgents. . . seem to be gaining broad acceptance" in Iraq, and that "more than half of Iraqis say killing U.S. troops can be justified in at least some cases."[62] Along the same lines, the *Associated Press* addressed the fears of American military leaders concluding that Iraq's resistance forces "have enough popular support among nationalist Iraqis angered by the presence of U.S. troops that they cannot be militarily defeated," as "a closer examination paints [many] insurgents as secular Iraqis angry at the presence of U.S. and other foreign troops."[63]

One can clearly deduce two countercurrents in the mainstream editorializing and reporting above: one pronounced approach which attacks resistance fighters as working against the interests of Iraq, and the other admitting that resistance groups gain legitimacy from the support and participation of large segments of the Iraqi population. Seldom has this contradiction of reporting been acknowledged forthright in the American press, however.

Despite the occasional admissions of the nationalist resistance to the U.S., corporate media has largely ignored such motivations in favor of more simplistic negative labels. The media's overwhelmingly tends to frame Iraqis struggling against occupation as anti-democratic, anti-American, and terrorist. Such polemic attacks overshadow rare admissions of Iraqi nationalism as the main driving force behind attacks on American troops. Disregard for nationalist underpinnings of resistance is underscored many times over. As one *Washington Post* editorial argues: "Analysts who reduce the war in Iraq to a nationalist 'resistance' against a U.S. occupation should be pressed to explain the events of the past couple weeks: the brutal murders of election officials, the bombings of schools where voting was due; the bloodcurdling threats against those who approached the polls."[64] Such an assessment is highly problematic. The claim that those who rely on repressive, violent means somehow cannot also "resist" U.S. occupation should be rejected outright. Violent resistance movements have never been able to completely prevent civilian deaths when attacking occupying armies; and many groups, in fact, make little effort to do so. This does not mean, however, that these groups are not motivated by a general commitment to nationalism, or a specific belief that nationalistic resistance requires the killing of foreign occupiers.

The hesitancy in acknowledging the nationalist goals behind anti-occupation resistance has the effect of obscuring the fact that most Iraqis are vehemently opposed to the occupation. Rather than considering that many Iraqis may support rebellion (violent and non-violent) as a countervailing force against the occupation, the American media has been more interested in the pro-war U.S. perspective that frames resistance in areas like Falluja as "a growing problem that gnawed at the Iraq occupation force for months."[65]   This is a significant development in that non-corporate media outlets have often chosen to emphasize nationalist motivations for attacks on the U.S. In *Common Dreams*, William Pfaff drives home such nationalist motivations, citing a study done by the Project on Defense Alternatives based upon interviews with Iraqis and studies of Iraqi public opinion. Pfaff concludes that "U.S. military operations meant to quell or defeat the resistance actually provoke it. . . a large overall majority [of Iraqis] want the United States out. . . . Strong majorities among both Sunnis and Shiites oppose the occupation, and significant minorities in both groups support attacks on U.S. troops. The factors driving these attitudes," according to the Defense Alternatives report, "are nationalism, the coercive practices of the occupation, and the collateral effects of military operations."

The substantive difference between explanations for the motives of Iraqi resistance, as seen in corporate reporting and Independent-Left sources, reveals much about the ideologies driving those sources. Many anti-war activists and media figures take the view that resistance to the U.S. is needed to ensure Iraq's independence. Defending a continued opposition to the U.S., Laith Said of *Al Jazeera* focuses on the Iraqi people's disillusionment with foreign occupation, specifically the people of Falluja: "If there is no seeming end to the American-led occupation, then why should there be an end to the resistance? Needless to say, many of the residents [of Falluja], including teenagers, who have been robbed of normalcy, will join the resistance, not out of hatred or zealotry, but simply to eject the disruptive American presence and restore normalcy in their own city."[66]

Anti-Occupation Resistance Examined

Contrary to pro-occupation media rhetoric, opinion polls reveal that it is the American military presence itself, which is disproportionately viewed by Iraqis as the primary threat to their country's national security. Tens of thousands of Iraqis have protested the American presence in their country, a strong indicator of the strong opposition to the U.S.[67] At the same time, rebellious groups seem to have gained strength in numbers, according to the Iraqi government. The interim head of Iraq's intelligence services estimated that there were over 200,000 "active fighters" and "sympathizers" fighting the U.S. in 2005, 40,000 of which were "full-time fighters," and 200,000 of which were "part-time" fighters.[68] This estimate contradicts the "dead ender" figures presented by the Bush administration and repeated in the mass media of only 5,000 to 20,000 rebel fighters.[69]

It is revealing to review the opinions of the Iraqi people concerning the role not only of armed resistance, but that of the U.S. occupation in its alleged efforts to establish Iraqi sovereignty and independence. What limited polling that has been done reveals largely the opposite of what the American mass media has told the American public about the humanitarian nature of the U.S. occupation. Such polling also raises interesting questions about the level of legitimacy   The claims of Fareed Zakaria and others that Al Sadr's resistance is not supported by the public, the argument that "the insurgency" is spearheaded by Saddam loyalists, and the theory that foreign terrorists play a leadership role in the Iraqi rebellion—all of these claims are thrown into question when reviewing Iraqi public opinion. Consider one *Associated Press* published poll conducted in mid-2004 throughout Baghdad, Basra, Mosul, Hillah, Diwaniyah, and Baqubah. Its findings question, point by point, the claims made in the American media about the importance of the U.S. presence and the maliciousness of Iraqi resistance:

- 85 percent of the poll's respondents had either little or no confidence in the Coalition Provisional Authority.

- 90 percent of Iraqis saw coalition forces as "occupiers," as opposed to two percent who saw them as "liberators."
- 86 percent thought that the U.S. should have either left Iraq "immediately" (as of May 2004) or right after the January 2005 elections.
- When asked what contributed most to their sense of security, 71 percent of respondents said it was either their friends, neighbors, or family, as opposed to 1 percent who said it was coalition forces.
- 49 percent of Iraqis felt either "Not Very Safe" or "Not Safe At All" in U.S. occupied Iraq.
- 62 percent of those surveyed thought it was "very likely" that the Iraqi police and army could maintain security without the help of coalition forces.
- At a time of increasing attacks by Al Sadr's Mahdi Army against coalition forces, 81 percent of Iraqis reported having a "better" or "much better" opinion of Moqtada al Sadr than they previously had.
- Contrasting al Sadr to the U.S. favored interim Prime Minister Ayad Allawi, 67 percent of Iraqis somewhat or strongly supported al Sadr, as opposed to 61 percent who either somewhat or strongly *opposed* U.S. imposed Prime Minister Ayad Allawi's leadership.
- 64 percent of Iraqis felt that the anti-occupation attacks of Moqtada al Sadr and his followers made Iraq "more unified" than the country had previously been.
- Contrary to the portrayal of Iraq's resistance groups as comprised of many foreign fighters, 61 percent of respondents either somewhat or strongly disagreed that violent attacks throughout the country were "an effort of outside groups to create instability" in Iraq.
- In contradiction to the media's theory that most resistance fighters are loyal to Saddam Hussein, only 25 percent of respondents either somewhat or strongly agreed that violent attacks in the country "are an effort to reinstate the old regime," while only 32 percent of respondents either somewhat or strongly believed that those who attack coalition forces "are angry because they lost the privileges they had under Saddam Hussein."
- To the contrary, 79 percent believed that violent attacks "have increased because of a loss of faith in coalition forces."
- Finally, reinforcing the strength of Iraqi nationalism as anti-occupation in nature, 68 percent of respondents either somewhat or strongly believed that Iraqi "national dignity requires the attacks" on coalition forces.[70]

As the above evidence suggests, corporate media coverage of the war has been largely one-sided in reaffirming the American occupation, and ignoring Iraqi public opinion, which is more skeptical of the occupation and the stereotypes employed against resistance groups. Sustained attacks on Iraqi resistance groups are intended more to placate domestic elites in the U.S. than anything else, as the Iraqi public clearly does not share the American media's assessment that "insurgents" constitute the primary threat to Iraqi safety.

"Terrorists" and "Foreign Jihadists"

Establishment media outlets are quick to equate attacks against American soldiers with terrorism. Islamist forces attacking the U.S. are often the prime target of Bush administration rhetoric and media commentary. *Time* magazine claimed—prior to his death—that much of the "resistance is being spearheaded by Jihadists loyal to al-Zarqawi."[71] Behind this phrasing is the assumption that foreign Islamist forces and Iraq's Sunni based resistance factions are working intimately together. This is well represented in another *Time* news story which predicted in December of 2005 that "those violently opposing the U.S. occupation may be splitting into two: Iraqi nationals and Al-Qaeda foreigners."[72] While one can argue that the two forms of resistance are loosely affiliated in that they both oppose the U.S. occupation of Iraq, substantive evidence demonstrating that they share a similar vision for Iraq, or are working together in a hierarchical command structure are lacking, to say the least.

The negative "terrorist" label is one of the most effective attacks against resistance fighters, since it elicits condemnation on an emotional level, rather than on a level of intellectual debate. Another strength of the label is that it is accurate (at least when applied to attacks on infrastructure or civilians), although it also obscures the United States' own responsibility for inciting or partaking in terrorism in Iraq. U.S. responsibility for terrorism is a subject American reporters avoid like the plague. Shepard Smith of *Fox New's Studio B* focuses in black and white language exclusively on, "these bad guys, these insurgents—they're terrorists."[73]   Chris Wallace, on *Fox News Sunday*, attacked "terrorists" for having "stepped up attacks on Iraq's new [interim] government."[74] David Asman of *Fox News Live* puts a different slant on "terror" in the region, asking his guest Lt. Col. Bill Cowan "what is the connection between the Syrian government and terrorists fighting in Iraq?[75]

Rod Nordland and Babak Dehghanpishek of *Newsweek* deplore "insurgents" for having "effectively created a reign of terror throughout the country" in which "Everyone is vulnerable."[76] The "insurgents'" "campaign of terror"[77] has created what *Newsweek* deems a "climate of fear," in which Iraqis are perpetually terrorized, and no one knows when or where new attacks will originate.[78] Implications that the United States may be destabilizing Iraq by participating in the violence are omitted from media commentary, even when American actions lead to the deaths of thousands of Iraqis, civilians and combatants alike. In this sense, the Progressive-Left press has framed the U.S. as a terrorist state. Mass media sources, on the other hand, systematically deny the notion that the United States engages in terrorism.

Most corporate media commentary neglects background motivations of Islamist terror groups. Writing for the *New York Times*, Daniel Benjamin and Gabriel Weimann portray terrorists in Iraq as intent on "winning" the conflict by "seizing cities and towns, killing American troops, and destabilizing the country with attacks on the police, oil pipelines, and reconstruction projects."[79] While terrorist attacks do, by definition, encompass such actions, claims that terrorist groups are concerned with "winning" outside of any tangible grievances with the U.S. are serious misrepresentations that must be shed. The myth of the terrorist who lacks any real reason for their actions outside of irrational fanaticism was a particularly large problem in portrayals of the war in Afghanistan, and continues to be a problem in the war with Iraq. In order to promote a more extensive and rich debate, long-standing U.S. policy throughout the Middle East must be taken into account when understanding the ideology and agenda behind Islamist groups.

Beneath the labeling of resistance forces as "terrorist" lies another problem of internal inconsistency. Traditionally, terrorism has been defined as attacks on civilian populations in the effort to coerce or intimidate a populace into submission, and it such a label that American media has chosen to appropriate. American media, however, often inaccurately label attacks on the U.S. troops in Iraq as terror, rather than as acts of warfare. Such was the case when Michael Holmes of *CNN* criticized "terror attacks. . . on American invaders," ignoring the traditional distinction when defining terrorism as attacks on civilian rather than military targets. Nonetheless, it is crucial to make such a distinction when determining what does and does not constitute terrorism. The Bush administration and the mass media definition of terrorism as any attacks against the American military is inherently problematic.

Challenges to politicized definitions of terrorism that define only enemies of the U.S. as terrorist have been relegated to the margins of the corporate media. Hence, Sean Gonsalves of the *Cape Cod Times* suggests that, "U.S. forces were not fighting 'terrorists' in Iraq but nationalists using low-tech terror tactics against a vastly superior U.S. military. Gonsalves continues: "Neocons have turned reality on its head, convincing the true believers that the U.S. occupation of Iraq is reducing terrorism. It should be clear to anyone without ideological blinders on that U.S. military presence in Iraq is actually fueling terrorism."[80]

The labeling of nationalist fighters as intrinsically "terrorist" because of their resistance to the U.S. occupation should be discarded in favor of a more complex understanding of nationalistic motivations driving the attacks. This has been done from time to time in the mainstream press, although much less so than should be the case. Jim Sciutto of *ABC World News Tonight*, for example, explains that "many of the insurgents in Falluja are not hard-core terrorists, but people who've joined the cause after losing relatives to U.S. attacks—or who simply want to defend their homes."[81]

The claim that resistance groups engage in terrorism by primarily targeting civilians has been challenged by other intelligence sources as well. A report from the Center for Strategic and International Studies entitled "The Developing Iraqi Insurgency" examined the period from September 2003 through October 2004, analyzing the number of resistance attacks and people killed, to find that only 4.1 percent of the attacks in that period were directed against civilians, as opposed to 75 percent which were directed against coalition forces.[82] Writing in the Progressive magazine *Left Hook*, Junaid Alam argues that "This reality is at striking odds with the general picture painted in the press of a narcissistic, mindless and sinister insurgency simply bent on chaos and destruction."[83] As Patrick

Cockburn of the *Independent* of London reports, the split within resistance groups is "between Islamic fanatics, willing to kill anybody remotely connected with the government, and Iraqi nationalists who want to concentrate on attacking the 130,000 U.S. troops in Iraq."[84]

It has become popular to marginalize resistance groups as foreign in origin. Drawing from military sources, *MSNBC News* postulates that "foreign fighters" are migrating to Iraq primarily from Saudi Arabia and Syria, in addition to a number of other countries.[85] Mainstream news outlets repeatedly report the "foreign fighters" thesis promoted by the Bush administration without strong reservations. The *Washington Post* and *ABC News* transmitted the claims of American political and military leaders who argue that the number of "foreign fighters" in Iraq is on the rise.[86] Other sources have made similar claims, but independent of citing military leaders. In one instance, Rowman Scaborough of the *Washington Times* maintained that, "The war in Iraq is increasingly looking more like a showdown with Osama bin Laden's al Qaeda followers than a battle primarily against Saddam Hussein loyalists." Citing "foreign jihadists" who have "crossed the border with Syria to join the al Qaeda network in Iraq led by Abu Musab Zarqawi," Scarborough addressed the "scores of captures of Zarqawi's terrorists" who have been detained, particularly in U.S. Operation Matador and ensuing operations, as a sign of a "sobering reality" in which "Zarqawi has in place a larger number of cell leaders and planners" and "a sizable terror network since the March 2003 invasion."[87]

Prior to Zarqawi's reported death at the hands of the U.S. military, Michael Ware of *Time* magazine claimed that, "the Jordanian-born al-Zarqawi and his network of hard-line Jihadis have long been *the driving force* [emphasis added] of the insurgency, transforming it from a nationalist struggle to one fueled by religious zealotry and infused with foreign recruits."[88] The *Los Angeles Times* labeled Zarqawi Iraq's "Insurgency mastermind."[89] Such arguments have gained a sympathetic ear amongst members of the Bush administration, who have maintained that "Islamic radicals" are "trying to enslave whole nations and intimidate the world."[90] While the harsh condemnations of Islamist terrorist cells such as Al Qaeda is clearly appropriate in light of their terrorist attacks on civilians, to portray them as the "driving force" behind resistance to the U.S., capable in power and scope of "enslaving whole nations" is grossly inaccurate at best. Available evidence suggests that these Islamist forces account for only a very small number of Iraq's resistance forces, rather than *the* dominant force. One report from the Center for Strategic International Studies estimates that only between 4 and 10 percent of resistance fighters are from outside of Iraq,[91] while the *Los Angeles Times* itself admits, contrary to its "insurgency mastermind" claims, that during the Falluja campaign, "of the more than 1,000 men between the ages of fifteen and fifty-five who were captured. . . just fifteen are confirmed foreign fighters."[92]

Evidence of foreign "masterminding" of resistance has generally been difficult to come by. The statistics cited above suggest that the behavior of a very small minority of Zarqawi inspired "foreign terrorists" is not representative, by and large, of other resistance groups, which have been primarily concerned with expelling American forces from Iraq, rather than promoting sectarian violence and full blown civil war. As the International Institute for Strategic Studies estimates, there are only approximately 1,000 "foreign Islamic Jihadists" currently in Iraq, out of an estimated 40,000—200,000 part-time and full-time fighters, hardly enough to lead a resistance movement so large.[93] According to one British report inside of Falluja in October of 2004, foreign fighters were in short supply, as 99 percent of those opposing the occupation were estimated to be local residents.[94] This is consistent with other critical appraisals of the conflict. For example, Scott Ritter argues in *Al Jazeera* that, "There is simply no substance" to the "legend" of Al Zarqawi as the terror mastermind in Falluja. Ritter concludes that during the November U.S. siege, "Rather than extremist foreign fighters battling to the death," U.S. "marines are mostly finding local men from Falluja who are fighting to defend their city from what they view as an illegitimate occupier."[95] Still, this did not prevent reporters from focusing disproportionately on the Al Zarqawi phenomenon—disproportionately, at least, in terms of his lack of influence over nationalist resistance groups. *Time* magazine, for example, published a major story in December of 2005 entitled, "The Rise of an Evil Protégé," with a menacing picture of a pixilated al-Zarqawi. The story argued that Zarqawi was "turning Iraq into a breeding ground for al Qaeda foot soldiers," while also quoting an American intelligence analyst who claimed he was trying to "assume the mantle of bin Laden" in Al Qaeda's leadership.[96]

Attacks on "foreign fighters" often fail to examine the historical backgrounds and motivations of those involved in Islamist terror. When one delves deeper into the matter, a more detailed understanding emerges. Take for example one study done by the Saudi Arabian government and an Israeli think tank, which analyzed the backgrounds and motivations of many of these foreign fighters entering Iraq. The report found that most of these fighters were not long-time terrorists, but had become polarized by the Iraq war, as "the vast majority of [non-Iraqi] Arabs killed in Iraq have never taken part in any terrorist activity prior to their arrival in Iraq."[97] Such an analysis suggests that, rather than longtime terrorists entering Iraq and attacking the U.S., most of these individuals had little past experience with terror attacks, and were, in fact, radicalized by the occupation itself.

Who is a Terrorist?

The "Iraqi insurgents equals terrorists" argument promulgated throughout the mainstream press is an interesting one, worthy of serious analysis, at least in so far as it reveals the propagandistic nature of American media coverage. A clear trend has emerged in corporate reporting on the "insurgency." Iraq's "insurgents" are consistently labeled as terrorists, while U.S. forces, often engaging in similar activities, have not been labeled as such. American forces are also guilty of killing thousands of civilians when targeting "insurgent strongholds," and on a radically larger level than any resistance fighters have achieved. Just as Iraq's resistance factions have kidnapped Iraqis and assassinated and tortured them, so too has the U.S. been implicated in torturing and executing Iraqis, and in supporting and training militias that, in targeting the "insurgents," have killed thousands of innocent civilians. The lack of a consistently applied definition of terror is evident within media framing. "Insurgents" are labeled terrorists when they kill Iraqi civilians while targeting the U.S.; conversely, U.S. forces are not considered terrorists as they kill Iraqi civilians while targeting "insurgents."

The lack of ideological consistency in defining terror constitutes a significant roadblock to an evenhanded discussion of the escalating violence in Iraq. Classifying those who resist occupation automatically as "terrorists" does not deal with the underlying reality of what terror really is; rather, it blurs the difference between radical anti-Americanism and terrorism as seen in the actions of groups like Al Qaeda, and attacks directed primarily at the U.S. military, rather than civilians. Clearly, a single standard for defining terror, regardless of who is involved in targeting civilians, is needed when reviewing the activities of U.S. forces and resistance groups.

A New Kind of Resistance Neglected

The extraordinary amount of commentary over Iraq's violent resistance groups has also led to a massive imbalance between the reporting on different forms of resistance to occupation. Scarcely has Iraq's mass anti-war movement been referred to as a nonviolent resistance in the American mass media. Nonviolent resistance is not often referenced in mainstream reporting, at least not on par with more sensational violent opposition to the U.S. All this, despite the fact that tens of thousands of Iraqis have shunned violence in their protests of the Iraq war and the American occupation. In cities like Najaf, Kufa, and Nasiriyah, Iraqis joined together despite ethnic differences, Sunnis and Shiites together, to protest the U.S.[98] In support of Moqtada al Sadr, tens of thousands of Shiites demonstrated in Baghdad demanding a specific timetable for withdrawal of coalition troops, despite media claims that Sadr is not supported amongst many Shiites.[99]

Nonviolent Iraqi resistance was antagonistic to American government appointees as well. Protests in cities such as Najaf opposed the interim government of former Prime Minister Ayad Allawi.[100] Rather than supporting the "transfer of power" under the interim Iraqi government established in 2004, Iraqis nonviolently demanded direct elections, a stipulation in which the Bush administration stridently opposed until Iraq's Shia revolt forced the administration to recant.[101] Anti-occupation demands were often inspired by religious leaders such as Ali al Sistani, who issued a widely followed fatwa against the Bush administration's plans to handpick a new government rather than allowing for direct elections of Iraq's political leaders. Iraq's growing labor movement has also made claims of its own in favor of improving the conditions of Iraq's workers. Working through the Iraqi Federation of Trade Unions, various industrial unions began to organize worker committees in numerous Baghdad factories in opposition to the repressive labor laws originally passed by Saddam Hussein, and later left in place by CPA head Paul Bremer III.[102] Many of the early anti-occupation demonstrations were organized by the Union of Unemployed in Iraq, showing that many Iraqi workers were disenfranchised under the U.S. neoliberalization campaign.

While the media reported on various anti-occupation protests throughout Iraq since the 2003 invasion, the context of such reports were limited. Reporters and editors did frame such protests as part of the growing nonviolence movement, but more as single incidents of protest and dissatisfaction. The idea of a collective solidarity uniting Iraqis against the United States was lost in favor of media promises, explicitly rejected by most Iraqis, that the U.S. was stabilizing and democratizing Iraq.

A Civil War Begins:
Iraq's Militias and U.S. Involvement

The violent eruptions throughout Iraq in late February of 2006 were heralded as evidence that the country was headed toward civil war, if it was not there already. The main catalysts for the growth in sectarian conflict that month were a number of attacks, one of which was a suicide bombing on February 21 of a bus in Baghdad that killed fourteen people and injured nine others. This bombing was followed by another two attacks, one a car bombing on February 22 in a crowded Shiite area in Baghdad, which killed twenty-two people and injured another twenty-eight, and the other attack against the Askari Golden Dome Shrine in Samarra on February 23. Thousands of Iraqi demonstrators assembled near the shrine in protest of the bombing. The *Associated Press* explained that the bombing was staged by "insurgents" dressed as police and likely members of "Sunni extremist groups."[103] Others directly implicated Musab Al Zarqawi and Al Qaeda with the bombing.[104]

Attacks against both Iraqi Shiites and Sunnis were seen not only in Samarra, but throughout much of the country. In Baghdad, gunmen fired upon a funeral procession of an *Al-Arabiya* reporter who was killed covering the Askari Golden Shrine bombing. At least one security guard and two Iraqi soldiers who were escorting the procession were killed after a car bomb struck their military patrol. In Baqubah, at least forty-seven people were murdered after being pulled from their vehicles, shot, and dumped in a nearby ditch. The dead, both Sunni and Shiite, were on their way to attend a protest of the Askari bombing. Protests exploded throughout the major cities of Basra and Baghdad. In Basra, Shiite militia members fired their rifles and rocket propelled grenades at a number of guards in front of the Iraqi Islamic Party office.

At least twenty-five Sunni mosques were attacked in Baghdad alone within one week of the Askari bombing, three of which were completely burned to the ground. Shiite protestors torched one Sunni Shrine that housed the seventh century tomb of Talha bin Obeid-Allah, who had been a friend of the prophet Mohammad. All told, 184 mosques were attacked, with estimates of at least 1,300 Iraqis dead within a week of the Askari bombing.[105] These attacks represented not only a danger to Iraqi life, but to the country's cultural and religious history. The Askari shrine was the tomb of the tenth and eleventh Imans of Shia Islam, and regarded as an important historical site by Iraqi and Middle Eastern Shia alike. In attempting to crack down on sectarian violence, the Iraqi government announced a strict curfew throughout Baghdad and neighboring provinces in which all travel except that of military, police, and emergency vehicles was forbidden. The curfew initially appeared to have the intended effect of curtailing the violence, as Sunni leaders, at first hesitant to meet with Shiite officials for peace talks, returned to the discussion table in order to try and ease countrywide tensions. Unfortunately, sectarian violence has continued since as the country has fallen further into civil war.

Predictions of Civil War

Although the Bush administration consistently proclaimed progress in the occupation of Iraq, American media outlets could not afford to ignore the obvious reality that the country was slipping again into a period of heightened ethnic violence. The *Associated Press* reported that the Askari bombing "seemed to push Iraq closer to all-out civil war,"[106] while the *Chicago Tribune* worried that "Iraq seemed to be teetering dangerously on the brink of the civil conflict that many have long feared is inevitable."[107] The *New York Times* also spoke of "the prospect of a full-blown civil war" in light of fears that ethnic tension may spread to other countries with Sunni-Shiite demographic splits, such as Lebanon, Bahrain, Oman, Kuwait, Syria, UAE, Yemen, and Saudi Arabia. Such fears have been followed by media promises that the U.S. is opposed to the civil war, and will do all it can to prevent it.[108] Shortly after the Askari shrine bombing, Richard Engel of *NBC* (stationed in Iraq) reported that the U.S. is having a difficult time trying to stop civil war.[109] Aparisim Ghosh of *Time* wrote that the "murderous rage" that has taken hold of Iraq represents a trend that "The U.S. may be powerless to stop." Ghosh continued: "the violence threatens to spoil the overriding U.S. objective in Iraq: brokering the formation of a broadly representative government."[110] By late 2006, the *Associated Press* reported that violence in Baghdad had reached "Civil War Proportions."[111] Morgues in Baghdad were reportedly so crowded that "Bodies [were] being turned away."[112]

In general, American mass media outlets urged against a U.S. withdrawal from Iraq, as they argued that it would cast the country further into despair and civil conflict. Zaki Chehab spoke in the *Washington Post* of averting an Iraqi civil war, but only through scuttling plans for an immediate U.S. withdrawal. Withdrawal, according to Chehab, "is not an option the U.S. can or should entertain. It would give Abu Musab Zarqawi and his small band of foreign fighters the opportunity to claim victory...and lead to greater instability throughout the region."[113] While these news outlets and their reporters were right to be concerned with the danger of civil war, they neglected the U.S. role in supporting, sponsoring, and training Iraqi militias which were exacerbating ethnic violence and engaging in terrorist atrocities.

The Rise of Militias and "Counterinsurgency"

In January of 2006, Iraqi police discovered the bodies of twelve men who were executed and dumped into three separate areas of Baghdad's Shia suburb of Shula. The executions were but a few of many that have occurred throughout Iraq in the last few years as a result of the re-emergence of sectarian violence in Iraq. In January of 2006, four Iraqi patrol officers of the Iraqi Interior Ministry were also detained and arrested at an Iraqi Army checkpoint after it was found out that they were planning on kidnapping and killing a Sunni man. These four men were subsequently shown to be a part of an Iraqi death squad tied to the Badr Organization, which is a part of SCIRI (the Supreme Council for Islamic Revolution in Iraq), which is a Shia-based, Iranian supported political party operating in Iraq. As U.S. Major General Joseph Peterson explained of the four officers: "They responded truthfully, telling the soldiers that they were taking the Sunni man away to be shot dead."[114] Although this incident represented the first "official" evidence of death squad operations, the use of such groups in sectarian-driven executions and assassinations has been ongoing for years.

In January of 2005, *Newsweek* reported that the Bush administration was considering the possibility of the use of mercenary forces, (often referred to as death squads) throughout Iraq, in an attempt to counter the growth in resistance groups, as well as suspected sympathizers.[115] This plan was dubbed the "Salvador Option," as it was modeled after the past U.S. practice of supporting paramilitary forces in El Salvador from the 1970s through the early 1990s. According to *Newsweek*, the "Pentagon proposal would send Special Forces teams to advise, support and possibly train Iraqi squads, most likely hand-picked Kurdish Peshmerga fighters and Shiite militiamen." *Newsweek* reported that these squads would then target suspected "insurgents" and "insurgent sympathizers," much as El Salvador's paramilitaries did, in order to create a general atmosphere of "fear of aiding the insurgency," according to one military source involved in revealing the Salvador Option. As the official explained, "The Sunni population is paying no price for the support it is giving to the terrorists. . . from their point of view, it is cost-free. We have to change that equation."[116]

Claims throughout the mainstream press concerning these "counterinsurgency" units went something like this: the U.S. government will support "counter-terrorist strike squads" (the language used by *Newsweek*) in order "to target Sunni insurgents and their sympathizers."[117] Secretary of Defense Donald Rumsfeld denied the existence of the "Salvador Option," claiming that it is the "responsibility of the commanders there and the coalition and the Iraqi government to see that the Iraqis are trained up to provide security for that country."[118]

In the case of El Salvador, the Reagan and Carter administrations provided billions in funding to government forces and paramilitaries that targeted opponents of the government, violent and nonviolent. As with the U.S. war against Iraqi resistance, the Salvadoran government also alleged that the use of "counter-insurgency" forces would be used only to destroy dangerous guerilla fighters who were threatening national security and stability. In reality, the Salvadoran paramilitaries acquired a well-deserved reputation as one of the most brutal counterrevolutionary, terrorist forces throughout Latin America. With the support of the U.S., the Salvadoran military and its paramilitary forces embarked upon a campaign that often targeted civilians for violent repression and murder.

The use of violence against the Salvadoran rebel forces, suspected sympathizers, and critics of government highlights a reality confronting most "counterinsurgency" campaigns—namely the lack of interest in separating guerilla forces from civilians. The case of El Salvador posed questions which are important, but not discussed in media commentary: is it possible to distinguish between guerilla forces and civilians when the majority of a population that is vehemently opposed to their own government? What are the implications when one targets for repression nonviolent protestors and dissidents who are exercising their right to protest their government?

Despite the protests of human rights organizations throughout the hemisphere, the Salvadoran government and its paramilitaries targeted civilians during their attacks, relying on execution, massacres, torture, and kidnappings. Women, children, refugee workers, union members, university staff, students, church social workers, priests, nuns, hospital patients, doctors, and nurses were just some of the people killed by paramilitary forces. *Amnesty International* received "regular, often daily, reports identifying El Salvador's regular security and military units as responsible for the torture, 'disappearance,' and killing of noncombatant civilians from all sectors of Salvadoran society."[119] One such report was the massacre at El Mozote, where an estimated 700-1,000 Salvadorans, mostly the elderly, women, and children, were murdered by paramilitary forces. All told, estimates from human rights organizations (including the UN Truth Commission) estimated that as many as 60,000 to 75,000 Salvadoran civilians were killed between 1979 and 1992, primarily as a result of the terrorist atrocities of U.S. supported paramilitaries.[120]

Paramilitaries in Iraq

In early 2005, a number of activists and critics throughout the Progressive-Left media loudly condemned U.S. consideration of the "Salvador Option" in Iraq. Most may not have known the plethora of evidence that would emerge within the next year confirming U.S. support for these "counter-insurgency" units. The American press generally declined to grant extensive coverage, and sometimes actively denied that the U.S. was supporting "counterinsurgency" units and ethnic militias in Iraq. Ziad Khalaf of the *Associated Press* maintained that, "both Sunnis and the US fear the rise of such militias,"[121] while *Newsweek* chose to acknowledge their links with the U.S., but re-frame these militias as "counterterrorist strike squads."[122] On the other hand, Anthony Shadid of the *Washington Post* was one of the most critical in the mass media of the militias, attacking them for "instill[ing] a climate of fear" and for having "beaten up and threatened government officials and political leaders," as he characterized the militias as "security forces" that "claim de-facto territory and authority."[123]

While reporting on U.S. financial and tactical support for ethnic militias and "counterinsurgency" units is not a major concern for mass media outlets, it has been a major focus for Progressive-Left media. Arun Gupta is one of the most ardent critics in the Progressive press of the terror groups. Gupta explains that, when the Shiite government came into power, they cleared out many ex-Baathist military commanders and replacing them with leaders from the Badr Brigade, a militia that is an outgrowth of SCIRI, which gained substantial political representation after the 2004 and 2005 elections.[124] The new government, Gupta reported, began to sponsor a slew of paramilitaries: "they have all sorts of various brigades, one called the Wolf Brigade, the Scorpion Brigade, the Lion Brigade, another the Fearless Warriors. And they sound like death squads. And they are death squads. They go around with masks. They're conducting raids, especially throughout Baghdad."[125] Gupta also warned of the plan by U.S. National Security Advisor Stephen Hadley and other American leaders to initiate a "Shia-on-Shia" civil war, specifically through efforts to provoke the (Shia-comprised) Badr militia to declare war on Moqtada al Sadr's (Shia-based) Mahdi militia. The Mahdi army's stepped up attacks against U.S. military forces, which hit new heights in 2006 and 2007, set the stage for the Bush administration's attempts to provoke civil war within the Shia community. Gupta also criticized the American media for ignoring the humanitarian implications of the plan to foment civil war in Iraq. Instead of considering the human consequences of a "Shia-on-Shia" divide and conquer policy, the American media instead focused "on the modalities of the [2007 U.S.] surge of 21,500 troops [sent to Baghdad]: how many more troops to deploy, what is their specific mission, how long can a surge be sustained."[126]

At times, media editorializing was rather harsh of American support for ethnic militias and "counterinsurgency" squads, although this represented more the exception than the rule. The *Washington Post*, for example, condemned the U.S. and Iraqi governments for supporting the groups: "of all the bloodshed in Iraq, none may be more disturbing than the campaign of torture and murder being conducted by U.S. trained government police forces...Iraqi Interior Ministry commando and police units have been infiltrated by two Shiite militias, which have been conducting ethnic cleansing and rounding up Sunnis suspected of supporting the insurgency."[127]

In the Independent-Left media, skepticism was sustained on a more frequent level. In *Common Dreams*, Tom Hayden criticized the U.S. for its war on "Sunnis and other 'diehards,'" as he argued that "[the U.S. prefers] a political settlement that brings the nationalist resistance, including the Sunnis, into negotiations rather than war."[128] In *Z Magazine*, Nicolas Davies drew attention to a UN report suspicious of the militias linked to the Interior Ministry, highlighting the "corpses [that] appear regularly in and around Baghdad and other areas. Most bear signs of torture and appear to be victims of extra judicial executions."[129] Anthony Shadid of the *Washington Post* reported that Shiite and Kurdish militias loosely allied with the U.S. have initiated "a wave of abductions, assassinations, and other acts of intimidation, consolidating their control over territory across northern and southern Iraq and deepening the country's divide along ethnic and sectarian lines."[130] These parties operate with U.S. and Iraqi government funding, although largely independent of both entities, allowing the Bush administration and Iraq's leaders a strong degree of plausible deniability, so as to create a separation between militias and "counterinsurgency" groups on one side, and the U.S. and the Iraqi government on the other. Hundreds of bodies have been found in rivers, sewage treatment plant, garbage dumps, and various other locations, as Sunni resistance factions, and Shia and Kurdish militias target their political enemies for assassination.

The Special Police Commandos

The White House considers the Special Police Commandos (headed by former Baathist General Adnan Thabit) as a vital part of the campaign to root out resistance groups. Ex-Baathist and former Interim Prime Minister Ayad Allawi stood strongly behind the commandos, in what marked an ironic twist of events where former Ba'athists were put in charge of fighting Sunni-based resistance groups. Donald Rumsfeld also supported the group, arguing in front of the Senate Appropriations Committee that they are the "forces that are going to have the greatest leverage on suppressing and eliminating the insurgency."[131] The Police Commandos, as an outgrowth of the Iraqi Badr Militia, gained a reputation throughout Iraq for their reliance on torture and execution of those suspected of aiding or taking part in the "insurgency."

The Bush administration and Iraqi government, however, turned to the militias allegedly in order to fill the power vacuum that was left after the collapse of the Baath regime. The *New York Times* and the *Associated Press* referred to the Wolf Brigade (a part of the Badr Organization, organized as a part of the Supreme Council for the Islamic Revolution of Iraq) as one of many "counter terrorism" commando units.[132] Quite the contrary, the Wolf Brigade militia has an extensive record of terrorist atrocities, despite its assistance to the U.S. military in "counterinsurgency" operations in Mosul. Shiite militias (including the Wolf Brigade) were implicated with the deaths of at least 539 Iraqis who were executed between April of 2004 and October of 2005.[133] Rupert James of *Newsday* reported that the Bush administration wanted to incrementally replace American troops in Iraq with "Iraqi security forces" including various commando units mentioned above, in order to reduce American casualties. Rupert identified the Volcano Brigade (which is an outgrowth of SCIRI) as one example of U.S. outsourcing of "counterinsurgency" operations. One government official wishing to remain anonymous explained that "no one can talk openly about the Volcanoes because we could easily be killed," as execution by commando units and militias has become commonplace throughout Iraq.[134] Salah Matlaq, a Sunni politician and opponent of SCIRI stated that "Each sector of [Iraq's] police" retains forces affiliated with the Badr Brigade and SCIRI. These forces comprise a separate police entity from the ministry, but "are able to operate on their own, using police cars, uniforms and weapons for Badr operations, while people in leadership positions can say, some of them truthfully, that they don't know about it."[135] The Badr Brigade, along with the Mahdi Army (claiming inspiration from Moqtada al-Sadr) has a pattern of engaging in torture; many of their detainees are beaten severely with blunt objects, other bodies are discovered with holes drilled in them. Most of their victims are found wearing handcuffs, showing that they were defenseless at the time of death.[136]

Fueling Ethnic Tensions

The U.S. has not escaped criticism when it comes to supporting militias fueling ethnic tensions. Nahrain Toma of the human rights group *Bethnahrain*, explains that "Nobody wants to do anything with the Americans anymore. . . . Why? Because they gave power to the Kurds and to the Shiites" and their militias. "No one else has any rights."[137] Majid Sari, an adviser for the Iraqi Defense Ministry in Basra speaks critically of the U.S./Iraqi effort to institutionalize the militia forces: "They're [the militias] taking money from the state, they're taking clothes from the state, they're taking vehicles from the state, but their loyalty is to the parties [they serve]." As for those who challenge them, "the next day you'll find them dead in the street."[138]

The *Guardian* of London reported that in the few months preceding March 2006, "more than 7,000 people have been killed by death squads. . . . Reports of government-sponsored death squads have sparked fear among many prominent Iraqis, prompting a rise in the number leaving the country."[139] Andrew Buncombe and Patrick Cockburn of the *Independent* of London explained that, "hundreds of Iraqis are being tortured to death or summarily executed every month in Baghdad alone by death squads working from the Ministry of the Interior."[140]

In a fundamental questioning of mainstream media reporting, opponents of U.S. support for militias and "counterinsurgency" forces were often uncompromising in their condemnations of the U.S. Edward Herman, argued in *Z Magazine* that the U.S. is fueling ethnic tensions and violence through an informal imperial policy of divide and conquer:

> The Bush war has already started a civil war as part of the evolving occupation strategy. The character of the occupation, with its murderous use of firepower and harsh treatment of the populace, has steadily enlarged and consolidated a resistance. Having failed to get a puppet effectively installed without even nominal democratic forms, the Bush war managers opted for a tacit alliance with the Shiites and Kurds, who would be given nominal and possibly a modicum of real power via an electoral process, but with much of the legal and power arrangements of the occupation left intact and with the United States staying on to protect the new quasi-rulers from the Sunni-based insurgency. This provoked and institutionalized a civil war, with the occupation maintained as the military arm of one side. Thus the idea that the United States should stay on to avert a civil war is a laugher – it produced the resistance and then moved on to a tacit alliance with the Shiites and Kurds to fight the Sunnis on behalf of

the latter two groups while trying to train and arm them to be able to pacify the Sunnis on their own.[141]

There is a great contradiction between rhetoric throughout the mainstream press that promotes an image of the U.S. as dedicated to preventing civil war, and the occasional admissions within that same media system that the U.S. itself is fueling ethnic tensions, civil war, and terrorism in Iraq. A serious exploration of U.S. support for militias and death squads should be an essential goal of any balanced media system. To date, such a discussion has not taken place.

Notes

1. Jeffrey Gettleman, "4 From U.S. Killed in Ambush in Iraq," *New York Times*, 1 April 2004, 1(A); Bill Carter and Judith Steinberg, "To Portray the Horror, News Media Agonize," *New York Times*, 1 April 2004, 12(A).

2. Dahr Jamail, "Vigilant Resolve," *Dahr Jamail's Iraq Dispatches*, 5 February 2004, http://www.dahrjamailiraq.com/covering_iraq/archives/000197.php (7 Sep. 2005).

3. Jamail, "Vigilant Resolve," 2004.

4. Russell Mokhiber and Robert Weissman, "Contractors and Mercenaries: The Rising Corporate Military Monster," *Counterpunch*, 23 April 2004, http://www.counterpunch.org/mokhiber04232004.html (3 Sep. 2005).

5. Bill Berkowitz, "Mercenaries 'R' Us," *Alternet*, 9 August 2005, http://alternet.org-story/18193/ (15 Nov. 2005).

6. Sean Rayment, "'Trophy' Video Exposes Private Security Contractors Shooting Up Iraqi Drivers," *Telegraph*, 27 November 2005, http://www.telegraph.co.uk/news/main .jhtml?xml=news/2005/11/27/wirq27.xml&sSheet=news/2005/11/27/ixworld.html   (28 Nov. 2005).

7. CNN.com, "High Pay—and High Risks—for Contractors in Iraq," 2 April 2004, http://edition cnn.com/2004/WORLD/meast/04/01/iraq.contractor/ (4 Oct. 2005).

8. Carter and Steinberg, "To Portray the Horror," 2004.

9. Gettleman, "4 From U.S. Killed," 2004.

10. Gettleman, "4 From U.S. Killed," 2004.

11. Gettleman, "4 From U.S. Killed," 2004.

12. Colin McMahon, "Iraqi Mob Mutilates 4 American Civilians," *Chicago Tribune*, sec. 1, 1 April 2004, 1; Washington Times Staff, "Four Americans Mutilated," *Washington Times*, sec. 1, 1 April 2004, 1.

13. Colin Freeman, "Horror at Fallujah," *San Francisco Chronicle*, 1 April 2004, http://www.sfgate.com/cgi-bin/article.cgi?f=/c/a/2004/04/01/MNGH35UO801.DTL&hw =Horror+at+Fallujah&sn=001&sc=1000 (8 Mar. 2006).

14. Dexter Filkins, "In Die Hard City, G.I.s are the Enemy," *New York Times*, 4 November 2003, 1(A).

15. James Glanz and Edward Wong, "U.S. is Expanding Iraqi Offensive in Violent Area," *New York Times*, 24 November 2004, 1(A).

16. Edward Wong, "Attackers Hit Oil Pipelines, Police, and a U.S. Convoy," *New York Times*, 10 June 2004, 13(A).

17. Filkins, "In Die-Hard City," 2003.

18. David Ignatius, D. "What Bush Can Do to Salvage Iraq," *Washington Post*, 5 November 2004, 25(A).

19. Barbara Starr, *CNN Headline News*, CNN, 7 October 2004.
20. Todd Pitman, "Insurgent Attacks Reportedly Halt Iraq Oil Exports," *Associated Press*, 30 August 2004.
21. Edward Cody, "To Many, Mission Not Accomplished," *Washington Post*, 3 June 2004, 1(A).
22. Patrick McDonnell, "U.S. Attacks an Iraqi City with Double-Edged Sword," *Los Angeles Times*, 14 September 2004, 6(A).
23. Patrick McDonnell and T. Christian Miller, "Allawi Says He Regularly Meets with Insurgents to Halt Violence," *Los Angeles Times*, 30 August 2004, 6(A).
24. Nancy Gibbs, "Digging in for a Fight," *Time*, 3 May 2004, http://www.time.com/time/magazine/article/0,9171,994058-1,00.html (20 Dec. 2006).
25. Jackie Spinner, "For Iraqis, Not Much to Celebrate in 2004," *Washington Post*, 1 January 2004, 19(A).
26. Robert F. Worth, "Sides in Falluja Fight for Hearts and Minds," *New York Times*, 17 November 2004, 13(A).
27. Patrick E. Tyler, "G.I.'s in a Desert Town Face Rising Iraqi Hostility," *New York Times*, 30 May, 2003, 1(A).
28. John F. Burns, "Bremer Raising Pressure to End Iraqi Uprisings," *New York Times*, 19 April 2004, 1(A).
29. Peter Jennings, *ABC Nightly News*, ABC, 19 January 2005.
30. Charles Krauthammer, "Free to Dance in Iraq," *Washington Post*, 4 February 2005, 17(A).
31. MSNBC News, "Anti-American Voices Grow Louder in Iraq," 2 April 2004, http://msnbc.msn.com/id/4651377/ (15 Sep. 2005).
32. CBS News, "Spate of Attacks in Iraq Continue," 15 September 2004, http://cbsnews.cbs.com/stories/2004/09/16/iraq/main643801.shtml (15 Sep. 2004).
33. Jeffrey Gettleman, "Anti-U.S. Outrage Unites a Growing Iraqi Resistance," *New York Times*, 11 April 2004, 11(A).
34. Associated Press, "Iraqis Increase Calls for U.S. to Leave," *Truthout*, 12 April 2005, http://www.truthout.org/docs_2005/printer_041305D.shtml (2 July 2005).
35. Al Jazeera, "U.S. Losing Fight for Muslim Minds," 25 November 2004, http://english.aljazeera.net/NR/exeres/67B9E924-7A3C-4CAE-BB6F-0CBA0D4C39D8.-htm (24 Nov. 2004).
36. Will Dunham, *ABC World News Tonight*, ABC, 26 October 2004.
37. Eric Schmitt, "In Iraq, U.S. Officials Cite Obstacles to Victory," *New York Times*, 31 October 2004, 1(A).
38. Eric Schmitt and Robert F. Worth, "Marine Officers See Risk in Cuts in Falluja Force," *New York Times*, 18 November 2004, 1(A); Editorial, "The Larger Battle in Iraq" *New York Times*, 15 November 2004, 22(A).
39. Editorial, "Explosion in Mosul," *Washington Post*, 22 December 2004, 26(A).
40. Editorial, "Ballots, the Insurgent's Enemy," *Los Angeles Times*, 30 November 2004, 12(B).
41. "Ballots, the Insurgents Enemy," 2004.
42. Alissa J. Rubin, "Troops Target Mosul Rebels," *Los Angeles Times*, 17 November 2004, 1(A).
43. McDonnell and Miller, "Allawi Regularly Meets with Insurgents," 2004.
44. Victor Davis Hanson, "Stop Talking: Kill the Insurgents," *New Republic*, 7 June 2004, 13.
45. Thomas J. Nagy, "The Secret Behind the Sanctions, How the U.S. Intentionally Destroyed Iraq's Water Supply," *Progressive*, September 2001, http://www.progressive.-

org/mag_nagysanctions (25 Mar. 2007).

46. Wolf Blitzer, *Wolf Blitzer Reports*, CNN, 18 October 2004.

47. Liz Sly, "2nd Iraq Official Slain," *Chicago Tribune*, sec. 1, 14 June 2004, 1.

48. Thom Shanker, "Hussein's Agents Behind Attacks, Pentagon Finds," *New York Times*, 29 April 2004, 1(A); Douglas Jehl, "U.S. Officials See Hussein's Hand in Attacks on Americans in Iraq," *New York Times*, 31 October 2003, 1(A); Alan Sipress, "Hunt for Hussein Led to Insurgent Hub," *Washington Post*, 26 December 2003, 1(A).

49. Jacquelyn S. Porth, "Bremer Says Iraqi Resistance not Centrally Directed," *Global Security*, 12 June 2003, http://www.globalsecurity.org/wmd/library/news/iraq/2003/06/Iraq-030612-usia01.htm (3 Jul. 2005).

50. Editorial, "Divide to Conquer: The Racist Media on Iraq," *Covert Action Quarterly*, Spring 2004, 31.

51. Fareed Zakaria, "The Holes in a 'Shia Strategy,'" *Newsweek*, 20 September 2004, http://www.msnbc.msn.com/id/5973045/site/newsweek/ (25 September 2004).

52. Jim Hoagland, "Stick with January 30," *Washington Post*, 2 December 2004, 35(A).

53. Richard A. Oppel, Jr., "In Northern Iraq, the Insurgency has Two Faces, Secular and Jihad, but a Common Goal," *New York Times*, 19 December 2004, 30(A).

54. Spencer Ackerman, "Welcome Back Sadr," *New Republic*, 26 August 2005, https://ss1.tnr.com/p/docsub.mhtml?I=w050822&s=ackerman082605 (2 Oct. 2005).

55. Michael Ledeen, "The Fattest Terrorist," *National Review*, 15 May 2004, http://www.nationalreview.com/ledeen/ledeen200405251028.asp (3 Oct. 2005).

56. Fareed Zakaria, "Our Last Real Chance," *Newsweek*, 19 April 2004, http://www.fareedzakaria.com/articles/newsweek/041904.html (14 Oct. 2005).

57. Steven Vincent, "The Ungovernable Shiites," *National Review*, 8 April 2004, http://www.nationalreview.com/comment/vincent 200404081542.asp (12 Oct. 2005).

58. Liz Sly, "No. 1 Question: How to Deal with Sadr?," *Chicago Tribune*, sec. 2, 21 January 2007, 4.

59. Zaki Chehab, *Inside the Resistance: The Iraqi Insurgency and the Future of the Middle East*, (New York: Nation, 2005), 25.

60. Patrick Cockburn, "The Military Progress Claimed by Bush is Largely Illusory," *Independent*, 1 December 2005, http://comment.independent.co.uk/commentators/article-330424.ece (1 Dec. 2005).

61. Edward Wong, "On Baghdad Streets, Loyalty to Rebel Cleric is still Fierce," *New York Times*, 4 October 2004, 10(A).

62. Cesar G. Soriano and Steven Komarow, "Poll: Iraqis Out of Patience," *USA Today*, 28 April 2004, http://www.usatoday.com/news/world/iraq/2004-04-28-poll-coverx.htm?-POE=click-refer (15 Nov. 2005).

63. Associated Press, "Iraq Insurgency Larger Than Thought," *USA Today*, 8 July 2004, http://www.usatoday.com/news/world/iraq/2004-07-08-insurgency-countx.htm (27 Nov. 2004).

64. Editorial, "Iraq's Election," *Washington Post*, 30 January 2005, 6(B).

65. Dexter Filkins and James Glanz, "Rebels Routed in Falluja: Fighting Spreads Elsewhere in Iraq," *New York Times*, 15 November 2004, 1(A).

66. Laith Said, "Violence in Iraq and US Presence," *Al Jazeera*, 26 June 2005, http://english.aljazeera.net/NR/exeres/554FAF3A-B267-427A-B9EC54881BDE0A2E.htm (26 Jun. 2005).

67. Dexter Filkins, "Demonstrators in Iraq Demand that U.S. Leave," *New York Times*, 10 April 2005, 1(A).

68. Al Jazeera, "Spy Chief Says 200,000 Fighters in Iraq," 3 January 2005, http://english.aljazeera.net/NR/exeres/554FAF3A-B267-427A-B9EC54881BDE02E.htm (3 Jan. 2005).

69. Associated Press, "AP: Iraq Insurgency Larger Than Thought," *USA Today*, 8 July 2004, http://www.usatoday.com/news/world/iraq/2004-07-08insurgency-count_x.htm (19 Nov. 2005); Washington Times, "Insurgents Number 20,000 in Iraq," 18 March 2005, http://washingtontimes.com/upi-breaking/20050318-093102-3216r.htm (11 Jun. 2005).

70. Associated Press, "Public Opinion in Iraq: First Poll Following Abu Ghraib Revelations," *MSNBC.com*, 14-23 May 2004, http://www.msnbc.com/id/5217741/site/newsweek/ (25 Oct. 2005).

71. Romesh Ratnesar, "Can This War Be Won?" *Time*, 4 October 2004, 34; Richard A. Oppel Jr., "In Northern Iraq, the Insurgency has Two Faces, Secular and Jihad, but a Common Goal," *New York Times*, 19 December 2004, 30(A).

72. Michael Ware, "Insurgent vs. Insurgent?" *Time*, 12 December 2005, 5.

73. Shepard Smith, *Studio B*, Fox News, 9 November 2004.

74. Chris Wallace, *Fox News Sunday*, Fox News, 19 September 2004.

75. David Asman, *Fox News Live*, Fox News, 4 January 2005.

76. Rob Nordland and Babak Dehghanpisheh, "Hell to Pay," *Newsweek*, 8 November 2004, 28.

77. Robert F. Worth, "Sides in Falluja Fight for Hearts and Minds," *New York Times*, 17 November 2004, 11(A).

78. Rob Nordland, "No Place is Safe," *Newsweek*, 4 October 2004, 31.

79. Daniel Benjamin and Gabriel Weimann, "What the Terrorists Have in Mind," *New York Times*, 27 October 2004, 31(A).

80. Sean Gonsalves, "Terrorists in Iraq or Nationalists?" *Cape Cod Times*, 30 August 2005, http://www.capecodonline.com/cctimes/edits/seang.htm (20 Dec. 2006).

81. Jim Sciutto, "Answering Questions about Iraq," *ABC World News Tonight*, 12 November 2004, http://abcnews.go.com/WNT/story?id=247934&page=1 (14 Dec. 2005).

82. M. Junaid Alam, (18 April 2005), "Does the Resistance Target Civilians?" *Left Hook*, http://lefthook.org/Politics/Alam041605.html (19 Apr. 2005).

83. Alam, "Does Resistance Target Civilians?" 2005.

84. Patrick Cockburn, "Stop Killing Iraqis, Nationalists Warn Islamic Fanatics," *Independent*, sec. 1, 11 April 2005, 25.

85. Lisa Myers, "Who Are the Foreign Fighters in Iraq?" *MSNBC.com*, 20 June 2005, http://www.msnbc.msn.com/id/8293410/ (2 Jul. 2005).

86. ABC News, "More Foreign Fighters Entering Iraq: U.S. General," 28 March 2005, http://www.abc.net.au/news/newsitems/200503/s1332344.htm (22 September 2005); Susan B. Glasser, "'Martyrs' in Iraq Mostly Saudis," *Washington Post*, 15 May 2005, 1(A).

87. Rowan Scarborough, "War in Iraq looks like last stand for Al Qaeda," *Washington Times*, 11 May 2005, http://www.washingtontimes.com/national/20050511-121123-9220r.htm (17 Aug. 2005).

88. Michael Ware, "The New Rules of Engagement," *Time*, 12 December 2005, 36.

89. Mark Mazzetti and Josh Meyer, "In a Battle of Wits, Iraq's Insurgency Mastermind Stays a Step Ahead of U.S.," *Los Angeles Times*, 16 November 2005, 1(A).

90. Associated Press, "Bush Stresses Terror Threat and Urges Support for Iraq War," 6 October 2005.

91. Tom Regan, "The 'Myth' of Iraq's Foreign Fighters," *Christian Science Monitor*, 23 September 2005, http://www.csmonitor.com/2005/0923/dailyUpdate.html (20 Dec. 2006).

92. John Hendren, "Few Foreigners Among Insurgents," *Los Angeles Times*, 16 November 2004, 1(A).

93. Gonsalves, "Terrorists in Iraq or Nationalists?" 2005.

94. BBC News, "Inside Besieged Falluja," 18 October 2004, http://news.bbc.co.uk/2hi/middle_east/3748966.stm (18 Oct. 2004).

95. Scott Ritter, "The risks of the al-Zarqawi myth," *Al Jazeera*, 14 December 2004, http://english.aljazeera.net/NR/exeres/9FA18AFB-F2C9-4678-8E6A-3595D91B83A1.htm (14 Dec. 2004).

96. Tim McGirk, "The Rise of an Evil Protégé," *Time*, 19 December 2005, 49, 50.

97. Bryan Bender, "Study cites seeds of terror in Iraq," *Boston Globe*, 17 July 2005, http://www.boston.com/news/world/articles/2005/07/17/study_cites_seeds_of_terror_in_i raq/ (17 Jul. 2005).

98. Associated Press, "Thousands of Shiites, Sunnis Protest U.S. Occupation," *Common Dreams*, 20 May 2005, http://www.commondreams.org/cgi-bin/print.cgi?file=headlines05/0520-03.htm (20 May 2005).

99. Anthony Shadid, "Tens of Thousands of Iraqis Demand U.S. Withdrawal," *Washington Post*, 10 April 2005, 2(A).

100. Al Jazeera, "Iraqis Protest as US Plans Assault on Najaf," 11 August 2004, http://english.aljazeera.net/NR/exeres/554FAF3A-B267-427A-B9EC-54881BDE0A2E.htm (11 Aug. 2004).

101. BBC News, "U.S. Downplays Rift with Iraq Shia," 16 January 2004, http://news.bbc.co.uk/2/hi/middle_east/3402859.stm (1 Nov. 2005).

102. David Bacon, "Iraqi Unions Defy Assassinations and Occupation," *Truthout*, 10 August 2005, http://www.truthout.org/issues_05/printer_081005LA.shtml (6 Sep. 2005).

103. Ziad Khalaf, "Shrine Attack Brings Reprisals and Fear," *Associated Press*, 22 February 2006, http://ww5.salon.com/wire/ap/archive.html?wire=D8FU64380.html (22 Feb. 2006).

104. CBS News, "Al Qaeda Blows it," 24 February 2006, http://www.cbsnews.com/stories/2006/02/23/opinion/main1341727.shtml (24 Feb. 2006).

105. Ellen Knickmeyer and Bassam Sebti, "Toll in Iraq's Deadly Surge: 1,300," *Washington Post*, 28 February 2006, 1(A).

106. Ziad Khalaf, "Mosque Attack Pushes Iraq Toward Civil War," *Associated Press*, 22 February 2006, http://abcnews.go.com/International/wireStory?id=1650745 (23 Feb. 2006).

107. Liz Sly, "Iraq's Unity Teeters after Blast at Shrine," *Chicago Tribune*, sec. 1, 23 February 2006, 1.

108. Michael Slackman, "Chaos in Iraq Sends Shock Waves Across Middle East and Elevates Iran's Influence," *New York Times*, 27 February 2006, 9(A).

109. Richard Engel, *NBC Nightly News*, NBC, 23 February 2006.

110. Aparisim Ghosh, "An Eye for an Eye," *Time*, 6 November 2006, 18, 20.

111. Sameer N. Yacoub, "Violence in Baghdad has Reached 'Civil War Proportions,'" *Associated Press*, 11 November 2006, http://www.truthout.org/cgi-bin/artman/exec/view-.cgi/66/23801 (15 Apr. 2007).

112. Associated Press, "Baghdad's Morgues so Full, Bodies Being Turned Away," 12 November 2006, http://www.truthout.org/cgi-bin/artman/exec/view.cgi/66/23812 (15 Apr. 2007).

113. Zaki Chehab, "Civil War can be Averted," *Washington Post*, 11 December 2005, 3(B).

114. Cnn.com, "U.S.: Iraqi death squad members detained," 17 February 2006, http://edition.cnn.com/2006/WORLD/meast/02/16/iraq.main/index.html (17 Feb. 2006).

115. Michael Hirsch and John Barry, "'The Salvador Option,'" Newsweek, 15 January 2005, http://www.msnbc.msn.com/id/6802629/site/newsweek/ (18 Feb. 2006).

116. Hirsch and Barry, "Salvador Option," 2005.

117. Hirsch and Barry, "Salvador Option," 2005.

118. Donald Rumsfeld, "Secretary Rumsfeld Joint Media Availability with Russian Defense Minister Sergey Ivanov," *Department of Defense*, 11 January 2005, http://www.pentagon.gov/transcripts/2005/tr20050111-secdef1961.html (18 Feb. 2006).

119. Amnesty International, "Torture in the Eighties," 1984, 155-56.

120. William Blum, *Killing Hope: U.S. Military and CIA Interventions Since World War II* (Monroe, Me.: Common Courage, 1995), 359; BBC News, "U.S. Role in Salvador's Brutal War," 24 March 2002, http://news.bbc.co.uk/2/hi/americas/1891145.stm (15 February 2008).

121. Ziad Khalaf, "Mosque Attack Pushes Iraq Toward Civil War," *Associated Press*, 22 February 2006, http://abcnews.go.com/International/wireStory?id=1650745 (22 Feb. 2006).

122. Hirsch and Barry, "Salvador Option," 2005.

123. Anthony Shadid and Steve Fainaru, "Militias on the Rise Across Iraq," *Washington Post*, 21 August 2005, 1(A).

124. A. K. Gupta, "Unraveling Iraq's Secret Militias," *Z Magazine*, May 2005, 33-37.

125. Amy Goodman and A. K. Gupta, "U.S. Funding Iraqi Militias Led by Baathists as Part of Counter-Insurgency Operation," *Democracy Now!* 21 April 2005, http://www.democracynow.org/article.pl?sid=05/04/21/1418219 (21 Apr. 2005).

126. A. K. Gupta, "Bush's Iraq Strategy for 2007: A Second Civil War or Genocide," *Z Magazine*, February 2007, http://zmagsite.zmag.org/Feb2007/gupta0207.html (15 Apr. 2007).

127. Editorial, "Iraq's Death Squads," *Washington Post*, 4 December 2005, 6(B).

128. Tom Hayden, "Why the U.S. is Supporting Civil War," *Common Dreams*, 26 August 2005, http://www.commondreams.org/views05/0826-22.htm (26 Aug. 2005).

129. Nicolas J. S. Davies, "The Dirty War in Iraq," *Z Magazine*, November 2005, 5.

130. Shadid and Fainaru, "Militias on the Rise," 2005.

131. Gupta, "Unraveling Iraq's Secret Militias," 2005.

132. New York Times, "Q & A: Iraq's Militias," 9 June 2005, http://www.nytimes.com/c/cfr/international/slot2_060905.html (19 Oct. 2005); Sinan Salaheddin, "Government Accused of Death Squads in Iraq," *Associated Press*, 7 October 2005, http://www.truthout.org/docs_2005/100705Q.shtml (7 Oct. 2005).

133. Salaheddin, "Government Accused of Death Squads," 2005.

134. James Rupert, "Some See U.S. Backed Iraqi Guards as Death Squads," *Newsday*, 16 November 2005, http://www.newsday.com/news/nationworld/world/ny wopoli14451-4708nov16,0,5638540.story?coll=ny-worldviews-toputility (25 Nov. 2005).

135. Rupert, "Some See U.S. Backed Iraqi Guards," 2005.

136. Rupert, "Some See U.S. Backed Iraqi Guards," 2005; Shadid and Fainaru, "Militias on the Rise," 2005.

137. Shadid and Fainaru, "Militias on the Rise," 2005.

138. Shadid and Fainaru, "Militias on the Rise," 2005.

139. Jonathan Steele, "Baghdad Official Who Exposed Executions Flees," *Guardian*, 2 March 2006, http://www.guardian.co.uk/Iraq/Story/0,,1721366,00.html (10 Nov. 2005).

140. Andrew Buncombe and Patrick Cockburn, "Iraq's Death Squads: On the Brink of Civil War," *Independent*, 26 February 2006, http://news.independent.co.uk/world/middle-_east/article347806.ece (26 Feb. 2006).

141. Noam Chomsky, Edward Herman, and Anthony DiMaggio, "Q & A on the Iraq War," *Z Magazine*, 29 November 2005, http://www.zmag.org/content/showarticle.cfm?ItemID=9215 (29 Nov. 2005).

6

Free Speech Fatalities

Detained in 2002, Dilawar was merely one of many Afghans suspected of attacking American troops. However, Dilawar's case was especially tragic in that he did not live to see his name cleared following his arrest. His death was disturbing considering that most American military interrogators did not seriously suspect him of taking part in a missile attack against American troops—the original reason for which he was detained.[1] Dilawar, like a number of other Iraqi and Afghan prisoners, was tortured during his incarceration by American military forces. Chained to the ceiling by his wrists for days, his legs were beaten over one-hundred times in less than twenty-four hours.[2] These injuries were so extensive that they eventually led to his death.

Alongside many other detainees' stories of abuse published in such influential newspapers as the *Independent* of London, the *New York Times*, and the *Chicago Tribune*, Dilawar's story raised serious questions about American treatment of prisoners of war. The issue of the military's treatment of detainees becomes all the more important when looking at the *Newsweek*-Koran "scandal."

Newsweek and the Koran Flushing "Scandal"

On May 2005, *Newsweek* reported that American interrogators at Guantanamo Bay prison placed copies of the Koran in toilets, and in one instance, flushed one down the toilet.[3] The story elicited strong condemnations and criticisms of *Newsweek*; the paper was charged with unprofessional journalism and unfairly inciting riots that killed American soldiers in Afghanistan. The Bush administration assailed *Newsweek* along similar lines. Scott McClellan, former White House Spokesperson, argued that *Newsweek*'s "story has damaged the image of the United States abroad and damaged the credibility of the media at home."[4] McClellan claimed that Americans "share in the outrage that this report was published in the first place."[5] Secretary of State Condoleeza Rice blamed the story for having "done a lot of harm" to the U.S. image: "it's appalling that this story got out there. . . . The sad thing was that there was a lot of anger that got stirred by a story that was not very well founded."[6]

The *Newsweek* Koran scandal is particularly relevant in light of abuses uncovered at U.S. military prisons in Iraq, Afghanistan, and Guantanamo Bay, Cuba. In response to growing media and government criticisms, *Newsweek* retracted its charges that the Koran was flushed down a toilet by American interrogators. *Newsweek* editor Mark Whitaker announced: "Based on what we know now, we are retracting our original story that an internal military investigation had uncovered Quran abuse at Guantanamo Bay. . . . We've called it an error. We've called it a mistake."[7]

A number of pundits attacked *Newsweek* for its challenges to the U.S. military's human rights record. Bill O'Reilly explained: "The American press is far too cavalier when it comes to publicizing alleged wrongdoing by the U.S.A. . . . The truth is that some news agencies can't wait to get dirt on the military so they can embarrass the Bush administration. Ideological reporting is rampant in this country and it is getting people killed."[8] Daryl Kagan and Barbara Starr of *CNN Live Today* conversed over *Newsweek*'s reporting, citing the paper's failure to pursue more than one military source (the paper used only one anonymous source) in confirming the Koran charge. Kagan and Starr indicated that they trusted the military to look into the charges over suspected wrongdoing.[9] *CNN* programs such as *Crossfire* also addressed the mounting "scandal." Cliff May, the President of the Foundation for Defense of Democracies argued: "The media, I think, are in crisis right now. . . . This case was terrible reporting."[10] Bay Buchanan faulted *Newsweek*:

> They didn't go for the second source to confirm this report. They went out with a report that was extremely sensitive, almost a tender—a tinderbox out there when it comes to U.S.-Muslim relationships. They dropped it out there with absolute disregard for doing what would be standard in journalism, I believe, really basic journalism and it resulted in seventeen deaths so far. Is there not some cause for some serious accountability here?[11]

Buchanan continued: "Isn't it time for *Newsweek* to take some responsibility for this awful mistake?"[12]

The punditry's condemnations of *Newsweek* fell within a narrow line of criticism, since most attacks focused on the paper's failure to secure two sources for the allegation, and the use of an anonymous source for such a controversial charge. Pundits generally did not dispute U.S. mistreatment of prisoners of war, but only the specific charge that U.S. interrogators or guards flushed Korans down the toilet. There is clearly room to fault *Newsweek* for its relatively low journalistic standards in confirming the Koran-flushing charge; however, the intense focus on the failure to secure multiple sources in the *Newsweek* story neglects a larger pattern of U.S. mistreatment and torture of prisoners in the "War on Terror."

Political leaders like Condoleeza Rice and Scott McClellan are able to attack the story as "appalling" and having "damaged the image of the United States" because reporters and editors throughout mass media lack the will to stand up against administration propaganda. In reality, U.S. forces have an extensively documented record of mistreating the Koran, as well as engaging in torture against detainees. That American political leaders could deny such violations with impunity is more a sign of the lack of independence of media outlets than an indication of media malfeasance.

By going on the defensive in the Koran flushing "scandal," media reporters and editors allowed the Bush administration to obscure the U.S. record of torturing prisoners and desecrating the Koran. While debating minor details regarding the Koran-flushing charge, pundits missed the larger trend of American forces' violation of the Geneva Conventions in the Iraq and Afghan wars, as seen in U.S. human rights abuses. Far from unfounded, the claims of U.S. mistreatment of prisoners are well documented in recent years. Specifically related to abuse of the Koran, the Pentagon itself admitted to at least five separate instances of the U.S. military having "mishandled" the Islamic Holy Book at Guantanamo Bay prison.[13] Guards have been implicated for writing obscenities inside copies of the Koran, kicking them across the floor, stepping on them, throwing them at walls, and tearing them.[14] Contrary to Rice's claims, if there is anything "appalling" about the Koran flushing "scandal," it is that the administration was allowed to skirt U.S. responsibility for well-documented mistreatment of the Koran.

Skepticism toward official denials of mistreatment of prisoners should always be in order, regardless of the occasional journalistic mistake in citing sources. In 2002 and 2003, the Red Cross released reports detailing human rights violations relating to American military personnel's abuse of the Koran.[15] The Red Cross also criticized the U.S. military for behavior that was "tantamount to torture" in its dealings with detainees.[16] Any balanced reporting on the *Newsweek* "scandal" would need to highlight the armed forces' documented mistreatment of the Koran in a number of other instances. Sadly, the "scandal" was not situated within such a reality.

The charges made by human rights organizations against the U.S. military and the Bush administration are numerous. There have been reports of the use of dogs to bite Iraqi prisoners. In one instance, sergeants reportedly competed by using dogs to find out who could scare prisoners more, as dogs were used in "psychologically breaking [detainees] down."[17] Reports of "routine" beating of Iraqi prisoners by the Army's 82nd Airborne Division have also emerged, as the abuse was sometimes pursued to "gather intelligence," and at other times simply for amusement.[18]

The Bush administration was criticized by human rights groups for authorizing through Executive Order controversial interrogation tactics including: use of sleep deprivation, reliance on loud music in "sensory overload," placing detainees into "stress positions," and forcing detainees to strip naked.[19] Evidence of military misconduct and torture by American troops at Abu Ghraib and Guantanamo has emerged throughout the "War on Terror." At the same time, the

Bush administration has authorized controversial interrogation tactics and skirted its responsibility for upholding the Geneva Conventions when it comes to prisoners detained in times of war.

The Bush administration's labeling of its detainees in the "War on Terror" as "enemy combatants" rather than prisoners of war (an attempt to circumvent the protections of the Geneva Conventions afforded to POWs), the Justice Department's 2002 advisement to the White House that the torture of suspected Al Qaeda members "may be justifiable" under certain circumstances, as well as the Bush administration's slow reaction to reports that Iraqi prisoners were systematically abused by U.S. officers all raise serious questions about the scope of U.S. human rights abuses in the "War on Terror."[20] Helen Thomas, a senior journalist in the White House Press Corps, was one of the few reporters in the mainstream to point out what she considered to be unfounded attacks on *Newsweek*: "There's a sense of hypocrisy that pervades the huffing and puffing by the Bush administration officials as they rush to criticize *Newsweek*. Where was their outrage when they saw the photographs of the shameful mistreatment of the prisoners of war at the Abu Ghraib facility, with forced nudity, humiliation, sexual harassment, brutal interrogation, dogs?"[21] Thomas' skepticism was leveled at a time when official reports confirmed U.S. responsibility for human rights violations of those held in Iraq under the U.S. A report filed by U.S. Major General Antonio M. Taguba charged that between October and December of 2003, there were acts of "sadistic, blatant, and wanton criminal abuses" committed against detainees of Abu Ghraib.[22]

Chronicling the Assault on Dissent

George W. Bush was not happy during the April 2006 White House Press Correspondents Dinner. Bush had come into the dinner—filled with 2,700 attendees, including noted celebrities, political officials, and White House Press reporters—with his own assumptions about the legitimate bounds of criticism of his Presidency. At the event Bush joked about his own personal difficulties with the English language, and even had a look alike (Steve Bridges) come on stage to play his "inner monologue," as the actor mildly poked fun at the President. What Bush, and most White House reporters were not prepared for, however, were the serious criticisms that were laid at their feet by *Comedy Central* comedian and host Stephen Colbert. Along with *Daily Show* host John Stewart, Colbert was well known as a caustic critic of the Bush administration, the war in Iraq, and the general state of corporate media reporting in the U.S. today. His appearance at the Correspondents dinner offered more of the same in terms of his biting humor and not-so-veiled criticisms and hostility directed against the White House and the mainstream media.

Throughout his keynote speech, Colbert mocked the Bush administration for its low public approval ratings, authorization of NSA wiretaps, failure to find Weapons of Mass Destruction in Iraq, and the general deterioration of social order in Iraq. Mockingly, Colbert spoke approvingly of the belief that "the gov-

ernment that governs best is a government that governs least, and by these standards we have set up a fabulous government in Iraq." Colbert also placed significant blame for the WMD debacle on the mainstream media. Speaking critically of reporters' deference to the Bush administration's pre-war claims about
Iraq, Colbert stated: "Let's review the rules. Here's how it works. The president
makes decisions, he's the decider. The press secretary announces those decisions, and you people of the press type those decisions down. Make, announce,
type. Put them through a spell check and go home."[23]

By the end of Colbert's tirade against the press and the President, Bush was
no longer smiling. A number of guests sitting near the President later confirmed
that he had been offended by Colbert's attacks. That President Bush was so
shocked by Colbert's comments itself may be a serious indicator of the failure of
the mainstream press to regularly direct critical questions at the President—for if
such questions were common amongst reporters questioning Bush, why take
them so personally? One thing was for certain: Colbert's tone was far more
harsh and critical than Bush and his Press Secretaries were used to when it came
to their White House Press Corps briefings. *Chicago Sun Times* TV critic Doug
Elfman claimed that, "For perhaps the first time, the president was forced to sit
and listen to a litany of criminal and corruption allegations." Elfman faulted the
White House Press Corps, which he referred to as "the unthinking and unblink-
ing herd of pack journalists," for "virtually ignoring Stephen Colbert's keynote
speech," claiming that "The truth is [that] many in the media. . . didn't report
much on Colbert's funnier, harsher jokes. . . shocking lines were barely covered
by any traditional [media] organ," outside of a few exceptions like *Editor &
Publisher* magazine and *USA Today*.[24] The tendency to downplay the harsher
parts of Colbert's speech is far from an isolated incident in media reporting and
editorializing when it comes to restricting anti-war dissent. Indeed, there is a
longstanding pattern of neglecting, glossing over, and sometimes actively attacking anti-war perspectives throughout the mainstream press. Such criticisms
are often viewed as a serious threat to the justifications for war put forth by
American political leaders.

Government and media aversion to anti-war dissent is commonplace during
times of war, and the political atmosphere surrounding the U.S. interventions in
Afghanistan and Iraq has been no different. The mainstream media has generally
been critical of anti-war dissent, as arguments that charge the U.S. with aggression, and human rights violations represent a diversion from official statements
and media framing which seek to reinforce the veracity of the Iraq war and its
"humanitarian motivations." This chapter is primarily concerned with analyzing
anti-war dissent, as well as the punishments leveled throughout the American
media aimed at restricting that dissent.

In a story run on June 20 2004 entitled, "Looking Back Before the War,"
Washington Post ombudsmen Michael Getler claimed that his paper did not de-
vote adequate attention to the anti-war movement as it was growing in late 2002
and early 2003. He summarized the paper's failure to cover the movement as
follows: "too many public events in which alternative views were expressed
[against the war], especially during 2002, when the debate [over war] was gath-

ering steam, were either missed, underreported, or poorly displayed" in the
mainstream press. Getler admitted that various protests against the war (inside
and outside the U.S.) in the pre-war period did not receive front-page coverage
he felt they deserved: he considered this a major problem for a paper priding
itself in presenting a diversity of views regarding the war.[25] Such introspection
seems less common amongst most mainstream reporters, most of whom promote
the notion that mainstream reporting and editorializing strikes a balance between
different perspectives.

The claim that the American media is disinterested in rigorous criticisms of
U.S. involvement in foreign conflicts has gained more legitimacy in recent
years. Richard Sambrook, Director of *BBC News* World Service and Global
News division criticizes the American media for having "wrapped themselves in
the flag" and for failing to perform "the role the public expects of them—to ask
difficult questions, to press, to verify" the legitimacy of government statements
about war.[26] Sambrook's view is reinforced when one considers the nationalistic
pressures driving reporters and editors after the 9/11 attacks and throughout the
"War on Terror." Numerous pundits and commentators have demonstrated
strong skepticism of anti-war views throughout the Iraq war, as a "Fox Effect"
was said to have taken its toll on the television news networks. Joe Scarborough
of *MSNBC* complained of "leftist stooges for anti-American causes" who "are
always given a free pass," as he asked, "Isn't it time to make them stand up and
be counted for their views?"[27] Talk radio conservative Michael Savage discounted anti-war protestors by arguing that, "They are absolutely committing
sedition or treason."[28] In his diatribe, Savage insisted that the American government must not only "arrest the leaders of the Anti-War Movement," but also
resurrect the Aliens and Seditions Act of 1918 that made criticisms of the government during times of war illegal.[29] Bill O'Reilly of *Fox News* helped lead the
effort to downsize dissent by assailing the "nutty Left" for actions that "alienate"
it from "regular Americans."[30]

Distrust of anti-war views is based on the assumption that the United States
is committed to fighting a "just war" in Iraq, and that those who question that
"just" war are "harming America." Columnists David Brooks and William
Safire of the *New York Times* have taken such an approach. Implying that criticisms of the Iraq war equal support for the Baath regime, Brooks argued that,
"We can argue about what would have been the best way to depose Saddam,
but...this insatiable tyrant needed to be deposed."[31] Safire concurred, claiming
that those who criticized the administration's war were "prepared to let Saddam
remain in power."[32] Along the same line of thought, Brit Hume of *Fox News'*
Special Report claims that it is "irresponsible" to talk of a withdrawal from Iraq.
Fred Barnes of the conservative *Weekly Standard* seems to agree, as he views
condemnations of the war as largely motivated by the Democratic party's efforts
to gain a "cheap political advantage" in the post-2004 election period.[33] Anthony
Pagden argues in the *Los Angeles Times*: "When either detractors or defenders
of American foreign policy represent the U.S. as an expansionist empire imposing some latter-day version of the 'white man's burden' on the world, they are
not just being historically misleading, they are courting political danger."[34]

Attacks on dissent are not restricted only to conservative media commentators and editorialists. At the onset of the Iraq war, *CBS News* anchor Dan Rather argued that "It's not a time to argue" over the legitimacy of the invasion, while admitting that, during the Afghan war, the media "didn't ask enough thorough questions" (he claims this is "usually the case in war time").[35] Rather, however, was simply reiterating his longstanding position on the inappropriateness of dissent in times of war, as he argued during the Afghan war that, "George Bush is the president. He makes the decisions. . . wherever he wants me to line up, just tell me where."[36] Peter Beinart of the *New Republic* professed a similar point of view, stating shortly after the September 11 attacks that, "This nation is now at war. And in such an environment, domestic political dissent is immoral without a prior statement of national solidarity, a choosing of sides."[37]

Dissent is also limited when it comes to those who argue that the U.S. is indirectly fueling anti-American hostility and contributing to the likelihood of terrorist attacks on American soil. Thomas Friedman, the well-respected establishment liberal from the *New York Times*, contends that, "After every major terrorist incident, the excuse makers come out to tell us why imperialism, Zionism, colonialism, or Iraq explains why the terrorists acted. These excuse makers are just one notch less despicable than the terrorists and also deserve to be exposed."[38] Friedman's comments hardly seem intended to promote an open forum for discussion of the root causes of terrorist attacks, (at least with those who claim the U.S. may be inciting terrorism). Such open debate should be the goal in any democratic media system. Quite the contrary, Friedman's comments fall in line with administration justifications that absolve the U.S. in any blame for fueling the anti-Americanism of groups like Al Qaeda, while attacking those who do not agree as anti-American.

Rather, Friedman, and Beinart's comments show that denunciations of antiwar perspectives are not limited to conservatives in the press. Liberal news mediums like *CBS* and the *New Republic* subscribe to what amounts to strong support for authority and in the post-9/11 political climate, allowing only narrow limits from which to dissent against government policy. The adherence to official state doctrines proclaiming American commitment to democracy and justice, while simultaneously attacking anti-war views protected under the 1st amendment, constitutes is a serious problem from a democratic standpoint, as disagreement with elected officials never requires a permission slip from government. The freedom to disagree with political leaders and others without being blackballed from public discussion is supposed to be a guiding principle of American democracy and freedom of speech in the media. The media's uncomfortable reactions to anti-war dissent throw the alleged commitment to balanced reporting into serious question. Reporters, pundits, editors and owners have often shown that they would prefer to downplay or ignore anti-war protestors and their arguments rather than discuss their views rigorously and respectfully through open dialogue.

CBS and the *New Republic* are not the only liberal establishment outlets opposed to substantive criticisms of American foreign policy. Disapproval of anti-war views encompasses the entire mainstream media (liberal and conservative sources), as revealed by various quantitative studies. One study conducted by *Fairness and Accuracy in Reporting* (*FAIR*) showed a lack of interest in dissent to be a chronic problem for the T.V. networks during the initial stages of the Iraq war. In reviewing the period from March 19 to April 9 2003, when the war began, *FAIR* exhaustively studied nightly news programs including *ABC World News Tonight, CBS Evening News, NBC Nightly News, CNN's Wolf Blitzer Reports, Fox's Special Report with Brit Hume*, and *PBS's News Hour with Jim Lehrer*, showing that over two-thirds of all the on-camera sources used by the programs were pro-war. While 71 percent of the guests who appeared on these programs favored the war, only 10 percent of the guests were opposed.[39] The situation was more extreme prior to the invasion. *FAIR's* Steve Rendall explains that, of the guests "on the four flagship shows on each of the four [major] networks (*ABC, CBS, NBC, Fox News*) who spoke about Iraq over a two week period in February [2003]. . . less than 1 percent anti-war voices were heard."[40] *FAIR* found the same tendency toward marginalizing dissent during the war against Afghanistan. Analyzing *New York Times* and *Washington Post* editorials during the first three weeks after 9/11, *FAIR* found that "columns calling for or assuming a military response to the attacks were given a great deal of space, while opinions urging diplomatic and international law approaches as an alternative to military action were nearly non-existent. A total of forty-four columns in the *New York Times* and *Washington Post* clearly stressed a military response, against only two columns stressing non-military solutions."[41]

Anti-war critics have been portrayed as opponents of democracy and as pacifists. In the *Los Angeles Times*, conservative activist David Horowitz depicted anti-war protestors as anti-democratic, arguing: "the [anti-war] 'movement' is now in full attack mode against its own democratic government in a time of war. . . . This is no longer a loyal opposition. It is no longer the voice of a progressive future that once upon a time would have opposed misogyny, thuggery, and the depravity of regimes like Saddam Hussein's."[42] The *New York Times* labeled Barbara Lee (D-Ca), and anti-corporate globalization activist Kevin Danaher as "pacifists" shortly after the 9/11 attacks.[43] This was not the first reference to "pacifists" in the *New York Times*, as the paper ran a headline a few days earlier titled "Protestors in Washington Urge Peace with Terrorists," in reference to an anti-war demonstration that had recently taken place.[44] Other references to "pacifists" were more blatantly hostile. Michael Kelly of the *Washington Post* railed critics of the Afghan war, claiming that, "Pacifists are not serious people. . . and their arguments are not being taken seriously at the moment." Continuing his pro-war diatribe, Kelly invoked the right of self-defense: "In the situation where one's nation has been attacked—a situation such as we are now in—pacifism is, inescapably and profoundly, immoral. Indeed, in the case of this specific situation, pacifism is on the side of the murderers, and it is on the side of letting them murder again."[45]

The simplistic use of the "pacifist" label fails to address serious grievances of anti-war protestors. Reviewing the statements of Danaher and other anti-war figures attacked in the media, it becomes clear that the debate over war cannot be accurately characterized by the simple-minded dichotomy presented by the

Washington Post of the "good" pro-war advocates versus the "bad" anti-war "pacifists." In a column for the *Washington Post*, Danaher was given a chance to respond to the charges against him and other dissidents after 9/11. Elaborating upon the nuances of the anti-war-pro-war debate that have often been absent in the mainstream press, Danaher wrote:

> The perpetrators of the recent attacks can be apprehended and brought to justice without killing innocent civilians if we have the support of the world's governments. If America were to engage the world in setting up an effective international criminal court system, the support from other nations would be so strong it would be impossible for any country to shelter the perpetrators of mass violence.[46]

While the *Washington Post's* decision to allow Danaher a chance to respond to his attackers was a step in the right direction in terms of promoting dissent, most anti-war activists have not been allotted similar space to respond to their detractors, or to enunciate a cogent anti-war platform.

Reminiscent of the anti-"pacifist" approach in terms of its simplicity is the assumption that anti-war views are not worth addressing if the American public does not commonly hold those views. Rationalizing a failure to incorporate anti-war views, media outlets sometimes assume that the vast majority of the population does not harbor similar perspectives. This belief was widely reflected in the war against Afghanistan. Rena Golden, executive Vice President and General Manager of *CNN International* explains that censorship in that war "wasn't a matter of government pressure, but a reluctance to criticize anything in a war that was obviously supported by the vast majority of the [American] people."[47] When asked if there were any anti-war views amongst the American public after 9/11, Cokie Roberts of *National Public Radio* responded that there were "None that matter."[48] Similarly, Erik Sorenson, President of *MSNBC* claimed that "There has not been a lot of debate period," and that "most of the dissent we've had on the air is the opposite—conservatives like John McCain and Bill Bennett saying we should bomb more or attack Iraq."[49]

The assumption that Americans are not interested in anti-war views is problematic for a few reasons. First, this position neglects a significant number of Americans who *were* actually against the war. As former *MSNBC* talk show host Phil Donahue explained, "You cannot say that people willing to speak up [against the Afghan war] are not in existence. . . . There is just not a lot of enthusiasm for this on the [mainstream news] programs."[50] Second, the assumption that anti-war views are not represented amongst the American public overlooks the media's role in shaping pro-war opinions in the first place. Rather than media executives, reporters, and pundits asking "why should we cover anti-war views if the public does not believe in them?," the question posed could have been: "will public opinion swing in favor of the war if we refuse to expose Americans to peaceful alternatives to war, instead of just violent ones?" The media does not simply "reflect public opinion" in its reporting, but plays an active role in formulating that opinion. The mainstream media largely failed in its task of educating the public about the full range of views that existed after 9/11 in terms of potential U.S. responses. One of the most relevant questions, then, seems to be: how could Americans be expected to formulate informed opinions about prospects for war or peaceful alternatives to war if they were systematically denied such alternatives?

Smearing Cindy Sheehan

In 2005, Cindy Sheehan became a central figure in the anti-war movement. The mother of an army specialist who was killed in Iraq, Sheehan presented a problem for the Bush administration in a time of war. Her pain and anguish made her anti-war message difficult to discount, although that did not stop pundits from trying. After her son Casey was killed, Sheehan, along with a number of parents who lost their children in Iraq, had a chance to meet with President Bush. Unfulfilled after her discussion with the President, Sheehan dedicated the month of August to protesting the Iraq war outside of Bush's ranch in Crawford, Texas, as she attempted to obtain another appointment to meet with the President. Her protest gained nationwide media attention, as she vowed to sit outside of Bush's ranch until he agreed to meet with her again.

Many throughout the mass media took great strides to criticize Sheehan. Fred Barnes of *Fox News* labeled her a "crackpot," while Rush Limbaugh claimed that her "story is nothing more than forged documents...there's nothing about it that's real."[51] A popular method of attack against Sheehan was to label her a pawn of the anti-war movement. On *Fox News*, Bill O'Reilly characterized Sheehan as "in bed with the radical left," while William F. Buckley of the conservative *National Review* condemned her as "the mouthpiece. . . of howling at the moon, bile spewing Bush haters."[52] Charles Krauthammer denounced her for "hurting our troops and endangering our troops."[53] Krauthammer believes that anti-war critics like Sheehan "have to be attacked because they are libeling America, endangering America."[54]

Even liberal "supporters" of Sheehan in the mainstream press sometimes resorted to backhanded compliments. These "supporters" sympathized with Sheehan, while criticizing the anti-war movement in which she was involved. Farhad Manjoo of *Salon* claimed that, "the antiwar movement was dominated by lefties, and ineffective—until a grieving mother from California became its symbol."[55] Manjoo's discounting of the anti-war movement as fringe-based seems inappropriate considering that since 2004, public support for the Iraq war scarcely broke more than half the American public. Frank Rich of the *New York Times* criticized "the opportunistic left wing groups that have attached themselves to her like barnacles,"[56] while Leonard Pitts Jr. of the *Miami Herald* stated: "Sheehan has one quality most protestors lack: moral authority." Pitt's position seemed intended to create a dichotomy between those with and without "moral authority," based directly upon the proximity (or lack there of) of protestors to others who are directly involved in fighting the war.[57] Such distinctions, however, are not really of significance when looking at First amendment protections of the right to free speech, regardless of one's affiliation with the military.

Separating Sheehan from her anti-war supporters may very well marginalize the very anti-war movement she is attempting to mobilize. Sheehan made this point herself when refuting claims that she was being victimized or used by the anti-war movement, explaining: "the media are wrong. The people who have come out to Camp Casey to help coordinate the press and events with me are not putting words in my mouth, they are taking words out of my mouth."[58] The implication in the press that it is acceptable only for grieving parents like Sheehan to protest the war, implying that it is acceptable for one mother to dissent, but not for others to sympathize with and work with her is an effective way to dilute a broad-based anti-war movement. Then again, this may very well be the goal of many of those in the media who attack Sheehan and anti-war protest groups.

Christopher Hitchens is one of the many pro-war personalities in the media who helped lead the effort against the anti-war movement. Hitchens assailed Sheehan for "spouting sinister piffle." Labels such as "sinister" create distinctions between proponents of war and "evil" opponents of the U.S. occupation. Hitchens, while berating anti-war and progressive movements, has at times misapplied the negative labels on which he relies. Hitchens' attack against Cindy Sheehan's "cheerleader" Michael Moore for Moore's "spouting [of] fascistic nonsense"[59] is a deliberate effort to redefine free speech as an affront to American dignity. Terms like fascism, used to characterize anti-war dissent, demonize those who oppose war.

Fascism has traditionally been defined through governments that prioritize the state and the party over the individual—through efforts to merge a repressive and totalitarian state with the corporate capitalist system. It is difficult to uncover, even on the most tangential level, how activists like Michael Moore and Cindy Sheehan fit in under the context of this definition. As they lack any status as corporate or government leaders, and are exercising their First Amendment rights to dissent against government, these activists have nothing in common with fascists of modern history such as Adolf Hitler or Benito Mussolini. Such a vital distinction is lost in reckless efforts to link anti-war activists with some of the most repressive dictators and criminals in world history.

Railing the Rest

Cindy Sheehan is not the only personality subject to incendiary media rhetoric. After stating that the Iraq war was illegal under international law, U.N. Secretary General Kofi Annan became the subject of a firestorm of criticisms amongst television anchors, pundits, and columnists. The *Washington Post* attacked his statement as "inappropriate" and "counterproductive,"[60] failing to note that Annan's criticism was factually accurate. While discussing the issue with Geraldo Rivera on *Fox News*, Rita Cosby found it "stunning" that Annan would make such a claim against the war.[61] On *CNN*, Lou Dobbs spoke skeptically of the Secretary General's "incredible outburst"—this "bizarre statement" questioning the legal legitimacy of the conflict.[62] Dobbs' condemnation was driven, more than anything else, by an unwavering commitment to American political leaders, rather than to principals of international or national law. International law clearly outlaws military aggression outside of two pre-texts: self-defense, and U.N. Security Council authorization of the use of force, in which the United States could claim neither.

Anti-war celebrities are also regarded as attractive targets, since their mass appeal is a potentially powerful tool of the anti-war movement at a time when procedural "anti-war" views dominate the mainstream press. In one instance, Tony Snow, former talk show host for *Fox News*, derided actor Tim Robbins for protesting the invasion of Iraq. Robbins' claim that the media "has shoved the war down the public's throat" was met with hostility, as both Snow and Lloyd Grove of the *Washington Post* concurred that Robbins was a "complete fascist," who was "brainwashing" the American public against the war.[63]

Pro-war pundits also directed their attacks against prominent political officials who criticized the war. On *CNN Headline News*, Chuck Roberts and Linda Stoeffer postulated that Congresswoman Barbara Boxer's criticisms of Secretary of State Condoleeza Rice regarding the Bush administration's manipulation of intelligence regarding Iraqi weapons of mass destruction were motivated by aspirations for a higher political office.[64] Similarly, Bill O'Reilly assumed that the anti-war criticisms of Richard Clarke, the former counter-terrorism coordinator for the Bush administration, were motivated largely by a desire to sell his book, *Against All Enemies: Inside America's War on Terror*.[65] The criticism of anti-war figures for being motivated by personal gain (whether that is selling a book or running for higher office) is a classic means for limiting meaningful protest. By relying on such lines of superficial criticisms that frame anti-war activists as out for personal gain, pundits draw attention away from the substantive content of anti-war messages.

Punishing Anti-War Dissent

Media discomfort with anti-war perspectives is characterized by more than just verbal reprimand. For the limitation of substantive protest of government foreign policy to be effective, there must be clear, tangible penalties in place so as to discourage or deter debate outside the parameters of "acceptable" opinions. Prominent figures in the media have been subject to a number of punishments intended to skirt foundational anti-war opposition to the Bush administration. These punishments include intimidation, firings, and the use of censorship in order to limit messages questioning pro-war propaganda.

Major network reporters are heavily influenced by nationalistic pro-war pressures. *CNN* reporter Christiane Amanpour explained that she felt threatened by the Bush administration and those within the media who attempted to pressure *CNN* and other media outlets to climb on board in support of the "War on Terror."[66] Amanpour maintained that television networks were "intimidated by the [Bush] administration and its foot soldiers at *Fox News*. And it did, in fact, put a climate of fear and self-censorship in terms of the kind of broadcast work we did." The story of Jeremy Glick, an anti-war protestor whose father was killed in the September 11th terrorist attacks in New York, is also instructive of the heightened intimidation sometimes present in the post 9/11 period. *Fox News* coaxed Glick to appear on *The O'Reilly Factor* after he signed an anti-war petition against "Operation Enduring Freedom" in Afghanistan. Although it was less than six months after Glick's father's death, Bill O'Reilly brought Glick on the show, telling him repeatedly to "shut up," and physically threatening him with violence after Glick argued that the U.S. was killing innocent civilians in Afghanistan. On air, O'Reilly condemned Glick for spewing "vile propaganda" and for having "a warped view of this world and a warped view of this country."[67] Glick's position, which implicated the U.S. with supporting Islamist terrorists during the Soviet Union's war in Afghanistan, was too critical for O'Reilly to tolerate, as he cut Glick's microphone in mid-message. This would not be the last time O'Reilly would cut the microphone of a guest with whom he disagreed.

A Pattern of Firings

Intimidation of anti-war figures is furthered by the firing of those who rigorously challenge official statements and propaganda. Such firings sometimes include even proponents of the war who make occasional criticisms of those in power. Bill Maher is a case in point. The former host of the late night political talk show *Politically Incorrect*, Maher was known for his strong pro-war stance in the Afghan war, which he regarded as vital in fighting Islamist terror of groups like Al Qaeda. His lack of concern with civilian casualties in the conflict was expressed on many occasions after 9/11. Active disregard for civilians did not lead to any sort of reprimand by *ABC*, the carrier of *Politically Incorrect*. It was not until he became somewhat critical of the Bush administration's use of aerial bombing that Maher became a liability for *ABC*. Responding to the argument that the terrorists behind the 9/11 attacks were "cowards" Maher claimed: "We [the U.S.] have been the cowards, lobbing cruise missiles from 2,000 miles away. Staying in the airplane when it hits the building, say what you want about it, it's not cowardly."[68] By firing Maher, *ABC* sent a message to others throughout the press that criticisms of the heroism of American forces are not a legitimate part of the wartime debate.

Other media personalities with consistent records of anti-war criticism had similar problems keeping their jobs in the mainstream press. Phil Donahue's talk show on *MSNBC* was cancelled, although it was the highest rated program on the network's line up. An internal report unearthed in early 2003 explained a great deal about the mindset of *MSNBC* executives at the time they cancelled Donahue. The report framed Donahue as a major problem for the network in the run-up to war, as he represented a "difficult public face for *NBC* in a time of war," appearing to "delight in presenting guests who are anti-war, anti-Bush and skeptical of the administration's motives."[69] Jeff Cohen, *FAIR* founder and Senior Producer for the Donahue Show, recounts his experiences with *MSNBC*'s efforts to limit the public exposure of those attacking the war effort:

"In the last months of Donahue, we were ordered to book more right-wing guests than left-wing, more pro-war than anti-war to balance the liberalism of host Phil Donahue."[70] Having characterized Donahue as "a tired, left wing liberal out of touch with the current marketplace" of pro-war opinions, *MSNBC* dismissed him to make room for a new show hosted by conservative commentator Michael Savage, in "an attempt to expand the [network's] marketplace of ideas."[71] Savage's commitment to diversity was revealed after he was fired in mid-2003 for referring to an unidentified caller as a "sodomite" who should "get AIDS and die."[72]

The trend toward curtailing critical anti-war perspectives at *MSNBC* was not limited only to Donahue and his staff. *MSNBC* Host Keith Olbermann also complained that the network expressed unhappiness when he had two mainstream liberal guests on the show, Janeane Garofalo and Al Franken, within a period of three days between September 2 and September 4, 2003 out of a total of seven guests he had on air.[73] Such displeasure with even mainstream liberal perspectives revealed the extent to which the Fox Effect had taken hold of television news.

As the stakes underlying the "War on Terror" increased with the invasion of Iraq, the media remained intolerant of substantive anti-war dissent. Many prominent media figures were fired or encouraged to retire, including former *CBS News* anchor Dan Rather, former international correspondent for *NBC News* Peter Arnett, and Jon Leiberman, a former political reporter for *Sinclair Broadcasting*. Immediately following the onset of war, Peter Arnett was one of the first to be fired, as many throughout the media incorrectly perceived him as opposing the U.S. invasion.

A veteran reporter from the first U.S. war in the Gulf, Arnett was fired by *NBC* for his initial assessment of "Operation Iraqi Freedom." In an interview with an Iraqi satellite television, Arnett explained: "The first [U.S.] war plan has failed because of Iraqi resistance. Now they [American leaders] are trying to write another war plan. Clearly, the American war planners misjudged the determination of the Iraqi forces."[74] Soon after Arnett's assessment, critical voices sprang into action. *Fox News* said of Arnett: "He spoke out against American armed forces: he said America's war against terrorism had failed; he even vilified America's leadership."[75] John Gibson of *Fox News* claimed: "his comments seem to be supporting the Iraqi side."[76] He "seems to cheer the Iraqi resistance."[77] *NBC* joined suit, criticizing its own reporter for his statements. *NBC News* President Neal Shapiro said of Arnett's actions and comments: "It was wrong for Mr. Arnett to grant an interview to state-controlled Iraqi TV—especially at a time of war—and it was wrong for him to discuss personal observations and opinions in that interview. Therefore, Peter Arnett will no longer be reporting for *NBC News* and *MSNBC*."[78] *NBC* reporters who expressed overtly pro-war opinions throughout the invasion and occupation suffered no such reprimand for sharing their "insights" into the conflict.

Arnett was also fired from *National Geographic* as the organization cited his expression of "personal views" on Iraqi television as the reason for his dismissal. *National Geographic* released a statement which said that it "did not authorize or have any prior knowledge of Arnett's television interview with Iraqi Television, and had we been consulted, would not have allowed it." Arnett himself later apologized to television networks and the American people for his "misjudgment" of the initial stages of the Iraq war; however, this apology was likely more the result of intense nationalistic pressures than an acknowledgement on his part that he engaged in unprofessional reporting. In one public statement released after he was fired, Arnett argued that, "I am still in shock and awe at being fired. . . . I report the truth of what is happening here in Baghdad and will not apologise for it." Arnett's firing for expressing "anti-war views" is all the more ironic considering he was not an opponent of the war. Arnett explained that "I am not anti-war, I am not anti-military. . . . I said over the weekend what we all know about the war."[79]

Dan Rather also became the subject of the Bush administration and media attacks after *60 Minutes* ran a critical story of the President in late 2004 based on forged documents that alleged the President received special treatment while he served in the Texas Air National Guard. There was a perception amongst *CBS* reporters, editors, and executives that this story hurt the network professionally and in terms of credibility. A panel appointed by the network to look into the matter faulted those responsible for the story for their "rigid and blind" defense of the *60 Minutes* story.[80] *CBS Chairman* Leslie Moonves replied that, "We deeply regret the disservice this flawed 60 Minutes report did to the American public, which has the right to count on *CBS News* for fairness and accuracy."[81] After two weeks of defending the story, Dan Rather reversed course, personally apologizing for his "mistake in judgment" in the use of the forged documents.[82] In the nationalistic media climate of the 2004 elections, there were serious penalties to be paid for criticisms against the Bush administration—even Rather's criticisms—that lacked any direct connection to the post-9/11 foreign policy or Iraq.

As a major news anchor for a major news network, Rather's criticisms of the Bush administration could not be as easily ignored or brushed off as those of individual Op-Ed writers or newspaper editors. While the editors and columnists for papers like the *New York Times* and *Washington Post* were able to get away with supporting U.S. regime change in favor of Presidential hopeful John Kerry, there was a serious price to be paid for attacks such as Rather's, which was not merely an opinion, but was subject to empirical falsification. As punishment for the use of the counterfeit documents in the story, four *CBS* employees involved in the production were fired or asked to resign. The story was likely an important factor in forcing Dan Rather into retirement. At the heart of the National Guard "scandal" were two main problems. The first was *CBS*'s use of forged documents that were said to come from Bush's commander in the Texas Air National Guard, Lt. Col. Jerry Killian. The documents described Bush's supposed failure to take a physical during his National Guard service,[83] as well as the alleged efforts of Killian's superiors to get him to "sugarcoat" Bush's service record.[84] A second problem with the story, according to *CBS* president Andrew Heyward, was that *60 Minutes* rushed the piece onto the air. This meant that there was less time to expose potential problems with the story. Heyward explained, "In retrospect, we shouldn't have used the documents, and we clearly should have spent more time and more effort to authenticate them."[85]

Both of the problems mentioned by the media above are largely irrelevant. The story of Bush's special treatment in the National Guard was corroborated long before it became news in the *60 Minutes* piece in 2004. As one story run by the *Washington Post* in February of 2004 commented: "A review of Bush's military records shows that Bush enjoyed preferential treatment as the son of a then-congressman, when he walked into a Texas Guard unit in Houston two weeks before his 1968 graduation from Yale and was moved to the top of a long waiting list."[86] The *Washington Post* article went on to cite a *Boston Globe* story run in 2000, which found that between 1972 and 1973, Bush was granted permission to leave the Alabama National Guard in order to work on a Senate campaign.[87] In other words, it was not *60 Minute's* reporting of Bush's privileged position that got Rather and others fired, but only their use of counterfeit documents to corroborate a story that had already been well established for years.

And yet, only to highlight the misplaced punishment of Rather and others for reporting this story is to neglect a far more important lesson that should be learned from this "scandal." In the post-9/11 media climate, news anchors like Rather are castigated for errors in relatively trivial stories—at least trivial in the sense that the *60 Minutes* story had no direct relationship with the major campaign issue (the war in Iraq). Meanwhile, the Bush administration is exonerated in regards to scandals that are far more severe in scope. The *60 Minutes* "scandal" pales in comparison to other forged document stories, such as the Bush administration's reliance of counterfeit documentation in its allegation that Iraq had attempted to purchase "yellowcake" uranium from Niger—documents that were shown to be crude fakes shortly after the administration announced them to the public. To compare the Rather "scandal" with the Niger scandal in terms of their scope would be outlandish. And still, the *60 Minutes* story has been framed as a major humiliation for *CBS*, while the Bush administration's use of false documents and inaccurate intelligence (not only considering the yellowcake charge, but concerning Iraq's possession of weapons of mass destruction altogether) have not been interpreted by media so as to lead to greater skepticism of the Bush administration's justification for occupying Iraq. The attacks on Dan Rather reveal that even high-profile defenders of the Bush administration (recall his statements about the limits of dissent earlier in this chapter) can become the subjects of ridicule and attack when they criticize the President in a time of war.

The threat of being fired looms over the heads of those within the media who too rigorously promote views critical of the war and the President. Reporters without the star presence conferred by hosting a major network's nightly news are also in danger of losing their positions should they incorporate anti-war arguments into their reporting. *ABC News* Senior Correspondent Jim Wooten speaks of the fear among the White House press corps of asking critical questions: "There is, of course, among these ladies and gentlemen, an instinct for job protection. A clear understanding that if a question is too hostile, it could be the last time they got to ask one."[88]

Similar skepticism for tough critiques of the "War on Terror" exists outside of the White House press corps as well. Consider the story of John Leiberman, who was fired by *Sinclair Broadcastng* for his criticisms of the anti-Kerry film, *Stolen Honor: Wounds that Never Heal.* Sinclair planned on running the documentary on all of its sixty-two television stations, which are affiliated with *Fox, WB, NBC, ABC,* and *CBS.*[89] Sinclair owns more television stations than any other media corporation in the U.S. Although its stations are outside the major ten U.S. markets, they reach up to a quarter of a million households, which translates into enormous potential to influence American public opinion.[90]

The company's power in influencing opinion is driven home clearly in Robert McChesney and John Nichol's book, *Tragedy & Farce: How the American Media Sell Wars, Spin Elections, and Destroy Democracy.* McChesney and Nichols cite a nationwide survey done by the Annenberg Center, which found that the commercials for the Swift Boat documentary run on a number of stations in swing states had a significant effect on voters' perceptions of Kerry. According to the poll, "Independent voters [were] nearly evenly split over whether they [found] the ad believable; 44 percent [found] the ad somewhat or very believable, while 49 percent [found] the ad somewhat or very unbelievable."[91]

Sinclair was known for its pro-Republican stance before the *Stolen Honor* controversy. From 1996 to 2004, the *Sinclair Corporation* and its executives gave millions in contributions to Republicans running for office; in 2004, 97 percent of the contributions went to Republicans or the Republican Party.[92] *Sinclair* owners' conservative political views were clearly expressed when the company prohibited its *ABC* affiliates from running a *Nightline* program in which Ted Koppel read the names of American soldiers who died in Iraq. *Sinclair* criticized *ABC*'s choice as motivated by "a political agenda designed to undermine the efforts of the United States in Iraq. . . . We find it to be contrary to the public interest."[93] The station's anger with allegedly biased journalism was lost, however, after it decided to push forward with its openly anti-Kerry Vietnam documentary. At this point, biased journalism no longer seemed to be a problem for the network, as long as it favored the Bush administration.

It appears that former *Sinclair* reporter John Leiberman was punished for his opposition to the film. Leiberman was fired after criticizing *Sinclair* for "indefensible" conduct,[94] as he charged the station with playing "biased political propaganda,"[95] in what he considered an attempt to sway the 2004 Presidential election. The official reason given for Leiberman's firing was that he disclosed private company information to the media, although his charge that *Sinclair* was guilty of reliance on political propaganda probably played a larger part.

Sinclair's choice to run the documentary, compounded with its firing of Leiberman, left many convinced that the station was not committed to diversity of opinion or dissent. In retaliation, eighteen Democratic senators filed federal complaints condemning the planned broadcast of *Stolen Honor.*[96] Some Republicans even attacked *Sinclair.* Senator John McCain denounced the station's ban on the Nightline broadcast for attempting "to deny viewers an opportunity to be reminded of war's terrible costs."[97] McCain blasted the station for its "gross disservice to the public, and to the men and women of the United States Armed Forces."[98] After considerable bad press, *Sinclair* eventually backed down from running the entire anti-Kerry documentary, instead showing parts of it during a "news special" about the issue.[99] The controversy had done considerable damage to the reputation of a company that most of the American public probably did not even know existed before the 2004 election. Then again, the documentary may have also helped win the election for George W. Bush by promoting false attacks on Kerry and lending them credibility.

The Politics of Censorship: The Story of Michael Moore

Censorship is an extremely effective method for limiting anti-war views because it is so difficult to identify. Political leaders and media personalities often define censorship exclusively through government efforts to control or omit controversial content from newscasts and reports. Censorship of reporters and editors that originates from within corporate media is often left unconsidered. As a result of this narrow definition, many questions are left unanswered about the nature of corporate media censorship. How many books do publishers reject because they do not fit conventional norms that justify U.S. foreign policy? How many people are not invited as guest news analysts for television programs because they express controversial anti-war views? How many anti-war academics and polemicists are not considered for regular or guest newspaper columns? How many films never get made or distributed because they fail to conform to mainstream political perspectives?

Such questions are impossible to fully answer, since those censored usually do not get the chance to tell the American public their stories. On occasion, though, some stories of censorship are so blatant that it is hard to downplay them. Such was the case with Michael Moore's problems finding a distributor for his anti-war documentary *Fahrenheit 9/11.*

Miramax had originally funded Moore's project, although the company lacked permission from its parent company, *Disney*, to distribute the film upon completion. Former CEO Michael Eisner did not want *Disney* to be associated with this controversial film.[100] Eisner explained his reasoning as follows: "We're such a nonpartisan company. . . [consumers] do not look for us to take sides."[101] Michael Moore, however, explained the reluctance as a result of *Disney*'s suppression of anti-war messages. Moore stated, "I would have hoped by now that I would be able to put my work out to the public without having to experience the profound censorship obstacles I often seem to encounter."[102] This was not the first time Moore had problems with censorship. According to Moore, *Harper-Collins*, the publisher of *Stupid White Men*, originally threatened to shred his book in the wake of 9/11 if he did not remove a chapter that was critical of George W. Bush.[103] After drawing public attention to the issue, Moore was successful in releasing his book, although it came out six months late. In reflection, Moore claims: "I got lucky, but I wonder how many other people have been censored in the last five or six months: people we don't know about, people who don't have the forum that I have."[104]

Despite problems with censorship, both *Fahrenheit 9/11* and *Stupid White Men* were very lucrative for the corporate media outlets that distributed them. *Stupid White Men* made the *New York Times* bestseller list for over a year. *Fahrenheit 9/11* was also a financial success beyond most critics' expectations. Moore's success demonstrated that it is not that the American public is disinterested in anti-war views; in fact, they are often quite open to them when allowed exposure.

By finding alternative distribution, *Disney* kept away from the release of *Fahrenheit 9/11*, while still profiting from the venture. Although *Disney* only played a behind-the-scenes role in the film's release, the company still made over seventy million dollars from the project, as *Fahrenheit 9/11* became the most profitable documentary ever made, earning over $220 million from the time of its theatrical running through its release on DVD.[105] The negative reactions to Moore's works reveal a great deal about censorship in the mainstream media. Despite the fact that *Stupid White Men* and *Fahrenheit 9/11* were worth hundreds of millions of dollars, *Disney* and *HarperCollins* expressed few reservations in attempting to prohibit their release. It seems that fear of the political backlash of challenging the Bush administration was enough initially to scare *Disney* and *HarperCollins* out of supporting these projects.

Radical Nationalism at the Helm

The stories documented in this chapter share similarities in that they demonstrate the media's displeasure with those who are critical of the various aspects of the "War on Terror," particularly the wars in Afghanistan and Iraq. This displeasure is in large part the result of nationalistic pressures on the establishment press, as well as a general acceptance amongst many throughout the press that patriotism during times of war requires a curtailment of dissent challenging the official reasons for war. During the early phases of the Iraq and Afghan wars, even minimal dissent was at times considered unpatriotic. As the conflicts dragged on, nationalistic pressures often confined dissent within the "acceptable" framework of discussion proposed by the Democratic and Republican parties. However, nationalistic demands placed upon the American public do little to promote real dialogue and debate in the media and amongst the public. Nationalism as interpreted to limit dissent hurts informed discussion—at least if citizens understand greater levels of balance reporting as requiring the inclusion of not only pro-war views and pragmatic criticisms of war, but also challenges framing the war as illegal, immoral, or imperial. In this sense, the mass media has largely failed to promote a healthy dialogue between pro-war and anti-war voices.

Notes

1. Justin Huggler, "Afghan Prisoners Were 'Tortured to Death,' by American Guards," *Independent*, 21 May 2005, http://www.commondreams.org/headlines05/0521-01.htm (21 May 2005).

2. BBC News, "Q & A: U.S. Abuses in Afghan Jails," 22 May 2005, http://news.bbc-.co.uk/1/hi/world/south_asia/4570941.stm (22 May 2005).

3. CNN.com, "Newsweek Retracts Quran Story," 16 May 2005, http://www.cnn.com /2005/WORLD/asiapcf/05/16/newsweek.quran/ (16 May 2005).

4. Howard Kurtz, "Newsweek Retracts Koran Story," 16 May 2005, *Washington Post*, 1(A).

5. Kurtz, "Newsweek Retracts Koran Story," 2005.

6. Kurtz, "Newsweek Retracts Koran Story," 2005.

7. CNN.com, "Newsweek Retracts Quran Story," 2005.

8. Bill O'Reilly, *The O'Reilly Factor*, Fox News, 17 May 2005.

9. Daryn Kagan and Barbara Starr, *CNN Live* Today, CNN, 17 May, 2005.

10. Bay Buchanan, *Crossfire*, CNN, 17 May 2005.

11. Bay Buchanan, *Crossfire*, CNN, 17 May 2005.

12. Bay Buchanan, *Crossfire*, CNN, 17 May 2005.

13. Rupert Cornwell, "Pentagon Admits Five Acts of 'Mishandling' of Koran," *Independent*, sec. 1, 27 May 2005, 30.

14. Richard A. Serrano and John Daniszewski, "Dozens Have Alleged Koran's Mishandling," *Los Angeles Times*, 22 May 2005, http://www.commondreams.org/headlines0-5/0522-02.htm (22 May 2005).

15. Cam Simpson and Mark Silva, "Red Cross Told US of Koran Incidents," *Chicago Tribune*, 19 May 2005, http://www.truthout.org/docs_2005/052005B.shtml (22 May 2005).

16. Mark Matthews, "Powell says Bush was 'informed' of Red Cross Concerns," *Baltimore Sun*, 12 May 2004, http://www.baltimoresun.com/enws/nationalworld/balte.powe-ll12may12,0,2804533.story?coll=bal-news-nation (16 Oct. 2005).

17. David Dishneau, "Witness: Dogs Bit Abu Ghraib Detainees," *Associated Press*, 26 July 2005, http://www.truthout.org/docs_2005/072605Y.shtml (7 Aug. 2005).

18. Eric Schmitt, "3 in 82nd Airborne Say Beating Iraqi Prisoners was Routine," *New York Times*, 24 September 2005, 1(A).

19. New Standard, "President Authorized Abu Ghraib Torture, FBI Email Says," 21 December 2004, http://newstandardnews.net/content/index.cfm/items/1348 (21 Dec. 2004).

20. Mike Allen and Dana Priest, "Memo on Torture Draws Focus to Bush," *Washington Post*, 9 June 2004, 3(A).

21. Helen Thomas, "Newsweek Didn't Create White House Image," *Seattle Post-Intelligencer*, 24 May 2005, http://www.commondreams.org/views05/0524-26.htm (7 Dec. 2005).

22. Seymour M. Hersh, *Chain of Command: The Road from 9/11 to Abu Ghraib* (New York, NY: Harper, 2004), 22.

23. Anne Oldenburg, "Bush, Celebrities Attend Press Corps Dinner," *USA Today*, 1 May 2006, http://www.usatoday.com/news/washington/2006-04-30-bushdinner_x.htm (2 May 2006).

24. Editor and Publisher, "Colbert Lampoons Bush at White House Correspondents Dinner—President Not Amused," 29 April 2006, http://www.editorandpublisher.com/ne-ws/article_display.jsp?vnu_content_id=1002425363 (25 Apr. 2006); Oldenburg, "Bush, Celebrities Attend Press Corps. Dinner," 2006.

25. Michael Getler, "Looking Back Before the War," *Washington Post*, 20 June 2004, 6(B).

26. Jim Rutenberg, "Cable's War Coverage Suggests a New 'Fox Effect' on Television Journalism, " *New York Times*, 16 April 2003, 9(A).

27. Rutenberg, "Cable's War Coverage," 2003.

28. Rutenberg, "Cable's War Coverage," 2003.

29. Mark T. Harris, "Media's Pro-War Campaign," 28 May 2003, *Z Magazine*, http://www.zmag.org/content/print_article.cfm?ItemID=3688&sectionID-21 (25 Sep. 2005).

30. Bill O'Reilly, *The O'Reilly Factor*, Fox News, 16 December 2004.

31. David Brooks, "The Report that Nails Saddam," *New York Times*, 9 October 2004, 19(A).

32. William Safire, "You Lied to Us," *New York Times*, 2 June 2003, 21(A).

33. Brit Hume, *Special Report with Brit Hume*, Fox News, 1 February 2005.

34. Anthony Pagden, "Bush is No Emperor," *Los Angeles Times*, 14 November 2004, 1(M).

35. Larry King, *Larry King Live*, CNN, 14 April 2003.

36. Peter Hart and Seth Ackerman, "Patriotism and Censorship," *Extra!*, November/December 2001, www.fair.org/extra/0111/patriotism-and-censorship.html (15 Dec. 2004).

37. Peter Hart, "Covering the 'Fifth Column,'" *Extra!*, November/December 2001, http://www.fair.org/index.php?page=1083 (22 Dec. 2006).

38. Thomas L. Friedman, "Giving the Hatemongers No Place to Hide," *New York Times*, 22 July 2005, http://www.nytimes.com/2005/07/22/opinion/22friedman.html?ex=-1279684800&en=17fb5beb19b09d86&ei=5090&partner=rssuserland&emc=rss (22 Dec. 2006).

39. Steve Rendall and Tara Broughel, "Amplifying Officials, Squelching Dissent," *Extra!*, June 2003, 12-14.

40. Mariellen Diemand, "Media and Iraq: War Coverage Analysis," *Media Education Foundation*, 2004, http://www.mediaed.org/news/articles/mediairaq (23 Jul. 2005).

41. FAIR, "Op-Ed Echo Chamber," 2 November 2001, http://www.fair.org/activism/-nyt-wp-opeds.html (5 Dec. 2005).

42. David Horowitz, "In a Time of War, the Left is on Trial," *Los Angeles Times*, 10 January 2005, 9(B).

43. Evelyn Nieves, "In Bay Area, Pacifist Orthodoxy Faces Dissent," *New York Times*, 3 October 2001, 14(A); David Horowitz, "In a time of War, the Left is on Trial," *Los Angeles Times*, 10 January 2005, 9(B).

44. The New York Times, "Protestors in Washington Urge Peace with Terrorists," 30 September 2001, 2(B).

45. Michael Kelly, "Pacifist Claptrap," *Washington Post*, 26 September 2001, 25(A).

46. Kevin Danaher, "Justice, Not War," *Washington Post*, 29 September 2001, 27(A).

47. Kurt Nimmo, "'Yes, We Censored News About Afghanistan': The Lapdog Conversion of CNN," *Counterpunch*, 23 August 2002, http://www.counterpunch.org/nimmo-082-3.html (4 Oct. 2005).

48. Jonathon Lawson and Susan Gleason, "True Democracy and the War on Dissent," *Z Magazine*, 2006, http://www.zmag.org/lawson.htm (2 Oct. 2005).

49. Alessandra Stanley, "Opponents of War are Scarce on Television," *New York Times*, 9 November 2001, 4(B).

50. Stanley, "Opponents of War," 2001.

51. Frank Rich, "The Swift Boating of Cindy Sheehan," *New York Times*, 21 August 2005, 4(D).

52. John Nichols, "Cindy Sheehan's Tragic Critics," *Nation*, 17 August 2005, http://www.thenation.com/blogs/thebeat?bid=1&pid=13737 (20 Aug. 2005).

53. Media Matters for America, "Conservatives, others in the media launch smear campaign against Cindy Sheehan," 17 August 2005, http://mediamatters.org/items/2005-0817-0008 (20 Aug. 2005).

54. Media Matters, "Conservatives, others in media launch smear campaign," 2005.

55. Farhad Manjoo, "After Cindy Sheehan," *Salon*, 19 August 2005, http://www.salon.-com/news/feature/2005/08/19/antiwar/index_np.html?x (21 Aug. 2005).

56. Rich, "Swift Boating of Cindy Sheehan," 2005.

57. Leonard Pitts Jr., "A Question that Deserves to be Answered," *Miami Herald*, 26 August 2005, http://www.miami.com/mld/miamiherald/living/columnists/leonard-pitts/12 481085.htm (27 Aug. 2005).

58. Cindy Sheehan, "Hypocrites and Liars," *Truthout*, 20 August 2005, http://www.truthout.org/docs_2005/082005X.shtml (23 Aug. 2005).

59. Christopher Hitchens, "What Cindy Sheehan Really Wants," *Slate*, 19 August 2005, http://slate.msn.com/id/2124788/ (19 Aug. 2005).

60. Editorial, "Turn Back to Iraq," *Washington Post*, 6 November 2004, 22(A).

61. Rita Cosby and Geraldo Rivera, *Fox News Live*, Fox News, 19 September 2004.

62. Lou Dobbs, *Lou Dobbs Tonight*, CNN, 21 September 2004.

63. Tony Snow and Lloyd Grove, *Weekend Live*, Fox News, 19 April 2003.

64. Chuck Roberts and Linda Stouffer, *CNN Headline News*, CNN, 24 January 2005.

65. *Outfoxed: Rupert Murdoch's War on Journalism*, DVD, directed by Robert Greenwald (The Disinformation Company, 13 July 2004).

66. John Plunkett, (2003, September 16). CNN Star Reporter Attacks War Coverage. *Guardian*, http://www.guardian.co.uk/iraqandthemedia/story/0,1282,1043342,00.html (15 Apr. 2007).

67. *Outfoxed*, Greenwald, 2004.

68. CNN.com, "Bill Press: Don't Let Terrorists Kill Free Speech," 9 October 2001, http://archives.cnn.com/2001/ALLPOLITICS/10/09/column.billpress/ (3 Aug. 2003).

69. Steve Rendall and Anna Kosseff, "I'm Not a Leftist, But I Play One on TV," *Fairness and Accuracy in Reporting*, October 2004, http://www.fair.org/index.php?page=196-9 (19 Aug. 2005).

70. FAIR, "Too Many Liberals?" 27 October, 2005, http:www.fair.org/index.php?page=2707 (16 Jan. 2006).

71. FAIR, "MSNBC's Double Standard on Free Speech," 7 March 2003, http://www.fair.org/activism/savage-donahue.html (3 Jul. 2005).

72. Associated Press, "MSNBC Fires Michael Savage after Anti-Gay Comments," *USA Today*, 7 July 2003, http://www.usatoday.com/news/nation/2003-07-07-talk-host-fired_x.htm (26 Jun. 2005).

73. FAIR, "Too Many Liberals?" 2005.

74. CNN.com, (2003, April 1). Just Fired, Peter Arnett Hired by British Paper. *CNN.com*, http://www.cnn.com/2003/WORLD/meast/03/31/sprj.irq.arnett/ (5 Jun. 2005).

75. Jim Rutenberg, "Battle Rages Between Fox News and MSNBC," *New York Times*, 3 April 2003, 6(C).

76. Patrick Martin, "Media Bosses Admit Pro-War Bias in Coverage of Iraq," *WSWS*, 2 May, 2003, http://www.wsws.org/articles/2003/may2003/med-m02.shtml (25 Mar. 2006).

77. Martin, "Media bosses," 2003.

78. PBS. (2003, March 31). PBS Newshour. *PBS News*, http://www.pbs.org/newshour/media/media_watch/jan-june03/arnett_3-31.html (5 Jun. 2005).

79. BBC, "U.S. network sacks top journalist," 1 April 2003, http://news.bbc.co.uk/2hi-/americas/2903503.stm (11 Dec. 2005).

80. CBS News, "CBS Ousts 4 for Bush Guard Story," 10 January 2005, http://www.cbsnews.com/stories/2005/01/10/national/printable665727.shtml (10 Jan. 2005).

81. CBS, "CBS Outs 4 for Bush Guard Story," 2005.

82. Howard Kurtz, "Rather Admits 'Mistake in Judgment," *Washington Post*, 21 September 2004, 1(A).

83. CBS News, "For the Record: Bush Documents," 20 September 2004, http://www.cbsnews.com/stories/2004/09/15/60II/main643768.shtml (21 Sep. 2004).

84. Hugh Aynesworth, "Bush Guard Papers 'Forged,'" *Washington Times*, 12 September 2004, http://washingtontimes.com/national/20040912-125608-4609r.htm (8 Oct. 2005).

85. Howard Kurtz, "Rather Admits 'Mistake in Judgment,'" *Washington Post*, 21 September 2004, 1(A).

86. Lois Romano, "Bush's Guard Service in Question," *Washington Post*, 8(A).

87. Romano, "Bush's Guard Service in Question," 2004.

88. Ralph Nader, "Why are Reporters Playing it Safe Where Bush is Concerned?" *Common Dreams*, 30 April 2005, http://www.commondreams.org/views05/0430-20.htm (30 Apr. 2005).

89. Juan Gonzales, "Broadcasting their Anti-Kerry Bias," *New York Daily News*, 12 October 2004, http://www.independent-media.tv/item.cfm?media_id=9368&fcategory_desc=Media%20Lies%20and%20Right%20Wing%20Bias (7 Jun. 2005).

90. Frank Ahrens and Howard Kurtz, "Anti-Kerry Film Won't Be Aired," *Washington Post*, 20 October 2004, 7(A).

91. John Nichols and Robert McChesney, *Tragedy & Farce: How the American Media Sell Wars, Spin Elections, and Destroy Democracy* (New York: New Press, 2006), 142.

92. Katie Benner, "Anti-Kerry Film Sparks DNC Response," 11 October 2004, *CNN*, http://money.cnn.com/2004/10/11/news/newsmakers/sinclair_kerry/?cnn=yes (5 May 2005).

93. Eric Boehlert, "Sinclair's Disgrace," *Salon*, 14 October 2004, http://www.truthout.org/docs_04/101604F.shtml (17 Oct. 2004).

94. Howard Kurtz, "Sinclair Fires Critic of Plan to Broadcast Anti-Kerry Film," *Washington Post*, 19 October 2004, 1(C).

95. CNN.com, "Sinclair Fires Reporter for Criticizing Anti-Kerry Program," 19 October 2004, http://www.cnn.com/2004/ALLPOLITICS/10/19/sinclair.kerry/ (21 Oct. 2004).

96. CBSnews.com, "Sinclair Journo Fired for Stand," 19 October 2004, http://www.cbsnews.com/stories/2004/10/19/politics/main650166.shtml (24 Oct. 2004).

97. CBSnews.com, "Sinclair Journo Fired for Stand," 2004.

98. Buzzflash, "Sinclair Broadcasting: A History of Partisan Politics," 20 October 2004, http://www.buzzflash.com/alerts/04/10/ale04070.html (26 Oct. 2004).

99. Ahrens and Kurtz, "Anti-Kerry Film Won't Be Aired," 2004.

100. Edward Jay Epstein, "Paranoia for Fun and Profit," *Slate*, 3 May 2005, http://www.slate.com/id/2117923/ (17 Dec. 2005).

101. Charlotte Higgins, "Fahrenheit 9/11 Could Light Fire under Bush," *Guardian*, 17 May 2004, http://www.guardian.co.uk/uselections2004/story/0,13918,1218376,00.html#-article_continue (13 Dec. 2005).

102. CBSnews.com, "Disney Blocks Anti-Bush Film," 5 May 2004, http://www.cbsnews.com/stories/2004/05/05/entertainment/main615648.shtml (12 Dec. 2005).
103. BBC, "I was Censored, Says Satirist Moore," 27 February 2002, http://news.bbc.co.uk/1/low/entertainment/arts/1844723.stm (14 Dec. 2005).
104. BBC, "I was Censored," 2002.
105. Epstein, "Paranoia for Fun and Profit," 2005.

7

A World of Orwellian Doublethink

"You cannot simultaneously prevent and prepare for war."
—Albert Einstein

"I just want you to know that, when we talk about war, we're really talking about peace."
—George W. Bush, June 18 2002

George Orwell once said that, "If liberty means anything at all it means the right to tell people what they do not want to hear."[1] These words were included in the original preface to the first edition of his classic work, *Animal Farm*. Orwell understood that freedom of speech, as well as the free exchange of conflicting ideas, are essential in a democratic society. It was the lack of concern with such freedoms, displayed amongst political and social elites, that Orwell was committed to fighting. Orwell encountered many difficulties in his attempts to communicate what were often considered unpopular political messages in his day. He was turned down by numerous publishers in his attempts to release *Animal Farm*, as the work, while finished in February of 1944, was not released until a full 18 months later. When the book was finally published, the preface was cut, as Orwell was put on the defensive in light of the popularity of the Soviet Union amongst the Allied powers at the end of World War II.

Orwell's suspicion of communist reactionaries and their sympathizers was confirmed after *Animal Farm* was released, as his work was subject to a number of negative criticisms by those who viewed it mainly as an attack on the Soviet Union. In anticipation of critical reviews, Orwell explained that, "At any given moment there is an orthodoxy, a body of ideas which it is assumed that all right-thinking people will accept without question. . . anyone challenging the prevailing orthodoxy finds himself silenced with surprising effectiveness. A genuinely unfashionable opinion is almost never given a fair hearing."[2] The same could be said today concerning the prevailing pro-war orthodoxy in the American mass media. Anti-war views rarely receive adequate attention in the preoccupation with "progress" in the Iraq war. Various opponents of government propaganda have been quieted in the media through the use of intimidation and punishment.

Orwell addressed many aspects of censorship that are still relevant today. Regarding the conscious choice to self-censor, Orwell states, "the chief danger to freedom of thought and speech. . . is not the direct interference of the [British] Ministry of Information or any official body. . . the sinister fact about literary censorship in England is that it is largely voluntary. Unpopular ideas can be silenced, and inconvenient facts kept dark, without the need for any official ban."[3] Orwell's warning is relevant in other capitalist democracies aside from Britain, especially when reflecting on the strength of self-censorship in the American press, as its corporate entities traditionally conform to conventional views supporting the Iraq war, while remaining outside the realm of direct government influence and control.

A Short Background

George Orwell was the pen name under which Eric Arthur Blair wrote his polemics and political literature. Although he only lived to be forty-six (1903—1950), Orwell made an invaluable contribution to the understanding of government and media propaganda. Orwell understood that imperialism was antithetical to democratization, which is why he dedicated his life and his literary career to opposing it. As has commonly been misunderstood about Orwell, his works did not merely target communist totalitarianism, but also took aim at the very heart of British imperialism and capitalist expansion and dominance. Books such as *Burmese Days*, *Animal Farm*, and *1984*, and essays such as *Shooting an Elephant*, *Rudyard Kipling*, and *Why I Write*, addressed the dangers of imperialism within the context of Soviet expansionism *and* European colonial dominance. In his essay on the English pre-fascist *Rudyard Kipling*, Orwell speaks with disdain of the economic forces that drive the quest for imperialist dominance, particularly in light of Kipling's "romantic ideas about England and the empire."[4] Condemning Kipling's coining of the "White Man's Burden," which rationalized colonial dominance with racist notions of European superiority, Orwell replied: "It is no use pretending that Kipling's view of life, as a whole, can be accepted by any civilised person. . . . Kipling is a jingo imperialist, he is morally insensitive and aesthetically disgusting."[5]

Orwell was blunt in his attacks on colonialism, which he considered to be a rather evil endeavor. As author and lecturer Christopher Hitchens states, Orwell's "writings on colonialism are an indissoluble part of his lifelong engagement with the subjects of power and cruelty and force, and the crude yet subtle relationship between the dominator and the dominated."[6] In his essay *Shooting an Elephant*, Orwell reflected on his experiences as a sub-divisional police officer in the town of Moulmein during the British occupation of Burma:

At that time I had already made up my mind that imperialism was an evil thing and the sooner I chucked my job and got out of it the better. Theoretically—and secretly, of course—I was all for the Burmese and all against their oppressors, the British. As for the job I was doing, I hated it more bitterly than I can perhaps make clear. In a job like that you see the dirty work of Empire at close quarters.[7]

As Hitchens explains, Orwell's support for "decolonization without conditions"[8] also encompassed other rising powers other than the British, as he understood the "imperial successor role that the U.S. was ambitious to play."[9] In this sense, it should be understood that the transition after World War II from colonial to neocolonial political power and dominance was a trend that did not escape Orwell's attention. As colonial acquisitions became more and more unpopular near the end of the war, it became clear that rising powers needed to find more indirect means of exerting their authority over newly emerging, weaker nation-states throughout the Third World.

Misrepresentations of Orwell

Seldom have novels been as misunderstood and misapplied on such a wide level as Orwell's works, *Animal Farm* and *1984*. Orwell's political writings have come to mean many things to many different people, and political thinkers of all stripes have attempted to co-opt his work in order to reinforce their political ideologies. As Andrew Anthony explains in the *Observer* of London, Orwell has "been adopted by just about every political colour in the spectrum, from revolutionary red to Little-England blue, from hard-core Trotskyites to gung-ho neoconservatives, from utopian anarchists to old-fashioned High Tories."[10] The use of *1984* in the quest to demonize Soviet bloc communism in favor of corporate capitalist expansion is a practice that Orwell surely would have appalled. As mentioned above, Orwell was an opponent of both state communism *and* capitalism—although he did consider himself a socialist. In the preface to the 1947 Ukrainian edition of *Animal Farm*, Orwell denounced those who viewed the Soviet Union as a force for economic justice and revolution: "Nothing has contributed so much to the corruption of the original idea of socialism as the belief that Russia is a socialist country and that every act of its rulers must be excused, if not imitated."[11]

In reviewing *1984*, it is necessary to establish that the work, highlighting a nightmare world of repression, empire, double standards, and power politics, encompassed the entire globe, rather than just the Soviet bloc. Out of the three totalitarian super-states in *1984*, Oceania should be of particular interest to the West in that it included the United States, Latin America, and the British Empire. The concept of "permanent war" is employed throughout *1984*, as each one of the three main superpowers, Oceania, Eurasia, and Eastasia, is continually changing alliances in an attempt to gain strategic dominance over the other two. In *1984*, the government of Oceania attempts to draw attention away from brutal and totalitarian repression at home by demonizing foreign enemies. This vilification of "enemies" is undoubtedly relevant within the context of the "War on Terror," particularly in reference to the countries labeled as part of the "Axis of Evil" by the Bush administration. The applicability of Orwell's tale of endless war has not been lost today in many understandings of the "War on Terror" which view the Bush administration as attempting to indoctrinate the public so as to justify aggressive and illegal war, as well as reinforce a permanent "War on Terror" with no clear end or exit plan in sight. In citing George Orwell, Nancy Snow, author of *Information War* and *Propaganda Inc.* claims: "The slogan 'war on terrorism' remains a convenient state tactic to control public opinion, expand the climate of fear, and shut down opposition to war in Iraq and elsewhere. . . to many, we live in a climate of fear that chills dissent from the state's declaration of war."[12]

Of course, government and media propaganda have always been essential in efforts to convince citizens within democracies of the veracity of officially espoused war aims. The war in Iraq is only the most recent in a longstanding effort on the part of the government and the media to portray the U.S. as unconditionally committed to spreading justice, freedom, human rights, and democracy throughout the globe. In this sense, the mass media serves its role well in deterring dissent directed against the war. While the media should obviously not be considered the direct equivalent of the government "thought police," in *1984*, the American media has performed a vital role in reinforcing the pro-war orthodoxy at the expense of radical anti-war criticisms. By marginalizing anti-war activists from public discourse, the mass media sends a clear message that coverage of dissent is not a priority if such views frame the U.S. government as a repressive and malicious force in world affairs. The negative responses to criticisms of the Iraq war discussed in chapter 6, including the Korean *Newsweek* "scandal," the smearing of Cindy Sheehan, the attempted censorship of Michael Moore, and the expulsion of Phil Donahue from *MSNBC*, reflect the larger trend of policing media discourse in favor of pro-war doctrines.

Numerous American and British corporate media outlets have used Orwell in their diatribes against the Left. *Time* and *Life* Magazine saw Orwell's work as an attack against the English labor party, ignoring the long-standing support Orwell had extended to it. Other conservative newspapers like the *Wall Street Journal* and the *Economist* saw *1984* primarily as anti-communist,[13] contrary to Orwell's original intentions. In his essay *Why I Write*, Orwell dispelled such misinterpretations, and confirmed his commitment to socialism, as he recounted that, "Every line of serious work I have written since 1936 has been written, directly or indirectly, *against* totalitarianism and *for* democratic socialism, as I understand it."[14] Orwell elaborated: "My recent novel is NOT intended as an attack on Socialism or on the British Labour Party (of which I am a supporter), but as a show-up of the perversions to which a centralized economy is liable and which have already been partly realized in Communism and Fascism. . . . I believe also that totalitarian ideas have taken root in the minds of intellectuals everywhere. . . The scene of the book is laid in Britain in order to emphasize that the English-speaking races are not innately better than anyone else and that totalitarianism, if not fought against, could triumph anywhere."[15]

Admitting that *1984* was meant to be taken as a parody, Orwell also warned readers about "the direction in which the world is going at the present time," as he considered the trend toward totalitarianism as something that increasingly "lies deep in the political, social, and economic foundations of the contemporary world system."[16] Orwell was referring in large part to the growing hostilities between the United States and the Soviet Union after World War II, the expansionist ambitions of both powers having laid the context for the Cold War period that lasted until the fall of the communist bloc in 1991. In his work, *George Orwell: A Life,* Bernard Crick discussed the possibility and danger of an East-West standoff characterized by increasingly repressive, dictatorial societies, in which the United States and the Soviet Union would be included. In appropriating the terminology of *1984,* Crick states that, through Orwell's paradigm:

> The two principal super states will obviously be the Anglo-American world and Eurasia. If these two great blocks line up as mortal enemies it is obvious that the Anglo-Americans will not take the name of their opponents and will not dramatize themselves on the scene of history as Communists. Thus they will have to find a new name for themselves. The name suggested in *Nineteen Eighty-Four* is of course Ingsoc, but in practice a wide range of choices is open. In the USA the phrase "American" or "hundred percent American" is suitable and the qualifying adjective is as totalitarian as any could wish.[17]

It is through the debunking of the myth of Orwell as an anti-socialist, pro-capitalist, that one must proceed if they are to gain a basic understanding of the ways in which Orwellian doublethink applies to the American government and corporate media's reliance on pro-war perspectives and propaganda.

Understanding Orwellian Doublethink

George Orwell first used the concept of "doublethink" in *1984,* although it is still relevant today in explaining contradictions in American government and media propaganda. Orwell defined doublethink as the reliance on inherently antagonistic thoughts in the construction of one's ideology. Orwell considered such antagonisms to include the main slogans of the government of Oceania, also known as "The Party," which were: "War is Peace," "Freedom is Slavery," and "Ignorance is Strength."[18] Orwell considered doublethink as the attempt "to hold simultaneously two opinions which cancel[led] out, knowing them to be contradictory and believing in both of them. . . to forget whatever it [is] necessary to forget, then to draw it back into memory again at the moment it [is] needed, and then promptly forget it again."[19] Through "reality control," propagandists are "conscious of complete truthfulness while telling carefully constructed lies."[20] In Oceania, it was the responsibility of the Ministry of Truth to propagandize and indoctrinate the public into believing in the contradictory promises and statements of the government. Winston Smith, the protagonist of *1984,* works for the Ministry of Truth, which controls the newspapers, television programs, and other media sources throughout Oceania.

Like the corporate media today, the Ministry of Truth played a vital role in attempting to erase controversial views that challenged official government positions and propaganda on issues related to war and peace. However, corporate media, operating in a democratic society, is not reliant on violent repression of dissidents; rather, those who vigorously challenge official justifications for war are typically weeded out through a pattern of verbal attacks and firings, and suppression and omission of controversial views. This is a major point of distinction that must be made between totalitarian societies as seen in *1984*, and democratic societies like the United States. Like the Ministry of Truth, the American mass media typically relies on the selective use of framing to portray government motives as unworthy of challenge. This has clearly been the case amongst more conservative media outlets such as *Fox News*, the *Washington Times*, and the *Weekly Standard*, as well as in liberal establishment sources. The crucial difference, though, that must be taken into account when considering the relationship between the Ministry of Truth and Oceania's government, as contrasted with the corporate media and its relationship with American government—is the form of ownership of the press. While the government directly controlled the ministries in 1984, corporate media has traditionally operated independently, outside the scope of direct official control. Noam Chomsky characterizes corporate media outlets as institutions, not owned by the government, but playing an important role in "controlling [public] opinions and attitudes." Chomsky declares: "these corporations are not just taking orders from the government but are closely linked to the government, of course":[21]

> the press faces powerful pressures that induce it, and often almost compel it, to be anything but free. After all, the mainstream media are part of the corporate sector that dominates the economy and social life. And they rely on corporate advertising for their income. This isn't the same as state control, but is nevertheless a system of corporate control very closely linked to the state.[22]

Orwell also spoke of the structural biases inherent in corporate ownership of the media in which Chomsky speaks. Identifying the narrow spectrum of thought in Britain's media, and discrediting the myth of a corporate "free press," Orwell commented that, "the degree of freedom of the press existing in this country is overrated. Technically there is great freedom, but the fact that most of the press is owned by a few people operates in much the same way as state censorship."[23] Such structural impediments to the exchange of a wider range of ideas concerning the legitimacy of the Iraq war inevitably limit the degree to which journalists pose questions challenging official wartime motives.

Orwell felt that corporate ownership was a main cause of censorship of controversial ideas. In his discussion of the limits of journalistic freedom, he wrote that, "Any writer or journalist who wants to retain his integrity finds himself thwarted by the general drift of society rather than by active persecution." Orwell was talking, among other trends, about "the concentration of the press in the hands of a few men," specifically in terms of "the grip of [the] monopoly on radio and the films" in his day.[24] Today, corporate media conglomeration has been shown at times to rely on doublethink to a degree that may have been unexpected even in Orwell's life. Corporate consolidation of the media has continued unabated in recent decades, as fewer and fewer corporations promote a monopoly, not only on media ownership, but on the very ideas that influence and shape public opinion in regards to the "War on Terror."

War is Peace:
The Myth of the Peaceful War Machine

Much of the doublethink in corporate reporting of the Iraq war could very well fit within the pages of Orwell's *1984*. The belief that wars of aggression can be fought in "self defense" is welcomed by U.S. leaders and by the media. The idea that the United States can pursue a large number of wars, one after another, always under the banner of "self-defense," has also been a main characteristic of military propaganda. One of the most poignant examples is illustrated in the 1947 name change of the "Department of War" into the "Department of Defense." In this case, Orwellian doublethink was effectively employed in order to mask expansionist ambitions under the justification of defending the U.S. from Soviet imperialism. Today, the doublethink "war is defense" ideology is applicable to the conflict in Iraq and beyond. The belief that "Operation Iraqi Freedom" was intended to protect Americans against weapons of mass destruction and the "threat" of a Baath Party-Al Qaeda alliance is an important part of this trend. Charles Weingartner remarks on the perception that increases in military spending are always and inherently "defensive" initiatives by explaining: "Everyone, including generals (at least publicly) is 'against' war":

> According to the military, we need to spend more and more money every year for weapons systems not to be prepared to conduct a war but to 'protect the peace.' This form of lunacy seems always to have been popular, but after almost forty years of media assisted training in paranoia, the American public now 'requires' any presidential candidate to vow a commitment to national defense.[25]

Doublethink in the "War on Terror" began with the Bush administration's portrayal of the United States as simultaneously committed to peace *and* permanent war. The contradictory trends were apparent from the beginning, even if many Americans chose not to notice, as President Bush characterized the U.S. is "a peaceful nation,"[26] while also explaining that, "Our war on terror begins with Al Qaeda, but it does not end there. It will not end until every terrorist group of global reach has been found, stopped and defeated."[27] The shock at the 9/11 terrorist attacks may very well have been enough to obscure this Orwellian framing, as many Americans seemed to ignore the long-term implications of Bush's plans for war without visible end in favor of the short-term goal of bringing the 9/11 attackers to justice. On the other hand, American perceptions seem to have changed to a significant degree as the "War on Terror" continues. As the war in Iraq progresses, many Americans wonder whether it is possible for Americans to live in peace while at the same time committing to a "War on Terror" with no concrete end in sight—a "war for peace" which may continue for decades to come.

While the Bush administration's plans for peace through war initially elicited few criticisms throughout much of the corporate press, media also relied on doublethink in framing the U.S. as committed to the "humanitarian bombing" of Afghanistan. *CNN* described "Operation Enduring Freedom" as "combining humanitarian action with a military campaign,"[28] specifically in reference to the 37,500 food packages that were dropped alongside cluster bombs in Afghanistan each day throughout October 2001 and after. The U.S. food drops of only two million packages (each of which could only feed one Afghan for one day), as U.S. leaders cut off U.N. food shipments to millions of Afghans, was not considered a major focus of reporting in terms of implicating the U.S. in massive human rights violations. For example, Tom Fenton of *CBS News* interviewed a soldier who praised the operation by explaining: "Your adrenaline starts pumping, and you know you're doing a good thing for your country—and you're doing a good thing for the people down below you."[29] Support for the "humanitarian" food drops coincided well with the rhetoric of President Bush, who congratulated himself for the United States' "charitable offer" to the Afghan people, explaining that: "the oppressed people of Afghanistan will know the generosity of America and our allies. As we strike military targets, we'll also drop food, medicine and supplies to the starving and suffering men and women and children of Afghanistan."[30]

What was largely ignored in the positive reporting of U.S. "generosity" was that the drops were *not* part of a humanitarian campaign, considering that U.S. bombing cut off food to millions of Afghans, while only supplying food to thousands. How such a program could be classified as humanitarian was challenged by many independent media outlets, which perceived the effort as a ploy on the part of the Bush administration and corporate media to transform potentially massive human rights violations into support for human rights. Conversely, independent American news outlets like Alternet linked the campaign to "Afghanistan's Coming Humanitarian Disaster."[31] Some foreign press outlets were quick to criticize the program as well, as George Monbiot of the *Guardian* of London clarified some of the misconceptions of American reporters concerning the extent of this "aid" program.

> If you believe, as some commentators do, that this is an impressive or even meaningful operation, I urge you to conduct a simple calculation. The United Nations estimates that there are 7.5 million hungry people in Afghanistan. If every ration pack reached a starving person, then one two hundredth of the vulnerable were fed by the humanitarian effort [for one day]. The US Department of Defense has announced that it possesses a further two million of these packs, which it might be prepared to drop. If so, they could feed 27 per cent of the starving for one day.[32]

Another use of Orwellian doublethink is evident in the mass media's framing of U.S. actions in Iraq as inherently "peaceful," in opposition to the violent actions of Iraq's guerilla resistance. The image of the U.S. as a peaceful superpower, its leaders hating war, yet spending over $400 billion dollars a year on the military, and retaining American military personnel in 80 percent of the countries throughout the world, and 725 bases in thirty-eight countries (as of 2004), is prevalent in the establishment press and elite intellectual culture.[33]

The "war is peace" doctrine has been repeatedly invoked in order to construct the myth of a "peaceful" nation that is forced into war. At the time of the invasion of Iraq in March 2003, *Newsweek* ran the headline: "How to Win the Peace,"[34] in an Orwellian attempt to portray American militarism and violence as peaceful endeavors. The use of the "war equals peace" doublethink approach reappeared in a report from James Cox of *USA Today*, entitled, "War Machine under Pressure to Produce Peace and Security."[35]

Numerous other examples follow those given above. In one such incident, Zidan Khalaf of the *Associated Press* described the attempts by the American army to pacify Iraqi guerilla groups as part of "the U.S. strategy to restore peace in Iraq."[36] The *Associated Press* did not consider this "peace strategy" as encompassing U.S. responsibility for the deaths of tens of thousands—and potentially over a hundred thousand—Iraqi men, women, and children, as has been suggested by a recent study printed in the British Lancet medical journal. The preoccupation with escalating the violence in the "counterinsurgency" campaign (at the expense of rebuilding Iraq's shattered infrastructure) was not a primary consideration when the *Associated Press* elaborated upon U.S. efforts to "restore peace" to Iraq. A similar pattern persevered throughout the bombing of Falluja in November, 2004—In which an estimated between 60 and 70 percent of the houses and buildings in Falluja were destroyed,[37] and during the Iraqi elections of January 2005. *CBS News* portrayed "the battle of Falluja" as "a turning point in the struggle by the United States and the Interim Iraqi Government of Prime Minister Iyad Allawi to consolidate the country and hold *peaceful* elections" [emphasis added].[38]

The goal of "bringing peace" to Iraq was not considered compromised by the widespread destruction visited upon Falluja and other major cities by the U.S. In the Orwellian tradition, major papers like the *New York Times* and the *Los Angeles Times* attempted to compensate for U.S. responsibility for the destruction of Falluja and the collapse of social order throughout Iraq, with such headlines as "After Leveling City, U.S. Tries to Build Trust" and "In City's Ruins, Military Faces New Mission: Building Trust."[39] In "building trust" amongst those from the city it had just destroyed, the U.S. was said to be concerned with "maintaining moral superiority in the minds of the populace by stressing that the fighting was the insurgents' fault," rather than the fault of the U.S.[40] Such pro-war propaganda demonstrated the lengths to which the American media's Orwellian language had reached. By focusing on the "hearts and minds" campaign of Marines in Falluja to woo residents and "build trust,"[41] after dispossessing hundreds of thousands of people, papers like the *Los Angeles Times* displayed a masterful stroke of doublethink propaganda, effectively exonerating the U.S. as the party responsible for destroying the city.

This pattern of Orwellian doublethink continued in the post-2005 election period. The *Washington Post's* editorials prescribed that "the new government [of Iraq] must clearly establish that violence will not be a means of political leverage in a democratizing Iraq,"[42] and that Iraq must "establish itself as a democracy that distributes power among its various communities through ballots rather than force."[43] The *Post's* comments were easily on par with such peculiar demands as those of former Deputy Defense Secretary Paul Wolfowitz that "all foreigners should stop interfering in the internal affairs of Iraq."[44] Such framing suggests that violence only exists if the U.S. is not the party responsible, and outside incursion only takes place when the U.S. is not a party to such activities. Within this doublethink framework, proponents of the occupation of Iraq rhetorically challenge violence and aggression only when the United States is not responsible. The Oceania government of *1984* would have embraced such double standards wholeheartedly.

Sometimes the media's Orwellian doublethink charged anti-war protestors with responsibility for the violence in Iraq and for supporting the 9/11 terrorist attacks. Take for example, one editorial by William Hawkins of the *Washington Times*, in which he condemned anti-war groups such as ANSWER, Global Exchange, and others. According to Hawkins, ANSWER

> was formed to oppose going into Afghanistan to destroy the main al Qaeda base and the Taliban regime that had given it a home. In effect, ANSWER wanted to protect the thugs behind the murder of 3,000 people in New York and Washington. This is the same view as the other main sponsor of the September 24 [2005 anti-war] rally, the group United for Peace and Justice [UFPI].

Citing UFPI and other anti-war organizations, Hawkins argued: "These groups are not coming to the nation's capital to promote 'peace.' They are aligned with the planet's most violent despots and killers. Like Mr. Bush, they understand what is at stake in Iraq and how important America's 'imperialist' power is to world stability and progress. They just want none of it, preferring a new Dark Age where America suffers precipitous decline in isolation and defeat."[45] Should readers take Hawkins' words seriously, they would be left with the impression that anti-war protestors somehow support and encourage Al Qaeda's war against the U.S., even though many were calling for the nonviolent apprehension of members of the terrorist network. One might also think that protestors are guilty of escalating the conflict in Iraq by opposing the necessary steps U.S. leaders planned on taking to escalate the "pacification" of Iraqi resistance. Hawkins' statements are important in that, along with many other pundits, he situates the war in Iraq within the "imperialist" framework of debate, while also dedicated to democracy and human rights.

Possibly Imminent War

Media doublethink has a primary audience in mind: the political, economic, and social elites responsible for formulating U.S. foreign policy. American elites must be aware, at least on some level, of the contradictions in such an imperial philosophy if they are to effectively obscure those contradictions when promoting official statements and propaganda. This should hardly be considered a "conspiracy theory" explanation, as individuals often attempt to reconcile their beliefs with conflicting realities. The trend is commonly noted in fields like Psychology in reference to the concept of "cognitive dissonance," where individuals hold two contradictory ideas or beliefs in their mind simultaneously.

Those promoting Media doublethink have attempted to straddle the line between unrealistic portrayals of current events described in government propaganda, and more realistic accounts of what is really happening in the world. One of the best examples of the effort to walk this fine line was seen in the media's treatment of the longstanding policy of members of the Bush administration to invade Iraq—a policy objective that spans back to well before Bush took office in 2000. In undertaking this balancing act, the *New York Times* warned of "*possibly imminent* military action against Iraq" [emphasis added] in the weeks before the invasion.[46] This problematic phrasing signified more than just bad use of language; it was representative of the media's attempts to reconcile two conflicting stories: the propaganda approach taken by the Bush administration, which claimed that war was a last option and that the U.S. would do everything possible to deter the need for an invasion, and the reality, that members of the Bush administration had long favored an attack on Iraq not only immediately after 9/11, but years before Bush took political office. It is clear that the Bush administration was committed to war with Iraq long before March 2003, as the Downing Street Memo and other political statements from former members of the Bush administration reveal.

Albert Einstein once said that, "a country cannot simultaneously prevent and prepare for war." Mass media outlets like the New York Times, which portrayed the U.S. as both intent on war and hopeful to prevent it, largely ignored this insight. The *New York Times* was supportive of the Bush administration's attempts to convince the American public that the war on Iraq was not a choice made by American leaders, but rather a decision forced upon the U.S. after countless patient efforts to resolve the weapons of mass destruction "threat" through peaceful overtures. Despite these efforts, it remained obvious to many who critically followed the pre-war political climate that the Bush administration had already decided to go to war with Saddam Hussein, and that the goal had always been to overthrow the Baath regime. This revelation is difficult to deny in light of the Blair administration's admission in July 2002 that "military action" was "now seen as inevitable."

Prominent figures such as Richard Clarke, the former White House Anti-Terrorism Chief, and Paul Wolfowitz, former Deputy Secretary of Defense, explained the long-term plans to attack Iraq in detail. Clarke recounted a conversation he had with Secretary of Defense Donald Rumsfeld shortly after the 9/11 attacks, in which Rumsfeld expressed his desire to use the attacks as a justification for bombing Iraq.[47] Wolfowitz also admitted that, in his meeting with Bush administration officials two days after 9/11, "On the surface of the debate it at least appeared to be about not *whether* but *when*" an attack on Iraq would take place [emphasis added].[48] These admissions were the opposite of President Bush's public promises, faithfully reported by media, that the President had "not made up" his mind about military action in the weeks before the attack,[49] and his claim that the war was somehow "forced upon" the U.S. contrary to the wishes of the Bush administration.[50]

Freedom is Slavery:
The Fallacy of Democratic Imperialism

A final use of Orwellian doublethink by media involves the admission of antagonistic policy goals in terms of U.S. motivations in Iraq. Establishment sources sometimes sent conflicting signals regarding what American leaders really wanted from war in Iraq. On the one hand, the media spoke in high regard of a "vision" of the Bush administration of ending the totalitarian rule of Saddam Hussein and imposing democracy in Iraq. On the other hand, from time to time it was lucidly admitted that the United States had selfish motivations outside of promoting justice and human rights. Considering such schizophrenic portrayals, it may be difficult for many readers to know which messages to take seriously and which to disregard. Sometimes it was admitted within the same news article that the U.S. was an imperialist power, yet also committed to democracy. Other times, readers were left to try and put together the pieces of a puzzle that did not seem to fit. For instance, what little polling was done of the Iraqi people consistently revealed a pattern of negative attitudes toward the U.S. occupation. Polling research showed that most Iraqis were overwhelmingly against American occupation by 2004, and that they viewed the U.S. as an occupier rather than a liberator.[51] Yet at the same time, corporate media outlets, by ignoring the implications of their own polling information, continued to promote the idea of the U.S. as a liberator and democratizer in Iraq. This antagonism has not sufficiently been addressed in media reporting, unless Americans are to understand that when U.S. elites discuss "democracy," they are really referring to U.S. coercion, dominance, and empire.

Why War?
The Strategic Importance of Oil

Schizophrenia was rife throughout media appraisals and reappraisals of the reasons for war. At times, media outlets portrayed the Bush administration as dishonest in its motives for war, while still lending strong support to its promises for the future democratization of Iraq. The *New Republic* effectively spearheaded this initiative with editorials such as "Best Intentions: Why We Went,

What We've Found." In the article, Fouad Ajami, while admitting that the U.S. has been guilty of human rights violations at places like Abu Ghraib, continued to support the war in deference to the humanitarian rhetoric of the President, congratulating U.S. "leaders [who] took up the sword against Arab-Muslim troubles and dared to think that tyranny was not fated and inevitable for the Arabs."[52] The message implicit in this editorial was that, despite the administration's ultimate responsibility for human rights violations in Iraq, its members still deserved the benefit of the doubt in their humanitarian attempts to transform Iraq for the better. Such a view was presented under the assumption that the acts at Abu Ghraib were not supported by the Bush administration, but rather the isolated acts of soldiers whose behavior was not representative of the policy goals of U.S. leaders. Ajami argued that, "there can be no doubting the nobility of the effort. Abu Ghraib isn't the U.S. war, but merely the failure of a small number of our soldiers to honor the mission entrusted to them."[53] Many critics of Abu Ghraib maintained the opposite in light of the Bush administration's circumvention of the Geneva Conventions' protections of POWs during the war in Afghanistan, as well as other efforts of the Bush administration (noted in chapters 6 and 8), to ignore or downplay human rights violations on the part of the U.S. military.

Fareed Zakaria of *Newsweek* speaks of "a Jekyll-and-Hyde problem" in which the Bush administration "has wholeheartedly embraced the view that America must change its image in the Muslim world. It wants to stop being seen as the supporter of Muslim tyrants and instead become the champion of Muslim freedoms." At the same time, Zakaria admits that the administration has also subscribed to a "warrior ethos that believes in beating up bad guys without much regard for such niceties as international law."[54] Zakaria espouses a grand transformation in which the U.S. wants to shed its image amongst many critics as an oppressor, while also continuing its support of despotic regimes throughout the region, such as the Saudi royal family and the Egyptian government of Hosni Mubarak, among numerous others. The tension clearly evident here between espoused humanitarian goals and realist support for repressive leaders is unsurprisingly ignored in most media commentary.

Doublethink also encompasses specific admissions in the media that U.S. policy, at its core, is driven by a desire for economic domination, most notably seen in the concern with Iraq's oil reserves, which are amongst the largest in the world. A full seven months before the war started, the *Wall Street Journal* speculated over "the possibility of a long-term bonanza" for U.S. oil companies "in a region [the Middle East] that contains about two-thirds of the world's proven oil reserves, but is still largely closed to western companies." A preferable scenario for American companies, according to the *Wall Street Journal*, would entail a return to "A pro-American Iraqi government" that "keeps the country stable and united, opens up to Western companies, and starts raising oil output."[55] At about the same time, the *Washington Post* also drew attention to the "importance of Iraq's oil," as well as the possibility that "A U.S. led ouster of Saddam Hussein could open a bonanza for American oil companies long ban-ished from Iraq, scuttling oil deals between Baghdad and Russia, France, and other countries."[56]

It may be that the perception amongst many in the American media is that implanting democracy in Iraq is tantamount to privatizing or dominating Iraq's oil reserves and placing them under the jurisdiction and management of Western corporations. David Ignatius of the *Washington Post* combines these two antagonistic ideas (between democracy promotion and foreign control of Iraqi oil) in one of his columns, as he speaks favorably about the "unambiguously positive developments" of the Iraq invasion, in which surrounding Arab countries proposed to assist the U.S. by "send[ing] troops to protect Iraq's oil fields" during the U.S. occupation.[57] That the pursuit of oil could be pursued alongside humanitarian objectives was considered an axiom unworthy of question for those who allude to imperial interests. Columnists like Ignatius, for instance, cheered the U.S. for toppling "The region's most ruthless and feared dictator. . . his people gone from cowering at his seemingly magical powers to taunting his ghost,"[58] while concurrently celebrating U.S. administration of Iraqi oil.

Empire as Democracy

Some pundits throughout the media attempted to re-conceptualize imperialism as a force for good, rather than one of repression. Conservative Op-Ed writer Max Boot of *USA Today* claimed there was "no need to run away" from the label of American imperialism. Boot contended that, "In [the] contest for control of Iraq, America can outspend and outmuscle any competing faction." Since U.S. imperialism "has been the greatest force for good in the world during the past century" maintaining this position of prestige will "require selecting a new [Iraqi] ruler who is committed to pluralism, and then backing him or her to the hilt." Since "Iran and other neighboring states won't hesitate to impose their despotic views on Iraq; we shouldn't hesitate to impose our democratic views."[59] To Boot, democracy necessarily means the imposition of American military force and occupation on the Iraqi people. Boot is a strong proponent of the idea that pacification and occupation are a vital part of the reconstruction and rehabilitation of Iraq after over two decades of destruction and war. U.S. occupation and dominance, then, is something that is vital in ensuring pluralist democracy and national self-determination.

The naïve image of the right-wing, power-hungry imperialist who openly acknowledges malicious aspirations for world domination should be shed in favor of a more nuanced view which recognizes that both mainstream liberals and conservatives see imperialism as the desirable means and ends of U.S. foreign policy in terms of promoting democracy *and* ensuring hegemony. Aside from neoconservatives like Max Boot, John Lewis Gaddis, a professor of Political Science at Yale University, argues in the *New York Times* that the United States has "always had an empire. The thinking of the founding fathers was we were going to be an empire. Empire is as American as apple pie in that sense. The question is, what kind of an empire do we have? A liberal empire? A responsible empire?[60] The *New York Times* has occasionally been quite clear about the Bush administration's imperial plans for the Middle East, despite its editorial and reporting biases in favor of "liberating" Iraq. In one report, the paper described the importance of the "new influence" within the Middle East envisaged by the Bush administration, as it quoted one senior official who claimed: "What you are seeing is an impressive demonstration of American will and American capability." Some of President Bush's closest aides remarked within the article that the war "was about far more than just Iraq," in that it sought to demonstrate to the world that "the United States would never allow American military supremacy to be challenged in the way it was during the Cold War."[61]

Editorial content sometimes reinforced the same brazen commitment to power politics. In one example, Bill Keller, Executive Director of the *New York Times*, announced his support of the invasion of Iraq, since Saddam Hussein had "brazenly defied us and made us seem weak and vulnerable, an impression we can ill afford."[62] While such comments effectively spelled out the American formula for imperialism in the post-9/11 political atmosphere, widespread condemnation of such plans throughout the mainstream press were absent. Throughout the Iraq war, the media's reaction has been one of jubilation in terms of celebrating American democratic intentions. National newspapers favorably report the goals of occupation in terms of "promoting stability" and self-determination, and local papers have largely adapted to the discourse set in the national agenda-setting media. The U.S., then, is not considered a part of the problem in Iraq, but part of the solution. American leadership is a virtue, which must be nurtured, rather than attacked or ridiculed. In the wake of the invasion of Iraq, the *New York Times* reported on this role in greater detail, explaining the danger of developments in which "the [Middle East] region is testing American leadership in ways that would tax any administration."[63] The story referred to bombings in Saudi Arabia, in which Al Qaeda took credit for, as well as the alleged threat of Iran to U.S. national security.

As Andrew Bacevich depicted the invasion of Iraq in the *Los Angeles Times*: "Force has emerged as [the] preferred instrument of American policy. By initiating hostilities without explicit United Nations sanction and despite fierce opposition abroad, it [the U.S.] has shown that when it comes to using force, the world's sole superpower insists upon absolute freedom of action."[64] The understanding of American imperial ambitions was not relegated to "conspiracy theorists" in the dissident press. Conservative commentators such as William Kristol of the *Weekly Standard* bluntly announced that, "we need to err on the side of being strong. And if people want to say we're an imperial power, fine."[65] The "might makes right" philosophy of American military power had found a welcome home with a number of pundits and columnists in the mainstream press, liberal, centrist, and conservative.

Ignorance is Strength:
The Power of Propaganda in Modern Times

Orwell believed that political speech and writing in modern times "are largely the defence of the indefensible. Things like the continuance of British rule in India, the Russian purges and deportations, the dropping of the atom bombs on Japan, can indeed be defended, but only by arguments that are too brutal for most people to face."[66] Within the context of the invasions of Afghanistan and Iraq, rationalizations of American power politics often promoted contradictory notions that the U.S was fighting simultaneously for democracy and imperialism. Public support for the war could never have been so high without the Bush administration and media's promotion of the idea that the U.S. is democratizing Iraq by removing the dictatorship of Saddam through "shock and awe" and prolonged occupation. And while Orwellian framing of U.S. actions in Iraq may be inevitable amongst delusional political elites, such "understandings" of the nature of U.S. foreign policy are not necessarily shared by the general public. This reality will become more apparent in further discussions of American public opinion explored at length in Chapter 8.

Notes

1. George Orwell, *Animal Farm: A Fairy Story* (New York: Harcourt Brace, 1995), 171.
2. Orwell, *Animal Farm*, 163.
3. Orwell, *Animal Farm*, 162.
4. George Orwell, "Rudyard Kipling," in *A Collection of Essays by George Orwell* (Garden City, NY: Doubleday, 1954), 126, 129.
5. Orwell, *A Collection of Essays by George Orwell*, 123-24.
6. Christopher Hitchens, *Why Orwell Matters* (New York: Basic, 2002), 28.
7. George Orwell, "Shooting an Elephant," in *A Collection of Essays by George Orwell* (Garden City, NY: Doubleday, 1954), 155.
8. Hitchens, *Why Orwell Matters*, 28.
9. Hitchens, *Why Orwell Matters*, 34.
10. Andrew Anthony, "Orwell: the Observer Years," *Observer*, 11 May 2003, http://books.guardian.co.uk/departments/classics/story/0,6000,953217,00.html (4 Feb. 2006).
11. Jeffrey Meyers, *Orwell: A Wintry Conscience of a Generation* (New York: W. W. Norton, 2000), 245.
12. Nancy Snow, "Opinion Control on the Next War in Iraq," *Nancysnow.com*, 2006, http://www.nancysnow.com/infowar_excerpt.htm (12 Jun. 2006).
13. Bernard Crick, *George Orwell: A Life* (London: Secker and Warburg, 1980), 394.
14. George Orwell, "Why I Write," in *A Collection of Essays by George Orwell* (Garden City, NY: Doubleday, 1954), 318.
15. Sonia Orwell and Ian Angus, "Letter to Francis A. Henson (Extract)," in *The Collected Essays, Journalism and Letters of George Orwell: 1945-1950, Vol. 4* (New York: Hancourt, Brace, & World, 1968), 502.
16. Crick, *George Orwell: A Life*, 395.

17. Crick, *George Orwell: A Life*, 395.

18. George Orwell, *1984* (New York: Penguin, 1987), 6.

19. Orwell, *1984*, 37.

20. Orwell, *1984*, 37.

21. Noam Chomsky and David Barsamian, *Imperial Ambitions: Conversations on the Post 9/11 World* (New York: Metropolitan, 2005), 22.

22. Chomsky and Barsamian, *Imperial Ambitions*, 152.

23. Sonia Orwell and Ian Angus, "Freedom of the Park," in *The Collected Essays, Journalism and Letters of George Orwell: 1945-1950, Vol. 4* (New York: Hancourt, Brace, & World, 1968), 38.

24. Sonia Orwell and Ian Angus, "The Prevention of Literature," in *The Collected Essays, Journalism and Letters of George Orwell: 1945-1950, Vol. 4* (New York: Hancourt, Brace & World, 1968), 60.

25. Charles Weingartner, "What do we Know?" in *Beyond Nineteen Eighty-Four: Doublespeak in a Post-Orwellian Age*, ed. William Lutz (Urbana, Il.: National Council of Teachers of English, 1989), 34.

26. George W. Bush, "Presidential Address to the Nation," *White House Website*, 7 October 2001, http://www.whitehouse.gov/news/releases/2001/10/20011007-8.html (13 Jan. 2007).

27. George W. Bush, "Address to a Joint Session of Congress and the American People," *White House Website*, 20 September 2001, http://www.whitehouse.gov/news/release/2001/09/20010920-8.html (10 Jan. 2007).

28. CNN.com, "Agencies Question Afghan Aid Drops," 9 October 2001, http://archives.cnn.com/2001/WORLD/europe/10/09/gen.aid.agencies/ (5 Nov. 2006).

29. Seth Ackerman, "Afghan Famine On and Off the Screen," *Extra!* May/June 2002, http://www.fair.org/extra/0205/afghan-famine.html (11 Jun. 2006).

30. George W. Bush, "Presidential Address to the Nation," 2001.

31. Tamara Straus, "Afghanistan's Coming Humanitarian Disaster," *Alternet*, 12 October 2001, http://www.alternet.org/story/11704/ (10 Jan. 2007).

32. George Monbiot, "Folly of Aid and Bombs," *Guardian*, 9 October 2001, http://www.guardian.co.uk/Archive/Article/0,4273,4273413,00.html (10 Jan. 2007).

33. Chalmers Johnson, *The Sorrows of Empire: Militarism, Secrecy, and the End of the Republic* (New York: Henry Holt, 2004), 154.

34. Fareed Zakaria, "How to Win the Peace," *Newsweek*, 21 April 2003, 38.

35. James Cox, "War Machine under Pressure to Produce Peace and Security," *USA Today*, 11 April 2003, 1(A).

36. Ziad Khalaf, "U.S., Iraqi Officials Declare Success in Samarra Assault," *San Francisco Chronicle*, 2 October 2004, http://www.sfgate.com/cgi- bin/article.cgi?f=newsbin/-article.cgi?f=news/archive/2004/10/02/international1639EDT0565.DTL (11 Jan. 2007).

37. Joseph Kay, "Fallujah Residents Return to a Destroyed City," *World Socialist Website*, 30 December 2004, http://www.wsws.org/articles/2004/dec2004/fall-d30.shtml (9 Jan. 2007).

38. Tom Fenton, "High Stakes Showdown in Fallujah," *CBSnews.com*, 8 November 2004, http://www.cbsnews.com/stories/2004/10/18/opinion/fenton/main649837.shtml (8 Nov. 2004).

39. Tony Perry, "After Leveling City, U.S. Tries to Build Trust," *Los Angeles Times*, 7 January 2005, 3(A); Dexter Filkins, "In City's Ruins, Military Faces New Mission: Building Trust," *New York Times*, 16 November 2004, 10(A).

40. Perry, 2005.

41. Perry, 2005.

42. Editorial, "Iraq's Election," *Washington Post*, 30 January 2005, 6(B).

43. Editorial, "Don't Postpone Elections," *Washington Post*, 30 November 2004, 18(A).

44. Russell Mokhiber, "Scottie & Me," *Common Dreams*, 29 July 2003, http://www.commondreams.org/scottie/0729-11.htm (12 Aug. 2005).

45. William Hawkins, "Promoting Worldwide Defeat," *Washington Times*, 22 September 2005, http://www.washtimes.com/commentary/20050921-093438-2631r.html (22 Sep. 2005).

46. Felicity Barringer and David E. Sanger, "President Readies U.S. for Prospect of Imminent War," *New York Times*, 7 March 2003, 1(A).

47. Richard Clarke, *Against All Enemies* (New York: Free Press, 2004), 31.

48. Jason Leopold, "Wolfowitz Admits Iraq War Planned Two Days After 9-11," *Independent Media TV*, 1 August 2003, http://www.independent-media.tv/item.cfm?fmedia _id=1917&fcategory_desc=Paul%20Wolfowitz (25 Oct. 2005).

49. George W. Bush, "President George Bush Discusses Iraq in National Press Conference," *White House Website*, 6 March 2003, http://www.whitehouse.gov/news/releases/2-003/03/20030306-8.html (25 Oct. 2005).

50. George W. Bush, "State of the Union Address," *White House Website*, 28 January 2003, http://www.whitehouse.gov/news/releases/2003/01/20030128-19.html (25 Oct. 2005).

51. Associated Press, "Public Opinion in Iraq: First Poll Following Abu Ghraib Revelations," *MSNBC.com*, 14-23 May 2004, http://www.msnbc.com/id/5217741/site/newsweek/ (25 Oct. 2005).

52. Fouad Ajami, "Best Intentions: Why We Went, What We've Found," *New Republic*, 28 June 2004, http://www.tnr.com/doc.mhtml?i=20040628&s=ajami062804 (20 Jul. 2005).

53. Ajami, "Best Intentions," 2004.

54. Fareed Zakaria, "Uncle Sam: Jekyll or Hyde?" *Newsweek*, 6 June 2005, 33.

55. Bhushran Bahree, "Oil Industry Ponders Iraq Risks," *Wall Street Journal*, 30 August 2003, 7(A).

56. Dan Morgan and David B. Ottaway, "In Iraqi War Scenario, Oil is Key Issue," *Washington Post*, 15 September 2002, 1(A).

57. David Ignatius, "Regime Change's Regional Ripples," *Washington Post*, 10 April 2003, 25(A).

58. Ignatius, 2003.

59. Max Boot, "American Imperialism? No need to run away from the label," *USA Today*, 5 May 2003, http://www.usatoday.com/news/opinion/editorials/2003-05-05-boot_x.htm (13 Aug. 2005).

60. John L. Gaddis, "Kill the Empire! (Or Not)," *New York Times*, sec. 7, 25 July 2004, 23.

61. David E. Sanger and Steven R. Weisman, "Bush's Aides Envision New Influence in Region," *New York Times*, 10 April 2003, 11(B).

62. Bill Keller, "The Boys Who Cried Wolfowitz," *New York Times*, 14 June 2003, 15(A).

63. Steven R. Weisman, "The Mideast Thicket," *New York Times*, 17 May 2003, 1(A).

64. Andrew J. Bacevich, "The Nation at War: Force has Emerged as Preferred Instrument of American Policy," *New York Times*, 20 March 2003, 17(B).

65. Maureen Dowd, "Hypocrisy and Apple Pie," *New York Times*, 30 April 2003, 27(A).

66. George Orwell, "Politics and the English Language," in *A Collection of Essays by George Orwell* (Garden City, NY: Doubleday, 1954), 173.

8

Doctrines of Media and State: Hailing Humanitarianism, Dismissing Disaster

On January 9, 2006, *U.S. News & World Report* published an issue featuring an update on the progress of the United States in its occupation of Iraq. What seemed most relevant about this report was not so much how different or unique it was from other news stories coming out at the time, but how similar it was to the rest mainstream reporting in terms of the uniform promotion of the dangers of Iraqi "insurgency" and the importance of American heroism in Iraq. The *U.S. News* edition ran a number of stories discussing topics such as "insurgent" violence and "evolving American military tactics," and the 2005 parliamentary elections in the midst of re-emerging sectarian violence between Iraqi Shiite, Sunni, and Kurdish political and military groups.[1]

As one story indicated, the pacification of Iraqi resistance forces was getting much more difficult in light of the growth of violence directed at the U.S. occupation. In a piece entitled "Cracking an Insurgent Cell" Julian Barnes reported that "finding—and breaking—the ruthless killers of Iraq is not a pretty business," as the report provided "an exclusive look at how it's done."[2] Barnes' article, emphasizing "counter-insurgency" tactics, was printed alongside a picture of Iraqi soldiers as they detained two "insurgents" who appeared to be begging the officers, perhaps to be released from custody. The printing of the picture represented a clever use of imagery, as it reframed the conflict from one between American soldiers and guerilla resistance to one between Iraqi security forces and "insurgents" in the struggle for democracy and stability. The image of the two Iraqi soldiers, in a position of power over rebel forces, seemed to suggest that Iraqis were taking over security operations from the United States, thereby implying a homegrown legitimacy to the entire U.S. project in Iraq.

The magazine's cover displayed a more "human" side to the conflict, as it featured a picture of Jonathan Fox, an American soldier, who spoke with Iraqi children in a slum in Western Mosul. Inside the issue readers could see pictures of confiscated weapons and American troops cruising through Mosul on patrol with large caliber machine guns pointing into the blurred background. As is standard in much pro-military propaganda and reporting, the paper's aim was undoubtedly the promotion of a positive image of the American armed forces. In its chronicling of U.S. military operations in Mosul, the magazine's imagery reflected a sort of dual role for the armed forces—one of heroism, where American soldiers tirelessly fight secret terrorist threats, and another of compassion, where those same soldiers also take the time to play the role of friend to Iraqi children.

Aside from the valiant image of the war promoted within the paper, other portrayals were to follow. In assessing the U.S. plans for Iraq's future, Barnes wondered in one of the stories: "How should Americans balance winning the war against the insurgency with maintaining its image and values? And how should American soldiers balance letting the indigenous police and Army do things their way while making sure they comply with western standards."[3] As this statement indicated, the assumption of American paternalism was alive and well within the pages of U.S. News & World Report. This was perhaps best seen when the magazine spoke of "letting" the police and army work, while assuring that they "comply" with the Bush administration's standards, demands, and expectations, rather than those put in place by the Iraqi citizenry.

The issue of U.S. News & World Report was not selected for analysis because of its uniqueness when compared to other mainstream reporting, but because of its symbolism of a uniform trend in the American mass media of emphasizing U.S. humanitarianism and downplaying the arguments of those who argue that the U.S. is inducing humanitarian disaster in Iraq. Chapter Four extensively analyzed the many ways in which the United States is portrayed as a necessary, democratic, and stabilizing agent in Iraq. This chapter looks at arguments that the U.S. is responsible for escalating humanitarian disaster in Iraq. Addressing such views, regardless of how controversial some may consider them, is essential if the objective of media coverage is a full and rich debate over war. Traditional patterns of pro-war propaganda are analyzed throughout, alongside counter arguments made by those who present anti-war views. Mainstream media emphasizes a number of assumptions regarding occupied Iraq; these include: the importance of reconstruction, the construction of the image of a clean war against the "insurgency," and the assumption that the U.S. is committed to democracy enhancement in Iraq. Standard arguments repeated throughout the press mandate acceptance of the thesis that the U.S. is determined to rejuvenate the Iraqi state after years of war and sanctions. This chapter, however, takes an in-depth look at other views promoted in Progressive-Left media sources, which argue that torture, widespread destabilization, and the killing of tens of thousands (possibly hundreds of thousands) Iraqi civilians are major consequences of U.S. intervention.

Despite the persistence of elections, the U.S. remains very much in a position of authority in Iraq, as American media and establishment elites continually reaffirm the legitimacy of the United States' self-imposed role in regulating Iraqi political affairs. Such dominance is evident in a number of examples, such as when the administration began to push for neoliberalization of Iraq through the passing of the Bremer Laws (2003), as well as the introduction of an Iraqi law (which was passed by the Iraqi Parliament in 2007, but drafted largely in the United States) which allows for the partial privatization of Iraqi oil through the use of Production Sharing Agreements (PSAs).

Such paternalistic dominance was also evident in recent political developments, such as the Bush administration's pressuring of former Prime Minister Ibrahim a-Jaafari not to seek a second term, and the domineering negative appraisals of Prime Minister Nouri al-Maliki, as seen in a memo from National Security Advisor Stephen Hadley. The memo, faulting Maliki for the growth of sectarian violence in Iraq, spoke of the possibility that the U.S. might need to push for the reconfiguration of Iraq's parliament. It also expressed displeasure with Maliki's performance, wondering whether the U.S. and Maliki "share the same vision for Iraq," and judging that Maliki may not be "willing and able to rise above the sectarian agendas being promoted by others."[4]

The Construction of a Clean War

Perspectives criticizing the one-sided coverage of civilian casualties in Iraq seldom receive serious attention throughout media reporting, although there are a few important exceptions. One such exception was an episode of *Oprah Winfrey* aired on January 23 2006. Oprah's guests included Peter Bergen, terrorism expert and author of *Holy War Inc., Inside the Secret World of Osama bin Laden*, *CNN* Correspondent Michael Holmes, and Thomas Friedman, author and Op-Ed writer for the *New York Times*, among others.[5]

The guests shared many similarities in their support for U.S. policy in Iraq, and in their absence of bedrock challenges to the administration's central war claims. Friedman has long been known as a proponent of war and occupation, as was made apparent in analysis of his *New York Times* Op-Eds in chapter 4. Michael Holmes was intent to focus primarily on the "terror attacks. . . on American invaders," in contradiction to the traditional definition of terrorism as attacks on civilians rather than military targets. Perhaps the most critical perspective on this program, however, was that of Bergen, who spent the most time discussing the failure to make Iraqi civilian casualties a serious subject of criticism in the United States' media. In questioning Bergin, Oprah wondered why American media networks and papers traditionally shy away from discussing Iraqi civilian casualties, while American military casualties are meticulously documented. In contrasting *CNN International* (which has generally taken a more balanced approach to reporting both Iraqi and American casualties) with *CNN* in the United States, Oprah's question was an important one for a journalistic system that is known to place more of an emphasis on American casualties. In general, Bergen agreed with Oprah that the American press has reported casualties in a lopsided manner, asserting that the escalation of Iraqi deaths was one of the reasons why the U.S. is "not liked" by many Iraqis. Bergen felt that that the failure of Americans to become better informed about such Iraqi casualties was likely part of the reason for escalating hostility against the U.S. occupation.

Critics abroad have made similar criticisms of the lack of American concern with Iraqi casualties. Kim Sengupta from the *Independent* of London, for example, explained that the Bush administration was responsible for "having ignored the civilian casualties which would inevitably result from such a military operation [in Iraq]," as "the U.S. government appeared to be oblivious to the likely international consequences around the world of women and children being killed."[6]

The Story of Jessica Lynch

On April 14 2003, *Newsweek* ran a feature story about the "rescue" of Private Jessica Lynch from an Iraqi hospital in Nasiriya. The story was important, if for no other reason, because it put a human face on a conflict in a far away land. Titled "Saving Private Lynch," the story intended to draw a comparison between the Iraq war and World War II. The title was borrowed from the film "Saving Private Ryan," where Matt Damon's character is saved by Tom Hanks from certain death during an extended battle with Nazi forces. American media outlets generally presented a picture of Jessica Lynch as a captive of hostile Iraqi forces who also needed to be saved.

In its inside story, *Newsweek* spoke of "Jessica's Liberation," as "Special forces execute[d] a bold raid to save a private" who was allegedly under the captivity of enemy forces. In entering the Iraqi town of Nasiriya, "One detachment of Marines made a diversionary attack on another part of the city, while the main force landed at the hospital and began searching for Lynch."[7] The picture in *Newsweek* showed Lynch "On her way to safety" away from the hospital. The story referred to her as "the first U.S. prisoner to be rescued from behind enemy lines since World War II." The *Washington Times* reported that the Lynch operation "marked the first time in decades that Special Operations Forces had penetrated enemy lines and rescued a prisoner of war."[8] George Bush was reported to be "full of joy because of her rescue and full of pride because of her rescuers" although there were still "unsettling questions about Lynch's condition and her treatment in captivity."[9] A large number of news outlets repeated allegations that Iraqi soldiers abused Lynch during her captivity.

The Jessica Lynch story, as covered in mainstream news sources, is significant because it demonstrates how important facts are lost in the frenzy to cover wartime stories and when media outlets are pressured to climb on board in favor of an administration's propaganda. On a factual level, the story of Lynch's "rescue" from the "hostile" hospital personnel was shown to be inaccurate. Evidence later suggested that Lynch was not in danger when at the hospital, as she had been taken care of by a number of Iraqi doctors who attended to her wounds and aided in her recovery. Even Lynch herself later admitted that she felt the U.S. military "overdramatized" her evacuation from the hospital. *CNN* eventually reported, in contradiction to earlier stories that "the hospital staff said no Iraqi troops were in the hospital at the time [of her "rescue"]—and that they had unsuccessfully tried to turn Lynch over to American soldiers earlier." Lynch also told Diane Sawyer of *ABC*—contrary to earlier reports in the media—that she did not recollect ever being raped or being beaten during her stay in the hospital.[10]

Anti-war critics (Iraqi and American alike) have drawn upon the news coverage of Jessica Lynch as an example of the focus on American lives to the neglect of Iraqi deaths. One Iraqi interviewed by Cliff Kindy of the human rights group *Christian Peacemaker Teams* (*CPT*), asked why Americans hold Iraqi life so lightly. As one of the doctors stationed at the Nasiriya hospital, he had worked to take care of Jessica Lynch, only to witness invading troops treat hospital staff as if they were threatening Lynch's life. This, according to the doctor, stood in glaring contrast to the way American troops treated his nephew, who he explained had been killed at an American checkpoint. The man's nephew was shot during a sudden backup of highway traffic as he approached the military checkpoint. In hoping to avoid crashing into the cars in front of him, he swerved out of the line of traffic, and was killed by American troops who feared he was a suicide bomber. The young man's family later accused American soldiers of having "lost" the body so that there would be no way to prove they had made a mistake. Sadly, this Iraqi's story (in addition to thousands of others) have not received coverage anywhere near that of American troops who lose their lives in Iraq.

Throughout the Iraq war, establishment papers like the *New York Times* and *Washington Post* provide regular updates of American troop casualty counts, while neglecting a similar accounting of Iraqi civilian deaths. As Anthony Marro, an editor for *Newsday* admits: "We pay more attention to Americans deaths" than those of Iraqis.[11] "It is easier to report on people we know, we put more faces of the Americans, we know who they are." To be sure, it is easier for the American military (and the media) to verify the exact number of American military deaths as opposed to those of Iraqi civilians. However, the coverage of *CNN International* and *Al Jazeera* are clear cases of another standard amongst media channels seeking to present *both* Iraqi and American casualties with greater frequency. Specials like "Faces of the Fallen" and "Fallen Heroes" as seen in outlets like the *Washington Post* and *Fox News*, honor American servicemen and women without asking about the Iraqi civilian death toll. While the "Faces of the Fallen" are often shown in print and on television, gory images of those killed in combat are limited in the American press.

Statistical studies of television media coverage reinforce a pattern of discomfort with running bloody pictures of the casualties of war. A study by George Washington University's *School of Media and Public Affairs* analyzed 600 hours of news segments on *Fox News*, *ABC*, and *CNN* from March 20 through April 9, 2003, revealing that just 13.5 percent of the over 1,700 stories examined contained pictures of dead or wounded coalition soldiers, Iraqi soldiers, or civilians. Less than 4 percent of the over 500 images of combat contained dead civilians or soldiers.[12] Another study reviewing a six-month period following the 2003 U.S. invasion found that, of five major American newspa-

184   Chapter 8

pers, none printed a picture of a dead serviceman/woman, despite the fact that
559 American and allied forces died within that same period.[13]

Downsizing Civilian Casualties

Despite emphasizing American deaths, the American media has at times printed
information on the Iraqi death tolls. For example, the *Associated Press*, after
reviewing statistics gathered by Iraqi hospitals, police, military and government
officials, concluded in late 2005 that as many as 3,663 Iraqis were killed in the
previous six months.[14] Reports like this, however, are more the exception than
the norm, as coverage of Iraqi deaths is sparse and sporadic when compared to
more common coverage of American deaths. During the invasion of Iraq, major
American newspapers printed deceptive, flagrantly inaccurate portrayals of U.S.
promises to limit civilian casualties. In an Op-Ed for the *Washington Post*, Harold Meyerson argued:

> In the history of the planet, ours [the U.S.] is the only government to show its
> concern for human life through the precision of its bombs. Even the Iraqi gov-
> ernment, which is hardly shy about claiming or fabricating propaganda victo-
> ries, isn't contending that our air attacks on Baghdad have killed more than a
> relative handful of civilians. Plainly, our bombs are displaying a strategic so-
> licitude that seems beyond the capacities and inclinations of the men who run
> our nation. The careful avoidance of civilian targets—or military targets in ci-
> vilian neighborhoods—is of course a matter of military necessity. The Bush
> administration clearly understands that making a mortal enemy of the Iraqi
> people would be a disaster.[15]

The *Washington Post*'s reporting of the U.S. invasion of Iraq was also characterized by a reluctance to acknowledge large numbers of civilian casualties resulting during the invasion. A study of the invasion period from March 20 through
April 20, 2003 reveals that, by more than a two-to-one ratio, the paper's coverage favored American casualties over stories of Iraqi deaths.[16] This imbalance of
coverage is problematic in light of estimates showing that 1,367—1,620 Iraqi
civilians died (during the first month of the conflict alone), as opposed to only
139 U.S. troops who died within the first two months of the conflict.[17] Propor-
tional reporting on these deaths would have required nearly eleven times more
coverage of Iraqi casualties, although nothing approaching that amount of coverage was seen in the *Washington Post* or other American media.

When statistics on Iraqi deaths *are* given, they are often based upon the
most conservative and lowest projected civilian death figures, while higher
death count estimates receive less attention or even active ridicule. This practice
is unmistakable after reviewing the media's reaction to the Lancet reports. The
Lancet reports (released in 2004 and 2006) are an important component in the
debate, or lack thereof, over the number of Iraqi casualties. The studies questioned whether the U.S. has really targeted enemy "insurgents" with pinpoint
precision without killing large numbers of civilians. The Lancet reports' chal-

lenges to the myth that the U.S. has minimized collateral damage in Iraq is likely a main reason why the reports created such a controversy between critics and supporters of the Iraq war. By failing to adequately cover large estimates of Iraqi deaths in detail, media outlets implicitly indicate that they viewed studies projecting lower Iraqi casualty counts as more credible. This trend becomes more apparent when looking at the reactions to the *Iraq Body Count* project, as contrasted with reactions to the Lancet reports.

The Lancet reports, conducted by researchers at Johns Hopkins, the Bloomberg School of Public Health, and Columbia University, estimated that approximately 100,000 Iraqi civilians died in the 17.8 months (or one and a half years) after the 2003 invasion, and that approximately 650,000 Iraqis died through 2006 due to the escalation of post-invasion violence.[18] The surveys were conducted door-to-door in dozens of different neighborhoods, in which thousands of Iraqis were questioned.[19] Researchers intentionally left out the city of Falluja (in the 2004 study) so as to skirt any criticisms that this part of the sample would lead to an overestimate of the total fatalities in Iraq. In the 2004 study, women and children were cited as "frequent victims" in U.S. occupied Iraq. According to the *Los Angeles Times* summary of the 2004 Lancet report, 84% of the deaths were said to be due to coalition forces—95 percent of which were due to the so-called "precision guided" air strikes coming from the U.S. and its allies.[20] The 2006 report also found a large percentage (31 percent) of Iraqi deaths to be the fault of occupying forces. The risk of violent death was fifty-eight times higher from 2003 to 2004 than it had been before the collapse of Saddam's regime.[21] The 2006 report found that an estimated 2.5 percent of the Iraqi population had perished under U.S. occupation since 2003.[22]

The Lancet reports *were* reported in the American mainstream media, although they did not receive front-page coverage in the most prestigious national newspapers when they were released. These papers did not omit the reports from their coverage, but did not consider them feature-worthy material. Out of the three leading American newspapers, (the *Los Angeles Times, New York Times*, and *Washington Post*), only the *Washington Post* wrote its own piece on the first Lancet report. The other two papers instead picked up stories from British papers that had already written about the study. Out of the three newspapers, none ran this story as a feature (on page one) in their print versions, and none posted the story as a main headline in their Internet sites. The 2004 Lancet study received coverage on page A16 of the *Washington Post*, A4 of the *Los Angeles Times*, and A8 of the *New York Times*.[23] Stories that beat out the Lancet report in terms of gaining front-page coverage (on the day the report was first covered) included: Yasser Arafat's sickness, the surfacing of a new bin Laden tape, the impending U.S. attack on Falluja, and the death of eight U.S. marines in Iraq. In sum, the death of eight Americans was deemed a more salient issue than the estimated deaths of 100,000 Iraqis. Systematic burial of, and disregard for, the second Lancet report—pursued largely in the same fashion as with the original Lancet report—has been discussed at length elsewhere.[24] Stories deemed more important than the second Lancet report in major American newspapers included Madonna's adoption of a Malawian child, and the discovery of a 100,000 year-old Camel twice the size of today's average Camel, amongst other issues of marginal significance.[25] This disregard should not be viewed as "natural" or inevitable, in that leading British newspapers such as the *Guardian* and the *Independent* featured the stories on their covers, and framed the 2006 report's content in far more adversarial language than did American media outlets.[26]

Media organizations tended to dispute the Lancet's methodological soundness. George Monbiot of the *Guardian* of London explained, "In the U.S. and U.K., the [2004] study was either ignored or torn to bits. The media described it as 'inflated,' 'overstated,' 'politicized' and 'out of proportion'. . . . But the attacks in the press succeeded in sinking the study. Now, whenever a newspaper or broadcaster produces an estimate of civilian deaths, the Lancet report is passed over in favor of lesser figures. . . . We can expect the U.S. and U.K. governments to seek to minimize the extent of their war crimes. But it's time the media stopped collaborating."[27]

The charge that the studies were methodologically flawed was disputed by those involved in the study. Columbia University Professor and Lancet co-researcher Les Roberts took issue with the *Iraq Body Count's* low Iraqi death estimates (taken more seriously by American and Iraqi political leaders and media outlets): "The government in Iraq [has] claimed that since the 2003 invasion between 40,000 and 50,000 violent deaths have occurred. Few have pointed out the absurdity of this statement. . . it is a gross underestimate. . . if it were true, including suicides, South Africa, Colombia, Estonia, Kazakhstan, Latvia, Lithuania and Russia have experienced higher violent death rates than Iraq over the past four years. If true, many North and South American cities and Sub-Saharan Africa have had a similar murder rate to that claimed in Iraq. For those of us who have been in Iraq, the suggestion that New Orleans is more violent seems simply ridiculous."[28] Dr. Gilbert Burnham, one of the study's authors, recounted that "we used a standard survey method that is used all over the world to estimate mortality. . . . Going to the community for household surveys on mortality is the standard method used for calculating mortality." Burnham accounts for the radical difference between the estimates of Lancet reports and more conservative findings as seen in projects like *Iraq Body Count*, or *IBC* (which estimates Iraqi deaths only by those names which can be confirmed in media reports) fairly simply: "information collected in surveys always produces higher numbers than 'passive reporting' [as seen in the *IBC*] as many things never get reported. This is the easy explanation for the difference between *iraqbodycount.net* and our survey."[29] The "standard survey method" in which Burnham speaks of includes a standard research sampling size, as Michael O'Toole, the head of the *Center for International Health at Burnet Institute* in Australia reports that, "scientists say the size of the survey [sample] was adequate for extrapolation to the entire country."[30]

The summary of media coverage provided above is not meant so much to argue that the Lancet reports were without flaws or limitations. For one, they *were* estimates, rather than total tallies based on a body count (in contrast, *Iraq Body Count can* actually verify the deaths of each individual it lists within a very specific range of accuracy). However, a documented study of all or most of the deaths in Iraq is unfeasible at a time when sectarian and occupation violence are causing the country to spiral out of control.

The 1st Lancet study was also limited in that it only looked at the seventeen months after the March 2003 invasion, and did not encompass any statistics for the period including the last few months of 2004 and beyond. While the second study did much to compensate for the earlier study's limited period, both studies still failed to take into account any deaths that occurred after the 2003—2006 period. However, the Lancet reports still merit more extensive news coverage than they received in that they met the standard medical and scientific methodological requirements for studies estimating death tolls in war zones. For this reason alone they should have been a much larger focus throughout the media, and should not have been dismissed or downplayed as "exaggerated" or "false" based upon the negative political implications they posed for the Bush and Blair administration's occupation of Iraq.

A more balanced standard for reporting the projected Iraqi death toll is badly needed in the American media. The estimates President Bush cites for Iraqi casualties (which are virtually identical to the more conservative estimates of *Iraq Body Count*) were projected to be in the range of about 30,000 people (prior to the release of the second Lancet report). Bush's use of the 30,000 figure has been quoted more frequently and featured more often throughout the mass media, as reporters generally reacted to this study with less skepticism than they did the Lancet projects.[31] Disregard for the Lancet reports, and the relative lack of skepticism toward the *Iraq Body Count* estimates are important to address in light of admissions from those involved with *IBC* who explain that their estimates are limited in a number of ways. *IBC* admits that: "it is likely that many if not most civilian casualties will go unreported by the media [sources in which *IBC* relies] ... our own total is certain to be an underestimate of the true position, because of gaps in reporting or recording."[32]

Moral Violence and Challenges to "Collateral Damage"

Attempts to create a moral distinction between the violence of the U.S. and that of its enemies are seen throughout much of American media coverage of foreign wars. This trend is acknowledged from time to time, although most often it is not explicitly discussed. In one of the exceptions, George Will of the *Washington Post* expounded upon the distinction between legitimate and illegitimate violence when he asserted that, "the first task of the [U.S.] occupation [of Iraq] remains the first task of government, to establish a monopoly on violence."[33] Many Americans see their country as a purveyor of moral violence, as opposed to official enemies, which are said to use violence for pernicious purposes such as greed and lust for power. The concept of limiting "collateral damage" fits well within this system of thought, promoted by government officials, media, and part of the American public. According to this theory, American enemies such as the Iraqi "insurgents" are deemed terrorists because they actively target civilians, whereas American forces, in attempting to "promote democracy," reconstruction, and human rights, only kill civilians by accident in bombing campaigns targeting guerilla forces. The attempt to make this distinction is vital when considering the argument that the U.S. is promoting democracy, stabilization, and prosperity in Iraq.

As opposed to Islamist groups like Al Qaeda, which directly target civilians, American forces are said to target only rebel forces, although civilians inevitably are caught up in the attacks (to a supposedly small degree). The emphasis on limiting Iraqi civilian casualties has become a major theme driving reporting of the American invasion, and subsequently, the pacification campaign. The *New Republic* editors announced during the 2003 invasion in regards to the alleged limitation of collateral damage that "this supposedly cold-blooded [Bush] administration is making a remarkable, some might even say militarily dangerous, effort to spare Iraqi lives."[34] The *New York Times* reported the administration's motives in a similar fashion, as the U.S. sought to "Avoid a Siege"[35] in its drive toward the capital. A major headline from the paper read: "Battle for Baghdad like War Plan: Kill Enemy, Limit Damage, Provide Aid."[36] The claims of reporters, that the U.S. is concerned with limiting Iraqi casualties, are in accord with statements of government leaders who speak of limiting collateral damage. Former Pentagon Spokesperson Victoria Clarke, for example, argued that "We [the U.S.] go to great lengths to avoid unnecessary loss of [Iraqi] life," and that "most of our bombs are precision-guided," allowing American leaders to "choose targets carefully to avoid civilian casualties."[37]

Despite efforts to portray Iraq as a major security threat, the United States defeated the Baath regime with minimal resistance. No Iraqi tank was successful during the 2003 invasion in destroying an American tank, and no American warplane ever went up against an Iraqi fighter.[38] Media rhetoric announcing a commitment to limiting civilian damage was repeated throughout the early stages of the war, but also appeared later on as violence escalated against the growing "insurgency." However, media outlets sometimes contradicted promises of limiting collateral damage, using language that suggested that Iraq had suffered greater infrastructure damage as a result of the American campaign.

In reporting on the "fast, furious and relentless"[39] invasion toward Baghdad, U.S. forces found themselves "cruising to Baghdad"[40] and strengthening their "chokehold" on the city, as they proceeded in the "tightening of the noose" around the regime and the people of Iraq.[41] John F. Burns of the *New York Times* reported shortly before the war on the "deep-rooted fear" of the Iraqi people "of being obliterated in an Armageddon deployed by the world's greatest military power."[42] Such rare admissions of the large-scale dangers of American bombing, however, were not a central theme of wartime media reporting and propaganda.

Sustained resistance to American occupation was to surface shortly after the invasion, however, as many Iraqis attempted to force an end to the occupation. As attacks against the U.S. grew, so too did media reporting on the importance of fighting guerilla resistance. *Newsweek* summarized that: "defeating insurgencies is very hard. The preferred method down the ages has been extermination—

genocide and the elimination of whole villages and tribes, such brutal tactics are not an option for a democratic superpower."[43]

Although thousands were reportedly dying as a result of the cycle of violence, the notion that the U.S. was concerned with limiting collateral damage continued unabated. One of the most popular methods of promoting this notion was the framing of attacks on "insurgent targets." Headlines such as "U.S. targeting insurgents in Northern Iraq," "109 Insurgents Killed in major [Falluja] offensive," and "U.S. Bombs Insurgent Targets in Baghdad" were common in sources such as *CNN*, the *Los Angeles Times*, and the majority of media outlets.[44] Offensives were said to take place against "insurgent dominated areas" as the U.S. "put pressure on insurgent hideouts and bases."[45] "Rebel controlled" cities were attacked, giving the impression that those killed within those cities were consistently and overwhelmingly sympathizers with, or supporters of resistance groups.[46] In obliterating "insurgent havens," U.S. leaders assured Americans that they went "to great lengths in avoiding civilian casualties by carefully weighing intelligence and following strict protocols," bombing with "near-pinpoint precision."[47] Such promises were shown to be false considering the large number of civilians killed by American bombing, as indicated in the Lancet reports.

Mainstream reporters who were reliant on official sources often found it difficult to question those same sources of information in terms of their accuracy in estimating civilian deaths. This likely has much to do with the dramatic cut in money allocated in the corporate press toward international reporting, and the increasingly dangerous prospect of reporting on the ground in Iraq outside of the protection of American troops. Media critics Robert McChesney and John Nichols claim that commercial pressures to cut down on reporting expense have led media corporations to limit their reporting from within conflict zones: "U.S. news media have few if any reporters on the ground to provide context for the story. What this means is that there is less capacity for journalists to provide a counterbalance to whatever official story Washington puts forward."[48]

A major reason for the media's failure to challenge official claims has to do with the escalating violence throughout countries like Iraq. As sectarian tensions continue, and attacks between U.S. forces and resistance become worse, most reporters fear for their lives. They fear being abducted by terrorist groups, guerillas, or various militias, or being killed by American bombs. While such fear is understandable, it has led to less of a capacity to question official promises when it comes to alleged efforts to limit collateral damage. As Patrick Cockburn, one of the few reporters operating outside of military protection in occupied Iraq explains: "So dangerous is it to travel anywhere in Iraq outside Kurdistan that it is difficult for journalists to provide evidence of the slaughter house the country has become without being killed themselves."[49] The most important reason for journalists and editors disregard for Iraqi casualties likely has to do with their hesitance in challenging official propaganda concerning "collateral damage." Journalists are inclined to accept proclamations that the U.S. is unique in world history, particularly in its commitment to pursuing just wars and limiting civilian casualties and destruction.

Media reporting and framing in support of promised "precision attacks" implies two things about the nature of American bombing: 1. that "insurgents" and Iraqi civilians can largely be separated during bombing campaigns (hence the promotion of the concept of "precision bombing"); and 2. as a logical result of the use of "precision weapons," the U.S. has not, and is not killing large numbers of civilians in its occupation of Iraq. Studies such as the Lancet reports, however, have seriously questioned both assumptions, which is likely the main reason why they were neglected in media coverage.

News outlets outside the American mainstream media focus more attention on reporting stories highlighting civilian deaths in Iraq. Arab news stations like *Al Jazeera* show the effects of numerous bombing campaigns on the Iraqi people and infrastructure, emphasizing bloody images of civilians killed in the Iraqi conflict. Conversely, American mainstream media prefer to refrain from printing the most bloody and gruesome images, assuming that Americans cannot handle such bloody pictures, or that they are not interested in them in the first place. This difference in reporting has become a major point of contention between *Al Jazeera* and Western media outlets. Hafez Mirazi, Washington bureau chief of *Al Jazeera*, exemplifies *Al Jazeera*'s view on this issue well: "There is a feeling in our newsroom that you need to be as realistic as possible and carry the images of war and the effect that war has on people...if you are in a war, your population shouldn't just eat their dinner and watch sanitized images on TV."[50]

American reporters and editors call upon traditional notions of "objectivity," "professionalism," and "taste" in order to refrain from printing or airing the bloody pictures. The objective of reporting, according to Howell Raines, Executive Editor of the *New York Times*, is "to try to capture the true nature of an event, whether it's a disaster like the World Trade Center or war, but also do so with restraint and an avoidance of the gratuitous use of images simply for shock value."[51] This standard is generally adhered to in most reporting, although there are some dissenters from within the system. Veteran American war reporter Chris Hedges argues that media has a responsibility to show such gruesome images in order to fully educate the public about the brutality of war: "If we really reported war as it is, people would be so disgusted and appalled they wouldn't be able to watch. War is packaged and sanitized the same way the poisons of tobacco or liquor are packaged and sanitized. We see enough of the titillation and excitement to hold our interest, but we never actually see what wounds do to bodies." The divorce of war from bloody images and graphic violence does a great disservice to American understanding of the effects of the American occupation of Iraq, which has steadily grown more deadly since the early days of the invasion.

The problem with the Iraq war, Hedges explains, is that "We reveled in the power of the weapons, and we were never shown what those weapons did so that somehow the consequences of these machines of death were sanitized. That, I think, is always dangerous."[52] While Iraqis, human rights groups, and un-embedded reporters consistently claim that civilians are being targeted and killed in mass by American bombings, U.S. officials react in the negative, arguing that those who are killed are, by and large, "insurgents." When admitting that Iraqis have died due to U.S. actions, military officials claim that such deaths are unfortunate and accidental. Often, military officials react to reports of civilian deaths by claiming that civilian casualties cannot be substantiated with available evidence. Media reliance on official sources in regards to casualty counts and admissions (or lack thereof) of civilian deaths, and the reluctance or inability of reporters to go out into the field to verify claims of civilian deaths, means that most of the reports on civilian casualties fail to receive serious follow-up attention. Reporters and editors generally take the Bush administration and military planners' promises to use "pinpoint weaponry" and reduce "collateral damage" at face value, especially since they are not reporting from Iraq and are not in a position to directly challenge official claims with evidence collected from contrary, on-the-ground reporting.

There is another standard of reporting, however, seen in Independent-Left and foreign media outlets, which make it a higher priority to directly challenge official claims of minimizing collateral damage. Take, for example, one interchange between a reporter at the independent *Pacifica* radio network and an editor at the *Washington Post* in which they discuss the U.S. military's estimates of Iraqi dead. In response to the Pentagon's recognition that it keeps track of "insurgent" dead in Iraq, the *Pacifica* reporter combatively asked Bradley Graham, a staff writer for the *Washington Post*:

> Please explain how the Pentagon counts the number of insurgents killed from a jet traveling near supersonic speed at an altitude of 25—30,000 feet. At times, these numbers seem to come out of thin air, literally. When reports on the ground clearly contradict the claims that civilians are not killed in these attacks it throws into question all that we are told. How can a mere observer of events make heads or tails of what is really going on?

In response, Graham stated that: "For air strikes by high-flying, fast moving jets, the casualty counts appear to be derived from advance estimates of how many *bad guys* [emphasis added] were suspected of being at or in the targeted site just before it was struck...As for sorting out differing accounts after a particular incident, there's often nothing a reader can do at first except to keep an open mind and wait for further reporting to determine the truth."[53] The problem with Graham's hope that "further reporting" will provide a better picture, however, is that continued media over-reliance on official propaganda leads to chronic underemphasis and underreporting of Iraqi suffering and casualties.

The promotion of, and opposition to, terms like "collateral damage" is of major significance when looking at the differences between most mainstream reporting and Progressive-Left critiques of the bombing of Iraq. "Collateral damage" implies many of the deaths and the destruction that come along with bombing are unintended effects of U.S. actions. On this point many critics seriously challenge official justifications for war.[54] Questioning the attempt to distinguish between "intentional" and "unintentional" violence against civilians is useful when one reviews both sides of the debate over whether the U.S. is engaging in terrorism in Iraq. Dissident scholars and activists claim the U.S. is a leading terrorist state, while the mainstream press, political leaders, and many

mainstream academics wholeheartedly reject the charge as ludicrous or unfounded.

A standard definition of terrorism, declared by U.N. Secretary General Kofi
Annan, includes "any action. . . . if it is *intended* [emphasis added] to cause death
or serious bodily harm to civilians or non-combatants with the purpose of in-
timidating a population or compelling a government or an international organization to do or abstain from doing any act."[55] Such a definition is critical when
discussing terrorism. At the heart of the debate over terrorism and the U.S.
bombing of Iraq are two questions: 1. Is the killing of civilians really "unintentional" in the light of a U.S. bombing campaign which has led to a marked increase in Iraqi civilian deaths, to the disinterest of American leaders?; and 2. If
such killings are unintentional, how important is "intent" when looking at the
actual consequences of American bombings, which have killed at minimum
thousands of innocents throughout Iraq? Does the "unintentional" bombing of
civilians constitute an act of terror, if not according to the definition provided by
Kofi Annan, than at least according to a more expansive definition that defines
terrorism through creation of an environment where civilians fear for their lives
in light of military attacks that systematically fail to distinguish between military
and non-military targets? These questions have been passionately discussed
(with answers presented) throughout much Progressive-Left media commentary,
but such a dialogue has been absent in mainstream media reporting and editorializing.

Proponents of American bombing claim that Americans weapons are extremely precise in their targeting and that the death of civilians is unintentional,
but always regrettable. Critics of U.S. bombing maintain that such deaths can
never be fully unintended when American military planners and media pundits
already have a term established in advance to describe deaths resulting from
American bombing campaigns. For example, Howard Zinn claims that the killings of Afghan civilians during Operation Enduring Freedom were less accidental and more representative of reckless acts of terror. In the *Nation*, Zinn argued
about "precision bombing": "We have been waging a war on ordinary men,
women and children...these human beings have died because they happened to
live in Afghan villages in the vicinity of vaguely defined 'military targets'. . . .
the bombing that destroyed their lives is in now way a war on terrorism, because
it has no chance of ending terrorism and is itself a form of terrorism."[56] Zinn
argues against the notion that the United States was simply defending itself in
Afghanistan: "the term 'self defense' does not apply when you drop bombs in
heavily populated residential areas and kill people other than your attacker."[57]
Zinn points to past experiences where American bombing was largely indiscriminate, such as the first Gulf War, where over 90 percent of the bombs used
were not precision guided.[58]

Similarly, Gilbert Achcar claims that the use of terms like collateral damage
represent an attempt to deceive the American public over the realities of bombing heavily populated urban areas: "No civilized ethic can justify deliberate assassination of noncombatants or children, whether indiscriminate or deliberate,
by state or nongovernmental terror." Achcar equates bombing of civilians with

other terrorist acts of barbarism, as the use of concepts like collateral damage "not only cynically reduces the murder of innocents to something banal; it is a hypocritical attempt to excuse the murders that result from repetitive recourse to military force."[59] The challenges of Achcar and others to official U.S. humanitarian propaganda have unsurprisingly been overlooked amongst media organizations that are not only heavily reliant on official sources, but also extraordinarily gullible in accepting and embracing noble official justifications for war.

Major news outlets have quietly acknowledged, from time to time, that there are clear dangers to the people of Iraq in the face of "precision bombing." This point was perhaps best seen shortly before the March 2003 invasion, when the American news agencies in Baghdad ordered their journalists out for their own safety.[60] The orders for reporters to leave Iraq in anticipation of "shock and awe" showed that there was a strong concern amongst American journalists that Iraq was an unsafe place at the time of the invasion. U.S. bombing in Iraq is directed overwhelmingly in urban areas with heavily concentrated populations. Most of the fighting throughout Iraq has been between American troops and guerillas conducting hit and run attacks against the U.S. Iraqi fighters use the urban landscape in order to blend in with civilians in an attempt to avoid retribution by massive conventional bombing. While major American media outlets maintain that the concern with *not* killing large numbers of civilians in urban areas prevents the U.S. from unleashing its full military might on Iraqi resistors, Independent-Left media critics counter that bombing in urban areas is the primary reason why large numbers of civilians (in the tens of thousands) have died. Marc Herold, a University of New Hampshire professor and contributor to *Iraq Body Count* argues that: "The mantra that precision weapons will kill few people is false when the Pentagon is dropping them in civilian-rich areas. The U.S. military has carpet-bombed around Baghdad and in the northern areas where concentrations of Iraqi fighters are believed to exist."

As American forces bomb buildings throughout Iraqi cities, it is difficult to verify who exactly is in each building, or how many civilians are killed versus how many "insurgents." For example, the *New York Times* reported in 2003 that: "Every day, briefers at Central Command show high-tech images of buildings in and around Baghdad being blown to bits by America's advanced precision weaponry. Were there people inside? No one can say."[61] Even when targets *are* hit precisely, it is difficult, if not impossible, to know for certain whether civilians have been killed, and if so, how many. Admiral Stufflebeam explains that "smart bombs," dropped from B-2 bombers, have a specified margin of error rate of thirteen meters, or forty-two feet. Even when accurate, these bombs kill everyone within a 120-meter (396 foot) radius, and 790-foot diameter from the blast site. To be safe from serious shrapnel damage, individuals must be at least 365 meters away, or 1,204 feet, and to be safe from *all* effects a full 1,000 meters away, or 3,300 feet (three-fifths of a mile). Such revelations raise important questions about the indiscriminate nature of American bombing concentrated in dense areas with large populations.

"Precision Bombing" and the Case of Falluja

When looking at mainstream reporting, claims that the U.S. is committed to limiting Iraqi deaths were also repeated at length in the U.S. attacks against Falluja in 2004. The *New York Times* ran a headline in April of that year reporting that "A Full Range of Technology is Applied to Bomb Falluja," as the paper claimed that the U.S. wanted "to avoid civilian casualties," although conceding that the entire city had essentially become "a military target."[62] It was known in advance that mass bombing of Falluja would lead to major casualties if the city was not evacuated. In preparation for the bombing, media pundits and television hosts congratulated the U.S. for encouraging an evacuation from the city in preparation of the bombing. Shephard Smith of *Fox News Studio B* announced that "we told [the people of Falluja] we were coming so the innocents could get out of there."[63] Reports from the Red Cross in mid-November, revealed that not all civilians were believed to have escaped, as the organization estimated that approximately 800 civilians were "feared dead."[64] On the same day the *Red Cross* report was released, the *Washington Post* report on the bombing did not suggest that hundreds of civilians had died. The paper announced that, "Falluja looks like a city from which everyone has walked away."[65] The *Los Angeles Times* added the same, that "most civilians were cleared out, leaving a 'clean' battlefield."[66] Finally, the *New York Times* repeated the statement of former Prime Minister Ayad Allawi that, "the number of Iraqi casualties has not been officially announced," although Allawi "said he does not believe any civilians were killed in the offensive, which has left more than 1,200 insurgents dead."[67]

In general, a different picture emerged of the attack on Falluja depending upon which news sources viewers and readers were following. On the day the *Red Cross* report was released in the Independent-Left media outlet *Z Magazine*, other stories were deemed more important in the major papers discussed above. Stories that beat out the *Red Cross* report in terms of feature coverage included updates on second term cabinet changes in the Bush administration, Yasser Arafat's death, and celebrations of the tactical progress of the assault on Falluja. *Fox News* was amongst the most vocal in the speculations over the success of the attack on Falluja. *Fox News Live* posed the question: "How Will U.S. Forces Finish the Fight?," as host Rita Cosby announced that the U.S. takeover of the city in six days was "amazing."[68] *CNN Live* presented a similar question: "Will U.S. and Coalition Forces be Successful in Driving Forces Out of Falluja?"[69] The *New York Times* editorial staff celebrated the demolition of Falluja and forced expulsion of its people as "swift," "stunning," and ultimately, a "triumph."[70] Special privileging was allotted to eliminating "a major safe haven for insurgents," so as to more effectively "disrupt their operations."[71] The conflict in Falluja had become "a contest for the confidence of the Iraqi people,"[72] with the U.S. "liberating"[73] the city from the hands of the "insurgency" a major focus of reporting. The reality that the destruction of the city ignited Iraqi anger on a grand scale was left to more critical news outlets to make. In *Al Jazeera*, for example, Scott Ritter predicted the opposite of the euphoria in the mainstream American press, claiming that: "While the U.S. is unlikely to deliver a fatal blow to the Iraqi resistance, it is succeeding in leveling huge areas of Falluja, recalling the Vietnam-era lament that we had to destroy the village in order to save it."[74]

Iraq and Human Rights:
Torture, Mass Detainment, and Executions

As a human rights worker in Iraq, Cliff Kindy documented many horror stories about the deaths of Iraqi civilians—stories of people killed by bombs and urban warfare, others tortured while under detainment, and finally, some who had reportedly been executed by American troops. Working with the *Christian Peacemaker Teams* (*CPT*), Kindy risked his life by traveling to Iraq in order to promote nonviolence at a time when violence was escalating between resistance groups and the U.S. military. In documenting cases of human rights abuse, *CPT* was taking a stand against the escalating violence and destabilization of Iraq.

Working with *CPT*, Kindy was a vocal critic of the American occupation. Kindy's human rights work represented a departure from mass media reporting, which generally refuses to implicate the U.S. in inciting major human rights violations in Iraq. In November of 2003, Kindy met with a number of Iraqis near Ramadi to investigate charges that American troops had executed local Iraqi civilians. *CPT* determined after speaking with locals who had allegedly witnessed the incident that American troops, searching the area for "insurgents," had detained three young Iraqis who were thought to be hostile to the occupation.

Assuming there may have been resistance fighters in his [one of the Iraqi's] house, American soldiers split into two groups and entered opposite ends of his home. They initially cleared the women who were in the house and then continued their search. Apparently, there had been a shot fired in the house in confusion, which led the soldiers to begin firing as they thought they were being threatened. As it turned out, there were no resistance fighters in the house, and the initial shot had been from one of the groups of American soldiers. In the confusion, a few soldiers had been killed by friendly fire. We were told that in their frustration and anger, the surviving soldiers left the house, went outside, and proceeded to execute the three detainees. Afterwards, they called in the tank and air strike to level the house.[75]

Kindy spoke with a number of American soldiers, the coroner, neighbors, and family members of the deceased in verifying this potentially explosive story. Kindy recounted that: "Although all the details were not perfectly clear, we had enough information to bring attention to this abuse, so we called a press conference in order or the coroner and neighbors to testify."[76] Only *Al Jazeera*, *Al Arabiya*, and the *Associated Press* ended up running with the story, as an earthquake in Bam, Iran led most of the other media outlets that had planned on attending to cover the natural disaster instead. This meant that the *Associated Press* was the only western media outlet that covered the story.

Kindy equates the disinterest in stories questioning U.S. humanitarianism with more than just a preference for sensationalistic coverage (such as the Iranian earthquake). In an interview with one alternative American newspaper, Kindy stated that his organization faced censorship routinely when submitting controversial stories that were critical of the U.S. to Western news outfits:

> It was as if there was a filter role in the mainstream media. I got the impression that this was the type of information that they felt shouldn't be coming out. It wasn't really clear who was doing the filtering though. For example, we went to the offices of the *New York Times*, the *BBC*, and *Reuters* in Baghdad. We were consistently left with the impression that this was the kind of news that just wouldn't end up getting through to Western viewers. We would give them stories that were much hotter than the ones they were printing at the time, and we would be left with the impression of, "oh, that's nice. We'll be in touch," although we wouldn't hear back from them.[77]

Media coverage of U.S. human rights abuses in Iraq has become incredibly important in light of the Abu Ghraib scandal and other reports of human rights violations. While the mainstream media was heralded for breaking the Abu Ghraib story—which was a major embarrassment for the Bush administration—critics from outside the mainstream press were quick to point out flaws in the handling of the scandal. Sherry Ricchiardi of the *American Journalism Review* explained: "the media were awfully slow to unearth a scandal that ultimately caused international embarrassment for the United States and cast a shadow over the war in Iraq."[78]

Attacks on delayed reporting of U.S. human rights violations were based on the fact that groups like *Amnesty International* and *Human Rights Watch* had consistently complained about U.S. treatment of detainees at prisons in Afghanistan and at Guantanamo Bay well before serious attention was devoted to Abu Ghraib. Knowledge of American mistreatment of detainees at Abu Ghraib was certainly known at least five months prior to the breaking of the Abu Ghraib story. The *Associated Press*, for example, ran a story in late 2003 regarding allegations of torture. Even though U.S. Command in Baghdad stated in mid-January of 2004 that, "an investigation has been initiated into reported incidents of detainee abuse at a Coalition forces detention facility,"[79] it was not until 3 months later that *CBS* and the *New Yorker* ran stories about the Abu Ghraib scandal. Although the story did finally break by April of 2004, it had a difficult time surfacing in light of pressures from the U.S. military. *60 Minutes II*, the *CBS* news program that originally ran the story and many of the disturbing images that came along with it, held off on airing the program for two weeks because of a request by General Richard Myers. It was not until the *New Yorker* magazine announced that it would run the story that *CBS* decided to run with the piece.

Despite the decision of major newspapers throughout the country to feature cover stories on the Abu Ghraib scandal, few actually showed on the unedited pictures of naked piled Iraqi bodies, hooded prisoners placed in stress positions, and prisoners dragged by dog collars, among other photos that became so controversial and infamous throughout the world. Only a select number of newspapers printed the images in front-page stories, including the *Los Angeles Times*, the *Chicago Tribune*, and the *Washington Post*, and those were censored so as to avoid printing "obscene" images. One study done by American University scholars surveying 210 journalists in the U.S. found that most of those interviewed chose to self-censor in their reporting of the Abu Ghraib scandal by refusing to run "graphic" pictures, and by putting more grisly details regarding the abuses inside their papers, rather than on the cover.[80]

The *New York Times* decided not to print the pictures on its cover as the story broke, claiming at first that it wanted to wait to see if the images were authentic. Executive Editor Bill Keller summarized the papers coverage as follows: "our night crew was uncomfortable with their inability to independently verify that the pictures were legitimate. . . that held us for a day."[81] By the time the pictures were revealed as authentic, the *New York Times* decided not to print them, supposedly because they were no longer "timely." Keller explained that "by the time we had assurance that the pictures were genuine, they had been so widely distributed that we opted to run a couple pictures inside rather than front them" in the paper.[82] Claims about the lack of "timeliness" of printing the photos are difficult to take seriously in light of the large amount of attention accorded Abu Ghraib in the months following the initial reporting. More likely, the *New York Times'* editors—as with other major media—were concerned with avoiding the controversy of challenging U.S. humanitarianism in Iraq.

It was not only the military, however, that attempted to limit the reporting on the Abu Ghraib scandal. A number of commentators in the media attempted to downplay Abu Ghraib and the images that *were* actually run in the American media, by suggesting that the press was over-blowing the scandal and misrepresenting information when it came to the events surrounding the scandal. Rush Limbaugh claimed that the scandal "is not as serious as everybody is making it out to be. . . this is a pure media-generated story. . . . This is no different than what happens at the Skull and Bones initiation, and we're going to ruin people's lives over it, and we're going to hamper our military effort. . . . I'm talking about people having a good time, these people, you ever heard of emotional release? You [ever] heard of need to blow some steam off?"[83] In an interview with Seymour Hersh, Bill O'Reilly admitted that "there's no question about" whether Abu Ghraib constituted a major scandal and embarrassment for the U.S., but he also challenged a number of reports that over half of those held at Abu Ghraib demonstrated no ties with Al Qaeda or the "insurgency." O'Reilly questioned Hersh: "How do you wind up in a prison if you're just innocent and didn't do anything? I'm going to dispute [the] contention that we had a lot of people in there with just no rap sheets at all, who were just picked up for no reason at all."[84] Finally, *CNN's* Pentagon Correspondent Barbara Starr blamed the media for reporting the story. Starr justified her criticisms by labeling the photos, rather than the military's actions, as "inappropriate": "Let's start by reminding everybody that under U.S. military law and practice, the only photographs that can be taken are official photographs for documentation purposes about the status of prisoners when they are in military detention. That's it. Anything else is not acceptable. And of course, that is what the Abu Ghraib Prison scandal is all about."[85] It should be pointed out, however—contrary to Starr's claims—that public anger over the Abu Ghraib scandal was directed overwhelmingly at the mistreatment of prisoners, *not* at a soldier's choice to break Pentagon protocol by distributing the pictures.

Some journalists and editors throughout the mainstream press did feel that they made a mistake by not uncovering the tragedy sooner. Philip Taubman, the Washington Bureau Chief for the *New York Times* shared his evaluation: "We didn't do our job with this [scandal] until the photographs appeared on *CBS*." This, Taubman explained, represented "a failure of newsgathering" in regards to Abu Ghraib.[86] The *American Journalism Review* laid out a number of reasons for the media's failure to report Abu Ghraib sooner, citing such factors as "the Bush administration's penchant for secrecy and controlling the news agenda; dangerous conditions that limited reporting by Western reporters in much of Iraq," in addition to the nationalistic climate of the media after 9/11 and during the Iraq war which discouraged reporting presenting strong criticisms of the war effort and American troops in Iraq.[87]

The Bush administration and American military have generally reacted to Abu Ghraib so as to attempt to limit the future release of other materials implicating the U.S. with human rights violations at Abu Ghraib. In 2005, the Pentagon attempted to prohibit the release of emerging video evidence of U.S. abuse of prisoners at Abu Ghraib. The argument given was that such images could assist in the recruitment of Islamist forces, a trend which may threaten American lives in Iraq.[88] These types of restrictions on access to information will only make it more difficult for stories like Abu Ghraib to break in the future, as the military has emphasized its desire to cover up its human rights abuses, rather than work toward prohibiting them in a transparent fashion. Further restrictions on the part of the government have been followed by increased media efforts to reinforce military secrecy. In November of 2005, the *Washington Post* reported a feature story about secret overseas American prisons in Eastern Europe that were holding terrorist suspects. The paper withheld the locations of these prisons at the request of the U.S. government, citing the possibility that the release of such information might "disrupt counter-terrorism efforts."[89]

Media watchdog *Fairness and Accuracy in Reporting* protested the paper's refusal to print the locations of these bases: "Without the basic fact of where these prisons are, it's difficult if not impossible for 'legal challenges' or 'political condemnation' to force them to close. . . . Given that Vice President Dick Cheney and CIA Director Porter Goss [have sought] to exempt the CIA from legislation that would prohibit 'cruel and degrading treatment' of prisoners, and that CIA-approved 'Enhanced Interrogation Techniques' include torture techniques like 'waterboarding' [where prisoners are made to think they're drowning], there's no reason to think that prisons that operate in total secrecy will have fewer abuses than Abu Ghraib or Afghanistan's Bagram."[90]

The events at Abu Ghraib are not an isolated incident when it comes to the abuse of prisoners in Iraq. Evidence has since shown that the abuse and torture of prisoners was not restricted only to Abu Ghraib, but other jails, such as one in

Mosul, where detainees reportedly abused through practices such as sleep deprivation and physical assault, among other questionable behavior.[91] Evidence has also revealed that mass detainment of Iraqis in attempts to find Saddam Hussein and fight the "insurgency" was based upon questionable or non-existence evidence. The *Red Cross* estimated that by 2004, as many as 70—90 percent of detainees held in Iraq by the U.S. had been arrested "by mistake,"[92] meaning there was a lack of sufficient evidence to hold them or charge them with any crime. This estimate was similar in its projection to the conclusion of a report filed by Maj. General Antonio Taguba, which found that about 60 percent of the detainees at Abu Ghraib were not considered a security risk to the U.S. military.[93]

Hundreds were held at Abu Ghraib for extended periods, often without any evidence that they posed a security risk, according to one army report released in late 2003. As the *New York Times* reported: "some Iraqis had been held for several months for nothing more than expressing 'displeasure or ill will' toward the American occupying forces."[94] Children have not been exempt from detention either. An investigation by the *Sunday Herald* revealed that, in 2004, U.S. and allied forces in Iraq were holding over one-hundred children in facilities like Abu Ghraib, as some as young as ten claimed to have been raped and tortured.[95]

Human Rights Watch released similar documentation contending that "the abuse of detainees by the Iraqi police and intelligence forces has become routine and commonplace," as such practices as arresting suspects without warrants, and beatings of prisoners were said to be commonplace.[96] All this, contrary to the rules and procedures encompassed in the Iraqi Code of Criminal Procedures, which mandates that a defendant receive all the benefits of due process. *Human Rights Watch* reported that physical punishment of detainees includes "use of cables, metal rods, kicking, slapping, and punching...suspension from the wrists and earlobes. . . electric shocks to the earlobes and genitals. . . [prisoners] receiving little or no food or water for several days...[and] overcrowded cells," to name a few of the violations of prisoners' rights. Extortion is listed as a particularly large problem, as those who can afford to pay prison guards are reportedly set free, while others who cannot afford these bribes are denied access to legal defense.

2005 and 2006 were also important years for other revelations of U.S. abuse of detainees in the "War on Terror." James Risen, reporter for the *New York Times* and author of *State of War: The Secret History of the CIA and the Bush Administration*, reported on secret CIA detainment facilities where terrorist suspects are held. Risen explained: "Several CIA officials who are familiar with the way the interrogations of high value Al Qaeda detainees are actually conducted say that there are no doubts in their minds that the CIA is torturing prisoners."[97] Zaki Chehab, an editor for *Al Hayat* and author of *Inside the Resistance: The Iraqi Insurgency and the Future of the Middle East*, attributes U.S. treatment of detainees with growing resistance against the U.S. Through his reporting and research, Chehab uncovered evidence of serious human rights violations on the part of the U.S., such as the raping of Iraqi women in U.S. custody.[98] One woman was reportedly raped seventeen times in one day by Iraqi police forces,

who assaulted the women in the presence of American soldiers. One Iraqi journalist for *Al Jazeera* was arrested while filming in Samarra, and charged with
assisting resistance forces against the U.S. This reporter recaps his treatment
under detainment:

> I was constantly beaten and subjected to different kinds of torture. I was taken
> to the military base near Baghdad International Airport, where I stayed for two
> days with my head covered by a plastic hood. Often soldiers would put their
> guns to my head and threatened to shoot me. I was in constant pain from the
> frequent blows I received to my body and from having head knocked against
> the walls. Finally I ended up in Abu Ghraib, where I was subjected to similar
> experiences, which have now been seen by the world.[99]

Other attacks on prisoners uncovered in one military report of U.S. transgres-
sions includes the breaking of chemical lights on, and the use of phosphorous
liquid on prisoners, the beating of detainees with broom handles and chairs,
promises from soldiers to rape detainees, and the use of chemical lights to sod-
omize terrorist or "insurgent" suspects.[100]

In releasing the 2005 State Department's report on Iraqi human rights, the
New York Times cited "torture, rape, and illegal detentions by [Iraqi] police officers" as well as the "arbitrary deprivation of life, torture, impunity, [and] poor
prison conditions" as an integral part of the practices of Iraqi police and security
forces.[101] Citing a *Human Rights Watch* report, the paper highlighted the practices of police officers in Baghdad who "were systematically raping and torturing female detainees."[102] Such reporting from the corporate press shows that
American infringements upon Iraqi human rights have been an extensive focus
of American reporting. However, the extraordinary level of documentation of
systematic U.S. human rights abuses against Iraqis has not led American reporters and editors to question dogmatic claims that the U.S. remains unconditionally committed to democracy and security promotion in Iraq.

To argue that Iraqi and American use of torture has not been reported in the
mainstream press would be inaccurate. After all, it was the corporate press that
did break the Abu Ghraib story, and granted it extensive coverage, even if a focus on U.S. atrocities was prolonged due to military pressure and concerns with
appearing too critical of government during times of war. However, the practice
of reporting torture and abuse of prisoners has not led media outlets to rethink
their schizophrenic commitment to claiming U.S. devotion to human rights on
one hand, and explicit admissions of U.S. violations of those rights on the other.
Conversely, Progressive-Left media sources have taken the revelations of torture
as evidence that the U.S. is hurting democratic prospects in Iraq, rather than
furthering them. The editors of the *Nation* magazine attacked the official an-
nouncement of good intentions in Iraq as follows: "Given that the war in Iraq is,
in part, a war of images, the Abu Ghraib scandal represents a profound and perhaps irreversible defeat for the United States. Can any Iraqi now be expected to
believe US intentions are good? A more insulting, inflammatory message to the
world's Muslims and Arabs—and a more effective recruiting tool for groups
like Al Qaeda—can scarcely be imagined."[103] Similarly, Bob Wing argued in the

alternative online magazine *Counterpunch* that: "The tortures at Abu Ghraib have exposed to the world the utter moral bankruptcy of Bush's war. Far from being fought on behalf of Iraqi democracy, it is a war for U.S. supremacy in which racist dehumanization and brutalization of Arabs and Muslims play an absolutely central role."[104] Such blatant challenges to officially espoused humanitarian motives in Iraq were unthinkable in mainstream media commentary.

Iraqi Reconstruction Examined

Stories like that of "Baby Noor" are instrumental in constructing the image of a noble intervention. Noor was discovered by American troops in 2005 after they had searched a house in Abu Ghraib outside of Baghdad, only to find the baby suffering with paralysis and a tumor on her back that she developed after the infant was born with Spina Bifida. Later she was taken to the United States to receive treatment for her condition at Children's Healthcare of Atlanta. After her first operation, it was reported that Noor seemed to be on her way to recovery, although it was acknowledged that she would probably be in a wheelchair for the rest of her life. American media outlets used the story of Baby Noor to promote a charitable image of the United States in its occupation of Iraq. *CBS News* ran a story about Noor, quoting Helen Shepherd of Child Spring International (the charity group that brought Noor and her family to the U.S.), who explained that the baby's father and grandmother shed "tears of joy and relief when they learned she was out of surgery and in recovery." The baby girl's grandmother praised the United States, repeating "thank you America, thank you."[105] Shepherd reported that Noor's parents "are just feeling so blessed that things went well. . . they never expected so much help from the U.S. Army."[106]

Many Americans were likely left with the impression after following stories such as Baby Noor's that the U.S. is committed to promoting humanitarian objectives in Iraq. This media constructed image is incredibly important when looking at Iraqi reconstruction. Framing in the mainstream press methodically maintains that the United States is dedicated to serious reconstruction of Iraq. If anything is going wrong with reconstruction, it is the "insurgents" fault, rather than the United States. When the U.S. *is* blamed, it is typically for underestimating the time it will take for reconstruction, rather than for failing to adequately commit to reconstruction. This practice is represented in the "Paper of Record," which in late 2003 began to wonder about the feasibility of a quick "transition to a peaceful [Iraqi] nation," as there emerged, in light of growing resistance and slowly paced reconstruction, "reason to wonder whether" the "vision" of democracy "was unrealistically optimistic—at least on the time scale Mr. Bush and his aides once described."[107]

Reporters for the *New York Times* spoke of escalating "security costs" in explaining the slow pace of reconstruction projects aimed at rejuvenating water purification plants, oil pump stations, electric generators and power lines, schools, roads, and post offices, among other vital infrastructure projects.[108] Other explanations for the slow rate of reconstruction included "the rapid turn-

over of American officials in Iraq," as "all six U.S. agencies involved in the reconstruction effort lost all or some of their senior staff [in 2005]."[109] The *Washington Times* reported that "the government still lacks the personnel and exper-
tise to conduct proper oversight and management of military outsourcing in
Iraq," and cites "poor contractor performance" and retention of employees "with
insufficient qualifications or undesirable backgrounds," as well as a "lack of
government accounting" when it came to reconstruction funds and projects.[110] In
a similar fashion, the *Boston Globe* reported the persistence of "contractor delays" due to "higher security demands" and increased "efforts to quell the insurgency by improving living standards."[111]

As available evidence demonstrates, the reconstruction of Iraq has generally
fallen below the expectations of most critics and supporters of the war. This, in
large part, has to do with the redirection of reconstruction funds toward pacification of Iraqi resistance groups. Out of the only 18.4 billion dollars originally set
aside by the U.S. for reconstruction, half ended up redirected toward pacification.[112] 18.4 billion dollar commitment was initially directed at reconstruction,
despite the estimates of the World Bank that to return Iraq to its 1991 level of
development (at a time when it was already devastated by eight years of war
with Iran) would cost fifty-five billion dollars.[113] The World Bank's fifty-five
billion dollar figure, however, is likely to be a major underestimate of reconstruction needs, as Iraq was still suffering under deteriorating infrastructure in
mid-2006, when approximately forty-five billion dollars in aid had been allocated.[114] The U.S. Department of Energy estimated that "long-term reconstruction" of Iraq could cost one hundred billion dollars, if not much more.[115] In addition, the original amount set aside by the U.S. for reconstruction listed above is a
bit misleading, as a study by Ed Harriman revealed that Donald Rumsfeld and
Paul Bremer "made sure that the reconstruction of Iraq is paid for by the 'liberated' country," rather than by the United States itself. This meant that, out of the
initial twenty billion dollars set aside from rebuilding, most was paid for by Iraq,
with the U.S. fronting only about 300 million dollars.[116]

Large amounts (potentially billions) may have been wasted on projects with
little prospect of success (but of great value to reconstruction companies), as is
suggested by critics involved in the reconstruction process.[117] Corruption is considered a serious problem according to critical studies of the reconstruction effort. One estimate indicates that the U.S. embassy has had difficulty accounting
2.8 billion dollars in contracted commitments that were allocated in the first half
of 2005 alone.[118] Audits published as of January 2006 revealed that at least 12
billion dollars in funds spent by the U.S. and the interim regime were not adequately recorded or accounted for.[119]

With reduced levels of funding, Iraq has made limited progress in rebuilding.[120] By mid-2005, the U.S. General Accounting Office found that Iraqi power
levels were lower than they had been before the March 2003 invasion, with residents of Baghdad having access to electricity for no more than six hours a
day.[121] By May 2005, Iraq was producing only 2.1 million barrels of oil a day,
and exporting only 1.4 million, as contrasted with prewar levels of 2.6 million
barrels produced per day and 2.1 million barrels exported each day.[122] Iraq's

sewage treatment plants were also in disarray. Progressive critics of the war such as Christian Parenti reported that, over a year after the invasion, untreated sewage was still flowing into the major Iraqi rivers, leading thousands of residents drinking from the rivers to become sick. Parenti blamed the "delays in the sewage rehabilitation" throughout much of the country on the unwillingness of the U.S. and its contractors to bring Iraqis into the reconstruction process. As Gazwan Muktar, a retired electrical engineer explained to Parenti: "You need to have the people who spent years running these irrigation canals or power plants to be there. They know the tricks; they know the quirks. But the foreign contracts ignore Iraqis, and as a result, they get nowhere!"[123] Although infrastructure development largely fell below many critics' expectations, the Bush administration announced in late 2005 that it planned on terminating U.S. funding for most of the reconstruction regardless.[124] Brigadier General William McCoy stated: "The U.S. never intended to completely rebuild Iraq. . . . This [reconstruction] was just supposed to be a jump-start."[125]

The slowdown in reconstruction, coupled with the growth of violence, lack of central authority, deterioration of social order, and high unemployment in Iraq, mean that the raising of living standards and health levels are severely compromised. The United Nations Development Program, which surveyed 21,000 households in 2004, found that Iraqis endured high rates of infant and child mortality, low rates of life expectancy, and generally high levels of malnutrition.[126] Forty percent of urban homes complained that sewage still remained within the streets of their neighborhoods, while 37 percent explained that gunshots and other artillery fire were normal occurrences in the areas in which they lived, with shooting incidents taking place every day.[127] An internal staff report by the U.S. embassy in Iraq revealed a similar assessment. The embassy study, conducted by a joint civilian and military group in Baghdad, found that six of the country's eighteen provinces suffered under "serious" or "critical" conditions in terms of violent destabilization. A number of factors were cited, including increasing sectarian violence, the failure to form functioning governments, low levels of economic development, high unemployment, and a general "security situation marked by routine violence, assassinations, and extremism."[128] Food shortages throughout Iraq are especially important when looking at the post-invasion period, as the country has become less and less stable. While the number of children going hungry under Saddam Hussein and sanctions was estimated to be 4 percent, that number nearly doubled under U.S. occupation by March of 2005.[129] By other estimates released in 2005, 23 percent of Iraqi children between one-half a year and five years old suffered from chronic malnutrition, 12 percent from general malnutrition, and 8 percent from severe malnutrition.[130] Fewer than 55 percent of homes were said to have "safe and stable" access to clean water, whereas that number jumped to 80 percent in rural areas. Finally, 78 percent of homes listed "severe instability" as a major problem with which they were plagued.[131] U.S. media reporting, while conceding most of the points above, has failed to draw the obvious conclusion that the U.S. is primarily to blame for those breakdowns, as the major occupying power in Iraq.

When the U.S. is directly involved in inciting potential humanitarian crisis, its role is generally ignored or downplayed in media coverage. Such was the case in late 2005, when the *Independent* of London reported that the United States was "cutting off food and water" to areas where Iraqi civilians lived, forcing them "to flee before attacks on insurgent strongholds."[132] The American media's reaction was largely muted on the day the story broke in the *Independent*. *USA Today*'s weekend edition contained no coverage; neither did papers like the *New York Times*, the *Washington Post*, the *Houston Chronicle*, the *Chicago Sun Times*, the *Chicago Tribune*, or *New York Newsday*, although the story was printed in the *Boston Globe* and the *Los Angeles Times* after it was picked up from *Reuters* news service.

Serous disagreement has ensued over the reasons for the "failure" of reconstruction in Iraq. As discussed above, corporate media sources often blamed developments such as growing "insurgent violence" and escalating "security costs," as well as other bureaucratic and organizational problems. A number of Progressive-Left media venues, however, argued that the U.S. consciously chose not to adequately commit to reconstruction. In this point there is a serious divergence between the mainstream reporting addressed above, which frames reconstruction failings on factors other than U.S. disinterest in rebuilding Iraq, and the Progressive-Left critiques of the Bush administration which claim that it is largely uninterested in reconstruction. Indeed, the mass media's framing of the reconstruction as "failing" already assumes that the U.S. is seriously committed to reconstruction, rather than using such high-minded rhetoric for propaganda purposes.

Critics throughout Progressive-Left media have suggested that the funds for reconstruction originally set aside were known to be inadequate in terms of rebuilding Iraq. Tom Englehardt and Nick Turse, for example, reported in September of 2005: "the reconstruction [of Iraq] is petering out, because the money is largely gone. . . . Water and sanitation projects have been particularly hard hit; while staggering sums, once earmarked for reconstruction, are being shunted to private security firms whose reconstruction funds were spent without competitive bidding amongst American companies, but handed out to companies like Halliburton with close ties to the Bush administration." Edward Herman argued in *Z Magazine* that: "The U.S. specialty is destruction, not reconstruction, in accord with the U.S. elite's longstanding giving of primacy to military means, and the use of force in dealing with target states. We save them by destroying them, and then move on to the next creative project. . . . In Iraq, there has been a lot of construction, but not much reconstruction. What have been constructed are massive U.S. military bases and facilities, repairs of oil extraction facilities, and protective walls in and around the Green Zone, which is essentially an occupied fortress within Baghdad. Not much has been done for Iraqi benefit."[133]

Iraqi Democracy:
Public Opinion and Elections

Media defenses of U.S "humanitarianism" in Iraq have generally failed to address mass Iraqi resistance to occupation, and the implications of such resistance for the legitimacy of "democracy promotion" claims. John Kampfner, producer for the *BBC News* program "War Spin" observes that, "In the [United] States, as far as I can ascertain, there is a presumption that politicians are right, and truthful and honest. That is the default from which everything else operates."[134] This default requires that certain questions about U.S. involvement in Iraq receive precedence, while others are not addressed. It is common, for example, to ask questions about how long it will take for democracy to come to fruition, or whether the costs in terms of monetary drain on the U.S. economy are worth it or not. However, some questions are deemed off limits. Some of those questions are included below:

• What does it mean to speak about the importance of "pacification" of Iraqi resistance to occupation and about bringing "democracy" to Iraq when the vast majority of Iraqis are against the U.S. presence in Iraq, and most actively support attacks on U.S. troops?

• How strong is the government's commitment to democracy abroad when the Bush administration is reluctant to even consider American opinion at home, where most of the public would like to see a move toward phased withdrawal, rather than prolonged, indefinite occupation?

• Can democracy be imposed or initiated from the outside, or is it inherently dependent, rather, upon domestic activism and struggle to be legitimate?

• How "democratic" were the elections in Iraq when the U.S. largely failed to involve the Iraqi people directly in the political process?

This question is perhaps most relevant at a time when the U.S. was claiming democracy promotion as its main pre-text for remaining in Iraq, and when evidence on the ground suggested otherwise. A poll from the *International Republican Institute* (*IRI*), for example, showed that, while 71.4 percent of Iraqis questioned intended on voting in the 2005 election, few Iraqis actually knew *what* they were voting for 54.5 percent of Iraqis questioned provided wrong answers to the question of what they were voting for, claiming they were either voting for a President (they were not), or that they "didn't know" who they were voting for, while only 28 percent correctly answered that they were voting for a transnational assembly.[135]

It is easy to argue that reporters should not try and answer such questions if they are interested in letting readers decide for themselves about the nature of the U.S. presence in Iraq. However, questions like these should, ideally, be represented on at least some level in media reporting if the goal is to promote open dialogue, and critical thought. Scholars and anti-war critics could easily be consulted in media reporting, if reporters and editors were to reconsider their commitment to propagandistic news coverage. Such fundamental questions about U.S. humanitarianism *have* arisen in dissident magazines and other news sources, but have been left out of mainstream reporting and editorializing on the Iraq war.

Incorporation of such questions into media discourse is vital if Americans are interested in the consent, or lack thereof, of the Iraqi people to occupation and to Iraqi democracy in general. Throughout the post-invasion period, Iraqis indicated overwhelmingly that they were, and are, opposed to what the Bush administration and U.S. are doing in Iraq:

- According to one poll conducted in 2004, 80 percent of Iraqis surveyed indicated that they lacked confidence in the Coalition Provisional Authority, while 82 percent disapproved of the U.S. and its allies occupying Iraq.[136]
- In another 2004 poll, 71 percent of Iraqis questioned said they felt that U.S. troops were occupiers, rather than "liberators." Sixty percent also felt that U.S. troops displayed disrespect for Iraqis when searching their homes, while over half indicated that killing U.S. troops "can be justified in at least some cases."[137]
- In a secret Ministry of Defense poll released in late 2005, 65 percent of Iraqis asked indicated that they supported attacks on British troops in southern Iraq, while 45 percent supported attacks on American troops; 82 percent were opposed to the occupation. This sentiment was reinforced in a 2006 poll, which found that six in ten Iraqis supported violent attacks against American troops.[138]
- In a poll released by the *Program for International Policy Attitudes* in January 2006, 87 percent of Iraqis surveyed said that they approved of an Iraqi government plan that endorsed a timetable for U.S. withdrawal. At the same time, only 23 percent believed that the U.S. would withdraw from Iraqi if it were asked.[139]
- Arab elites also have reservations over U.S. incursions into the Middle East. One U.N. Report endorsed by Arab intellectuals condemned the U.S. supported Israel occupation of the West Bank and Gaza, as well as the U.S. occupation of Iraq, as main factors in inciting mass public opposition to the U.S. throughout the region.[140]

Opposition to occupation is put forth in anecdotal evidence reported in the Progressive-Left media as well. Cliff Kindy recounts from his time speaking with Iraqis about the war:

From my experiences, the majority of the Iraqi people are against the occupation of Iraq. When I was traveling back to the U.S. through Amman Jordan in 2004, I met an Iraqi exile while I was waiting for my flight. He was Shia Muslim and had worked as a physician. He had lived in Jordan for many years after he was kicked out of Iraq; his son and wife were killed by Saddam Hussein's regime. I think that his story is really symbolic of the change in Iraqi opinion concerning the war and the occupation. He told me that originally he had been in favor of the U.S. invasion—that he saw it as a way for the country to open up politically and economically. By March of 2004 though, a year after the invasion, he had changed his mind completely (after he had gone back to Iraq). He had become so outraged with the occupation and with the U.S. that he told me he had decided to sell his house in Jordan, and go to Iraq and form a militia in order to kill American soldiers. His story is symbolic of the Iraqi people as a whole because many were in favor of the occupation when it came to getting rid of Saddam Hussein; but after almost a year and a half of lacking consistent access to fresh water, electricity, jobs, adequate health care, schools, and security, many Iraqis believe that they are worse off now than before the war. Most people I have encountered believe that the occupation has been a total disaster, and they just want the U.S. to leave Iraq. The resistance is much stronger now than it was a year ago; it has much more breath now that Iraqis are so fed up.[141]

Kindy's observations are critical in that they reveal a crucial distinction ignored in mainstream media reporting and editorials: namely the assertion that support for the overthrow of Saddam Hussein's dictatorship does *not* necessarily translate into support for a prolonged American occupation. Highlighting the lack of Iraqi consent to the continued occupation is crucial when debating the "promotion of democracy" in Iraq (at least if democracy is based fundamentally upon the public consent).

Consideration of prospects for democracy promotion should also be contingent upon an understanding of American public opinion, which is also largely opposed to the Bush administration's plans for a long-term occupation of Iraq. Consider the following public opinion polling results:

- In September of 2004, 54 percent of Americans asked indicated that U.S. troops should be brought home from Iraq within the next year; The preference was repeated a year later, when in November 2005, 63 percent of Americans polled said they favored "bringing most of our troops home in the next year," as opposed to only 35 percent who said U.S. troops should remain in Iraq until a stable government is set up.[142]

- By August of 2005, 57 percent of Americans questioned thought that the war in Iraq had made the U.S. "less safe from terrorism."[143]

- Most Americans also reacted skeptically to the reliance on the American military power in promoting democracy abroad. In one opinion poll released in September 2005, 74 percent of Americans questioned said that the goal of overthrowing Iraq's dictatorship and "establishing democracy" was not a sufficient reason for going to war, while 72 percent said the experience "made them feel worse about the possibility of using military force to bring about democracy in the future."[144]

- Most Americans feel, contrary to the propaganda of the Bush administration and media, that the Iraq war was unnecessary. In a poll released in June of 2005, only 37 percent of Americans approved of Bush's handling of the Iraq war, while 61 percent felt that the war was moving in the wrong direction. During that same month, only 42 percent of Americans surveyed said they thought the war was worthwhile. In a poll published in April 2006, 67 percent of respondents said they thought that the Iraq war was a war of choice, rather than one of necessity.[145]

- Finally, most Americans oppose U.S. long term plans in establishing military bases in Iraq. Another study released in April 2006 found that only 27 percent of those asked supported keeping permanent U.S. military bases in Iraq (which is the Bush administration's plan), although 51 percent felt that the U.S. plans to retain such bases regardless of public opinion.[146]

Most Americans may not be aware that the Iraqi public is opposed to the occupation of Iraq. This may have to do with the fact that the mainstream press, while occasionally reporting such opposition, has not placed this revelation on par with other major themes seen in media reporting which reinforce the American commitment to "democratizing" Iraq. Is the U.S. a viable agent in promoting democracy in Iraq, or is its disregard for Iraqi opposition to the occupation a sign of the hampering, rather than strengthening of democracy? The prioritization of such critical questions is vital when attempting to expand the parochial constraints apparent within most mainstream discourse on the "democratization" of Iraq. On this point, those throughout the American dissident press are looking to engage in constructive debate that has been ignored in elite media discourse.

Notes

1. Julian E. Barnes, "The Tipping Point," *U.S. News & World Report,* 9 January 2006, 30; Jill Carroll, "Politics, Mesopotamian Style," *U.S. News & World Report,* 9 January, 2006, 34; Farhad Ajami, "Identity Voting in Iraq," *U.S. News & World Report,* 9 January 2006, 35; Julian E. Barnes, "Cracking an Insurgent Cell," *U.S. News & World Report,* 9 January 2006, 36.
2. Barnes, "Cracking an Insurgent Cell," 36.
3. Barnes, "Cracking an Insurgent Cell," 40.
4. Michael R. Gordon, "Bush Aide's Memo Doubts Iraqi Leader," *New York Times,* 29 November 2006, http://www.nytimes.com/2006/11/29/world/middleeast/29cnd-militaryhtml?ex=1322456400&en=688e0331df987eec&ei=5088&partner=rssnyt&emc=r ss (18 Mar. 2007).
5. Oprah Winfrey. *The Oprah Winfrey Show,* ABC, 23 January 2006.
6. Kim Segupta, "Rumsfeld 'Ignored Fallujah Warnings,'" *Independent,* 26 October 2004, http://news.independent.co.uk/world/amercas/story.jsp? (26 Oct. 2004).
7. Jerry Adler, "Jessica's Liberation," *Newsweek,* 14 April 2003, 42.
8. Rowman Scarborough, "Special Ops Say Lives Were on the Line in Lynch Rescue," *Washington Times,* 9 June 2003, http://washingtontimes.com/national/20030609-122701-9940r.htm (12 May 2005).
9. Adler, "Jessica's Liberation," 44.
10. CNN.com, "Lynch: Military Played up Rescue too much," 7 November 2003, http://www.cnn.com/2003/US/11/07/lynch.interview/index.html (21 Nov. 2003).
11. Joe Strupp, "How Papers are Covering Iraqi Civilian Casualties," *Editor & Publisher,* 8 April 2003, http://www.editorandpublisher.com/eandp/news/article_display.j sp?vnu_content_id=1859190 (7 Apr. 2004).
12. Eric Boehlert, "Reality Check," *Salon,* 6 May 2004, http://dir.salon.com/storynewsfeature/2004/05/06/images/index.html?pn=1 (17 Nov. 2005).
13. Shelton Rampton and John Stauber, *The Best War Ever: Lies, Damned Lies, and the Mess in Iraq* (New York: Jeremy Tarcher, 2006), 24-5.
14. Associated Press, "3,663 Iraqis Killed in Past 6 Months," 14 October 2005, http://www.truthout.org/cgi-bin/artman/exec/view.cgi/37/14817 (14 Oct. 2005).

15. Harold Meyerson, "Smart Bombs, Dumb War," *Washington Post*, 27 March 2003, 21(A).

16. I undertook the study of Iraqi vs. American deaths by searching the *Lexis Nexis* database during the one-month period from March 20 through April 20, 2003. The keyword "Iraq" was used in order to pull stories from that period that addressed the U.S. invasion. In total, there were 32 headlines that addressed American deaths, as compared with only 14 addressing Iraqi deaths. This translated into a ratio of 2.3:1 in favor of covering American deaths.

17. Iraq Body Count, "Keeping Civilian Deaths in the Eye of the World," 14 April 2003, http://www.iraqbodycount.org/press/archive/php (15 Apr. 2007); Iraq Coalition Casualty Count, "Military Fatalities: By Month," http://icasualties.org/oif (15 Apr. 2007).

18. Rob Stein, "100,000 Civilian Deaths Estimated in Iraq," *Washington Post*, 29 October 2004, 16(A).

19. Times Wire Services, "Conflict May Have Killed 100,000 Iraqis, Report Says," *Los Angeles Times*, 29 October 2004, 4(A).

20. Times Wire Services, "Conflict May Have Killed 100,000 Iraqis, Report Says," 2004.

21. Elizabeth Rosenthal, "Study Puts Iraqi Deaths of Civilians at 100,000," *New York Times*, 29 October 2004, 8(A).

22. Paul Reynolds, "Huge Gaps Between Iraqi Death Estimates," *BBC News*, 20 October 2006, http://news.bbc.co.uk/2/hi/middle_east/6045112.stm (18 Mar. 2007).

23. Times Wire Services, "Conflict May Have Killed 100,000 Iraqis, Report Says," 2004.; Stein, "100,000 Civilian Deaths Estimated in Iraq," 2004.; Rosenthal, "Study Puts Iraqi Deaths of Civilians at 100,000," 2004.

24. Anthony DiMaggio, "Damage Control: American Corporate Media Disregards the Lancet Report...Again," *Z Magazine*, 17 October 2006, http://www.zmag.org/content/showarticle.cfm?ItemID=11201 (18 Mar. 2006); Media Lens, "Media Alert: Lancet Report Co-Author Responds to Questions," *Z Magazine*, 2 November 2006, http://www.zmag.org/content/showarticle.cfm?ItemID=11309 (18 Mar. 2007).

25. DiMaggio, "Damage Control," 2006.

26. DiMaggio, "Damage Control," 2006.

27. George Monbiot, "The Media are Minimizing US and British War Crimes in Iraq," *Guardian*, 8 November 2005, http://www.guardian.co.uk/Columists/Column/0,56-73,1636606,00.html (8 Nov. 2005).

28. Les Roberts, "Iraq's Death Toll is far Worse than Our Leaders Admit," 14 February 2007, *Common Dreams*, http://www.commondreams.org/views07/0214-21.htm (20 Mar. 2007).

29. David Cromwell and David Edwards, *Guardians of Power: The Myth of the Liberal Media* (London: Pluto, 2006), 60.

30. Doug Ireland, "Why U.S. Media Dismissed Lancet Study," 27 January 2005, *Common Dreams*, http://www.commondreams.org/views05/0127-23.htm (27 Jan. 2005).

31. Oren Dorell, "Bush Puts Deaths of Iraqis at 30,000.," *USA Today*, sec. 1, 12 December 2005, 1; CNN.com, "Bush: Iraqi Democracy Making Progress," 12 December 2005, http://www.cnn.com/2005/POLITICS/12/12/bush.iraq/index.html (12 Dec. 2005); Edward Epstein, "Bush says 30,000 Iraqis Dead Since Invasion Began," *San Francisco Chronicle*, 13 December 2005, http://sfgate.com/cgi-bin/article.cgi?f=c/a/2005/12/13/MNG50G76G31.DTL (13 Dec. 2005); CBSnews.com, "Bush: 30,000 Iraqis Killed in Iraq," 12 December 2005, http://www.cbsnews.com/stories/2005/12/12/politics/printable11170-45.shtml (12 Dec. 2005).

32. David Edwards and David Cromwell, "Paved with Good Intentions," *Media Lens*, 25 January 2006, http://www.medialens.org/alerts/06/060125_paved_with_good.php (25 Jan. 2006).

33. George F. Will, "A War President's Job," *Washington Post*, 7 April 2004, 31(A).

34. Editorial, "Counting Heads," *New Republic*, 7 April 2003, 6.

35. Michael R. Gordon, "Goal of U.S.: Avoid a Siege," *New York* Times, 3 April 2003, 1(A).

36. Eric Schmitt and Bernard Weinraub, "Battle for Baghdad like War Plan: Kill Enemy, Limit Damage, Provide Aid," *New York Times*, 3 April 2003, 1(B).

37. Victoria Clarke, "Pentagon Briefing," *CNN.com*, 8 April 2003, http://transcripts.cnn.com/TRANSCRIPTS/0304/08/se.06.html (15 Jun. 2003).

38. John H. Cushman Jr. and Thom Shanker, "A War Like No Other Uses New 21st Century Methods to Disable Enemy Forces," *New York Times*, 10 April 2003, 5(B).

39. Charles M. Madigan, "Fast, Furious, Relentless: Lightning-Quick Campaign Ousts Hussein in 4 Weeks," *Chicago Tribune*, sec. 1, 20 April 2003, 1.

40. Laurie Goering and Evan Osnos, "Marines Cruising to Baghdad," *Chicago Tribune*, sec. 1, 5 April 2003, 1.

41. Michael R. Gordon, "A Tightening of the Noose," *New York Times*, 4 April 2003, 1(A).

42. John F. Burns, "The Question on Every Mind in Baghdad: When Will it Be?" *New York Times*, 20 March 2003, 1(A).

43. Evan Thomas, Rob Nordland, and Christian Caryl, "Operation Hearts and Minds," *Newsweek*, 29 December, 2005, 37-38.

44. CNN.com, "U.S. Targeting Insurgents in Northern Iraq," 9 September 2004, http://www.cnn.com/2004/WORLD/meast/09/09/iraq.main/index.html (21 Jun. 2005); Edmund Sanders, "U.S. Bombs Insurgent Targets in Baghdad," *Los Angeles Times*, 28 September 2004, 8(A).

45. CNN.com, "U.S.: 109 Insurgents Killed in Major Offensive," http://www.cnn.com-/2004/WORLD/meast/10/01/iraq.main/index.html (1 Oct. 2004).

46. Fox News, "Iraqi Prime Minister: Fallujah Assault Imminent," 6 November 2004, http://www.foxnews.com/story/0,2933,137671,00.html (6 Nov. 2004).

47. Patrick J. McDonnell and John Hendren, "Fallouja Fight Among Deadliest in Years for U.S.," *Los Angeles Times*, 2 December 2004, 10(A); Kirk Semple, Kirk and Sabrina Tavernise, "U.S. Reports Iraqi Civilian Casualties in Anti-Insurgent Sweep," *New York Times*, 10 November 2005, 14(A).

48. John Nichols and Robert W. McChesney, *Tragedy & Farce: How the American Media Sell Wars, Spin Elections, and Destroy Democracy* (New York: New Press, 2005), 49.

49. Patrick Cockburn, "Iraq: A Country Drenched in Blood," *Independent*, 20 March 2007, http://news.independent.co.uk/world/middle_east/article2374380.ece (20 Mar. 2007).

50. PBS.org, "Two Different Wars: Comparing Arab and U.S. Coverage of the Iraq War," 4 April 2003, http://www.pbs.org/newshour/extra/features/jan-june03/media_4-3.html (20 May 2005).

51. David Carr, Jim Rutenberg, and Jacques Steinberg, "Telling War's Deadly Story at Just Enough Distance," *New York Times*, 7 April 2003, 13(B).

52. Chris Hedges, "We're Not Mother Theresas in Flak Jackets," in *Feet to the Fire: The Media After 9/11*, ed. Kristina Borjesson (New York: Prometheus, 2005), 517, 525.

53. Bradley Graham, "Enemy Body Counts Used," *Washington Post*, 24 October 2005, http://www.washingtonpost.com/wpdyn/content/discussion/2005/10/24/DI200510-2400588.html (3 Jan. 2007).

54. Howard Zinn, *Terrorism and War* (New York: Seven Stories, 2002).

55. Noam Chomsky, *Failed States: The Abuse of Power and the Assault on Democracy* (New York: Metropolitan, 2006), 36.

56. Howard Zinn, "The Others," *Nation*, 11 February 2002, http://www.thenation.com/doc/20020211/zinn (2 Aug. 2006).

57. Zinn, *Terrorism and War*, 24.

58. Zinn, *Terrorism and War*, 82.

59. Gilbert Achcar, *The Clash of the Barbarisms: September 11 and the Making of the New World Order* (New York: Monthly Review, 2002), 67.

60. Jim Rutenberg, "U.S. News Organizations Tell Employees to Leave Baghdad," *New York Times*, 19 March 2003, 17(A).

61. John M. Broder, "U.S. Military has No Count of Iraqi Dead in Fighting," *New York Times*, 2 April 2003, 1(A).

62. Eric Schmitt and Thom Shanker, "A Full Range of Technology is Applied to Bomb Falluja," *New York Times*, 30 April 2004, 10(A).

63. Shepard Smith, *Studio B*, Fox News, 9 November 2004.

64. Dahr Jamail, "Civilians Feared Dead in Fallujah," *Z Magazine*, 16 November 2004, http://www.zmag.org/content/showarticle.cfm?SectionID=15&ItemID=6662 (16 Nov. 2004).

65. Jackie Spinner, "Fallujah Battered and Mostly Quiet after the Battle," *Washington Post*, 16 November 2004, 13(A).

66. Patrick J. McDonnell, "Fight for Fallouja Began with a Ruse," *Los Angeles Times*, 16 November 2004, 9(A).

67. Christine Hauser, "UN Chief for Human Rights Raises Concern on Falluja," *New York Times*, 16 November 2004, http://www.nytimes.com/2004/11/16/international/middleeast/16cndfall.html?ex=1141016400&en=85a4c049f45d4ae0&ei=5070 (16 Nov. 2004).

68. Rita Cosby, *Fox News Live*, Fox News, 14 November 2004.

69. CNN Live. CNN, 8 November 2004.

70. Editorial, "Costly Troop Deficit in Iraq," *New York Times*, 22 November 2004, 30(A).

71. Eric Schmitt, "A Goal is Met. What's Next?" *New York Times*, 15 November 2004, 1(A); Patrick J. McDonnell and John Hendren, "Fallouja Fight Among Deadliest in Years for U.S.," *Los Angeles Times*, 2 December 2004, 10(A); Eric Schmitt and Thom Shanker, "Past Battles Won and Lost Helped in Falluja Assault," *New York Times*, 22 November 2004, 6(A).

72. Editorial, "Why We Must Take Falluja," *Los Angeles Times*, 12 November 2004, 13(B).

73. Sachi Koto, *CNN Headline News*, CNN, 14 November 2004.

74. Scott Ritter, "Squeezing Jello in Iraq," *Al Jazeera*, 10 November 2004, http://english.aljazeera.net/NR/exeres/718AE278-58EE-431F-8045-5A3F505021B8.html (10 Nov. 2004).

75. Cliff Kindy and Anthony DiMaggio, "Interview with Cliff Kindy of the Christian Peacemaker Teams," *Indy*, 6 October 2004, 7.

76. Kindy and DiMaggio, "Interview," 2004.

77. Kindy and DiMaggio, "Interview," 2004.

78. Sherry Ricchiardi, "Missed Signals," *American Journalism Review*, August/September 2004, http://www.ajr.org/article_printable.asp?id=3716 (12 Apr. 2006).

79. Ricchiardi, "Missed Signals," 2004.
80. Joe Strupp, "Study: Media Self-Censored on Iraq," *Alternet*, 18 March 2005, http://www.alternet.org/mediaculture/21538/ (20 Mar. 2007).
81. Ricchiardi, "Missed Signals," 2004.
82. Eric Boehlert, "Reality Check," 2004.
83. Dick Meyer, "Rush: MPs Just 'Blowing Off Steam,'" *CBSNews.com*, 6 May 2004, http://www.cbsnews.com/stories/2004/05/06/opinion/meyer/main616021.shtml (3 Apr. 2006).
84. Bill O'Reilly, "Inside Iraq's Abu Ghraib Prison," *FoxNews.com*, 4 May 2004, http://www.foxnews.com/story/0,2933,118955,00.html (13 May 2006).
85. Jeremy Scahill, "Missing the Scandal at Abu Ghraib," *Alternet*, 16 February 2006, http://www.alternet.org/story/32321/ (16 Feb. 2006).
86. Ricchiardi, "Missed Signals," 2004.
87. Ricchiardi, "Missed Signals," 2004.
88. Agence France Press, "Fearing Backlash, Pentagon Moves to Block New Abu Ghraib Photos," 13 August 2005, http://www.commondreams.org/headlines05/0813-02.htm (12 Apr. 2006).
89. FAIR, "The Consequences of Covering Up," December 2005, http://www.fair.org-/index.php?page=2715 (13 Apr. 2006).
90. FAIR, "The Consequences of Covering Up," 2005.
91. Andrew Marshall, "U.S. Troops Tortured Iraqis in Mosul, Documents Show," *Common Dreams*, 26 March 2005, http://www.commondreams.org/cgi-bin/print.cgi?file =headlines05/0326-01.htm (14 Apr. 2006).
92. Alexander G. Higgins, "Report: 70-90% held in error in Iraq," *Arizona Daily Star*, 11 May 2004, http://www.azstarnet.com/dailystar/printDS/21552.php (15 Apr. 2006).
93. Seymour Hersh, *Chain of Command: The Road from 9/11 to Abu Ghraib* (New York: Harper Perennial, 2005), 40.
94. Douglas Jehl and Kate Zernike, "Scant Evidence, Long Detention Cited for Iraqis," *New York* Times, 1(A).
95. Neil Mackay, "Iraq's Child Prisoners," *Sunday Herald*, 1 August 2004, http://www.truthout.org/docs_2005/printer_080405S.shtml (11 Apr. 2006).
96. Human Rights Watch, "Torture and Ill-Treatment of Detainees in Iraqi Custody," 2005, http://hrw.org/reports/2005/iraq0105/index.htm (5 May 2006).
97. James Risen, *State of War: The Secret History of the CIA and the Bush Adminis-tration* (New York: Free Press, 2006), 32.
98. Zaki Chehab, *Inside the Resistance: The Iraqi Insurgency and the Future of the Middle East* (New York: Nation, 2005), 106, 109-10.
99. Chehab, *Inside the Resistance*, 113.
100. Chehab, *Inside the Resistance*, 118.
101. Brian Knowlton, "U.S. Cites Array of Rights Abuses by the Iraqi Government in 2004," *New York Times*, 1 March 2005, 1(A).
102. Knowlton, "U.S. Cites Array of Rights Abuses," 2004.
103. Editorial, "The Horror of Abu Ghraib," *Nation*, 6 May 2004, http://www.thenatio-n.com/doc/20040524/lede (12 Mar. 2006).
104. Bob Wing, "Racist Imagery and Humiliation: The Color of Abu Ghraib," *Counter-punch*, 18 May 2004, http://www.counterpunch.org/wing05182004.html (11 Apr. 2006).
105. CBSnews.com, "Baby Noor 'A Real Delight,'" 10 January 2006, http://www.cbsnews.com/stories/2006/01/10/health/main1194568.shtml (17 Mar. 2006).
106. MSNBC.com, "Iraqi Baby Recovering from Surgery in U.S.," 9 January 2006, http://www.msnbc.msn.com/id/10771891/ (17 Mar. 2006).

107. David E. Sanger, "Bush's Task: To Prepare Americans for Long Fight," *New York Times*, 28 September 2003, 11(A).

108. James Glanz, "Funds Fade, Deaths Rise as Iraq Rebuilding Lags," *New York Times*, 31 October 2005, 8(A).

109. Paul Richter, "Rapid Personnel Shifts Hinder U.S. Efforts to Rebuild Iraq," *Los Angeles Times*, 17 November 2005, 1(A).

110. Hannah K. Strange, "Iraq Reconstruction Flawed, Say Experts," *Washington Times*, 26 July 2005, http://www.washtimes.com/upi-breaking/20040726-053029-5356r.htm (26 Jul. 2005).

111. T. Christian Miller, "Iraq Reconstruction Moving to Local Level," *Boston Globe*, 10 April 2005, http://www.boston.com/news/world/middleeast/articles/2005/04/10/iraq_-reconstruction_moving_to_local_level/ (19 Apr. 2006).

112. Ellen Knickmeyer, "U.S. has End in Sight on Iraq Rebuilding," *Washington Post*, 2 January 2006, 1(A).

113. Christian Parenti, "Fables of the Reconstruction," *Nation*, 30 August 2004, http://www.thenation.com/doc/20040830/parenti (22 Mar. 2006).

114. James Glanz, "Rebuilding of Iraqi Pipeline as Disaster Waiting to Happen," *New York Times*, 25 April 2006, http://www.nytimes.com/2006/04/25/world/middleeast/25/world/middleeast/25pipeline.html?ex=1303617600&en=d01c31229dfae9f2ei=5088&partner=rssnyt&emc=rss (25 Apr. 2006).

115. John Ward Anderson and Bassam Sebti, "Billion-Dollar Start Falls Short in Iraq," *Washington Post*, 16 April 2006, 11(A).

116. Chomsky, *Failed States*, 60.

117. Glanz, "Rebuilding of Iraqi Pipeline as Disaster Waiting to Happen," 2006.

118. Ed Harriman, "Cronyism and Kickbacks," *London Review of Books*, 26 January 2006, http://www.lrb.co.uk/v28/n02/harr04_.html (13 Mar. 2006).

119. Harriman, "Cronyism and Kickbacks," 2006.

120. Al Jazeera, "Limited Progress in Iraq Rebuilding," 1 August 2005, http://english.aljazeera.net/News/archive/archive?ArchiveId=13792 (3 Jan. 2007).

121. Al Jazeera, "Limited Progress in Iraq Rebuilding," 2005.; Andrew Gumbel, "White House to Withdraw Funding for Rebuilding Iraq," *Independent*, 3 January 2006, http://news.independent.co.uk/world/americas/article336300.ece (3 Jan. 2006).

122. Al Jazeera, "Limited Progress in Iraq Rebuilding," 2006.

123. Parenti, "Fables of Reconstruction," 2004.

124. Suzanne Goldenberg, "Bush Pulls the Plug on Iraq Reconstruction," *Guardian*, 3 January 2006, http://www.guardian.co.uk/Iraq/Story/0,2763,1676911,00.html (3 Jan. 2006).

125. Ellen Knickmeyer, "U.S. has End in Sight on Iraq Rebuilding," *Washington Post*, 2 January 2006, 1(A).

126. David Cortright, "Iraq: The Human Toll," *Nation*, 27 July 2005, http://www.thenation.com/doc.mhtml?i=20050801&s=cortright (12 Jun. 2005).

127. Cortright, "Iraq: The Human Toll," 2005.

128. Eric Schmitt and Edward Wong, "U.S. Study Paints Somber Portrait of Iraqi Discord," *New York Times*, 9 April 2006, 1(A).

129. BBC News, "Children 'Starving' in New Iraq," 31 March 2005, http://www.truthout.org/docs_2005/printer_033105Z.shtml (31 Mar. 2005); Jonathon Fowler, "Child Hunger in Iraq Said About Double," *Associated Press*, 31 March 2005, http://www.boston.com/news/world/articles/2005/03/31/child_hunger_in_iraq_said_abou t_double?mode=PF (31 Mar. 2005).

130. Chris Shumway, "Iraqis Endure Worse Conditions than under Saddam," *Z Magazine*, 19 May 2005, http://www.zmag.org/content/showarticle.cfm?sectionID=15&ItemID=7894 (19 May 2005).

131. Shumway, "Iraqis Endure Worse Conditions than under Saddam," 2005.

132. Bradley S. Klapper, "US Practice of Starving out Iraqi Civilians is Inhumane, says UN," 15 October 2005, *Independent*, http://news.independent.co.uk/world/middle_east/article319725.ece (15 Oct. 2005).

133. Noam Chomsky, Edward Herman, and Anthony DiMaggio "Q/A on the Iraq War," *Z Magazine*, 29 November 2005, http://www.zmag.org/content/showarticle.cfm?ID=9215 (29 Nov. 2005).

134. *Weapons of Mass Deception*, DVD, directed by Danny Schechter (Cinema Libre, 2004).

135. International Republican Institute, "Survey of Iraqi Public Opinion," 24 November-5 December 2004, http://www.iri.org/mena/iraq2.asp (4 Jan. 2007).

136. Thomas E. Ricks, "82% of Iraqis Oppose US Occupation," *Washington Post*, 13 May 2004, http://www.globalpolicy.org/ngo/advocacy/protest/iraq/2004/0513poll.htm (13 May 2004).

137. Cesar G. Soriano and Steven Komarow, "Poll: Iraqis out of Patience," *USA Today*, 28 April 2004, http://www.usatoday.com/news/world/iraq/2004-04-28-poll-cover_htm (28 Apr. 2004).

138. Sean Rayment, "Secret MoD Poll: Iraqis Support Attacks on British Troops," *Telegraph*, 23 October 2005, http://telegraph.co.uk/news/main.jhtml?xml=/news/2005/10 /23/wirq23.xml (23 Oct. 2005).; Program for International Policy Attitudes, "Most Iraqis Want U.S. Troops out Within a Year," 27 September 2006, http://www.worldpublicopinion.org/pipa/articles/home_page250.php?nid=&id=&pnt=250&lb=hmpg1 (15 Apr. 2007).

139. Program for International Policy Attitudes, "What the Iraqi Public Wants," 31 January 2006, http://www.pipa.org/OnlineReports/Iraq/Iraq_Jan06_rpt.pdf (31 Jan. 2006).

140. Jon Leyne, "Report Urges Arab World Reforms," *BBC*, 5 April 2005, http://news.bbc.co.uk/2/hi/middle_east/4413085.stm (5 Apr. 2005).

141. Cliff Kindy and Anthony DiMaggio, "Interview with Cliff Kindy," *Indy*, 6 October 2004, 7.

142. Pollingreport.com, "ABC News/Washington Post Poll, 23-26 September 2004, http://www.pollingreport.com/iraq.htm (15 Sep. 2006); and Harris Poll, "American's Confidence in Future of Iraq at New Low, Poll Shows," *Wall Street Journal*, 21 November 2005, http://online.wsj.com/public/article/SB113234687823301680uUqDGTKrDhI-QeDAlZhKP_tq7l4g_20061121.html?mod=tff_main_tff_top (27 Nov. 2005).

143. Dick Polman, "Majority of Americans have Lost Confidence in the War, Polls Show," *Common Dreams*, 14 August 2005, http://www.commondreams.org/headlines05/0814-01.htm (14 Aug. 2005).

144. Program for International Policy Attitudes, "Public Rejects Using Military Force to Promote Democracy," 29 September 2005, http://www.pipa.org/_admin/cms/fullPage.php?visit=1&id=87 (12 Oct. 2005).

145. Robin Toner and Marjorie Connelly, "Bush's Support on Major Issues Tumbles in Poll," *New York Times*, 17 June 2005, 1(A); Rupert Cornwell, "Bush Policies Blocked as US Mood on Iraq Sours," *Independent*, 17 June 2005, http://www.truthout.org/cgi-bin/artman/exec/view.cgi/37/11941/printer (17 June 2005); Program for International Policy Attitudes, "Two in Three Americans Call Iraq a War of Choice, Not Necessity," 25 April 2006, http://www.worldpublicopinion.org/pipa/articles/ home_page/179.php?nid =&id=&pnt=179&lb=hmpg2 (3 May 2006).

146. Program for International Policy Attitudes, "US Public Opposes Permanent Military Bases in Iraq, but Majority Thinks US Plans to Keep Them," 25 April 2006, http://www.worldpublicopinion.org/pipa/articles/home_page/177.php?nid=&id=&pnt=17 7&lb=hmpg2 (3 May 2006).

9

Catapult the Media

President George W. Bush once stated that, "in my line of work, you got to keep repeating things over and over and over again for the truth to sink in, to kind of catapult the propaganda."[1] Like the Bush administration, the American mass media has long been known for repetition when it comes to the promulgation of pro-war propaganda. The mainstream media's reliance on government propaganda was explored at great length earlier in this book. And yet, many criticisms of wartime media coverage fail to discuss constructive alternatives to the status quo of government-dominated reporting.

Focusing solely on criticisms of the U.S. media's one-sided framing of the events in Iraq is seriously limiting because it fails to identify alternative models of reporting which the American public may explore in their search of a wider diversity of news and views. The growth of independent, non-establishment media could do much to further media independence from entrenched political and economic interests.

A media system priding itself in greater levels of balance would require the incorporation of divergent and dissenting views, not merely on a nominal or infrequent level, but on a regular basis. The emergence of such a system, where a plethora of pro-war and anti-war views thrive, becomes less and less likely in the face of extreme corporate consolidation and conglomeration of media. As fewer and fewer corporations exercise more control over media markets, views reflected in the news are further homogenized, rather than diversified.

Some scholars have spoken critically of the "cast iron grid"[2] through which a state-centric approach to studying media and domestic and international politics takes precedence. "Indexing" could be seen as one example of this state-centric approach to the study of media, as the emphasis on elite disagreement as the basis for media criticism of government is of primary concern. In a break with this tradition, this chapter seeks to analyze national and transnational media systems that exist largely (if not entirely) outside of the U.S. political-military state apparatus that traditionally dominates news American reporting. Rather than merely "indexing" reporting and editorializing to reflect the major criti cisms of Republicans, Democrats, and military officials, these alternative media systems are less bound by the conventional dogmas that privilege official sources, and less likely to allow those sources to dominate news and editorial content.

In presenting alternative models of framing the Iraq war, the intention here is not to pick one over all others, but to recognize that many different media systems provide valuable insights suppressed by American mainstream media. The national media systems focused on in this chapter distinguish themselves in one way or another from American mainstream media in that they present substantive criticisms of the invasion and occupation of Iraq, rather than relying primarily upon the pragmatic, strategic criticisms described in chapter 4. For one, the more anti-war leaning parts of the British and Australian Press— particularly the *Guardian* and the *Independent* of London, and the *Sydney Morning Herald*—have more vigorously pursued a style of reporting that frames the news in ways that challenges the legitimacy of the U.S. presence in Iraq and casts a negative light on U.S. actions throughout the Middle East. The American independent media (or Progressive-Left media), is another example of a media system that seriously questions the validity of the U.S. role in the "War on Terror." These anti-war media aim to counter the propagandistic coverage in the American corporate media.

Unembedded, "unilateral" journalism is often a preferred method of reporting in alternative media paradigms. Unilteral reporters, such as Dahr Jamail, Rahul Mahajan, David Enders, Aaron Glantz, Christian Parenti, Patrick Cockburn and Robert Fisk—all reporting *outside* the U.S. mass media—pursue a substantively different method of reporting than American embeds, who get their news by traveling with the U.S. military. Unembedded journalists have risked their lives by reporting away from the protection of U.S. troops, as the case of Mazen Dana demonstrates. Their coverage, however, often reflects their strong level of independence from government-dominated narratives.

Five months after the 2003 U.S. invasion, and three months after President Bush declared that, "major combat operations have ended," Iraq remained an unsafe place for reporters. August 17, 2003 marked the death of Mazen Dana, a cameraman for *Reuters* news service who was reporting outside of the protection of the American military from a bridge outside the Abu Ghraib prison in west Baghdad. Awarded the International Press Freedom Award, and considered "one of *Reuters*' finest cameramen,"[3] Dana had considerable experience in wartime media coverage. Reporting in the West Bank for over two years on escalating Israeli and Palestinian bloodshed, Dana was no stranger to the perils of chronicling violent conflict. Dana was reassigned from the West Bank for his own security, after Israeli Defense Forces repeatedly assaulted him, breaking his hands twice and shooting him dozen of times with rubber bullets.[4]

Tragically, Dana's situation did not improve after he began reporting from Iraq, as he was killed by an American tank that fired a large caliber machine gun round into his chest.[5] Although American soldiers attempted to resuscitate him, it was too late, as he succumbed to extensive wounds, his camera having caught the whole attack in progress. Dana became another of the media's many casualties in covering the Iraq war, despite the fact that he had obtained permission to shoot from the bridge outside Abu Ghraib after talking with the prison's perimeter guards. The Pentagon's response to his death was similar to its answers to the deaths of other journalists at the hands of U.S. forces, as U.S. officials attempted to exculpate American soldiers for their role in his death. While declaring that the attack was "regrettable," the Pentagon also stated that the soldiers "acted within the rules of engagement."[6] In explaining their actions, soldiers on the ground who were responsible for the attack explained that they had mistaken Dana's camera for a missile launcher, as the Abu Ghraib prison had come under mortar attacks earlier in the day. The responses from the Pentagon and from soldiers involved in the incident were not surprising for those who were familiar with the military's refusal to place direct blame on the armed forces for the deaths of reporters. Nonetheless, their refusals did not lessen the fury of Dana's fellow journalists, as well as other media organizations in which Dana was involved. *Reuters*, the *Committee for the Protection of Journalists*, the *International Federation for Journalists*, and *Reporters Without Frontiers* collectively called on the U.S. government to reveal more details about the circumstances surrounding Dana's death. Tom Glocer, Chief Executive of *Reuters* commented that, "coming so soon after the death of Taras Protsuyuk" (another cameraman who had been killed by an American tank on April 8, 2003), Dana's death had motivated him to call "upon the highest levels of the U.S. government for a full and comprehensive investigation into this terrible tragedy."[7]

The story of Dana is central to the ongoing struggle between embedded reporters who have taken up positions within the American military in Iraq, and unembedded, "unilateral" journalists, who have questioned negative consequences of the embedding process. The question of journalistic ethics presented by embedding is only one of many points of contention between those in the American media who have willingly embedded themselves, not only with the U.S. military in Iraq, but also within ideological positions that reinforce the Iraq war, and others who seek to question the legitimacy of the U.S. role in world affairs. It is through this conflict that one must understand the drastically different interpretations of the Iraq war presented throughout different media systems. The increasingly popular practice of embedding journalists receives much attention throughout this chapter, particularly in light of the view that "professional" journalism is dependent upon media and government collaboration within the war zone.

Unembedded reporting is a main source of information driving progressive writings and reporting in the American Progressive-Left media. The independence from potential government censorship that unilaterals enjoy often translates into stronger criticisms of the U.S. occupation of Iraq. In addition, the independent reporting and anti-war views of *Al Jazeera*, the Arab news outlet based out of Qatar, stands out as an important example of critical journalism.

The alternative media systems seen in the U.S., Britain, Australia, and the Middle East have one important thing in common: they all base their independence from official propaganda, to a large degree, on unilateral reporting, in order to identify and highlight reports from, and perspectives on, Iraq that challenge the U.S. government's statements and promises. In the United States' assault on Falluja, for example, unembedded journalists for *Al Jazeera* evoked the anger of the Bush administration as they filed reports that American soldiers had killed Iraqi civilians—reports that traveled throughout the Arab World and incited hostility toward the U.S. government. As one of the most influential news organizations in the Middle East and the world, *Al Jazeera* receives the most attention in this chapter because it has presented perhaps the *most* powerful challenge to U.S. legitimacy in Iraq, considering its massive audience of tens of millions throughout the Arab World.

Progressive-Left Media

Saturday, July 12 2003 marked the death of the seventeenth Western journalist in Iraq between the period of March and July of that year. Twenty-four years old, Richard Wild had traveled to Iraq from Britain in order to fulfill his dream of becoming a war reporter. Shortly after interviewing the director of the Baghdad museum of natural history, Wild was gunned down on a busy street across from the museum while attempting to hail a cab. Wild was in the middle of completing a news story chronicling the looting of Iraq's precious antiquities during the March U.S. invasion. Sadly, Wild died shortly after he was taken to a nearby hospital by a local who witnessed the attack.[8] While the shots were fired from within a group of students, Wild's attacker, nonetheless, was not identified, and was able to escape in the confusion.

Many reporting on the incident suspected that Wild had become a target due to his communication with American troops on the streets of Baghdad and his apparent "military style" dress—both of which may have made attackers think he was an American soldier.[9] The British government's response to the attack evoked outrage amongst journalists who knew Wild, and particularly amongst his family. In response to his family's criticisms, the British Foreign Office answered that British forces were, as the *Telegraph* of London reports, "powerless to act at the time because coalition forces and Iraqi police had been too busy" with other military operations.[10]

Wild, like many other unembedded journalists working throughout Iraq, was at a security disadvantage in that, unlike embedded reporters, he did not enjoy the protection of American or British military forces. His death is a reminder of the danger that unilateral journalists place themselves in, in order to report free from government influence and censorship. Aaron Glantz, a unilateral reporter in Iraq for *Pacifica Radio*, reflects on the death of two journalists in mid-2005 at the hands of American forces: "Hearing these stories I think about my own time as an unembedded journalist in Iraq. In six months reporting from the ground, I never once had a gun pointed at me by an "insurgent," but on two occasions I felt personally threatened by an American soldier's machine gun."[11]

Independence from military censorship and guidelines comes not only at the cost of a reporter's physical safety, but with other disadvantages as well. In reporting outside of the corporate media establishment, journalists suffer from a slew of setbacks that make it difficult for them to compete with their corporate counterparts. This has been a major problem with Progressive-Left media, which, despite its critical unembedded reporting throughout Iraq, has been unable to compete with the U.S. mass media in terms of monetary resources and national audience size. David Enders, co-founder and editor for the *Baghdad Bulletin*, a weekly newspaper started by American reporters in Iraq, elaborates more fully on the disadvantages non-corporate media face during times of war. "Operating on a shoestring budget," Enders explains that his paper had to "run an extremely tight ship" just to raise enough money to cover the costs of printing the paper every week.[12] Largely unrecognized by the mainstream American press and the U.S. Coalition Provisional Authority in Iraq, Enders and his staff (along with other independent media networks operating throughout Iraq) were marginalized due to their lack of "credibility." Ignored at CPA press conferences and chastised by higher-level American military leaders in the field for lacking "real credentials" and for throwing "impartiality" to the wind, Enders was punished for his work at *Occupation Watch*, an anti-occupation, non-governmental organization and information network working in Iraq.[13]

Reporters who file critical stories also have to worry about being detained by the U.S. military. Ali Fadhill, *Guardian* reporter and winner of the Foreign Press Association Young Journalist of the Year Award was detained in Iraq by the U.S. after he investigated claims that millions of dollars worth of reconstruction funds controlled by the American and British government were "misused or misappropriated." American troops told Fadhill that they were searching for "insurgents" as they seized the videotapes from his home in Baghdad that he was planning on using in his news program. After invading his home, American soldiers fired shots into his bedroom where his wife and children were sleeping; subsequently, Fadhill was detained, hooded and questioned in relation to "insurgent" activity.[14]

Unembedded reporters are constantly in danger in Iraq, as the stories of Richard Wild and Ali Fadhill reveal. 2005 was a particularly deadly year for reporters, as sixty-three were killed throughout the world—twenty-four alone in Iraq.[15] Enders effectively recounts the dangers of reporting from a war zone, as his staff was forced "to contend with Kalashnikov-toting Iraqi gunmen and lumpy U.S. troops nearly shooting them up" at checkpoints.[16] In his reporting from the Iraqi Republican Palace, Enders detailed his experiences in May of 2003, less than two months after the fall of Saddam's government: "We walk around the grounds, wary of unexploded bombs or booby traps set by fleeing Iraqi troops. An unexploded grenade round sits on the sidewalk near the pool complex, which, along with the workout rooms, has been ransacked. . . . I wish I could have seen the country before the bombing and the invasion and the looting, the sheer megalomania of it all."[17]

Reporting for the *Truthout* news service (a major media outlet in the American Progressive-Left media), Steve Weissman claims that U.S. forces have failed to "protect journalists by training soldiers to recognize the difference between rocket launchers and TV cameras," their failure to pass on information concerning the locations of journalists in Iraq reporting away from U.S. troop positions, the refusal to hold soldiers accountable for killing journalists, and finally, the growing practice among U.S. forces of detaining unilateral journalists without charge in order to thwart critical reporting of potentially embarrassing incidents involving American soldiers.[18]

Unilateral reporters are also in danger of being attacked by Islamist and resistance groups operating throughout Iraq. As security throughout Iraq has deteriorated under the U.S. occupation, reporters are increasingly fearful for their lives. Robert Fisk worries about the possibility of being kidnapped as he travels outside the Green Zone in Iraq to conduct interviews and report stories: "If I go to see someone in any particular location, I give myself twelve minutes, because that is how long I reckon it takes a man with a mobile phone to summon gunmen to the scene in a car. . . the roads are infested with insurgents, checkpoints, hooded men and throat cutters. That's what it's like."[19] Maggie O'Kane of the *Guardian* shares similar experiences: "Since al Zarqawi's people started cutting off heads it is too dangerous for foreigners to go out. . . . We [reporters] no longer know what is going on but we are pretending we do. Any decent reporter knows that reporting from Baghdad now does a disservice to the truth."[20]

The U.S. government's attempts at discouraging independent anti-war reporting in Iraq (by promoting embedding and harassing unilateral reporters) is not surprising considering the strong challenge to U.S. occupation seen from non-embedded reporters. Christian Parenti, one of the many Americans who reported independently of U.S. troops in Iraq, painted a pessimistic picture of Iraqi society under American occupation: "after one year of occupation, Iraq—the birthplace of civilization—lies in ruins: occupied, violent, corrupt. . . and stalked by a gathering storm of religious fundamentalism irredentist nationalisms and criminal mayhem."[21] Citing an increase in repression against Iraqi women, Parenti further explained: "Many women and girls stay locked inside their homes for weeks at a time for fear that they will be assaulted on the street or because male relatives will not allow them to go out. Increasingly, those who do venture out wear veils."[22] Parenti's portrayal of the situation in Iraq shortly after the U.S. invasion stood in stark contrast to that of the mainstream media, which by-and-large portrayed the country, despite "modest" roadblocks, as on the path towards democracy and prosperity.

Other unilateral reporters have taken issue with mainstream American reporting of the war. Aaron Glantz, author of *How America Lost Iraq*, and reporter for the Progressive-Left *Pacifica* radio, claims that the mass media has neglected reporting on humanitarian crises gripping Iraq. Glantz focuses on the larger picture of Iraq's dire condition as a result of two U.S. wars that crippled their economy and led to the deaths of hundreds of thousands of Iraqis through sanctions: "The humanitarian situation in Iraq is a mess and needs to be reported. . . the long-term prognosis for the future of Iraq is not necessarily rosy. . . the water is so bad there that there is a possibility of an epidemic of cholera in Baghdad. . . parents are afraid to send their children to school because the streets are unsafe even during the day. Many people have been unable to return to work and the economy is a disaster after 25 years of war and sanctions."[23] Disagreeing with calls in the American mainstream media for an escalation of the "pacification"

of Iraqi resistance fighters as a means of getting Iraq back on track, Glantz instead predicts that such actions will "make the Iraqi people angry and make
more people join the resistance."[24]

The anti-war reporting of unilaterals on the ground leaves little question
over the scope of Iraq's infrastructure and security deterioration. By publishing
his blog online and reporting for Independent-Left publications such as *Z Magazine*, Dahr Jamail became one of the most well known journalists reporting out
of Iraq on the country's deteriorating security and living conditions. Jamail's
online dispatches provide a more thorough understanding of the problems confronting over twenty-five million Iraqis living under "brutal, chaotic lawlessness
caused by the American occupation."[25] Jamail blames the American mass media
in part for these conditions, for what he views as the "whitewashing [of] the
degrading situation" in cities like Falluja: as the town "begins to resemble a
concentration camp; the death toll of innocent Iraqis continues to escalate. . . the
American troops continue their aggressive operations—and all that comes
through here in this still peaceful-seeming land are flickering images of car-
bomb carnage."[26]

Reporting from Falluja, American journalist Rahul Mahajan made similar
assessments of the devastation of the November 2004 U.S. attack. Mahajan was
one of the few unilateral journalists to confirm reports of U.S. snipers targeting
ambulance drivers in the city during the American siege that was launched on
November 8 2004. Mahajan's recount of these assassinations is disturbing, as he
reported firsthand an ambulance, "with two neat, precise bullet-holes in the
windshield on the driver's side, pointing down at an angle that indicated they
would have hit the driver's chest. Another ambulance again with a single, neat
bullet-hole in the windshield. There's no way this was due to panicked spraying
of fire. These were deliberate shots to kill people in driving the ambulances."[27]
Strict limitations on reporters' access to Falluja have prohibited critical reporting
(such as that of Mahajan) of the American attack.[28]

The anti-war editorializing of Progressive-Left activists, writers, and journalists in the U.S. complements the critical views of many American unilateral
reporters in Iraq. Even before the invasion of Iraq, the anti-war leanings in Progressive-Left media were apparent. Writing for the *Nation*, David Cortright portrayed the invasion of Iraq as "illegal," "unjust," and "completely unnecessary,"[29] while Howard Zinn, writing for the *Progressive* magazine, classified the
conflict as "a war that is not a war but a massacre. . . mayhem caused by the
most powerful military machine on Earth raining thousands of bombs on a fifth-
rate military power already reduced to poverty by two wars and ten years of economic sanctions."[30] In *Z Magazine*, labor activist David Bacon assailed the
American occupation for exacerbating Iraq's economic and labor problems:
"Every day, the economic policies of the occupying authorities create more hunger among Iraq's working people, transforming them into a pool of low-wage,
semi-employed labor, desperate for jobs at almost any price."[31]

In the realm of independent television media, Amy Goodman has pioneered
an increasingly popular form of adversarial reporting and investigative journalism on programs such as *Democracy Now!* on the *Free Speech Television* net-

work. Goodman has long been interested in holding political officials and prominent mainstream media figures' feet to the fire by challenging pro-war propaganda. Goodman takes issue with corporate ownership and dominance of the media, as well as the resulting pro-war ideological apparatus that is supported by such dominance. Speaking of corporate consolidation, Goodman argues: "Since the first Gulf War, the media have become even more homogenized—and the news more uniform and gung ho. Six huge corporations now control the major U.S. media: *News Corporation, General Electric, Time Warner, Disney, Viacom,* and *Bertelsmann.*"[32] Goodman warns that narrow monopoly ownership has dire implications for professional journalism: "the lack of diversity behind the news helps explain the lack of diversity in the news."[33]

Speaking about the trend toward "sanitization of the news"[34] during times of conflict, Goodman believes that the mainstream press has conformed to the agenda of the major political parties: "The rules of mainstream journalism are simple: The Republicans and Democrats establish the acceptable boundaries of debate. When those groups agree—which is often—there is simply no debate. That's why there is such appalling silence around issues of war and peace...the media provides a forum for those in power. When there is an establishment consensus—such as during the period leading up to the [Iraq] war—the media just reflects that...but what about the nonofficial voices around the country and the world who have been consistently opposed to the invasion, the millions of people who took to the streets to say no to war? These voices have been almost completely excluded."[35] Attempting to rectify this marginalization of voices of dissent has been a main goal of networks such as *Free Speech T.V.* in general, and programs like *Democracy Now!* in particular. *Democracy Now!* is aired on over 400 public radio and television stations throughout the United States.

Anti-war activists in the independent media were quick to frame the prospects for going to war from an international law perspective. Doug Ireland, writing for *In These Times*, attacked the war plan as "a foolhardy project" that is "illegal under international law."[36] Ireland was referring to the illegality of preventive war under the United Nations Charter, which specifically outlaws the use of force outside of self-defense and Security Council authorization.

The question of the war's legality was not the only focus of Left anti-war reporting and editorializing. The Bush administration's misleading claims about Iraq's "threat" to U.S. national security were covered in in-depth refutations of U.S. weapons charges. Phyllis Bennis, a fellow at the Institute of Policy Studies painted a polar-opposite picture of that seen from the Bush administration rhetoric and in mass media reporting. Iraq posed no real threat to the U.S., Bennis claimed. Iraq lacked essential missile capability for attacking the U.S., and lacked the necessary delivery systems to use weapons of mass destruction. In Bennis' words, Iraq "simply was not a threat. They have been qualitatively disarmed and are probably now one of the weakest countries militarily in the entire region."[37]

Interpreting the motivations of the Bush administration in the Iraq war, dissident scholar Noam Chomsky argued that Saddam Hussein was a brutal tyrant, but added that he cannot be "anywhere near as dangerous as he was when the

U.S. and Britain were supporting him, even providing him with dual-use technology that he could use for nuclear and chemical weapons development, as he presumably did."[38] In identifying U.S. support for Saddam Hussein, Chomsky took a view opposite of the mainstream media establishment, which presented the United States as diametrically opposed to his crimes against humanity. Uncovering past support for Hussein during the Reagan and George H. W. Bush administrations—aid put forth by many of the same officials in office in the Bush administration today—has led many in the Progressive-Left media to question the alleged humanitarian motivations given for the Iraq war.

The question of whether most Iraqis oppose the U.S. occupation is not a major theme in pro-war propaganda. Daniel Ellsberg, the reporter who uncovered the Pentagon Papers during the Vietnam War discusses the notion of American exceptionalism in "promoting democracy" abroad by drawing a correlation between the Vietnam and Iraq Wars: "What we find very hard to perceive now as then, is that we are seen correctly by the Iraqis as foreign occupiers. Americans just can't see themselves in such terms. . . . From the beginning to end in Vietnam, almost no civilian or military person was ever able to perceive his relations with the people there as a relation between foreign occupier and either a collaborator or reluctant tolerator."[39]

The Progressive-Left and mainstream media coverage of the Iraq war are worlds apart. A more open mass media system would need to provide access to a wider range of views, including pro-war and anti-war views, so as to expose Americans to the widest range of opinions when deciding their stance on the Iraq war. This has not taken place, hence the growing audience for alternative voices as seen in those who follow the Progressive-Left media and international news sources discussed below.

While a wide range of views has been incorporated into American media when looking at *both* the corporate, mainstream press and the Progressive-Left media, there remains a large imbalance here. Mainstream media sources retain far greater monetary resources and control of the news medium; this translates into greater access and range in terms of their audience size. This has certainly been the case with progressive outlets like *Truthout, Z Magazine*, and the *New Standard*, which are all reliant on donations, rather than advertising, in order to operate.

Balancing Divergent Views:
British and Australian Media Examined

In assessing media framing of the Iraq war, what is left out of news reports is often as important as what is reported. Discussion, for example, of the U.S. use of weapons of mass destruction in Iraq was much more limited in the American mass media than it was in the American Progressive-Left press or in the British or Australian media. News readers and viewers who desired to learn more about the U.S. use of WMD would have found more coverage in some British and Australian newspapers, as they were some of the only English-speaking dailies that bothered to give the stories significant coverage. The *Observer* of London commented on "the shocking extent of live mines and unexploded cluster bombs" around Baghdad, Um Qatar, and Basra dropped by American and British planes, which litter[ed] Iraq 8 weeks after the conflict."[40] The *Guardian* of London reported that coalition forces also used thousands of tons of depleted uranium (DU), a waste product from enriched uranium, inside shells, bullets, and bombs against Iraqi troops. DU was declared illegal by the United Nations in 1994, due in large part to the fact that DU particles spread out over a wide area, as large as a few city blocks, and may be a hazard if they are inhaled, ingested, swallowed. The *Guardian* warned that, "when the dust settles: depleted uranium may be far more dangerous than previously thought"—further commenting that "we could be dealing with the fallout [in possible cancer developments] for many generations to come."[41] Such caution was of little surprise to many who followed the use of DU over the last ten years, as tens of thousands of Desert Storm veterans had been exposed to it in the first Gulf War, many of whom developed mystery illness thought to be related to the use of this radioactive ammunition.[42]

Perhaps most shocking of all the weapons of mass destruction stories that were downplayed in the American mainstream was the U.S. use of Mark 77 (firebombs) in Iraq. Mark 77 is known for its effects, which are startlingly similar to that of napalm. The *Sydney Morning Herald*, and the *Independent* and the *Daily Mirror* of London originally broke the story, reporting that the U.S. had used firebombs against Iraqi troops during "Operation Iraqi Freedom."[43] According to the *Independent*, "American officials lied to British ministers over the use of 'internationally reviled' napalm-type firebombs," not only during the 2003 invasion, but also in the assault against Falluja in November 2004.[44] A mixture of polystyrene and jet fuel, napalm was outlawed by the United Nations in 1980 due to its devastating effects that turn people into "human fireballs" and "melted corpses."[45]

The American mass media expressed little interest in the story, as the use of Mark 77 merited not a single mention in the headlines of the *New York Times* and the *Washington Post* between June 17 and July 10, 2005—when the story was reported by the *Independent*—according to a comprehensive search of the *Lexis Nexis* database. The omission of the United State's use of weapons of mass destruction was not limited to napalm. A search of *Lexis Nexis* found that the words "depleted uranium" were not mentioned in any headlines of reports coming from the *New York Times* or the *Washington Post* during March and April of 2003, when U.S. forces had used them. A search of headlines using the words "cluster bombs" also turns up few news reports, as *Lexis Nexis* revealed that these bombs were addressed only once by the *New York Times*—and not even in reference to the U.S. use, but in a story implicating Saddam Hussein's regime with still possessing cluster bombs.[46] On the other hand, the U.S. use of cluster bombs was referenced in the British press, as *Lexis Nexis* reveals that the *Guardian* ran ten stories about cluster bombs and six stories on DU in the same time period, while the *Independent* printed eight stories on cluster bombs and five stories on the use of DU.

Major media sources in the U.S. have been successful, not only in ignoring and downplaying U.S. use of WMD in Iraq, but also in narrowly defining what constitutes a weapon of mass destruction in the first place. U.S. use of incendiary and chemical weapons, or widespread conventional bombing are not defined as a reliance on weapons of mass destruction, even though the use of such weapons has led to a minimum of tens of thousands of deaths of Iraq civilians (see *Iraq Body Count* and the Lancet Report in chapter 8). Only foreign dictators who use such weapons are targeted for possessing weapons of mass destruction. As a result, the definition of what constitutes a WMD in media reporting is inherently loaded in favor of those who hold power in the United States. The theme was taken as axiomatic: official enemies use WMD, the U.S., conversely, uses "shock and awe" that somehow spares civilian casualties, even while media sources admit that tens of thousands are dying from such attacks.

The British and Australian media have been characterized by a broader spectrum of conventional and critical opinions concerning many aspects of the Iraq War. The British media consists of newspapers such as the *Sunday Times* and the *Telegraph*, which have been less critical of the war, in addition to a number of mainstream anti-war leaning papers including the tabloid the *Daily Mirror*, and daily papers including the *Guardian* and the *Independent*. Because an extensive analysis of the pro-war aspects of the British media has been explored in depth in other studies,[47] it will not be repeated here.

Australia's *Sydney Telegraph* (owned by Rupert Murdoch), and the *Sydney Morning Herald* have also countered each other in terms of their pro-war and anti-war dispositions respectively. Little of the sort can be said about the American mainstream media, with its most prestigious newspapers that have been overwhelmingly pro-war in their support and criticisms of the U.S. occupation of Iraq. An assessment of the editorial reporting of British and Australian journalists on issues regarding the Middle East reveals a foundational level of criticism of U.S. and British intentions in Iraq unseen in American mainstream media. Patrick Cockburn of the *Independent*, for example, disagrees with the argument that the U.S. is in Iraq to foster democracy: "the supposed handover of power" to the Iraqi interim government "has turned out to be no such thing." It "was always a misnomer. Much real power remained in the hands of the U.S. Its 140,000 troops kept the new government in business. . . . For all their declarations about Iraqi security the U.S. wanted to retain as much power in its own hands as it could."[48] Cockburn also takes issue with the assumption in the American media that Iraqi resistance groups are the enemy of the Iraqi people. "The simple reason for the rising strength of the Iraqi resistance," according to Cockburn, is that the overwhelming majority of Iraqis are "against the U.S. occupation" of Iraq, and see it as a means for stifling Iraqi sovereignty.[49]

Robert Fisk, a veteran reporter of Middle East affairs for the *Independent*, calls high unemployment in Iraq, reaching upwards of 80 percent of the population, a "recipe for rage and rebellion." Taking issue with the International Monetary Fund and CPA's neoliberalization of Iraq's economy, Fisk believes that the "free market" model "cannot bring democracy" to Iraq, as it "has been proven repeatedly to spread unemployment, disaffection, and the hollowing out of meaningful self-government."[50] Fisk's skepticism is partly based upon a distrust of the CPA's Bremer laws (named after Paul Bremer, the head of the CPA in Iraq), which have sought to open up Iraq's economy to foreign investment by multinational corporations.

Fisk portrays the Iraqi state as in total disarray: "They have no control over their oil, no authority over the streets of Baghdad, let alone the rest of the country, no workable army or loyal police force."[51] Fisk's assessment of lawlessness in Iraq is longstanding, as he has reported in other stories that coalition forces control little of Iraq outside of the Green Zone in Baghdad.[52] The state of anarchy and unfolding civil war throughout much of Iraq makes it difficult for reporters to travel throughout the country without military escorts for fear of being kidnapped or killed. *Independent* editorial reporting has rendered the situation in Iraq along similar lines. One editorial dated early 2005 questioned the connection between the invasion of Iraq and the implementation of democracy as one that is "tenuous at best." Claiming democracy to be primarily a product of indigenous struggle, the *Independent's* editors argued that, "If something akin to democracy eventually transpires in Iraq, it will be thanks to the determination of Iraqis themselves—which is the only way democracy can come about anywhere, and endure."[53]

Fisk targets the American media specifically for criticism, denouncing it for its "lobotomized coverage" of the "War on Terror" and for its "incestuous" relationship with the government.[54] Fisk describes his experience with reporters who intentionally pull punches in their reports so as not to offend the government: "Over and over again. . . . I talk to my American colleagues [reporting in the Middle East]. And what they tell me is fascinating. They really have a deep insight, many of them, into what's happening in the region, but when I read their reports its not there. Everything they have to tell me of interest has been erased."[55]

Part of the reason for this trend likely originates in journalists' attempts to self-censor and conform to pro-war ideology, and from fear of being labeled "anti-American" or "unpatriotic" should they question the government in times of war. Little else (short of editorial censorship back home) would explain why they deliberately change their news reports to reflect more conservative, pro-war and pro-American perspectives that contrast so much from their own views.

Fisk believes that the terrorist attacks against the U.S. and Britain, are, in part, motivated by Western injustices committed in the Middle East. While the *Washington Post* viewed the July 2005 London terrorist attacks as retaliation against the actions of "the democracies allied in combating Islamic extremism," Fisk took the opposite view by claiming that, while the attacks were clearly a crime against humanity, they were also a reaction to Western neocolonialism.[56] Explaining that the G8 Summit day was "obviously chosen, well in advance, as Attack Day," Fisk believes that these terrorist acts of aggression are likely an effort to force a British withdrawal from Iraq. Britain may very well become a target of terrorist groups like Al Qaeda because of its participation in the Iraq war, Fisk argues. He speaks critically of media apathy toward "children torn apart by cluster bombs, the countless innocent Iraqis gunned down at American military checkpoints," commenting on the mindset that frames the deaths of Iraqis as "collateral damage" and the death of American and British civilians as acts of terrorism.[57]

Fisk also believes that American behavior at Abu Ghraib is related to the backlash against the U.S.: "Whatever moral stature the United States could claim at the end of its invasion of Iraq has long ago been squandered in the torture and abuse and deaths at Abu Ghraib. . . the trail of prisons that now lies across Iraq is a shameful symbol not only of our cruelty but of our failure to create the circumstances in which a new Iraq might take shape. . . when this military sickness is allowed to spread, the whole purpose of democracy is overturned."[58] The Iraqi people seem to agree, as an *Associated Press* poll conducted after the Abu Ghraib revelations portrays the Iraqi population as not only extremely hostile to occupation by American and British forces, but interpreting national dignity as requiring the killing of American soldiers.[59]

Aside from Robert Fisk and Patrick Cockburn, another prominent anti-war critic in the British press is *Guardian* contributor Tariq Ali. A writer of fiction and nonfiction covering the Arab World, Ali has criticized U.S. foreign policy as imperialist and neocolonial in nature. Like Patrick Cockburn, Ali attributes the growing resistance in Iraq to the U.S. occupation. In his piece, "Resistance is the First Step Toward Iraqi Independence," Ali portrays resistance groups as driven in large part by a desire for independence from occupation. Resistance draws its strength, according to Ali, from "the tacit support of the population," without which "a sustained resistance is virtually impossible."[60] Since he considers the "transfer of power" to Iraqis to be little more than a "grotesque fiction," Ali advocates the "unconditional withdrawal of foreign troops" as "the only solution" to establishing Iraqi sovereignty.[61] Ali also agrees with Fisk about the problems confronting American journalism: "Journalists have accepted the official version [of war events]. Journalists go to press briefings at the Pentagon in Washington, and no critical questions are posed at all. It's just a news gathering operation, and the fact that the news is being controlled by governments who are waging war doesn't seem to worry many journalists too much."[62]

Like many critical Progressive-Left journalists in the U.S., Ali feels that "alternative information networks" existing outside of the mass media constitute "one of the most important developments in challenging the weight of the [mass] media."[63] Alternative news networks such as the progressive newswires *Common Dreams* and *Truthout* have provided an American audience to British skeptics like Ali and Fisk, and have likely significantly contributed to advancing transnational anti-war activism. Independent magazines such as *Multinational Monitor*, the *Progressive*, the *Nation*, *Z Magazine*, *Extra!*, *In These Times*, and the *New Standard*, and television and radio networks like *Democracy Now!* and *Pacifica* make available to the public a variety of anti-occupation viewpoints from around the world.

Questioning the alleged American push for "democracy" in Iraq, in light of the 2005 elections has often been a priority of the critical British reporters. Underscoring a point almost totally ignored in the American mainstream, *Guardian* reporter Jonathon Steele reported on the U.S. plan to appoint unelected "notables" in every province of Iraq who would attend caucuses in order to *select*, rather than elect, the members of the new Iraqi government as nothing more than a democratic "facade."[64] Addressing claims that the U.S. and Britain are occupying Iraq in order to gain control of the country's oil, Tariq Ali maintains: "The majority of Iraqis will not willingly hand over their oil or their country to the west. [Iraqi] politicians who try to force this through will lose all support and become totally dependent on the foreign armies in their country."[65] Steele and other British reporters' portrayals of the U.S. as diametrically opposed to Iraqi elections and democracy represent a serious departure from the American media portrayals of U.S. leaders as unconditionally and selflessly committed to furthering Iraqi democracy.

Like the British media, the Australian press has also generally been more balanced in its portrayals of the Iraq war. While the *Sydney Telegraph* has taken more pro-war editorial positions, the *Sydney Morning Herald* reports many controversial stories attacking the American campaign in Iraq. Aside from its reporting of American use of firebombs in Iraq, the *Sydney Morning Herald* also reported the explosive allegations that Interim Prime Minister Ayad Allawi murdered Iraqi prisoners "in cold blood." Paul McGeough reported that, according to witnesses on the scene, Allawi killed as many as six alleged "insurgents" who were blindfolded and handcuffed in a Baghdad police station shortly before the "transfer of power" to the interim authority in June 2004.[66]

Attending to possible charges of dishonesty against the "witnesses" to the event, McGeough reported that: while the witnesses were approached by the paper (rather than the other way around), "the witnesses did not perceive themselves as whistle-blowers. In interviews with the *Sydney Morning Herald* they were enthusiastic about such killings, with one of them arguing: "These criminals were terrorists. They are the ones who plant the bombs."[67] McGeough considered Allawi to be the strongman the Bush administration preferred to replace Saddam Hussein. McGeough framed Allawi's motivations for holding power in occupied Iraq as follows: "He wants the tools that Saddam had. Ominously, he is restructuring security and intelligence in the image of what Saddam had and his defence minister, Hazim Shaalan, caused some in Washington to blanch last week when he told *Newsweek*: 'We'll hit these people and teach them a good lesson they won't forget...we will cut off their hands and behead them.'"[68]

McGeough's accounts of events in Iraq consistently question the Bush administration's viewpoint of the "progress" of democracy. He is critical of the validity of Iraq's 2005 election, maintaining that the large-scale Sunni boycott of the election, the inaccuracy of voter rolls (as a result increasing lawlessness and violence that have deterred voter registration), and illegal U.S. occupation and supervision have all tested electoral legitimacy.[69]

Fellow *Sydney Morning Herald* reporter Tony Kevin also condemns what he sees as the "indiscriminate effects" of American attacks "on civilians and civilian homes and infrastructure—acts that are morally indefensible by any civilized standard." In his news story, "All the Makings of a War Crime," Kevin condemned the U.S. for its bombing of Falluja. Since Falluja became a symbol for Iraqi resistance to the U.S., it was "made an example"—its residents punished by massive bombing that destroyed much of the city. Kevin added, "The message the siege of Falluja sends is brutally simple: resist us and we will destroy you."[70]

McGeough considers the U.S. "war of attrition" against Iraq to be similar to the campaign conducted by Israel against the occupied Palestinian territories. As attacks against the U.S. continue, its forces pursue policies of collective punishment, McGeough argues, including the indefinite mass detainment of Iraqis without charge, the surrounding of some cities with barbed wire, the razing of the homes of suspected "insurgents," as well as the bombing of large urban areas. McGeough predicts that "the longer this continues, the greater the risk for Washington that more ordinary Iraqis will shift from fearing the insurgents to sympathizing or participating with them."[71] As the final section of this chapter discusses, the coverage of the *Al Jazeera* network, while balancing contrasting viewpoints of the Iraq war, has also been profoundly critical of American objectives in the "War on Terror" and the neoliberalization of Iraq. This is well reflected in the network's presentation of anti-occupation views and bluntly worded anti-war propaganda.

Al Jazeera's Challenge to "The War on Terror"

April 12, 2003 was a bad day for journalists in Iraq. Only three weeks into the U.S. Iraq invasion, American troops had already reached Baghdad to find only limited resistance in their occupation of the city. That Iraqi resistance was lighter than expected did not translate into a safer environment for journalists, however, as three reporters were killed on this day alone, one from *Abu Dhabi TV*, another from the Spanish channel *Telecino*, and the last from the *Al Jazeera* network. All three journalists had one thing in common; they were not traveling with, or protected by, the U.S. military.

In the Iraq war, many journalists have decided to risk their lives by asserting their independence from the U.S., reporting from positions well removed from embedded reporters and their military escorts. Tarek Ayyoub of *Al Jazeera* was one of the reporters who were unable to escape U.S. bombs falling on Baghdad. Stationed at *Al Jazeera*'s Baghdad office, Ayyoub and other *Al Jazeera* staff provided in depth reporting from the conflict zone—reporting that was far more critical of the U.S. than the vast majority of the coverage seen in the Western media, particularly from American major media outlets. Unfortunately, Ayyoub paid the ultimate price for providing critical information, after he was killed by a U.S. plane that launched a missile strike against Baghdad's *Al Jazeera* office. The office was destroyed despite the fact that the station had alerted the Pentagon numerous times to their presence at that location.

The Pentagon explained that the attack was in retaliation to fire that had allegedly originated from the area around the *Al Jazeera* office. The Pentagon also explained the motivation for the U.S. tank attack on the fourteenth and fifteenth floors of the Palestine Hotel (which killed *Reuters* cameraman Taras Protsyuk) by claiming it was in response to sniper fire and other attacks from the

Hotel area. Such claims, however, were challenged by numerous reporters on location who explained that they had neither seen nor heard such fire.[72]

Understandably, *Al Jazeera* reporters, editors, and staff took the death of Ayyoub rather personally, many perceiving the attack to be a punishment for *Al Jazeera*'s critical reporting of the U.S. invasions of Afghanistan and Iraq. Samir Khader, Senior Producer for *Al Jazeera* felt the objective of the attack was to convey the message to the news channel that "you're not siding 100 percent with the U.S. against Saddam Hussein, so we are going to punish you."[73] Baghdad correspondent Majed Abdel Hadi believed that "We were targeted because the Americans don't want the world to see the crimes they are committing against the Iraqi people."[74] The perception that *Al Jazeera* was deliberately targeted was shared by a number of people throughout the world who felt that the U.S. targeted the Arab news channel that was, and continues to be, most critical of the legitimacy of the "War on Terror." Reporters Without Borders released a report stating: "We can only conclude that the U.S. Army deliberately and without warning targeted journalists," while Robert Fisk of the *Independent* of London commented that the attacks "look very much like murder."[75]

Many saw the attack as an attempt to put *Al Jazeera* back on the "correct" path of reporting in terms of refraining from serious criticisms of the invasion, although Bush administration officials heavily disputed that view. Faisal Bodi, Senior Editor at *Al Jazeera* and columnist for the *Guardian* stated: "from the outset of the [Iraq] war, reporting followed two tracks, the "embed" line laid by Centcom (U.S. Central Command), and the independent line by news providers like *Al Jazeera*." Such unilateral reporting enjoyed "a greater degree of access to Iraqi towns and cities," allowing unembedded journalists "to report more independently than those journalists dependent on the armed forces for their personal safety and communication equipment."[76]

Competing Notions of Professional Journalism: A Brief History of *Al Jazeera*

Al Jazeera was formed in 1996 with funding from the government of Qatar in an attempt to create a more independent, critical kind of reporting than had been seen in most news outlets throughout the region traditionally reporting at the pleasure of repressive Arab governments. *Al Jazeera* is not what many Americans think of when they picture a free and independent media. Receiving its support from the Emir of Qatar, the channel's financial backing stands in radical contrast to corporate media outlets, which are owned and run by private investors rather than sponsored directly by government funding. *Al Jazeera* enjoys a strong degree of journalistic freedom, however, from the head of the Qatari royal family, Sheik Hamid bin Khalifa al Thani, who committed the kingdom to limited liberal reforms after taking power from his father in 1995. Thani abolished the government ministry of information as a sign of faith that he was committed to promoting *Al Jazeera*'s journalistic independence. The channel's freedom from government censorship and regulation stands in marked contrast to most media throughout the Arab world, which are controlled by government ministries and owned by the state so as to minimize voices that are critical of government.

Highlighting *Al Jazeera*'s journalistic independence and freedom does not mean that the station is without serious flaws. As many scholars who have studied the outlet agree, *Al Jazeera* is curiously silent when it comes to criticizing the Qatari constitutional monarchy in which it relies to exist.[77] In addition, funding from the Sheik hardly makes *Al Jazeera*'s ownership structure democratic, as it is reliant primarily upon the "benevolence" of Qatar's ruling family rather than upon public funds as allocated by a democratically elected government. Still, there exists a great chasm between *Al Jazeera*'s independent and critical reporting of not only American and Israeli foreign policy, but the activities of dictatorial, repressive Middle Eastern regimes, as contrasted with state-owned media throughout the Muslim world and their sympathetic, supportive coverage of dictators and autocrats.

Some may view it as ironic or contradictory that *Al Jazeera* could possess so much journalistic freedom while also being funded by the Qatari royal family. Nonetheless, the channel's independence is in large part the outcome of al Thani's refusal to interfere with *Al Jazeera*'s editorial and reporting policies, in opposition to the many requests of American, Israeli, and Arab leaders to curb its criticisms of Western and Middle Eastern leaders.

Reaching tens of millions of viewers, *Al Jazeera* has demonstrated its extraordinary power in influencing the opinions of many throughout the Middle East and the world, particularly in terms of reinforcing opposition to the war in Iraq and lending legitimacy to hostility toward the U.S. involvement in the affairs of countries such as Afghanistan, Saudi Arabia, and Israel and the Palestinian occupied territories. Western media have criticized *Al Jazeera* for a perceived lack of "objective" news reporting and for its anti-war propaganda. The channel's reporting has been attacked for being unprofessional, subjective, substandard, unbalanced, irresponsible, pro-terrorist, and for arousing passions throughout the Arab world against the United States and Israel. Bill O'Reilly, host of *Fox New*'s *O'Reilly Factor*, labels the station as a "propaganda network that's bent on encouraging violence and is sympathetic to terrorists."[78] Writing for *Slate News*, Lee Smith makes a more subtle criticism, arguing that, to leave questions of objective reporting to *Al Jazeera* journalists "is a problem; sometimes they are interested in truth and objectivity, and oftentimes they are not."[79]

Al Jazeera got into hot water with Western officials after airing a number of tapes carrying political messages from bin Laden to the station's audience. Western leaders in the U.S. and Britain were quick to label the network a supporter of Al Qaeda, as *Al Jazeera* was considered an accomplice to spreading "anti-American," "pro-terrorist" messages to the masses throughout the Muslim world.

Al Jazeera attempts to assert its own agency in relation to its coverage of important news stories. The channel seeks to steer clear of the control of any government aiming to influence or censor its reporting. Although many have condemned *Al Jazeera* for inciting popular rebellion and discontent throughout the Middle East against the U.S. and Britain, the reality of the situation is that *Al Jazeera*'s relationship with its Arab audiences has been mutually reinforcing—as the network seeks to report on issues important to the Arab masses, it thereby gains legitimacy as a network in tune with the needs and views of its viewers.

Mohamed Zayani, Associate Professor of critical theory at the American University of Sharjah in the UAE, lays out three primary reasons for *Al Jazeera*'s popularity throughout the Arab world: 1. the station's "aggressive field reporting" as seen in the way it pursues stories in a timely manner; 2. its "commitment to unedited news" as apparent in its "tendency to broadcast live, uncut pictures" of unfolding crises; and 3. its reputation for "honesty and fairness of its reporting."[80] The final reason likely relates in part to *Al Jazeera*'s lack of fear when it comes to challenging government propaganda and actions throughout the Arab world and beyond. Along the same lines, Mohammed El Oifi, Associate Professor of International Relations at the Institut d'Etudes Politiques de Paris claims that *Al Jazeera*'s popularity arises, to a large extent, from its willingness to reject common dogmas promoted by governments in the region. "The channel's tendency to deal with issues that are often considered taboo, including the radical critique of Arab rulers, and above all the channel's notable tendency to align itself with public opinion," are amongst the major reasons for *Al Jazeera*'s success.[81]

Al Jazeera's reporters see themselves as attempting to combine the practice "objective" news reporting with what many might see as contradictory attempts to challenge the legitimacy of the U.S. and its support for oppressive Arab regimes throughout the region. Samir Khader summarizes this position well: "the message of *Al Jazeera* is to educate the Arab masses on democracy, respect the other opinion, [with] free debate, no taboos. Everything should be dealt with, with openness."[82] *Al Jazeera* has constructed a vastly different definition of objective reporting as something that, while encompassing a variety of fundamentally conflicting viewpoints, seeks to challenge the legitimacy and authority of all governments covered in its reporting.

Al Jazeera also considers "objective" reporting to include the broadcasting of graphic images of civilian deaths at the hands of the Israeli military in the occupied territories and U.S. forces in Iraq, as well as the transmitting of bin Laden message tapes to Arab audiences. The channel has long argued that objectivity requires the transmission of all newsworthy information, no matter how graphic or controversial, so as to promote informed debate over the issues at hand. In reality, *Al Jazeera*, like all other media outlets, fails to achieve objectivity or neutrality, as its criticisms of most governments throughout the Middle East and many in the West show its antagonistic, critical relationship with government and political leaders. However, *Al Jazeera* has been more balanced than many Western media outlets in that, while it is very critical of the U.S. and the "War on Terror," it also makes serious efforts to televise the positions of pro-war pundits and political leaders from the United States, Israel, and the Middle East.[83]

If one considers more balanced reporting of the news as something that can be achieved by exposing viewers to a wider spectrum of debate, then *Al Jazeera* has been far more balanced than its competitors in the Arab World. The channel has traditionally operated without restrictions from the Qatari government, and is well known throughout the Arab world for its open mindedness in exploring multiple sides of complex issues such as Israel's occupation of the West Bank and Gaza Strip, and the U.S. invasion of Afghanistan and Iraq.[84] As Nabeel Khoury, Spokesmen for the U.S. State Department, explains: "*Al Jazeera* has been critical [of the U.S.], but at the same time they have been quite open to us, inviting U.S. government officials to speak directly on their channel and express the American point of view."[85]

Al Jazeera is also wildly popular, in part, because of its promotion of the idea of pan-Arab unity. As Mohamed Zayani discusses: "Al Jazeera has effectively put an end to an era marked by what may be described as a one-size-fits-all media. Issues now lend themselves to a different perspective—in fact an Arab perspective that has been absent" from much reporting throughout the region.[86] *Al Jazeera*'s reporting, however, should not be expected to serve as the primary agent of democratization through pan-Arab transformation of the Middle East. Rather, the station seems to serve more as a catalyst for change in terms of questioning the state borders throughout the Middle East that were drawn after the end of formal colonial rule. *Al Jazeera* seems to be most effective in providing a means of informing the Arab world about important issues of the day. In this sense, it is a vital institution in a region that has traditionally suffered under extreme government censorship of the media and repression of popular movements critical of government actions and authority, often with the support of Western leaders.

Many national leaders throughout the region have tried to punish the network as a result of what they see as its biased and critical reporting against their governments' activities. But *Al Jazeera* has not singled out any one government; it has been critical of most governments in its reporting. *Al Jazeera* considers criticisms of no political regime (perhaps with the exception of Qatar) to be out-of-bounds, as it has been kicked out of a large number of countries and areas as a result, including Jordan, Kuwait, U.S. occupied Iraq, the West Bank, Iran, Sudan, Algeria, Tunisia, Saudi Arabia, and Bahrain. Aside from its critical reporting of the U.S., British, and Israeli foreign policies, *Al Jazeera* has made numerous efforts to show viewers "the other side" by broadcasting speeches and interviews from U.S. political officials including George W. Bush, former Secretary of Defense Donald Rumsfeld, former Secretary of State Colin Powell, Secretary of State Condoleeza Rice, and other high level representatives from the Pentagon and Centcom, as well as American allies such as former Israeli Prime Ministers Ehud Barak and Ariel Sharon, and British Prime Minister Tony Blair.

Rather than reinforcing Ba'athist propaganda at the expense of U.S. war aims in Iraq (a claim made by U.S. leaders), the network has been critical of the governments of *both* George Bush and Saddam Hussein. Hugh Miles, author of *Al Jazeera: The Inside Story of the Arab News Channel That is Challenging the West*, explains that, "Despite all the allegations of bias issued from both sides during the invasion of Iraq, the simple truth is that Al Jazeera did not favor anyone in the war. Like most Arabs, it opposed Saddam's regime and opposed the invasion."[87] Miles continues: "All the information the channel received, whether it came from Coalition Central Command or from the Iraqi Ministry of Information, was treated with equal skepticism. . . information coming from the Iraqi Minister of Information, Muhammad Said al-Sahaf, and information from coalition spokesmen, Brigadier General Vincent K. Brooks. . . was treated as equally unreliable."[88]

Pro-War Propaganda:
The Embedded Approach

The embedded approach to reporting in Iraq has emerged as a disciplinary institution against critical anti-war reporting. During the first Gulf War in 1991, the first Bush administration attempted a much cruder version of embedding, in which the U.S. military physically restricted the American press from entering combat areas by herding them into journalistic pools which were not allowed to view the conflict up close. This approach to limiting field reporting gave way to a more "open" version of embedding in the 2003 invasion of Iraq, as hundreds of reporters were allowed to travel with coalition forces.

To the approval of the Pentagon and the Bush administration, embedding became the preferred method of reporting for establishment journalists in Iraq. Jim Wilkinson, Director of Strategic Communications at U.S. Central Command conveys the psyche of most mainstream American reporters well, stating: "There are two types of reporters in the world today: Those who are embedded and those who wish they were embedded."[89] Assessments of the embedded approach have been overwhelmingly positive throughout the U.S. mass media. Eric Burns of *Fox News Watch* argues that embedded journalists have been successful in "balancing the needs of the press, the military, and the public."[90] Jane Hall of the American University agrees, arguing that embedding "showed journalists can be trusted" by the military to report on the war in a way that conforms to the government agenda.[91] Rem Rieder, editor of the American Journalism Review celebrates: "it is clear that the great embedding experiment was a home run as far as the news media and the American people are concerned."[92]

Embedded reporters' protection by the American military has come with a price, as reporters agree to forego most serious challenges to the U.S. invasion and occupation, in turn normalizing the U.S. presence in post-Saddam Iraq. Chris Hedges, a veteran war reporter for the *New York Times* explains that embedded reporting translates into "look[ing] at Iraq totally through the eyes of the U.S. military."[93] As reporters embedded in Iraq eat, sleep, and share meaningful experiences with American troops, they develop a close bond with the troops.

Embeds rely on U.S. and British military forces to provide them with security as well. Army Major General Buford Blount explains that, in this relationship, "a level of trust develops between the soldier and the media that offers nearly unlimited access" to the battlefield.[94] However, reporters who embed themselves also become subject to significant restrictions in their capacity to report stories in a way that is critical of the U.S. Reporters become subject to the potential discipline of U.S. or allied armed forces, as they are forced to sign contracts allowing the military to review all their reporting, and allowing for government censorship of potentially controversial, antagonistic, or hard-hitting reporting, graphic coverage of civilian casualties being one of the most pertinent examples. Jon Rosen's experiences with the U.S. army put this reality into better perspective. Rosen, an American freelance reporter who spent two weeks embedded with the U.S. Army near the Iraqi-Syrian border, found out the hard way what happens when embeds challenge the military censors. Rosen's reports of the U.S. Army's practice of mass detainment of Iraqis in hopes of gathering information on resistance activities was most unwelcome by his unit's commander and public affairs officer. After publishing his findings with the *Asia Times*, Rosen was blacklisted from the embed program. Such was Rosen's punishment for criticizing the occupation and the behavior of American troops, as his reports claimed that over 90 percent of the Iraqis detained by the U.S. Army were innocent of any charges.[95]

But Rosen's experience is not identical to that of most embedded reporters, who have taken well to military guidance of their reporting. Jim Axelrod of *CBS News*, for example, displayed his attachment to the Third Infantry position from which he was reporting by adopting the language of his unit. After one military intelligence briefing, Axelrod reported that "we've been given orders," quickly rephrasing that "soldiers have been given orders," although his equation of his interests as a reporter with those of his unit left little doubt that embeds have failed to serve as impartial observers in this conflict.[96]

Despite acknowledging some reservations about the program, Axelrod was strongly in favor of the embedding process: "This will sound like I've drunk the Kool-Aid, but I found embedding to be an extremely positive experience. . . . We got great stories and they [the military and Bush administration] got very positive coverage."[97] Such an admission begs the important question: is the goal of media coverage primarily to provide the American military and political leaders with positive coverage, or to fairly assess the situation in Iraq independent of official positions and government censorship? Expectations that media serve as a "fourth estate," holding political and military leaders accountable, and exposing deceptions, fabrications, and outright lies are clearly not served by the deferential coverage discussed above.

Danny Schechter, founder of *MediaChannel.org*, comments on the close relationship between reporters and troops, explaining: "Most embedded reporters claimed that they were not really restrained, but rather assisted in their work by Pentagon press flacks. This is probably true—and the reason the system worked so well."[98] Most embeds' conformity with pro-war, pro-military perspectives, then, represents a voluntary choice to "get on board" in the war effort, rather than focus upon critical aspects of the war.

Embedded reporting has been primarily concerned with controlling the flow of information reaching the American people, in effect, shaping the public's perceptions of the war in a way that reinforces the legitimacy of the war effort and the Bush administration's public pronouncements about the "progress" of the war. What better way to accomplish this goal than by turning media reporters and soldiers into allies? As the Rosen example indicates, the embedded approach represents the antithesis of investigative journalism. In contrast, investigative journalism and muckraking have traditionally been interested in exposing government deception and misinformation, rather than getting on the good side of invading and occupying forces—hence the pertinent question posed by those critical of the program: "embed" or "in bed?"

The *BBC* acknowledges about the embed program that, "While the [U.S.] military sees [embed] propaganda as a weapon in itself, a journalists role is to cut through the half truths."[99] Paul Workman, an unembedded reporter in Iraq for the *Canadian Broadcasting Corporation* (*CBC*) feels that, "by keeping 'unilateral' journalists out of Iraq. . . the Americans have succeeded in reducing independent reporting of the war, and I believe that was exactly their plan from the beginning." As a result, Workman concludes, Americans are "more likely to see a glorified view of American power and morality, in a war much of the world considers unnecessary, unjustified or plain wrong, and is being covered at every crossroads, at every captured bridge, by a press corps that's sleeping with the winner."[100]

In making a deal with the military censors, embeds are rewarded by the U.S. government for taking a tactical, pragmatic approach to evaluating the war's progress (or lack thereof) at the expense of critical reporting and foundational questioning of U.S. foreign policy that is seen in outlets like *Al Jazeera*. The Project for Excellence in Journalism (PEJ) elaborates on this development in its content analysis of U.S. television reporting during the first few days of the Iraq war. PEJ's breakdown of U.S. television reporting on March 21, 22, 24, 2003—the "days in which ground troops began the push into Iraq, and first encountered serious resistance"—found that almost half of embedded reports focused on military action rather than on stories revealing the negative repercussions of the invasion on Iraqi civilians and American soldiers.[101] While approximately half of stories filed and aired were about combat operations, there was not one story that discussed or addressed in detail a scenario where U.S. weapons were used against the Iraqi people.

The discounting of the human consequences of war means that "punches get pulled" in embedded reporting on the conduct of American and British troops in Iraq.[102] As a result, Greg Mitchell of *Editor & Publisher* explains: "one usually has to look abroad, or to non-embeds, for eyewitness accounts of American boys behaving badly."[103] As one embedded reporter recounts in his web-blog, soldiers "frankly resent" any critical or "bloody" stories run by embeds concerning U.S. involvement in Iraq.[104] This, to a large degree, helps explain the rise in popularity of independent new outlets like *Al Jazeera* in the Arab World, as the network has not been afraid to tackle criticisms of the American presence in the Middle East.

Questioning Western Humanitarianism

Al Jazeera has become a force to be reckoned with as it continues to grow in popularity, in large part as a result of its foundational critiques of the U.S. incursions into the Arab World. It is through this fierce opposition and independence that *Al Jazeera* has been viewed as antagonistic to the interests of the Bush administration, and has become subject to the attempted discipline of not only the U.S. government and the corporate media, but the Iraqi government and surrounding Middle Eastern countries as well.

While much of the Western media tended to uncritically favor the war effort in the first few years of the conflict, *Al Jazeera* adamantly opposed the notion that the war was motivated by humanitarian purposes. Hugh Miles explains: "never once in the twenty-one days of conflict did *Al-Jazeera* acknowledge that invading Iraq had anything to do with democratization"[105]—a marked contrast from American mainstream sources, which overwhelmingly reinforced the idea that the U.S. was concerned with liberating Iraqis from Saddam Hussein (hence the label used in the media: "Operation Iraqi Freedom"). Conversely, *Al Jazeera* allocated significant airtime to experts and activists who were hostile to the U.S. invasion, to the dismay of American leaders.[106]

With only a short review of some of the channel's headlines, one begins to see the gulf that separates *Al Jazeera*'s ideological frames from those of U.S. news outfits such as *ABC, NBC, CBS, CNN,* and *Fox News.* Common incendiary headlines from *Al Jazeera*'s website (english.aljazeera.net) that were reported throughout the war include, "Will U.S. fabricate WMD evidence?"; "U.S. More Keen on Oil than Iraqi People"; "[Iraqi] Governing Council Selected Not Elected"; "U.S. 'Exaggerated' Foreign Fighters in Iraq"; "Arabs Voice Fears of US Interim Government"; "Mosul Residents Tire of U.S. Presence"; "Many Killed in Ramadi, Falluja Raids"; "U.S. Troops 'Preventing Aid' to Falluja"; "Scores Dead as Falluja Resists U.S. Onslaught"; and "U.S. Soldiers Kill Protestors in Falluja," to name merely a few.

Al Jazeera's editorials have also presented serious challenges to the U.S. In one example shortly after the beginning of the 2003 invasion, the channel claimed that the "U.S. and British occupation of Iraq is regarded as the re-emergence of the old colonialist practices of the western empires in some quarters. The real ambitions underlying the brutal onslaught are still highly questionable—and then there are the blatant lies over weapons of mass destruction originally used to justify the war."[107] Furthering its case against the Bush administration's WMD claims, *Al Jazeera* argued: "There is growing evidence that intelligence information was manipulated to support a political decision already taken. A combination of U.S. direct control of Iraqi oil and a long-term military presence in Iraq, in addition to the U.S. bases in surrounding countries, would enable the U.S. to have more control over world oil supplies and policies."[108]

Al Jazeera's criticisms of the U.S. encompass not only the Bush administration's weapons of mass destruction claims and its strategic plans for Iraq and the Middle East, but also the issue of Iraqi civilian casualties resulting from the

U.S.-British bombing campaign and occupation, and what is seen as the illegiti-
macy of Iraqi elections conducted under foreign occupation. Concerning the
humanitarian disaster in Iraq, *Al Jazeera* has consistently criticized the U.S.
for having killed and injured many Iraqi civilians in reporting that has given the
impression that the U.S. either recklessly or deliberately targeted civilians and
public infrastructure. In an editorial condemning the 2005 elections, Mohammed
al-Obaidi argued that any election conducted under U.S. supervision "is a violation of all international law. International charters that regulate the relationship
between occupier and occupied do not give occupying authorities the mandate to
instigate a change in the country's social, economic, and political structure."[109]

   Al Jazeera's ideological opposition to the U.S. invasion has resulted in a
substantial number of official government attacks against the channel. Mohammed El-Nawawy and Adel Iskandar, authors of *Al Jazeera: The Story of the
Network That is Rattling Governments and Redefining Modern Journalism*, explain: "many U.S. officials have accused *Al Jazeera* of inciting public demonstrations as a consequence of its coverage."[110] Former Secretary of State Colin
Powell condemned Al Jazeera for "give(ing) an undue amount of time and attention to some vitriolic, irresponsible kinds of statements" that question the justifications for U.S. actions in the "War on Terror."[111] Former Secretary of Defense
Donald Rumsfeld also attacked *Al Jazeera* for "manipulating world opinion" in
opposition to the Bush administration.[112] Many American news organizations
followed suit. Writing for the *National Review*, William F. Buckley Jr. fumed
that *Al Jazeera* "should be put out of business" because of its "poison" news
dispatches and "anti-American and anti-Israel" leanings.[113] In an editorial for the
Wall Street Journal, Dorrance Smith, former executive producer for *ABC's
Nightline* postulated: "the collaboration between the terrorists and *Al Jazeera* is
stronger than ever. . . *Al Jazeera* and terrorists have a working arrangement that
extends beyond a modus vivendi."[114]

   Smith and Buckley's statements, like the attacks of the Bush administration,
rely on denigrations intended to discredit the news organization, without presenting any tangible grievances other than a general dissatisfaction with *Al
Jazeera's* reputation as a news outlet that is critical of the United States. Any
grievance made on those grounds—and without evidence—is questionable considering that media have traditionally been expected to reflect a diversity of
views (of which anti-war arguments is clearly one) in reporting on the "War on
Terror." That *Al Jazeera* is reflecting and magnifying opposition to the U.S.
presence in Iraq (opposition that will continue whether *Al Jazeera* exists or not)
suggests that such attackers of the station are uncomfortable *more* with Arab
opposition to the U.S., than with the reporting of critical news outlet reflecting
that opposition.

The Casualties of War

Aside from its ideological opposition to the U.S., *Al Jazeera*'s reporting on spe-cific events throughout the "War on Terror" also aroused significant opposition from the Bush and Blair administration's, the Iraqi interim government, and much of the Western media. The network's coverage of Iraqi civilian and American military casualties throughout the war in Iraq is a case in point. *Al Jazeera* encountered serious resistance from Western governments and media after it chose to broadcast graphic pictures of Iraqi and Afghan civilian casual-ties as well as American and British Prisoners of War who were killed in the early days of the 2003 invasion of Iraq. The network exacerbated Western ap-prehension when it decided to broadcast images of American and British sol-diers killed in combat in late March 2003. Those images caused many viewers to question the human consequences of the war.

Predictably, reactions to the footage were overwhelmingly negative throughout much of the United States, Britain, and Iraq, particularly among those in high level government and media positions. Rumsfeld condemned *Al Jazeera*, claiming that the network had "a pattern of playing propaganda, over and over and over again," in what he considered—erroneously—to be manufac-tured images of civilian deaths that allegedly never took place.[115] Other military leaders leveled similar charges. Senior Military Spokesperson Mark Kimmitt attacked stations like *Al Jazeera* that are allegedly "showing Americans inten-tionally killing women and children." According to Kimmitt, outlets that make such claims "are not legitimate news sources," as these charges constitute "propaganda" and "lies" rather than factual reporting of events in Iraq.[116]

And yet, the claim that *Al Jazeera* is unprofessional because it discusses execution charges on the part of the U.S. military is highly circumspect. Other more conservative and pro-war sources such as the *Times* of London, along with many other world news sources, have come forward to level similar charges that U.S. forces have executed civilians. These charges have also been backed up by Iraqi police reports. As Hala Jaber and Tony Allen of the *Times* reported in De-cember of 2005, U.S. troops were implicated in executing eleven people in Abu Sifa, a village near the town of Balad. An Iraqi police report indicated that the Iraqis were killed after an American raid on the house, in which troops were hoping to catch an Al Qaeda suspect. Reports on the ground explained that vil-lagers searched the house after American soldiers left, only to uncover the bod-ies buried beneath the rubble. As the *Times* reported, "Women and children were blindfolded and hands bound. Some of their faces were totally disfigured."[117] The autopsy report from the hospital also indicated that all the victims were killed from bullet wounds.[118]

Attempts to discipline *Al Jazeera* have been made a priority by the Bush administration and other leaders who correctly view the station's reporting as critical of their legitimacy. In an attempt to censor *Al Jazeera*'s reporting, the Pentagon called *Al Jazeera*'s Washington bureau chief and suggested that the station end its broadcasting of any graphic pictures of American soldiers who had been captured or killed in Iraq. A British Ministry of Defense spokesperson

also released a statement on behalf of the Blair administration stating: "we deplore the decision by *Al Jazeera* to broadcast such material and call upon them
to desist immediately."[119] Finally, the interim Iraqi regime appointed by the
United States punished *Al Jazeera* for its independent reporting by shutting
down its Baghdad office and expelling the news organization from Iraq for one
month in August of 2004. Interim Foreign Minister Hoshyar Zebari defended the
action by deriding *Al Jazeera* for "one-sided and biased coverage" of news in
U.S. occupied Iraq. The Iraqi government's distrust of *Al Jazeera* was again
shown when the Iraqi Interior Ministry demanded of the lawyer representing *Al
Jazeera* that the station sign an agreement with the Iraqi government guarantee-
ing it would limit its criticisms of the U.S. occupation and the interim regime.[120]
As of 2007, *Al Jazeera* is still expelled from Iraq as a result of its anti-war reporting.

The American media also attacked *Al Jazeera* and other media outlets for
presenting graphic images of dead soldiers and civilians. The *New York Times*
called for "more sensitivity and less stridency on *Al Jazeera's* part" in terms of
its "sensational news coverage" and the "graphic details of its Iraq war coverage."[121] The *New York Times* rejected what it considered "the gratuitous use of
images simply for shock value."[122] Substituting for Wolf Blitzer on *CNN's Wolf
Blitzer Reports*, Daryn Kagan lambasted *Al Jazeera* by claiming that it "adds to
the sense of frustration and anger and adds to the problems in Iraq, rather than
trying to solve them."[123] Notice here that Kagan's assertion projects *Al Jazeera*
as a force that is fueling public resentment of the U.S., rather than reflecting
such resentment. Aaron Brown of *CNN's Newsnight* portrayed the conflict over
the use of graphic war images as "a question of taste," as he considered gory
images of the dead to be "too pornographic" for American consumption.[124] Regarding the well publicized execution of a Falluja resistance fighter by American troops, *NBC* Vice President Bill Wheatley stated that, "Generally speaking
NBC doesn't show specific acts of violence if too graphic. . . it is not a question
of bias, but one of taste."[125]

Alternative assessments of *Al Jazeera's* reporting by some in the U.S. military further drive home the monumental differences between the American
mainstream press and critical media outlets like *Al Jazeera*. Lt. John Rushing,
former press officer for U.S. Central Command (Centcom) in Qatar discussed
the Western media' failure to extensively cover civilian casualties, sharing his
reaction to a few incidents when *Al Jazeera* reported on Iraqi deaths:

> The night they [Al Jazeera] showed the POWs and the dead soldiers it was
> powerful because America doesn't show those kinds of images. Most of the
> news in America doesn't show really gory images, and it was revolting and
> made me sick to my stomach. And then what hit me was, the night before, there
> had been a bombing in Basra and *Al Jazeera* had shown equally if not more
> horrifying images. . . and it didn't affect me as much, and it upset me that I
> wasn't as bothered as I was the night before [when they showed American
> casualties].[126]

Rushing's account suggests that there has been a dehumanizing effect in terms of the neglect displayed toward Iraqi civilian deaths.

Efforts in the U.S. media to de-emphasize Iraqi civilian deaths should be contrasted with efforts to thoroughly expose Americans to bloody images that tend to reinforce U.S. war aims. Consider, for example, the Bush administration's proud showcasing of the bloody, mutilated faces of Uday and Qusay Hussein (Saddam Hussein's sons), which were circulated shamelessly throughout American media outlets such as *CNN* and *Fox News* for hours on end in late 2003. The Bush administration's capture of Uday and Qusay was met with ecstasy in the media, as emphasizing graphic images of dead bodies was not considered "too pornographic," but in fact perfectly acceptable, seeing as those shown were the "bad guys." Reporters expressed no interest in "taste" as influencing their decisions to show gory images, when the goal of such reporting was to reinforce pro-war propaganda.

Why Do Governments Distrust *Al Jazeera*?

Government leaders claim that they dislike *Al Jazeera* because of unfair, biased reporting. Such claims, of course, are erroneous. *Al Jazeera* is no more biased than any other media outlet. Kenton Keith, former US ambassador to Qatar states that the network, "no more than other news organizations, has a slant. Its slant happens to be one most Americans are not comfortable with. . . but the fact is that *Al Jazeera* has revolutionized media in the Middle East" through its openness and willingness to criticize those in power, regardless of their country of origin.[127] What seems to disturb many American and Middle Eastern leaders about *Al Jazeera* is not its bias or criticisms of other governments, but its challenges to their own. It is important to remember that, before the September 11 attacks and the Iraq war, the station had actually garnered much praise from the U.S. State Department because of its willingness to challenge undemocratic governments in the region.[128] It was not until *Al Jazeera* targeted the U.S. for criticism that it became uncomfortable with the channel's reporting.

Al Jazeera derives its legitimacy overwhelmingly from the people of the Middle East. It is the closeness to its Arab base of thirty-five to forty million viewers,[129] and the attention it pays in its reporting to their main concerns that has made the station a major power in terms of reflecting and influencing public opinion. The legitimacy that *Al Jazeera* enjoys seems to greatly outweigh that of most of its competitors. *Al Jazeera*'s website, as well as its television reporting is among the most popular in the Arab World in the Iraq war. The network's massive audience and public support greatly contrasts with that of American networks such as *Fox News*, *CNN*, which average far fewer followers in the Middle East. Indeed, nothing like *Al Jazeera* has ever been seen throughout the Middle East. As *CBC News* explains, "the network's very existence is revolutionary. Unlike state-controlled television in most Arab countries, *Al Jazeera* broadcasts the voices of ordinary people."[130] It is this revolution in the Arab World's access to critical information and anti-war propaganda, provided by *Al Jazeera*, that the Bush administration is committed to dismantling.

The Demonstration Effect

Many throughout the Middle East and the world felt that the U.S. intentionally assaulted *Al Jazeera* and its journalists in Iraq and Afghanistan in order to make an example of the station. Journalists from *Al Jazeera* have been detained by American forces and charged with collaborating with terrorists. Sami Muhyi al-Din al-Hajj, a cameraman for *Al Jazeera* in Iraq, was detained by the U.S. and held at Guantanamo Bay. It was reported in September of 2005 that U.S. interrogators promised Sami would be released if he spied on fellow reporters at *Al Jazeera*. The interrogators claimed that such surveillance was necessary since Al Qaeda members had infiltrated *Al Jazeera*.[131]

Evidence has also surfaced suggesting that the Bush administration may have considered bombing the *Al Jazeera* headquarters in Qatar. The *Daily Mirror* of London reported in November 2005 about the contents of a leaked memo from Downing Street that allegedly described a conversation between George Bush and Tony Blair (in April 2004) in which Blair attempted to convince the President *not* to bomb *Al Jazeera*.[132] One source for the *Mirror* report alleged that the conversation was "humorous, not serious," while White House Spokesperson Scott McClellan answered the charge by claiming that, "we are not interested in dignifying something so outlandish and inconceivable with a response."[133] Of course, McLellan's response did not amount to definitive proof that the Bush administration had not considered targeting *Al Jazeera*. Short of a declassification of the Blair administration's memo, little will probably put this controversy to rest in terms of confirming or demolishing the charges that the Bush administration was intent on bombing *Al Jazeera*.

Rather than working to promote transparency in government planning (by declassifying the document in full), the British government moved to punish the individual suspected of leaking it, leading many to wonder if the Bush and Blair administrations had something to hide. Cabinet Office civil servant David Keogh was charged under Britain's Official Secrets Act with the leak, as the memo was considered a "damaging disclosure" for the Blair government.[134] Likewise, all other British papers were threatened under the gag order not to publish the contents of the memo.[135]

The government's refusal to declassify the document was met with skepticism by some political officials, as the question of whether the Blair and Bush governments were deceiving their respective constituencies became more and more pertinent. Peter Kilfoyle, former Defense Minister under the Blair government called for the declassification of the document, maintaining that: "I think they ought to clarify what exactly happened on this occasion. . . . If it was the case that President Bush wanted to bomb *Al Jazeera* in what is after all a friendly country, it speaks volumes and it raises questions about subsequent attacks that took place on the press that wasn't embedded with coalition forces."[136]

Regardless of whether the U.S. bombings of the network offices in Afghanistan or Iraq were deliberate or accidental, the implications of the attacks on independent media are the same for any news outlet contemplating critical reporting of the United States outside of embedded positions. When asked by reporters for a justification for the U.S. bombing of *Al Jazeera*'s Baghdad office, former Pentagon spokesperson Victoria Clarke explained to reporters that American troops had done nothing wrong by "exercise[ing] their inherent right to self-defense. . . Baghdad is not a safe place, you should not be there."[137]

Assertions that reporters should not be covering conflicts from outside U.S. military censorship and protection are discouraging for those who value unembedded reporting during times of war, as it reveals the Bush administration's discomfort with unilateral reporters' challenges to the occupation of Iraq. Such discomfort inevitably has a chilling effect on unilateral reporters, as they realize that the U.S. has not made protection of unembedded journalists in Iraq a real priority. Indeed, the bombings of *Al Jazeera* throw into question the entire assumption that it is possible to separate civilian targets from military ones, or that the Bush administration and military planners have much of an interest in doing so in the first place. The lack of seriousness of the U.S. military's investigation into the attack on the Palestine Hotel demonstrates this reality clearly.[138] *Al Jazeera*'s journalists are also under great danger of being detained without charge by coalition forces in retaliation for their independent reporting. As David Enders explains in his book, The Baghdad Bulletin "Working as an independent journalist [in Iraq] is dangerous. . . . Journalists from *Al Jazeera* are arrested more often than employees of any other agency, generally after they show their press passes."[139]

Many media analysts believe that the bombings of *Al Jazeera* and other media offices during the Iraq and Afghanistan wars were meant to deter independent reporters from covering U.S. initiated conflicts. Scholar and media critic Philip Knightley argues that "those [reporters] who try to follow an objective, independent path [in Iraq] will be shunned" by the Bush administration, "and those who report from the enemy side will risk being shot. . . the Pentagon is determined that there will be no more reporting from the enemy side...and that a few deaths among correspondents who do so will deter others."[140] Mohammed Burini, *Al Jazeera*'s correspondent in Mosul attested to this perceived problem after the station's Baghdad office was hit: "after hitting our office, everybody was scared. They [Iraqis] didn't want to receive us, because they said, 'you are targeted, so if you start your machines here the American airplanes will target you.'"[141] The message to unembedded reporters is this: either embed yourselves under the control of the U.S. military or work at your own peril and risk being killed by U.S. or resistance groups. This message poses a serious challenge to reporters looking to provide adversarial, independent reporting in the Iraq war, while concurrently challenging government statements.

The U.S. also tried to discipline *Al Jazeera* by pressuring the government of Qatar to put the channel up for sale to a private buyer.[142] The logic behind the sale of *Al Jazeera* is clear enough: subject the station to market discipline in order to assimilate it within the U.S.-led neoliberal framework of corporate globalization, of which the invasion of Iraq is a major part. Private ownership of *Al Jazeera* would place great pressure on the news outlet to curtail its opposition to U.S. policy in the Middle East in two ways: 1. by threatening the station's funding should corporate advertisers decide to boycott *Al Jazeera* in retaliation for controversial reporting, and 2. by reinforcing the neoliberal ideology that states that media reporting, like other vital public services, exists *not* primarily to educate the public (*Al Jazeera*'s goal), but for profit gain (the corporate media's main goal).

As *Al Jazeera* attempts to expand its audience size with the introduction of an English-language news channel, the debate over the channel's influence amongst Western audiences will inevitably become more relevant. As the *International Herald Tribune* speculates over the possibility of *Al Jazeera*'s English channel: "Will the English-language service be able to persuade enough satellite and cable services to carry it, particularly in the United States market? Will advertisers sign up, or will they prefer to steer clear of associations with *Al Jazeera*?"[143] These questions are important to consider when one reflects on the traditionally strong relationship between corporate advertisers and the corporate press and the Bush administration. Sadly, U.S. media carriers have refused to carry *Al Jazeera* as of 2007, likely out of fear of alienating themselves from advertisers and angering the Bush administration and other American political leaders.

The elimination or censorship of the most influential and independent news source in the Arab world would deal a strong blow to the chances of strengthening informed opinion and debate throughout the Middle East regarding important issues of the day. *Al Jazeera* has performed a valuable service by highlighting the activities of repressive Arab regimes that have often been able to skirt public accountability.

Attacks against *Al Jazeera*, at their core, are attacks against the ability of the Arab World to openly and democratically debate the legitimacy of the U.S. presence in the region. As Walid al-Omary, West Bank Bureau Chief of *Al Jazeera* explains: the station's "biggest contribution to change in the Arab World" has come in the form of a "broadening of the Arab perspective. Before us, no one was saying anything about Arab leaders or Arab corruption. . . now I believe that the Arab world is moving towards more democratic changes."[144] *Al Jazeera*'s goal, as the old adage goes, is to remind its viewers of the power of knowledge. By equipping its viewers with the information needed to challenge and question government, *Al Jazeera* has performed a vital service. The negative repercussions of attempts to eliminate the network will be felt for years to come, should such efforts succeed.

Notes

1. Bill Gallagher, "Bush Lies, Propaganda Falling Flat," *Common Dreams*, 10 January 2006, http://www.commondreams.org/views06/0110-36.htm (3 May 2006).

2. Chadwick F. Alger, "The World Relations of Cities: Closing the Gap between Social Science Paradigms and Everyday Human Experience," *International Studies Quarterly*, 34 (1990), 493-518.

3. Sarah Lyall, "Death Brings Demand for Public Inquiry," *New York Times*, 18 August 2003, 11(A).

4. Steven Weissman, "Dead Messengers: How the U.S. Military Threaten Journalists," *Truthout*, 22 June 2005, http://www.truthout.org/docs_2005/022805A.shtml (25 Jun. 2005).

5. Amy Goodman, *Exception to the Rulers: Exposing Oily Politicians, War Profiteers, and the Media That Love Them* (New York: Hyperion, 2004), 187.

6. Goodman, *Exception to the Rulers*, 187.

7. Lyall, "Death Brings Public Inquiry," 2003.

8. David Enders, *Baghdad Bulletin: Dispatches on the American Occupation* (Ann Arbor, Mi.: University of Michigan, 2005), 38-40.

9. Jonathon Steele and Owen Bowcott, "Reporter Killed Covering his First War," *Guardian*, 7 July 2003, http://www.guardian.co.uk/Iraq/Story/0,2763,993003,00.html (25 Jun. 2005); Enders, *Baghdad Bulletin*, 38-40.

10. Lee Gordon, "Anger Over Failure to Investigate Reporter's Shooting," *Telegraph*, 11 November 2004, http://www.telegraph.co.uk/news/main.jhtml?xml=/news/2004/07/1-1/wirq.xm (15 Jun. 2005).

11. Aaron Glantz, "Stop Shooting Journalists," *Common Dreams*, 12 July 2005, http://www.commondreams.org/views05/0712-20.htm (12 Jul. 2005).

12. Enders, *Baghdad Bulletin*, 2-3, 67.

13. Enders, *Baghdad Bulletin*, 33.

14. Guardian, "US Troops Seize Award-Winning Iraqi Journalist," 9 January 2005, http://www.guardian.co.uk/frontpage/story/0,,1682246,00.html (12 Jun. 2005).

15. Reuters, "Last Year Deadliest for Journalists Since 2005," 4 January 2006, http://www.truthout.org/cgi-bin/artman/exec/view.cgi/47/16696 (4 Jan. 2006).

16. Enders, *Baghdad Bulletin*, 2.

17. Enders, *Baghdad Bulletin*, 19.

18. Steve Weissman, "Kill the Messenger, Hide the News," *Truthout*, 22 June 2005, http://www.truthout.org/docs_2005/062205B.shtml (22 Jun. 2005).

19. Tom Engelhardt, "'Hotel Journalism' Not the Essence of What's Happening in Iraq," *TomDispatch.com*, 3 November 2005, http://www.commondreams.org/views05/1-103-24.htm (3 Nov. 2005).

20. Englehardt, "Hotel Journalism," 2005.

21. Christian Parenti, *The Freedom: Shadows and Hallucinations in Occupied Iraq* (New York: New Press, 2004), 2.

22. Parenti, *The Freedom*, 23.

23. Aaron Glantz, *How America Lost Iraq* (New York: Penguin, 2005), 82-4.

24. Glantz, *How America Lost Iraq*, 235-36.

25. Dahr Jamail, "Daily Life in Baghdad, From Afar," *Dahr Jamail's Iraq Dispatches*, 22 May 2005, http://dahrjamailiraq.com/weblog/archives/dispatches/000248.php#more (22 May 2005).

26. Dahr Jamail, "Dahr Jamail on Living in Two Worlds," *Dahr Jamail's Iraq Dispatches*, 20 May 2005, http://dahrjamailiraq.com/weblog/archives/dispatches/000246.php#more (20 May 2005).

27. Raul Mahajan, "Eyewitness Account from Fallujah," *Z Magazine*, 11 April 2004, http://www.zmag.org/content/print_article.cfm?itemID=5304&sectionID=1 (2 May 2005).

28. Dahr Jamail and Jonathon Steele, "Our Guernica," *Z Magazine*, 27 April 2005, http://www.zmag.org/content/print_article.cfm?itemID=7743sectionID=15 (27 Apr. 2005).

29. David Cortright, "What We Do Now: A Peace Agenda," *Nation*, 21 April 2003, 11.

30. Howard Zinn, "A Chorus Against War," *Progressive*, March 2003, 19.

31. David Bacon, "Occupation and Human Rights," *Z Magazine*, 17 April 2004, http://www.zmag.org/content/showarticle.cfm?ItemID=5349 (17 Apr. 2004).

32. Goodman, *Exception to the Rulers*, 153.

33. Goodman, *Exception to the Rulers*, 153.

34. Goodman, *Exception to the Rulers*, 201.

35. Goodman, *Exception to the Rulers*, 206-08.

36. Doug Ireland, "Not So Fast," *In These Times*, 30 September 2002, 12.

37. Phyllis Bennis, "No Cause for War," *Multinational Monitor*, January/February 2003, 30.

38. Noam Chomsky and Michael Albert, "Albert Interviews Chomsky on Iraq," *Z Magazine*, 5 September 2002, http://www.zmag.org/Sustainers/content/200209/05chomsky.cfm (13 Nov. 2005).

39. Daniel Ellsberg, "The Courage to Talk Withdrawal," *Common Dreams*, 9 June 2005, http://www.commondreams.org/views05/0609-31.htm (9 Jun. 2005).

40. Kamal Ahmed, "Revealed: How Cluster Bombs Now Litter Iraq," *Observer*, sec. 1, 1 June 2003, 1.

41. Ian Sample and Nic Fleming, "When the Dust Settles," *Guardian*, sec. 1, 17 April 2003, 9.

42. Paul Brown, "Uranium Hazard Prompts Cancer Check on Troops," *Guardian*, 25 April 2003, http://www.guardian.co.uk/uranium/story/0,7369,943340,00.html (25 Apr. 2003); Guardian, "Depleted Uranium," 25 April 2003, http://www.guardian.co.uk/uranium/story/0,7369,943633,00.html (25 Apr. 2003).

43. Sydney Morning Herald, "U.S. Defends Using Napalm-Like Firebombs," 8 August 2003, http://www.smh.com.au/articles/2003/08/08/1060145827920.html (8 Aug. 2003).

44. Colin Brown, "U.S. Lied to Britain Over Use of Napalm in Iraq, " *Independent*, 17 June 2005, http://news.independent.co.uk/uk/politics/article226119.ece (17 June 2005); Paul Gilfeather, "Fallujah Napalmed," *Mirror*, 28 November 2004, http://www.sundaymirror.co.uk/news/tm_objectid=14920109&method=full&siteid=1066948&headline=fallujahnapalmedname_page.html (28 Nov. 2004).

45. Mike Whitney, "Covering Up Napalm in Iraq," *Truthout*, 28 June 2005, http://www.truthout.org/docs_2005/070105M.shtml (28 Jun. 2005).

46. Steven R. Weisman, "U.S. Says Blix Played Down Details of Banned Weapons," *New York Times*, 11 March 2003, 12(A).

47. David Cromwell and David Edwards, *Guardians of Power: The Myth of the Liberal Media* (London: Pluto, 2006).

48. Patrick Cockburn, "One Year After the 'Transfer' of Power, Iraq is a Lawless, Bloody No Man's Land," *Independent*, sec. 1, 28 June 2005, 2.

49. Patrick Cockburn, "A Year On, America Knows the Man for Whom Iraqis Would Not Fight is Irrelevant," *Independent*, sec. 1, 13 December 2004, 22.

50. Robert Fisk, "Robert Fisk in Lebanon and Iraq," *Independent*, sec. 1, 22 December 2004, 25.

51. Robert Fisk, "We'll Go on Cheering Democracy—and the Iraqis Will Go on Dying," *RobertFisk.com*, 30 January 2005, http://www.robert-fisk.com/articles453.htm (22 Jun. 2005).

52. Robert Fisk, "The Government Rules Only in the Capital," *Z Magazine*, 22 July 2004, http://www.zmag.org/content/showarticle.cfm?SectionID=15&ItemID=5918 (10 Jul. 2005).

53. Editorial, "Don't Be Fooled: Middle East Democracy has only the Most Tenuous Link with War in Iraq," *Independent*, sec. 1, 8 March 2005, 28.

54. Robert Fisk, "Covering the Middle East," in *Tell Me Lies: Propaganda and Media Distortion in the Attack on Iraq*, ed. David Miller (London: Pluto, 2004), 220.

55. Robert Fisk, "Covering the Middle East," 216-17.

56. Editorial, "Murder in London," *Washington Post*, 8 July 2005, 22(A).

57. Robert Fisk, "The Reality of this Barbaric Bombing," *Independent*, 8 July 2005, http://news.independent.co.uk/world/fisk/article297623.ece (8 Jul. 2005).

58. Robert Fisk, "America's Shame, Two Years on from 'Mission Accomplished,'" *Independent*, sec. 1, 8 May 2005, 21.

59. Associated Press, "Public Opinion in Iraq: First Poll Following Abu Ghraib Revelations," 14-23 May 2004, http://www.msnbc.com/id/5217741/site/newsweek/ (25 Oct. 2005).

60. Tariq Ali, "Resistance is the First Step Toward Iraqi Independence," *Guardian*, sec. 1, 4 November 2003, 18.

61. Tariq Ali, "The Withdrawal of Foreign Troops is the only Solution," *Guardian*, 12 August 2004, http://www.guardian.co.uk/comment/story/0,3604,1281233,00.html (12 Aug. 2004).

62. Tariq Ali and David Barsamian, *Speaking of Empire and Resistance: Conversations with Tariq Ali* (London: New Press, 2005), 5-6.

63. Ali and Barsamian, *Speaking of Empire and Resistance*, 33.

64. Jonathon Steele, "Why the U.S. is Running Scared of Elections in Iraq," *Guardian*, 19 January 2004, http://www.guardian.co.uk/Iraq/Story/0,2763,1126178,00.html (13 Jun. 2005).

65. Tariq Ali, "Out with the Old, in with the New," *Guardian*, 7 February 2005, http://www.guardian.co.uk/comment/story/0,3604,1407210,00.html (12 Jun. 2005).

66. Paul McGeough, "Allawi Shot Prisoners in Cold Blood: Witnesses," *Sydney Morning Herald*, 17 July 2004, http://www.smh.com.au/articles/2004/07/16/1089694568-757.html?oneclick=true (17 Jul. 2004).

67. McGeough, "Allawi Shot Prisoners in Cold Blood," 2004.

68. Paul McGeough, "All Eyes on the Main Who Stepped into Iraqi Inferno," *Sydney Morning Herald*, 30 June 2004, http://www.smh.com.au/articles/2004/06/29/108848796-5015.html (30 June 2004).

69. Paul McGeough, "Voter Turnout Won't Be Enough to Legitimize Election," *Sydney Morning Herald*, 20 January 2005, http://www.commondreams.org/hcadlines05/012-0-02.htm (20 Jan. 2005).

70. Tony Kevin, "All the Makings of a War Crime," *Sydney Morning Herald* 8 November 2004, http://www.commondreams.org/views04/1108-26.htm (8 Nov. 2004).

71. Paul McGeough, "Fight to the Death," *Sydney Morning Herald*, 20 December 2003, http://www.smh.com.au/articles/2003/12/19/1071337160499.html (3 May 2005).

72. Phillip Knightly, "History or Bunkum?," in *Tell Me Lies: Propaganda and Media Distortion in the Attack on Iraq*, ed. David Miller (London: Pluto, 2004), 102.

73. *Control Room*, DVD, directed by Jehane Noujaim (Lion's Gate, 26 Oct. 2004).

74. Goodman, *Exception to the Rulers*, 181.

75. Amy Goodman, "Killing the Messenger," *Third World Traveler*, 2004, http://www.thirdworldtraveler.com/Amy_Goodman/Killing_Messenger_TETTR.html (16 May 2005).

76. Faisal Bodi, "Al Jazeera's War," in *Tell Me Lies: Propaganda and Media Distortion in the Attack on Iraq*, ed. David Miller (London: Pluto, 2004), 267.

77. Mohamed Zayani, "Introduction: Al Jazeera and the Vicissitudes of the New Arab Mediascape," in *The Al Jazeera Phenomenon: Critical Perspectives on New Arab Media*, ed. Mohamed Zayani (Boulder, Co.: Paradigm, 2005), 10.

78. Bill O'Reilly, "Fox Out, Al Jazeera In," *BillO'Reilly.com*, 20 July 2004, http://www.billoreilly.com/pg/jsp/general/genericpage.jsp?pageID=334 (11 Apr. 2005).

79. Lee Smith, "Documenting Al Jazeera: In Control Room, Not All Conspiracy Theories are Created Equal," *Slate*, 12 April 2004, http://slate.msn.com/id/2098668/ (4 May 2005).

80. Mohamed Zayani, "Introduction: Al Jazeera and the Vicissitudes of the New Arab Mediascape," in *The Al Jazeera Phenomenon: Critical Perspectives on New Arab Media*, ed. Mohamed Zayani (Boulder, Co.: Paradigm, 2005), 4-5.

81. Mohammed El Oifi, "Influence Without Power: Al Jazeera and the Arab Public Sphere," in *The Al Jazeera Phenomenon: Critical Perspectives in New Arab Media*, ed. Mohamed Zayani (Boulder, Co.: Paradigm, 2005), 74.

82. *Control Room*, DVD, directed by Jehane Noujaim (Lion's Gate, 26 October 2004).

83. Samuel Abt, "For Al Jazeera, Balanced Coverage Frequently Leaves No Side Happy," *New York Times*, 16 February 2004, 2(C).

84. Abt, 2004.

85. *Control Room*, 2004.

86. Zayani, "Introduction," 31.

87. Hugh Miles, *Al Jazeera: The Inside Story of the Arab News Channel That is Challenging the West* (New York: Grove, 2005), 274.

88. Miles, *Al Jazeera*, 243.

89. Donna Leinwand, "CENTCOM: Heavy on Message, Light on News," *USA Today*, 4 April 2003, http://www.usatoday.com/news/world/iraq/2003-04-04-centcomusat_x.htm (18 Mar. 2005).

90. Eric Burns, *Fox News Watch*, Fox News, 12 December 2004.

91. Burns, *Fox News Watch*, 2004.

92. Danny Schechter, "Blogging the War Away," *Z Magazine*, July-August 2003, 66-7.

93. Barabara Bedway, "Chris Hedges on 'Distorted' War Coverage," *Editor & Publisher*, 2 April 2003, http://editorandpublisher.com/eandp/newsarticle_display.jsp?nu_content_id=1853701 (18 Jul. 2005).

94. Robert Jensen, "Embedded Reporters View Point Misses Main Point of War," *Dissident Voice*, 16 June 2003, http://www.dissidentvoice.org/Articles5/Jensen_Inbeds.htm (4 Mar. 2005).

95. Michael Massing, "Iraq, the Press, and the Election," *Mother Jones*, 22 November 2004, http://www.motherjones.com/news/dailymojo/2004/11/11_523.html (22 Nov. 2004).

96. Robert Jensen, "The Military's Media," *The Progressive*, May 2003, 22.

97. Goodman, *Exception to the Rulers*, 170.

98. Schechter, "Blogging the War Away," 66-7.

99. BBC News, "How 'Embedded' Reporters are Handling the War," 25 March 2003, http://news.bbc.co.uk/1/hi/uk/2885179.stm (1 Aug. 2005).

100. Paul Workman, "Embedded Journalists Versus 'Unilateral' Reporters," *CBC*, 7 April 2003, http://www.cbc.ca/news/iraq/canada/correspondents_workman030407.html (12 Jul. 2005).

101. Project for Excellence in Journalism, "Embedded Reporters: What Are Americans Getting," 2 May 2005, http://www.journalism.org/resources/research/reports/war/embed/-default.asp (2 May 2005).

102. Greg Mitchell, "Why Most Embeds Don't Tell All," *Reclaim the Media*, 11 January 2005, http://www.reclaimthemedia.org/print.php?story=05/01/11/4572908 (5 May 2005).

103. Mitchell, 2005.

104. Mitchell, 2005.

105. Miles, *Al Jazeera*, 242.

106. Mohammed El-Nawawy and Adel Iskandar, *Al Jazeera: The Story of the Network that is Rattling Governments and Redefining Modern Journalism* (Cambridge: Westview, 2003), 182.

107. Al Jazeera, "War Diary: Day 7," 26 March 2003, http://english.aljazeera.net/NR/exeres/8245212D-39CC-4E6E-80FF-2E1F29F72BC5.htm (23 Jun. 2005).

108. Najib Ghadban, "The War on Iraq: Justifications and Motives," *Al Jazeera*, 10August 2003, http://english.aljazeera.net/NR/exeres/FC73D48E-EE6F4C4EBD67C8C-1BD67C8C1179E97CC.htm (23 June 2005).

109. Mohammed Al-Obaidi, "Why Iraqis Should Boycott Elections," *Al Jazeera*, 3 December 2004, http://english.aljazeera.net/english/DialogBox/PrintReview.aspx?NRORIGINALURL=% (14 Apr. 2005).

110. El-Nawawy and Iskandar, 30.

111. El-Nawawy and Iskandar, 176.

112. Danny Schechter, "Watch Out World: Al Jazeera is Going Global," *MediaChannel.org*, 26 April 2005, http://www.commondreams.org/views05/0426-34.htm (26 Apr. 2005).

113. William F. Buckley, "Shut Up, Al-Jazeera," *National Review*, 1 February 2005, http://www.nationalreview.com/script.printpage.asp?ref=/buckley/wfb200502011314.asp (13 Mar. 2005).

114. Schechter, "Watch Out World," 2005.

115. El-Nawawy and Iskandar, 181.

116. Jeremy Scahill, "Bush Wanted Al Jazeera Gone and he Wanted it Then," *Nation*, 12 December 2005, http://www.truthout.org/cgi-bin/artman/exec/view.cgi/38/15772 (15 Dec. 2005).

117. Hala Jaber and Tony Allen Mills, "Iraqis Killed by US Troops 'on Ramage,'" *Sunday Times*, 26 March 2006.

118. Jaber and Mills, "Iraqis Killed by US Troops 'on Rampage,'" 2006.

119. Miles, *Al Jazeera*, 248.

120. Laura Flanders, "Arab CNN First Berated, then Bombed by U.S.," *Alternet*, 14 November 2001, http://www.alternet.org/story/11921/ (25 May 2005).

121. Editorial, "Banning Bad News in Iraq," *New York Times*, 10 August 2004, 22(A).

122. Knightly, "History or Bunkum?" 104.

123. Daryn Kagan, *Wolf Blitzer Reports*, CNN, 12 April 2004.

124. Amy Goodman, "Interview with CNN's Aaron Brown," *Democracy Now!*, 4 April 2003.

125. Morand Fachot, "Conference Report: Arab Media Take Center Stage," *Transnational Broadcasting Studies Journal*, 2004, http://www.tbsjournal.com/printer%20friendly/newsechange_fachot.htm (3 Jun. 2005).

126. *Control Room*, Noujaim (2004).

127. Cameron W. Barr, "Top Arab TV Network to hit U.S. Market," *Christian Science Monitor*, 26 December 2002, http://www.csmonitor.com/2002/1226/p01s04-wome.html (1 May 2005).

128. Isabel Hilton, "And Now, the Other News," *New York Times*, 6 March 2005, 7(A).

129. El-Nawawy and Iskandar, *Al Jazeera*, 34.

130. CBC News Online, "Al-Jazeera Television," 14 March 2003, http://www.cbs.ca/d-isclosure/archives/030401.html (23 Jul. 2005).

131. Al Jazeera, "Al Jazeera Cameraman 'Asked to Spy,'" 26 September 2005, http://english.aljazeera.net/News/archive/archive?ArchiveId=15328 (Nov. 25, 2005).

132. Kevin Maguire and Andy Lines, "Exclusive: Bush Plot to Bomb his Arab Ally," *Daily Mirror*, 22 November 2005, http://www.mirror.co.uk/news/topstories/tm_objectid-=16397937&method=full&siteid=94762-name_page.html (22 Nov. 2005).

133. Robert Barr, "Report: Bush Talked of Bombing Al Jazeera," *Associated Press*, 22 November 2005, http://www.sfgate.com/cgi-bin/article.cgi?file=n/a/2005/11/22/internati-onal/i075621S41.DTL&type=printable (22 Nov. 2005).

134. Barr, 2005.

135. Washington Post Blog, *Washington Post*, 23 November 2005, http://blog.washing-tonpost.com/worldopinion/roundup/ (23 Nov. 2005).

136. Jeremy Scahill, "The War on *Al Jazeera*," *Nation*, 5 December 2005, http://www.-thenation.com/doc/20051219/scahill (5 Dec. 2005).

137. Goodman, "Killing the Messenger," 2004.

138. Weissman, "Kill the Messenger," 2005.

139. Enders, *Baghdad Bulletin*, 107.

140. Knightly, History or Bunkum?, 104.

141. *Control Room*, Noujaim, 2004.

142. Steven R. Weisman, "Qatar's Quest: Finding a Buyer for Al Jazeera," *New York Times*, 31 January 2005, http://www.iht.com/articles/2005/01/30/news/qatar.html (31 Jan. 2005).

143. Eric Pfanner and Doreen Carvajal, "The Selling of Al Jazeera TV to an International Market," *New York Times*, 31 October 2005, http://www.nytimes.com/2005/10/31-/business/31jazeera.html?ex=1168232400&en=78a169ce329dccd5&ei=5070 (31 Oct. 2005).

144. Miles, *Al Jazeera*, 332.

10

Afghanistan and 9/11:
The "War on Terror" Declared

In his 2002 State of the Union Address to Congress, President Bush proudly announced: "the last time we met in this chamber, the mothers and daughters of Afghanistan were captives in their own homes, forbidden from working or going to school. Today women are free, and are part of Afghanistan's new government." The United States "saved a people from starvation and freed a country from brutal oppression," and "America and Afghanistan are now allies against terror. We will be partners in rebuilding the country."[1] In accord with the statements of the President, the American press uncritically disseminated his promises regarding Afghan reconstruction, enhancement of women's rights, and democracy promotion.

To be sure, mainstream media coverage did also emphasize humanitarian problems throughout Afghanistan at certain points. However, the repetition of official declarations concerning Afghanistan characterized most reporting in light of media over-reliance on official sources. At times, critical questions were asked about the potential human consequences of war with Afghanistan after 9/11. In one example, Jack Kelley of *USA Today* argued shortly before the U.S. invasion in 2001 that the looming war against Afghanistan carried with it a large risk for the Afghan people: "The stakes are clear. Those left starving will presumably blame the nation whose bombs made them refugees, as will Muslims around the world who see their plight on TV."[2]

More often the negative effects of the war on the Afghan people were lost or neglected in the rush to war. Media outlets were primarily concerned with "fighting terror" after the shocking attacks of 9/11. A shortage of reporting on the deterioration of Afghanistan continued long after the end of "Operation Enduring Freedom"—through the 2004 presidential and 2005 parliamentary elections—as news commentators and pundits applauded a "landmark election for representatives to the [Afghan] national parliament and local legislators."[3] Responsibility for the deterioration of social order was blamed primarily on Afghan "militants trying to derail the vote," while American and NATO forces were spoken highly of for "providing security" at polling and ballot counting locations.[4]

The elections were taken as a "demonstration of how much the country has changed since the ruling Taliban were toppled."[5] News organizations like *CNN* focused on newly acquired voting rights for women, among other achievements. The continued subjugation and repression of women on the part of the Northern Alliance, however, was often lost or downplayed in the praise. By 2005, the *New York Times* conceded that Afghanistan had fallen "out of the headlines," as news organizations became more concerned with events unfolding in Iraq and elsewhere. Stories about post-Taliban repression became less a focus of reporting after the end of major U.S. combat operations in Afghanistan in late 2001.

Contrary to official propaganda, the story of Ali Mohaqiq Nasab reveals a great deal about the state of Afghanistan after the fall of the Taliban. As an editor for Haqooq-i-Zan (an Afghan women's magazine), Ali consistently took a stand against conventional cultural norms relegating women to the status of second-class citizens. He criticized harsh government punishments, such as the stoning to death those who abandon Islam, and the mandatory punishment of 100 lashes for adultery. Ali also took issue with the belief that men and women are unequal before the law.

As someone who spoke out against corporal punishment and legally sanctioned sexual discrimination, Ali's challenges were, and continue to be considered a serious threat to the legitimacy of the new conservative Islamic Republic of Afghanistan. Ali's experience is just one of the many recent examples of what happens to those who are charged with spreading "un-Islamic materials" and "blasphemy."[6] After a Presidential advisor brought charges against him, Ali's case was taken to the Afghan Supreme Court, where he was tried for violating a 2004 media law signed by Hamid Karzai which banned from publication any materials considered an insult to Islam. The prosecutor in Ali's trial originally pushed for the death sentence, intending the case to be "a lesson for him and others" of what happens when one challenges traditional interpretations of "proper" adherence to the principles of Islam.[7]

Fortunately, Ali was not sentenced to death, although the Afghan Supreme Court did sentence him to two years in prison for exercising little more than what would be considered a standard free speech right in other countries. An equally extreme attempt to punish Abdul Rahman, an Afghan who converted from Islam to Christianity, was also seen in 2006. Rahman was arrested after being charged with violating the Afghan constitution, which, based upon Sharia (Islamic law), mandated that those who reject Islam receive the death penalty. Such was the harsh reality of day-to-day existence in what *USA Today* referred to as the "freshly minted democracy" of Afghanistan.[8] Indeed, the idea, presented in media framing, that Afghanistan is on the march toward democracy is an unrealistic whitewash of the repressive reality the Afghan people have endured in terms of the growth of state terror, and coercion, escalating warlord violence, social deterioration, and increasing attacks against women.

Post-Taliban "Democracy":
Afghanistan as a Failed State

The major American media have quietly acknowledged that there are a number of major problems in Afghanistan today. Media outlets, however, generally choose to portray the country, despite a few snags, as working toward democratic empowerment. Americans can read in mainstream newspapers that Afghanistan is stabilizing out of its own volition, although with some U.S. assistance. The main catalysts for the depiction of Afghanistan as an "emerging democracy" were the 2004 and 2005 Presidential and Parliamentary elections, which resulted in the first elected government in that country. According to *Business Week*, elections represented a "First step. . . on the path to democracy."[9] The *Washington Post* asserted that, through elections, "the Afghan people took another step toward lasting peace and prosperity while dealing a blow to terrorism."[10] Neo-Conservative columnist Charles Krauthammer and William Safire vociferously celebrated the "miracle" of Afghan democracy.[11] The United States was said to be "directly responsible for this outbreak of freedom in a Muslim land," as Safire explained that Muslims too, "can be democrats."[12] Such a paternalistic, condescending framing of Afghan democracy as inferior to American democracy was also seen in the reporting of the *New York Times*, which depicted the "students" of "Afghan Democracy 101" as under the tutelage of the United States.[13] The top-down approach to "imposing democracy" represents a serious departure from those who criticize U.S. involvement in Afghanistan from the late 1970s to this day as harmful in terms of hampering Afghan rights and freedoms.

Despite whatever past neglect the U.S. displayed toward Afghanistan, American leaders were said to be in the midst of a major change in their policy goals. Charles Norchi of the *Boston Globe* spoke optimistically of "a new start in Afghanistan" where "the goal is a stable and responsible state that will not breed terror."[14] Such reporting implied that the Northern Alliance, which controls much of Afghanistan, could be trusted in promoting stabilization, human rights, and democracy. Were consumers of American media to closely follow reporting on Afghanistan, however, they would have seen two clear, but antagonistic trends within the coverage: 1. Reporting closely followed the Bush administration's celebrations of a "new" Afghanistan that was said to be on the right track in terms of promoting human rights, reconstruction, and democracy. This Afghanistan, despite facing major hurdles, was working successfully toward peace and stability; and 2. More critical appraisals in the mainstream press, where readers could learn of a different Afghanistan—a land with a weak government—what some considered a failed state in terms of its reliance on the illicit drug trade due to its weak central economy. This land was characterized as increasingly unstable and insecure; as it lacked much of the basic infrastructure needed in any functioning society.

The picture of Afghanistan as deserted by the U.S.—a picture that was of less use to an administration interested in promoting the image of U.S. commitment to nation building—received less and less prominent attention as the war in

Iraq raged on. As a result, many looking for better reporting on the desolate conditions in Afghanistan were increasingly forced to look to more critical sources in the Progressive-Left media, international media, and human rights organizations for much of their information.

Overall, U.S. spending levels on "reconstruction" in Afghanistan have been far less than those committed to Iraq. After twenty-five years of war, as well as massive foreign intervention, Afghanistan has been left to a large degree with little working infrastructure; its cities lie in ruins as a result of civil conflict, with millions of refugees and internally displaced, hundreds of thousands of which are children, forced to live near landfills and markets in neighboring Pakistan.[15] The state is in need of a minimum of tens, if not hundreds of billions of dollars in reparations, should it ever come to resemble a state with properly functioning infrastructure and stable central authority. A report from a British Parliamentary Committee warns that Afghanistan may disintegrate as a result of Western sponsored destruction and neglect: "there is a real danger if these resources [needed for reconstruction] are not provided soon that Afghanistan—a fragile state in one of the most sensitive and volatile regions of the world—could implode, with terrible consequences."[16]

U.S. aid to Afghanistan averaged between only one and two billion dollars a year from 2002 to 2005, and the funding has fallen far short of the amounts needed for rebuilding and restoration of vital services. In 2003, the Bush administration initially failed to request *any* funds at all for rebuilding Afghanistan until Congress stepped in to fund an emergency 300 million dollars for the task.[17]

Figure 10.1

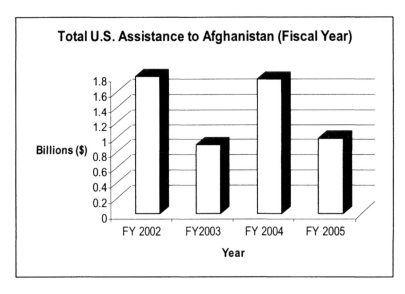

Total U.S. Assistance to Afghanistan (Fiscal Year)

Figure 10.1 Continued

Sources
James Dao, "Afghan Officials Say Aid has been too Slow," *New York Times*, 25 July 2002, 6(A).
Cnn.com, "Afghanistan Set for 1 Billion Boost," 25 August 2003, http://www.cnn.com-/2003/world/asiapcf/central/08/25/us.afghan/ (15 Apr. 2007).
U.S. State Department, "Foreign Aid: An Introductory Overview of U.S. Programs and Policy," *Congressional Research*, 15 April 2004, http://usinfo.state.gov/usa/infousa/infousa/trade/files/98-916.pdf (15 Apr. 2007).
U.S. State Department, "Foreign Aid: An Introductory Overview of U.S. Programs and Policy," 23 May 2005, *Congressional Research Service*, http://www.fas.org/sgp/crs/row/98-916.pdf (15 Apr. 2007).

To put U.S. funding levels into better perspective, the U.S. spends on average at least three billion dollars a year (by conservative estimates) on aid to Israel, one of the wealthiest, most prosperous countries in the Middle East.[18] Total U.S. aid to Afghanistan from 2002 to 2005 is the equivalent to approximately two years of aid to Israel. Such limited financial support for rebuilding means that vital infrastructure projects are typically left incomplete.

By 2002, the interim Afghan government was so under funded that it could not even afford to pay back salaries for government employees.[19] By June 2002, over 6 months after the end of major U.S. military operations, only 870 million dollars of the promised 1.8 billion dollars in reconstruction pledges from the U.S. had been received, and 350 million dollars of that money had been used to pay for activities related to overthrowing the Taliban in 2001. In short, six months after the war, Afghanistan was only supplied with $520 million by the U.S. for reconstruction.[20] By mid-2002, American journalists were reporting that social programs attempting to provide much needed food aid, health care, and school reforms had fallen "woefully short of money."[21] No serious reconstruction projects had yet begun at that time.

By late 2002, Afghanistan, which had some of the best roads before the Soviet/American intervention, had become reliant on U.S. funding for repairing major roads, although the 180 million dollars allocated was only enough to fund the renewal of 660 miles of highway, with another 650 million dollars still needed to fix main roads alone.[22] Of about 13,000 miles of roads nationwide, only 2,000 were paved, of which a mere 20 percent were "in good shape."[23] Inadequate funding for reconstruction has remained a problem in following years. The World Bank estimated by late 2006 to early 2007, that the top twenty-five international donors had allocated a mere 1.7 billion dollars for reconstruction, of which only 860 million dollars had been allocated to the Afghan government, and only 214 million dollars for investment projects.[24]

Afghanistan's economy has generally performed very poorly after so many years of foreign intervention, violence, and destruction. Exports from 2002-2003 amounted to a miniscule 100 million dollars,[25] while government revenues and expenditures for 2004 to 2005 were estimated at only 300 million and 609 million dollars respectively.[26] Sovereignty no longer remained with the central gov-

ernment either—as governing power was decentralized amongst regional warlords who are responsible for "a rise in rural lawlessness," according to reports
from the American press.[27] Meanwhile, Hamid Karzai, the U.S. favored candidate who was victorious in the 2004 Presidential election, retains only limited
power in the central government. Mitchell Prothero of *Salon* magazine reported
that Karzai "has lost credibility, not just because of the perception that he is a
pawn of the West, but because of his reluctance to confront warlords," many of
which gained representation in the central government after the 2005 election.[28]

As one of the poorest countries in the world, the Afghan standard of living
is exceptionally low. Basic human rights such as access to clean water, electricity, health care, and other services are systematically neglected. As of late 2004,
less than 20 percent of Afghans had access to clean water; only 6 percent had
electricity; and half of the population suffered under chronic malnutrition.[29] Afghanistan ranks close to the bottom of the list of all states when looking at life
expectancy and infant mortality; its education system is described as "the worst
in the world," and a third of its people "suffer from anxiety, depression, or post-
traumatic stress."[30] Despite these statistics, Afghanistan is still thought of as
something of a success story in mainstream reports.

What Happened to Women's Liberation?

As a young woman living in Kabul, Farishta's experiences with sexual abuse
and violence are by no means unique, making them all the more tragic. In a war-
plagued society where women often fear for their lives, Farishta displayed remarkable courage by sharing her story. On October 9, 2003, she was assaulted
by a local militia leader near her village and raped. Her family was powerless to
do anything, forced to watch as the terror unfolded. But Farishta is not the only
woman in her neighborhood who has suffered under warlord rule. A number of
other witnesses stepped forward to charge the same commander who attacked
Farishta with kidnapping other women and girls and committing acts of sexual
aggression and violence against them. As a local government administrator,
Farishta's perpetrator, like so many others throughout Afghanistan, seems to
enjoy immunity from punishment. *Amnesty International* elaborates upon this
problem of impunity, as the family members of the abused are themselves
threatened, beaten and sometimes even killed for asking too many questions and
for challenging warlord violence.

Farishta provides a glimpse into her experiences with the nightmare of sexual violence:

> I'm suffering from what happened to me. I was washing dishes in the spring
> well close to my home. I felt a touch on my shoulder, turned around and saw it
> was the local commander of the village. He grabbed me, threw me on the
> ground and raped me. The whole village could hear my screams, saw what was
> happening to me but would not help me. My father-in-law and three brothers-
> in-law came running to help me and were beaten and threatened by the com-
> mander and his men. They were released but the commander told them he

would not touch them now but that he would make sure he would kill them. We left that same night and walked through the mountains to Kabul. This man and his brother have raped many women in this district. He has been commander of this area for four years and many families have left because of his violence, looting and killing. I don't want our story to remain a secret. We want everyone to know. For many years we have complained but no one listens to us. We have complained to the authorities and many others. The authorities cannot do anything in our area as the commander is the one who is the authority.[31]

Nooria also wants the world to know of her experiences; she wants the injustices committed against women to come to an end. Nooria was twenty years old as well when she was assaulted and battered by her estranged husband. At sixteen years old, Nooria was told that she was to be wed, although her consent was never secured by her family or by her husband-to-be. Forced into an arranged marriage, her husband began to abuse her immediately. On the day of her wedding, he physically assaulted her, claiming that the neckline of her dress was too "revealing." This first attack was to be only one of many, as Nooria was effectively put on house arrest, beaten whenever she would leave the house without permission. After enduring a miscarriage due to her husband's beatings, and carrying another child to term despite continued physical abuse, Nooria decided that she had suffered enough. Unconcerned with the shame that it would bring upon her family, Nooria fled her abusive husband, although her family was initially hesitant to accept her. By mid-2005 though, Nooria had returned to her husband, after being pressured by her family not to seek a legal separation, since the disgrace that comes along with divorce likely meant that her two younger sisters would be unable to marry. In a traditional society where family honor necessitates permanent marriage regardless of abuse, Nooria and countless others are forced to live under increasingly repressive conditions. *Amnesty International* generalizes Nooria's experiences to the rest of Afghanistan:

> Nooria's story is by no means unusual. Countless Afghan women suffer violence from a husband or male family member. Like Nooria, they have no means of support and protection from the state or their families. Very few women will go to court. Most are unaware of their rights and the stigma attached endangers not only the victim but also the reputation of her family. Some fear reprisals from angry husbands and even from their own families—some have even been killed.[32]

The low status of Afghan women is often overlooked in media coverage that attempts to convey a general image of a newly democratic state that respects the human rights of Afghan citizens. The pattern whereby Afghan democracy is loudly proclaimed in headlines, and the desperation of the Afghan people quietly conceded within articles and on the back pages of newspapers, continued unabated during the 2004 and 2005 elections and after. It became popular to talk of "women's liberation" in political discourse, despite an increase in Islamist attacks on girls' schools, and the reinstatement of Taliban-esque rules mandating the covering of women in public.[33] Those who were interested in learning more about the increasing sexual repression in Afghanistan typically looked toward human rights groups, which have taken the strongest initiative in publishing detailed stories identifying the women who suffer under post-Taliban "democracy." The stories of Farishta and Nooria are but a few of the many cases of the human rights violations committed against women in Afghanistan—atrocities downplayed by the U.S. in its self-congratulatory quest for democratization. At a time when coming forward means that a woman may be targeted for violent reprisal, many choose to silently endure inhumane living conditions.

Human rights reports often deliberately refrain from publishing the names of victims, to protect them from possible punishment for speaking out. Even female candidates for public office have chosen to remain unnamed for fear of reprisals. One female candidate from Kandahar shares her experiences with intimidation as she ran for political office in the 2005 elections: "The phone calls were all threatening my life. They asked me to give up running for parliament or something would happen to me. They would kill me. I have told [international human rights groups] about the phone calls." By August, men had begun to physically threaten her on the street and at home: "I was really frightened. . . . I reported it to the security commander. . . . I am really scared now. I wasn't very worried about the phone calls. . . [but] these recent events have made me frightened. I don't go out at all. I don't know what I should do when the official campaign starts."[34]

Amnesty International reports that women have been targeted for assassination as a result of attempts to register to vote: "the risk of rape and sexual violence by members of armed factions and former combatants is still high," and "forced marriage of girl children, and violence against women in the family are widespread in many areas of the country."[35] *Human Rights Watch* states that little has changed for most of Afghanistan under the Northern Alliance's "routine" attacks on women: "the men who replaced the Taliban share the same views on women that made the Taliban so notorious. . . these warlords have had a chokehold on regional and local governments."[36]

American Progressive-Left media outlets have made it a major goal to highlight the repressive post-war situation of Afghanistan. Questions concerning human rights infringements and the failure of democracy have been a major focus of editorializing. In *Common Dreams* Jim Ingalls and Sonali Kolhatkar expressed major reservations about the argument that Afghanistan is transforming into a democracy. They cite a public opinion survey by the *Asia Foundation* in 2004, which found that 72 percent of Afghans who were questioned believed that "men should advise women in their voting choices," while 87 percent of those surveyed thought that "women would need their husband's permission to vote" in the upcoming election.[37] Such answers suggest a serious discrepancy between what many Americans and Afghan men consider to be the defining characteristics of democracy. Whereas Western nations traditionally lend support to the idea that men and women (at least in principle) should be treated equally and can make their own political decisions, the poll above suggests that many Afghans feel democracy authorizes male dominance over women when it comes to voting and other important aspects of economic, social, and political life.

The Northern Alliance "Alternative"

Much of American media reporting implies that Northern Alliance rule is something of an improvement over the extremism and repression of the Taliban. As American allies, North Alliance warlords' responsibility for atrocities is not typically a major concern for American reporters discussing Afghan "democratization," although such atrocities have been condemned from time to time in media reports. *USA Today* commends post-Taliban Afghanistan as a *"former* [emphasis added] cradle of radical Islamic fundamentalism," neglecting the Northern Alliance's role in the destruction of the country after the Soviet withdrawal in 1989, and its instatement of conservative Islamist rule.[38] Maseeh Rahman of the *Washington Times* also speaks highly of the election period, when "most Afghans appear[ed] eager to cast their votes, seeing it as an opportunity to end what they call 'gun rule.'"[39]

Increasingly, Progressive-Left media outlets are providing critical analysis of the deterioration of Afghan infrastructure and security. Jim Ingalls and Sonali Kolhatkar denounced the lack of Afghan civic involvement in setting up the 2004 elections: "the majority of Afghans played no part in decision-making regarding the schedule and structure of the elections, and will not benefit from the results." Ingalls and Kolhatkar summarize that "few [American] media outlets have dared to blame the U.S. for the more egregious fraud of imposing early elections on a still war-ravaged country where Northern Alliance warlords legitimized by Washington will continue to hold real power, regardless of who wins the vote."[40]

Opium: Afghanistan's Economic Lifeblood

One final note on Afghanistan's reconstruction pertains to the country's reliance on the opium industry. Reporters' coverage of the opium "problem" sometimes fails to provide a context for the crop's extraordinary importance to the nation's struggling economy (despite the danger it also poses as an addictive narcotic throughout Afghanistan and the world). While media organizations do sometimes highlight the negative effects of using defoliants on civilian populations, other equally important humanitarian issues fail to become major concerns.[41] Without pausing to ponder the economic implications, American media reports often emphasize the "progress," or lack thereof of the U.S. opium eradication effort. Western experts speak uncritically of the efforts to destroy Afghanistan's main economic staple.

One question is the standard in many of the reports: how effective has the U.S. been in eliminating these crops? In one example, the *Associated Press* reported that American officials "doubt that the vast amount of opium produced in Afghanistan can be significantly reduced without spraying." But in emphasizing the pragmatic question of "how best to get rid of Afghan poppy," the question of

what alternative industries exist to keep the Afghan economy running is discounted. For example, former Presidential candidate John Kerry argues in the
Wall Street Journal in favor of sending more troops to Afghanistan, so as to
combat a "resurgent Taliban" that has been "funded largely by a flourishing
opium trade," which increased by 50 percent in 2005. Kerry fails to offer any
sustainable alternatives to poppy cultivation, however, outside of extremely
vague advocacy of providing "alternative livelihoods for opium farmers."[42]
    Opium has long been the most lucrative crop for Afghan farmers, far more
profitable than any other agricultural alternative.[43] The destruction of this crop
would translate into the collapse not only of Afghanistan's illicit economy, but a
significant portion of its economy altogether. To be fair, some media commentators have moved to address this problem. Anne Applebaum of the *Washington
Post*, admitting that: "it isn't fashionable right now to argue for any legal form
of opiate cultivation," refuses to discount the importance of opium for Afghanistan's economy. By early 2007, "Afghanistan's opium exports account[ed] for
somewhere between one-third and two-thirds of the country's gross domestic
product."[44] Opium production has been further demonized, primarily due to
Taliban resurgence in Southern Afghanistan. The Taliban has been heavily reliant on opium production to fund its attacks on NATO and government forces,
and such attacks increased dramatically in 2006 and 2007.[45] Reports of the Taliban's expanded presence in Afghanistan have provoked American military leaders to consider extended tours of duty for American troops, as well as a possible
increase in troop numbers.

September 11th: What Changed in the Media?

It is considered common knowledge that September 11th led to major changes in
the way that Americans look at the world.[46] Many Americans attempted to shun
their parochialism and ignorance of world affairs by gaining access to more information about U.S. foreign policy, Middle East politics, global opinion of the
U.S., and other important issues. Book sales in the area of international affairs
and politics generally have increased in the years following the 9/11 attacks.
    The U.S. media, along with most of the public, viewed the 9/11 attacks as
an attack on the American way of life, and an attack on American values. In the
post-9/11 political environment, most throughout the media and public called for
violent retribution in punishing those responsible for killing 3,000 innocent victims who died in the World Trade Towers. The American public, shortly before
the war began, also overwhelmingly accepted the plans of the Bush administration to go to war with Afghanistan. Encouraged by the mainstream press,
Americans increasingly began to support the use of force, first against Afghanistan, and then against Iraq in the name of fighting terrorism.
    After the 9/11 terrorist attacks, a number of questions were promptly put
forth throughout the mainstream and dissident media, and in general dialogue
between citizens. How could this have happened? Who exactly were the attackers? Why was the U.S. targeted? One of the most important questions asked

was: how should the U.S. respond to the attacks? More specifically, the question seemed to be: how should the U.S. utilize its military to most effectively respond to the attacks? The American media and public's response to 9/11 overwhelmingly preferred a military response.

The question of why the U.S. was targeted was given high priority in media reporting and editorializing, although the answers presented were radically different depending on whether one looked at the mainstream or Progressive-Left press. To proclaim that the U.S. was a target because it was an unwanted occupying power in foreign lands was forbidden in most mainstream media commentary, as such explanations were seen as appeasement of the terrorists and defense of the terror attacks. Those who called for nonviolent solutions were increasingly attacked by media pundits who felt that critics of war were either justifying the attacks or siding with the terrorists. Those questioning war with Afghanistan were often thought of as "un-American" or unpatriotic.

After 9/11, the media deemed Osama bin Laden to be the mastermind behind the terror attacks. His capture was framed as the most important step in reducing or eliminating the threat of radical Islamist terrorism. Three years after 9/11, mass media outlets seemed to have changed their mind somewhat, framing bin Laden as one of many players in the world of Islamist terror cells, rather than the key player. The *Los Angeles Times*, for example, explored "the strategic failure to understand and combat Al Qaeda's evolution" as Osama bin Laden was said to "serve more as an inspiration figure than a CEO" for international terrorist networks.[47] Years after the 9/11 attacks, media outlets acknowledged that Islamist terror attacks were occurring throughout the world "with little or no direct contact with leaders" such as bin Laden and Ayman al Zawahiri (a close affiliate of bin Laden). Whereas after September 11 *CNN* considered bin Laden to be "at the center of an international coalition of Islamic radicals,"[48] it later reconsidered the point, reporting that his wealth was overstated, and that he was not "thought to be directly financing his terror group with his personal wealth."[49] As of 2004, the *New York Times* divulged that there existed a "far more complex picture of Al Qaeda's status" than was typically presented, granting that bin Laden and Zawahiri were only a few of the many individuals involved in the group.[50]

The mainstream media's acknowledgement that Islamist terrorist networks such as Al Qaeda were (and continue to be) more complex than the conventional view that portrayed bin Laden as the "terrorist mastermind" were seen in a number of critical works. An authority on decentralized Islamist networks, award-winning journalist Jason Burke enlightened his readers on the state of Islamist militant groups like Al Qaeda:

> even when it was most organized in late 2001, it is important to avoid seeing 'al Qaeda' as a coherent and structured terrorist organization with cells everywhere, or to imagine it had subsumed all other groups within its networks. This would be to profoundly misconceive its nature and the nature of modern Islamic militancy. Bin Laden's group was only one of very many radical Islamic outfits operating in and from Afghanistan at the time.[51]

Burke concluded: "This is not to say that al Qaeda does not exist, but merely that the labeling implies that bin Laden's group is something it is not. To see it as a coherent and tight-knit organization, with 'tentacles everywhere'. . . is to misunderstand not only its true nature but the nature of [decentralized] Islamic radicalism."[52] Al Qaeda is not one unitary, central organization, operating with top-down structured cells throughout dozens of countries. Rather, the Islamism of Osama bin Laden and Ayman al Zawahiri often serves more as a sort of inspiration for other islamist groups and their members (Abu Musab al Zarqawi being one of the most prominent examples). Such groups likely maintain only loose affiliations with Al Qaeda, rather than close organizational ties. At other times, Islamist groups operating throughout the Middle East and elsewhere completely shun groups like Al Qaeda as dangerous extremists.

Burke's analysis of radical Islamist terror networks stands in marked opposition to the less-nuanced, simplistic presentations purveyed throughout much of mainstream dialogue on the Islamist threat immediately following 9/11. The perpetuation of the myth of Iraqi ties to Al Qaeda tie shortly before the 2003 invasion of Iraq stands perhaps as the most significant example of the overestimation of the Islamist threat.

Media Reactions to 9/11: Calls for War Begin

The question "Why do they hate us?" was allowed significant attention after the 9/11 attacks, although perhaps not in the way those Americans posing strong challenges to U.S. foreign policy would have expected. James Atkins displayed his apprehension for the way the question was answered in most media discussion in a piece in the progressive magazine *In These Times*, stating:

> There is now occasionally an editorial or a letter to the editor in this country suggesting that it might be time to ask ourselves if there just might be reasons other than our innate goodness for being hated. This always provokes a flurry of angry responses saying that whatever it might be, it certainly had nothing to do with our Middle East policy. But the anti-American feeling in the Middle East and South Asia has everything to do with U.S. policy. It is not because of our democratic and moral principles, but precisely because we are seen as having betrayed these principles in the Middle East that peoples of the area have turned against us.[53]

Many Americans may have been shocked by the argument that the United States had something to do with inciting the attacks; they often believed that their government was the victim of unprovoked aggression. Dan Rather's reaction to 9/11 is symbolic of this larger refusal to acknowledge that there might have been motivations for the attacks outside of "hate for American freedom": "They hate us because they are losers. They see us as winners. And those who see themselves as losers sometimes develop a deep and abiding hatred for those they see who are winners."[54] Rather's explanation, however, was limited in that it did not delve into the stated motives of Al Qaeda's inspirational leaders for why they had supported attacks on the U.S. Writing for the *Washington Post*, George Will explained in one Op-Ed that the U.S. was at battle with "the enemies of civilization," and that "Americans are slow to anger but mighty when angry, and their proper anger now should be alloyed with pride. They are targets because of their virtues—principally democracy, and loyalty to those nations which, like Israel, are embattled salients of our virtues in a still dangerous world."[55] Three years after the attacks, the *New York Times* repeated a similar view regarding the terrorists responsible for attacking Americans. The paper's editors deemed terrorism as "the tactic of preference for the self-obsessed radical movements of our age,"[56] rather than a tactic also adopted by the powerful nations against weaker ones or civilian populations.

Although many Americans did not want to hear explanations for the 9/11 attacks that implicated U.S. foreign policy in fueling anti-American hatred, many others did. One opinion poll released in early October 2001 indicated that, although Americans were content with patriotic expressions after 9/11, they were also interested in hearing dissenting voices that took a critical look at U.S. foreign policy. Approximately seven in ten questioned felt that peaceful protests should be allowed, while 75 percent of those asked thought that the media "should air the views of those who feel U.S. policies were to blame for the terrorist attacks."[57] The public received little to no access to such anti-war views in the mainstream press, however, during the run-up to the invasion of Afghanistan, or throughout the conflict itself. In this case, the mass media was actively in contempt of majority opinion, which favored consideration of nonviolent political solutions in addition to violent ones.

The lack of criticism of the violent counter-response to 9/11 led some observers outside the U.S. to react skeptically to media complicity in the drive for war. Robert Fisk of the *Independent* of London spoke critically of American journalists, who he felt were "cowardly, idle, [and] spineless" in their "lobotomizing" of stories regarding the "War on Terror."[58] Fisk criticized the relationship between American government and media as too comfortable, and characterized by too strong a degree of trust. He called "the relationship of the press and television to government" "incestuous. The State Department correspondents, the White House correspondents, the Pentagon correspondents, have set a narrative where instead of telling us what they think is happening or what they know is happening, they tell us what they are told by the spokesman. They have become sub-spokesmen. Spokesmen for the great institutions of state."[59]

The general reaction to 9/11 throughout the American mass media and political establishment was one that lacked critical self-reflection. There was a wholesale attempt after 9/11 to better "sell" what America was really all about, rather than question whether U.S. foreign policy had fueled distrust of the U.S. prior to the attacks. Rather, the government joined forces with the public relations industry to promote a positive image of the U.S. throughout the American press and abroad. In the month following 9/11, the administration hired Charlotte Beers, a well-known advertising and public relations executive to become the new Undersecretary of State for Public Diplomacy and Public Affairs. Beers had extensive experience in creating public-friendly images for her former employers, *Ogilvy & Mather and J. Walter Thompson*, which worked with high profile companies such as IBM, Jaguar, and American Express in their PR campaigns.

In efforts such as the "Shared Values" promotion, Beers was responsible for spreading images throughout the media of Muslims living peacefully and successfully in America in order to try and bridge the gap between the "American way of life" and the estranged "others" in the Muslim world. Beers' campaign was criticized by some media critics, as well as by members of Congress for ineffectiveness and deceptive marketing. Beers' efforts focused on communicating "the intangible assets of the United States—things like our belief system and our values."[60] Like other members of the current administration, Beers felt that "the gap between who we [Americans] are and how we wish to be seen...is frighteningly wide."[61] What was her solution?: focus on getting the Muslim world to accept a more positive image of the U.S. as a country committed to equal rights, tolerance, and democracy.

The campaign to "better sell" the U.S. image abroad obviously failed in that it ignored the divergent realities of American freedom at home and oppressive American policies abroad, as witnessed in such incidents as the Abu Ghraib scandal and other system-wide abuses on detainees' rights, as well as the loss of tens of thousands of civilian lives in bombing operations in Afghanistan and Iraq. While Beers eventually quit her post due to "health reasons," hers and the State Department's effort to enhance positive perceptions of the U.S. in the Muslim world was generally seen as a failure. By 2005, a full two years after the invasion of Iraq, a report by the Council on Foreign Relations revealed that distrust and suspicion of the United States was still "widespread in the Muslim world," mainly because of "anger at U.S. policies in Iraq, and its role in the Israeli-Palestinian conflict."[62]

PR efforts aside, it did not take long for the American media and political establishment to begin their calls for violent reprisal when the American people were most shocked (rightfully so) over the attacks on the Pentagon and the World Trade Towers. In an editorial titled "War Without Illusions," the *New York Times* editors concluded that there was "no doubt" that the 9/11 attacks represented "the opening salvos in the first American war of the twenty-first century. Less clear is just what sort of war this will be and how the United States can ensure that it prevails."[63] Within days of the attacks, television headlines such as "America at War" (*CNN*) were common, as were print titles including "It's War" (the front page of *New York Daily News*) and "Act(s) of War" (*USA Today* and *San Jose Mercury News*). Although no enemy had yet been identified, war was often seen as inevitable. Sebastian Mallaby argued in the *Washington Post* that a newly declared "War on Terrorism will be appallingly difficult," although "it is the least bad option."[64] Only four days after the 9/11 attacks, the *Washington Post* was already preparing for war, listing "a broad array of potential targets," including Iran, Yemen, Sudan, Syria, and North Korea, all of which were framed as accused of having "aided terrorists to one degree or another." The paper's editors argued that "It is impossible to imagine the United States 'winning' this war in any meaningful sense while Saddam Hussein remains in Iraq," while also lambasting Afghanistan as the "most likely first target for armed force," due to its "harbor[ing] of bin Laden."[65] No peaceful alternatives such as extradition were seriously considered in the media and political establishment, as calls for violent reciprocity quickly became the norm. In this explosive environment, anti-war activists who favored extradition through the presentation of evidence were labeled (depending on who was attacking them) as somewhere between naïve pacifists and "objectively pro-terrorist."[66]

Nonviolent Alternatives Denied

The relevant question in the mainstream media was not *whether* to use force, but *how* best to utilize it. This debate was, as the *Los Angeles Times* accurately described, "over the scope of the retaliation." Would the response be limited just to Afghanistan, or should it also encompass other countries that were (previous to 9/11) designated as "enemies" by the Bush administration and its allies? The *Los Angeles Times* elaborated: "Initially, Rumsfeld and his allies argued for a broad campaign against not only Afghanistan, but other states suspected of supporting terrorism, principally Iraq."[67] Eventually, major media outlets would transition to support the latter option, as the war against Iraq was framed as a vital step in protecting U.S. national security through the "War on Terror."

While most media outlets deferred to the American government's claims of "precision weapons" that limited "collateral damage," a few actively encouraged war crimes as a path to vengeance. On *Fox News*, Bill O'Reilly described what would happen if the Taliban refused to extradite bin Laden upon demand: "If they don't [give him up], the U.S. should bomb the Afghan infrastructure to rubble. . . the airport, the power plants, their water facilities and roads. . . taking out their ability to exist day to day will not be hard."[68] The vast majority of media commentators, however, did not openly call for the U.S. to commit war crimes—they just failed to condemn the U.S. for the deaths of thousands of Afghan civilians and the continued destruction of Afghan infrastructure.

The possibility of avoiding violence through the extradition of bin Laden and other Al Qaeda operatives was not taken very seriously. In the rush to war, newspapers and television news venues failed to draw attention to the Bush administration's reluctance to pursue offers by the Taliban to hand over bin Laden upon presentation of evidence. The administration's refusal to negotiate with the Taliban showed that it was dead-set on going to war, rather than committed to extraditing bin Laden through the use of diplomatic channels.[69] Most of the American media simply assumed without discussion that a nonviolent reaction was not feasible or desirable. A comprehensive analysis of *Washington Post* coverage from September 12 to October 6, 2001 (the period after the 9/11 attacks, but before the beginning of "Operation Enduring Freedom in Afghanistan) found that nonviolent alternatives were heavily downplayed. Headlines emphasized preparations for military action four times more often than headlines emphasizing negotiations with the Taliban over extradition of bin Laden. The "military action" frame was also emphasized six times as often as those headlines focusing on the opposition of allies to U.S. military action. In total, the military preparation frame dominated both allied opposition and negotiation frames by a margin of three-to-one.[70] On the occasions where anti-war activists or critics were addressed, it was usually to denigrate them. Michael Kelly of the *Washington Post*, for example, derided those calling for peaceful solutions, stating that, "Incredibly, in the light of 6,000 dead, some (mostly on the Left) have persisted in the delusion that we are involved here in something that can be put into some sort of normality—a crisis that can be resolved through legal or diplomatic efforts."[71] The *Washington Post*'s editors agreed, defining the "legitimate" expression of "self-defense" as requiring violent action.[72]

The "U.S. Strikes Back," but at What?

Most Americans assumed that the U.S. was largely bombing Al Qaeda bases and targets during "Operation Enduring Freedom" in retaliation for the 9/11 attacks. Sadly, this myth was not entirely dispelled in most media reporting until months after the completion of the bombing campaign. For the most part, Al Qaeda and Taliban leaders were not willing to wait around and be bombed by the U.S. in light of the United States' calls for blood. It was only after the completion of major operations in Afghanistan that media coverage more soberly appraised the failures of the U.S. in effectively targeting militants. The *New York Times* reported that, seven months after the end of "Operation Enduring Freedom," "raids [had] not found any large groups of Taliban or Al Qaeda fighters"[73]; "virtually the entire top leadership of the Taliban [had] survived the American bombing and eluded capture by American-backed forces."[74] International Security Specialist Paul Rogers provided an explanation for the failure to destroy the terror cells: "the Al Qaeda network anticipated a strong U.S. response to 11 September, and had few of its key forces even in Afghanistan."[75] Reports near the beginning of the conflict indicated that much of the Al Qaeda-Islamist network that *was* actually in Afghanistan had already scattered into neighboring countries such as Pakistan.[76] While the U.S. bombing campaign might have helped disperse parts of the network and its affiliates in Afghanistan, it did little to nothing in terms of dismantling or destroying them.

Afghan civilians and the Taliban, rather than Al Qaeda operatives, were the main targets of U.S. bombing in Afghanistan. By November of 2001, it was estimated that as many as 5,000 unexploded cluster bomblets lay throughout Iraq as a result of U.S. military operations.[77] Mark Hiznay of the Arms Division of *Human Rights Watch* warned that, "these unexploded bomblets have in effect become antipersonnel landmines. . . they pose an extreme hazard to civilians, not just now but for years to come."[78] On average, about 7 percent of the cluster bomblets failed to detonate. The danger of unexploded bombs, coupled with the fact that they are the same color as the "humanitarian" food packages dropped by the U.S. at the time, made them especially dangerous to Afghans on the verge of starvation. American bombing campaigns were often much more lethal than was let on by reporters and anchors who accepted the promise of the use of "precision weapons" from U.S. military leaders.

On October 22, 2001 alone, at least twenty-five Afghan civilians were killed after a U.S. bombing of a village near Kandahar, despite reports from locals that there were no Taliban or Al Qaeda forces in the area.[79] Mushfeqa, one of the survivors of the attack, shared her experiences while she recovered at Quetta hospital from shrapnel injuries:

> It was at about 11 p.m. First, one plane came and dropped a bomb. We ran out of the home, because we were afraid to die there. Then, some went back inside. I was at the door, and some of the small children were outside. Then the plane came and it was firing. I saw my mother and my brother shot. My uncle ran to his car to turn off the lights. Then a bomb hit the car and he died. When the next bomb came, I was inside the room. I was injured from the shrapnel.[80]

In its coverage of the U.S.-Afghan war, the *Los Angeles Times* ran the umbrella headline "U.S. Strikes Back" above all its stories. But who was really targeted as the United States struck back? Reports throughout the major media admitted that American bombing was killing Afghan civilians, although the total tally for such deaths was rarely a feature of reporting. Most reporting seemed more interested in how the campaign was progressing, or failing to progress, in terms of capturing bin Laden and other suspected terrorists. Humanitarian concerns were generally allotted little attention. An examination of *New York Times* stories from October 7 to November 13, 2001 (the period of the U.S. bombing campaign against Afghanistan) shows that headlines emphasizing military operations or progress in "Operation Enduring Freedom" were run three times as often as those headlines addressing the potential for humanitarian disaster resulting from American bombing. Headlines reporting military progress outnumbered headlines addressing Afghan civilian deaths (numbering 3,000 in the month of military operations) by an astounding margin of eighteen-to-one.[81]

In such a fiercely pro-war climate, some pundits explained that concern with civilian casualties, limiting damage to infrastructure, and reconstruction should not be a major focus of reporting or U.S. strategy. Charles Krauthammer stated that "the American instinct for generosity is legendary, and we appear to be outdoing ourselves" by committing to rebuilding the country. Yet, in the same opinion piece, he lucidly wrote that, "Our objective in Afghanistan is to destroy the Taliban...we are not in Afghanistan to nation-build. We should do only as much as is necessary to leave behind a structure stable enough to prevent the return of the Taliban. . . . It is equally important to rid ourselves of the illusions of 'humanitarian war' that beguiled us during our holiday from history in the 1990s. This is going to be a long twilight struggle: dirty and dangerous, cynical and self-interested...war is an act of destruction, not urban renewal."[82]

In light of American bombing, media outlets began to promote a "bread and bombs" approach to reporting following the U.S. cut-off of food to millions of Afghans. The American bombing effectively prohibited the United Nations and other humanitarian aid organizations from trucking food in for millions of hungry Afghans. Attention in the dissident press was drawn to the Afghan people's long history of suffering under war. In *Z Magazine*, Mohsen Makhmalbaf made reference to the over 2.5 million Afghans who had died as a result of violent conflict, famine, and a lack of social services in the last twenty-five years, as well as to the over six million refugees in Iran and Pakistan.[83] Makhmalbaf discussed dire conditions for "a country where 10 percent of the people have been decimated and 30 percent have become refugees; where currently one million are dying of hunger."[84]

Emphasis in mainstream reporting was largely the opposite. Newspapers spoke of wartime objectives in which the U.S. would "balance traditional firepower" by "mounting a humanitarian offensive" through food drops.[85] The difficulty in "trying to win the hearts and minds of people you are pounding with high explosives" was acknowledged in papers like the *Washington Post*, although this did not stop writers from repeating "humanitarian warfare" rhetoric promoted through the "bread and bombs" paradigm.[86] The *Washington Post* labeled American food drops as an important part of "the lifeline" to the Afghan people, as the paper spoke of the Bush administration's "moral imperative to save innocent lives in a theater where U.S. and Western forces are operating."[87] The editors at the *New York Times* asserted: "Mr. Bush has widely made providing humanitarian assistance to the Afghan people an integral part of American strategy. It is important for humanitarian and practical reasons, to minimize the suffering of innocent Afghan civilians."[88] Reporting at the *New York Times* largely followed the "humanitarian bombing" frame with headlines such as "U.S. Plane Crews Fight Hunger from the Sky" and "Food Falls from the Sky over Afghanistan, Strange but Welcome."[89]

However, it was also admitted in reporting that the 37,500 food rations dropped by the U.S. every day—each enough to feed only one person for one day—were falling far short in making up for the loss of humanitarian food shipments (from the United Nations and other humanitarian aid agencies) previously provided to millions of Afghans.[90] Overall, it was estimated in mainstream and independent media sources that, at the time of U.S. bombing, the number of Afghans in need of food had reached upward of 5.5 to 7.5 million people.[91] Despite the fact that the World Food Program described the Afghan predicament as one of "pre-famine conditions," media reports only trickled out describing those Afghans who fled to the Pakistani and Iranian borders and were forced to eat "grass and animal fodder"[92] to survive. Regardless, American media outlets continued to repeat the erroneous claim that the U.S. was committed to humanitarian aid during the height of the bombing.[93]

Those who took issue with the United States' claim to humanitarianism countered that it was ridiculous to argue for engagement in humanitarian intervention at a time when the Bush administration had moved to cut off aid to millions of people, while providing aid (ineffectively) to thousands. Mainstream news organizations turned a deaf ear to such claims. Instead of implicating the U.S. in creating a humanitarian crisis, the *Chicago Sun Times* saluted the Bush administration and the U.S. military for coming "closer than any other nation to warring within the confines of the Geneva Conventions."[94]

Rather than pushing the Secretary of Defense on the issue of potential mass starvation of thousands (or even millions), reporters were generally intent on asking tactical questions about American military superiority and the success of "Operation Enduring Freedom." A short excerpt from one Q & A session between reporters and Donald Rumsfeld and General Richard Myers reveals a lack of combativeness and skepticism in the face of this "bread and bombs" campaign:

QUESTION: General, the bomber aircraft—first, were ships used today? And were bomber aircraft, both bombs and cruise missiles used again today as they were yesterday?

MYERS: We will use some Tomahawk missiles today from ships. And there were no cruise missiles used from the bombers.

QUESTION: And, Mr. Secretary, might I add, are U.S. and British forces attacking Taliban troop concentrations as well as air defense and airfields and other sites?

RUMSFELD: There have been some ground forces targeted.

QUESTION: Mr. Secretary, the issue of air superiority, can you say whether or not that's been achieved? And do you have any sense of whether or not the Taliban has been cut off from communicating with its forces?

RUMSFELD: I think it would be too soon to say that the Taliban air defense and aircraft and airports have been fully disabled. That is not the case. We have not got enough battle damage assessment to answer the question, but I suspect that when we do get it, we'll find there's some additional work to be done.[95]

While a single reporter later briefly addressed the U.S. cutoff of food to millions of Afghans, the issue was quickly dropped after Rumsfeld cynically dismissed the problem by explaining that the few people who did get rations "would be appreciative."[96] The lack of sustained skepticism in the face of official potential humanitarian disaster revealed much about reporters' lack of commitment to adversarial, critical reporting on the food drop issue, and on the war in general.

Media Blackout and the Embedding Solution

In retrospect, it seems clear that the mainstream press was prohibited from, and refused to, engage in in-depth, on-the-ground reporting in Afghanistan. Numerous complaints were made that reporters lacked the access needed to accurately report on the conflict. Paul Friedman, Executive Vice President of *ABC News* complained that after the first few days of military action, "we—and therefore the American public—really have no idea how it's [the war] going, what's being done in our name and what effects it's having."[97] As with the first Gulf War, reporters were mostly prohibited from getting close to the battlefield in Afghanistan. Many throughout the press presented the embedding "solution" as the best option for covering the war. Dan Klaidman of *Newsweek*, for example, claimed: "It's a good start that the Pentagon at least embedded some reporters on the aircraft carriers, but the real test is whether they'll allow reporters with the air units and with the ground units when they go in."[98] The success of the military's embedding campaign was later seen in full effect in "Operation Iraqi Freedom," where American reporters were assigned to specific military units in order to cover the conflict.

War on Terror or War *of* Terror?

Shortly before the beginning of the bombing of Afghanistan in early October 2001, the *Times* of London posed a series of critical questions about the planned military project: "What can all this military muscle achieve?" The American enemy "is in the hills and caves of a rugged and desolate land. Its infrastructure is shot to pieces, its people face starvation, there is little left to bomb. . . . What if the terrorist chieftain is impossible to pinpoint? What if civilians die, rather than the terrorists"?[99] The *Times* editorial was prophetic in many ways, although it may have underestimated the number of available targets in Afghanistan, as the U.S. did not hesitate to bomb Taliban emplacements and a number of other targets in civilian heavy areas in place of suspected Al Qaeda targets.

Absent from mainstream American media commentary on the planned war was one question of vital importance: was this really a "War on Terrorism," or were civilians going to be caught in the attacks in significant numbers, as the *Times* editorial seemed to imply? Would the deaths of thousands of Afghan civilians constitute a reciprocal act of terrorism to that of the terrorists who attacked the U.S. on 9/11? While the *Times* piece was a step in the right direction in terms of critically posing such questions, most American news editors and journalists were not paying much attention to such concerns.

A number of critics of the war, however, certainly seemed to think such questions were of vital importance. Historian Howard Zinn and foreign policy critic Noam Chomsky both released books in the independent press arguing that the U.S. campaign in Afghanistan was an example of U.S. terrorism directed against innocent civilians.[100] However, the works of these scholars and other anti-war critics, while selling well in the United States, were generally not well represented in Op-Eds and editorials. There was little to no dialogue between the Progressive-Left media contributors and mainstream media pundits, reporters, and editors over the question of whether the U.S. was engaging in terror by killing civilians. The mass media's acceptance of the notion that the U.S. could fight a "clean war" suggested that civilians could be spared in the bombing, although the events that unfolded indicated that thousands of civilians died in the American retaliation. The question of whether bombing civilians constituted a "War of Terror," rather than a "War on Terror" was considered so ludicrous by mainstream reporters that it was not even considered. The claim that war itself (undertaken by the world's foremost military power) is a form of terrorism was a topic deemed out of bounds for discussion. This differed significantly from

Arab media outlets like *Al Jazeera*, which referred to the campaign as a "so-called War on Terror" rather than a clear-cut campaign to fight terrorism.

In the tradition of promoting clean war claims, the *Wall Street Journal* sought to prepare Americans for a "long campaign" in which "The U.S. wants to avoid civilian casualties [and prevent] adding to the misery of the Afghan people."[101] The *Washington Post* reported that the U.S. "unleashed fresh air strikes at military and terrorist targets"[102] rather than on civilians. The emphasis then, was on "aerial assaults on resources of the al Qaeda terrorist network of Osama bin Laden and Afghanistan's Taliban leadership."[103] Such reporting seemed to imply that civilians were not dying in large numbers in those attacks, although newspapers did acknowledge at times that civilian deaths resulted from American bombings.

The "clean war" myth promulgated by the American media differed greatly from reports in Progressive-Left media outlets and parts of the British media. The *Guardian* of London, for example, drew attention to human rights reports and national and international media sources collected by Marc Herold of the University of New Hampshire, which estimated that as many as 3,500 civilians were killed during the attacks, more than the number of Americans who died on 9/11.[104] In general, Marc Herold's study was the focus of much more attention in the independent American press than it was in the mainstream. In an article entitled "Tragic Errors in U.S. Military Policy" run in *Z Magazine*, Edward Herman asserted: "the idea that most of these civilians were killed by 'errant' bombs or targeting errors is the central and most important establishment lie—they were killed in accord with a deliberate policy of sending missiles to, and dropping bombs on, targets in populated areas based on reports of a Taliban or al Qaeda presence."[105] Large-scale civilian deaths, in the end, were inevitable when one understands that Taliban headquarters and facilities were located either within or close to many villages.[106]

This chapter set out to discuss the imbalance in media reporting over the conflict in Afghanistan. There was a heavy skew in mainstream reporting and editorializing in favor of the official claims that the U.S. was limiting civilian casualties, assisting in rebuilding Afghanistan, and targeting terrorists in their campaign. Nonviolent solutions to the 9/11 attacks, such as extradition, were largely ignored, despite American public opinion, which was overwhelmingly in favor of hearing and discussing non-violent alternatives. Taking into account this public inclination, one can easily conclude, as many already have, that media reporting and editorializing should have focused much more on providing a wide range of possible reactions, violent and non-violent, in the wake of the 9/11 attacks.

Notes

1. CNN.com, "Bush's State of the Union Address," 29 January 2002, http://archives.cnn.com/2002/ALLPOLITICS/01/29/bush.speech.txt/ (25 Jul. 2005).
2. Jack Kelley, "Afghan Refugees Say They Feel Targeted by US," *USA Today*, sec. 1, 12 October 2001, 2.
3. CNN.com, "Afghans Vote in Landmark Poll," 18 September 2005, http://www.cnn.-cnn.com/2005/WORLD/asiapcf/09/17/afghan.elections/ (18 Sep. 2005).
4. CNN.com, "Afghans Vote in Landmark Poll," 2005.
5. CNN.com, "Afghans Vote in Landmark Poll," 2005.
6. Doug Ireland, "Afghan Women's Mag Editor Jailed for Articles Against Stoning to Death and Lashing," *Z Magazine*, 24 October 2005, http://www.zmag.org/content/show-article.cfm?ItemID=8986 (24 Oct. 2005).
7. Committee to Protect Journalists, "Editor Goes on Trial for Blasphemy," 11 October 2005, http://www.cpj.org/news/2005/Afghan11oct05na.html (11 Oct. 2005).
8. Gregg Zoroya, "Pride Jitters Greet First Afghan Vote," *USA Today*, 7 October 2004, 1(A).
9. Stan Crock, Manjeet Kripalani, and A. Mangi, "A Treacherous Test for Afghan-Democracy," *Business Week*, 4 October 2004, http://zdnet.businessweek.com/magazine/-Content/04_40/l3902154.htm (3 Nov. 2005).
10. Achraf Ghani, "Voting for Afghanistan's Future," *Washington Post*, 23(A).
11. Charles Krauthammer, "The Afghan Miracle: Why isn't this Stunning U.S. Success Appreciated?" *Washington Post*, 10 December 2004, 37(A).
12. William Safire, "The Afghan Miracle," *New York Times*, 6 October 2004, 29(A).
13. David Rohde and Carlotta Gall, "Afghan Democracy 101: The Students are Keen," *New York Times*, 4 October 2004, 11(A).
14. Charles H. Norchi, "A New Start in Afghanistan," *Boston Globe*, 9 October 2004, http://www.boston.com/news/globe/editorial_opinion/oped/articles/2004/10/09/a_new_start_in_afghanistan/ (13 Nov. 2005).
15. David Rohde, "A Dead End for Afghan Children Adrift in Pakistan," *New York Times*, 7 March 2003, 3(A).
16. CNN.com, "Report: Afghanistan could Implode," 20 July 2004, http://www.cnn.com/2004/WORLD/europe/07/29/uk.afghan.iraq/index.html (4 Nov. 2005).
17. Michael Buchanan, "Afghanistan Omitted from U.S. Aid Budget," *BBC*, 13 February 2003, http://news.bbc.co.uk/2/hi/south_asia/2759789.stm (20 Oct. 2005).
18. David R. Francis, "Economist Tallies Swelling Cost of Israel to U.S.," *Christian Science Monitor*, 9 December 2002, http://www.csmonitor.com/2002/1209/p16s01-wmgn.htm (22 Sep. 2005).
19. Ahmed Rashid, "A Shortage of Aid Could Hinder the Return of Afghan Democracy," *Wall Street Journal*, sec. 1, 6 June 2002, 12.
20. Rashid, 2002.
21. Rashid, 2002.
22. John F. Burns, "Afghan Dream: A Smooth Road to Anywhere," *New York Times*, 19 September 2002, 1(A).
23. James Dao, "Afghan Officials Say Aid Has Been Too Slow," *New York Times*, 25 July 2002, 6(A).
24. World Bank, "Afghanistan Reconstruction Fund," 2007, http://web.worldbank.org/W/EXTERNAL/COUNTRIES/SOUTHASIAEXT/AFGHANISTANEXTN/0,,contentMDK:20152008~pagePK:141137~piPK:217854~theSitePK:305985,00.html (25 Mar. 2007).

25. US State Department, "Background Note: Afghanistan," December 2005, http://www.state.gov/r/pa/ei/bgn/5380.htm (11 Apr. 2006).

26. CIA World Factbook, "Afghanistan," *Central Intelligence* Agency, 2005, http://www.cia.gov/publications/factbook/geos/af.html (1 Nov. 2005).

27. James Dao, "Lawmakers Urge Bush to Expand Afghan Force Beyond Kabul," *New York Times*, 27 June 2002, 11(A).

28. Mitchell Prothero, "Afghanistan: Mission Not Yet Accomplished," *Salon*, 21 September 2005, http://www.salon.com/news/feature/2005/09/21/afghanistan/ (6 Nov. 2005).

29. Paul Richter and Paul Watson, "Afghan Vote a Bright Spot Amid Shadows," *Los Angeles Times*, 8 October 2004, 12(A).

30. Simon Tisdall, "The Good Luck of Traumatized Afghanistan," *Guardian*, 25 February 2005, 14.

31. Amnesty International, "Afghanistan: Women Still Under Attack—A Systematic Failure to Protect," 2005, http://web.amnesty.org/library/index/engasa110072005 (14 Dec. 2005).

32. *Amnesty International*, "Afghanistan: Women Still Under Attack," 2005.

33. Feminist Majority, "Three More Girls' Schools Attacked in Afghanistan," 29 September 2003, http://www.feminist.org/news/newsbyte/uswirestory.asp?id=8069 (7 Nov. 2005); David Rohde, "Rights Group Says Governor in Afghan West Abuses Power," *New York Times*, 5 November 2002, 15(A).

34. Human Rights Watch, "Campaigning Against Fear: Women's Participation in Afghanistan's 2005 Elections," 17 August 2005, http://hrw.org/background/wrd/afghanistan0805/index.htm (2 Dec. 2005).

35. Amnesty International, "Afghanistan: No Justice and Security for Women," 6 http://www.lwvny.org/amnesty_international_article.htm (22 Oct. 2005).

36. Nisha Varia, "Struggle for Rights," *Human Rights Watch*, 1 March 2005, http://hrw.org/english/docs/2005/03/01/afghan10229.htm (24 Sep. 2005).

37. Jim Ingalls and Sonali Kolhatkar, "Afghan Elections: U.S. Solution to a U.S. Problem," *Common Dreams*, 7 October 2004, http://www.commondreams.org/views/04/1007-31.htm (3 Dec. 2005).

38. Zoroya, "Pride, Jitters Greet First Afghan Vote," 2004.

39. Maseeh Rahman, "Afghan Voters Won't be Deterred," *Washington Times*, 4 October 2004, http://www.washtimes.com/world/20041004-123836-5105r.htm (15 Aug. 2005).

40. Ingalls and Sonali, "Afghan Elections," 2004.

41. Associated Press, "U.S. Drops Afghanistan Opium Spraying Plans," *MSNBC*, 25 January 2005, http://msnbc.msn.com/id/6867458/ (22 Nov. 2005).

42. John Kerry, "Losing Afghanistan," *Wall Street Journal*, 26 September 2006, http://www.opinionjournal.com/editorial/feature.html?id=110008993 (26 Sep. 2006).

43. Chris Johnson and Jolyon Leslie, *Afghanistan: The Mirage of Peace* (London: Zed, 2004), 110-34.

44. Anne Applebaum, "Ending an Opium War," *Washington Post*, 16 January 2007, 19(A).

45. Declan Walsh, "Taliban Attacks Double after Pakistan's Deal with Militants," *Guardian*, 29 September 2006, http://www.guardian.co.uk/pakistan/Story/0,,188378,00.html (29 Sep. 2006).

46. Jamal Nassar, *Globalization and Terrorism: The Migration of Dreams and Nightmares* (Lanham, Md.: Rowman and Littlefield, 2004), 1-21.

47. Douglas Frantz, Josh Meyer, Sebastian Rotella, and Megan K. Stack, "The New Face of Al Qaeda," *Los Angeles Times*, 26 September 2004, http://www.truthout.org/cgi-bin/artman/exec/view.cgi/4/6462 (26 Sep. 2004).

48. Cnn.com, "Bin Laden, Millionaire with a Dangerous Grudge," 27 September 2001, http://archives.cnn.com/2001/US/09/12/binladen.profile/ (13 Oct. 2005).

49. CNN.com, "Bin Laden's Wealth Not the Force Behind 9/11," 2 September 2004, http://www.cnn.com/2004/WORLD/meast/09/02/binladen.wealth.ap/index.html (2 Sep. 2004).

50. David Johnston and David E. Sanger, "New Leaders are Emerging for Al Qaeda," *New York Times*, 10 August 2004, 1(A).

51. Jason Burke, *Al Qaeda: The True Story of Radical Islam* (London: I. B. Tauris, 2004), 6.

52. Burke, *Al Qaeda*, 8.

53. James Akins, "Why Do They Hate Us?" *In These Times*, 24 December 2001, 11.

54. Dan Rather, "CNN Live with Larry King," *CNN*, 18 October 2001.

55. George F. Will, "The End of Our Holiday from History," *Washington Post*, 11 September 2001, 31(A).

56. Editorial, "Mr. Bush and the Truth about Terror," *New York Times*, 2 September 2004, 22(A).

57. Pew Research Center, "Americans Open to Dissenting Views on the War on Terrorism," 4 October 2001, http://www.pewtrusts.com/ideas/ideas_item.cfm?content_Item_id=774&content_type_id=18&issue_name=Public%20opinion%20and%20polls&issue=11&page=18&name=Public%20Opinion%20Polls%20and%20Survey%20Results (16 Aug. 2005).

58. Robert Fisk, "Fear and Learning in America," *Independent*, 17 April 2002, http://www.commondreams.org/views02/0417-02.htm (5 Dec. 2005).

59. Robert Fisk, "Covering the War," in *Tell Me Lies: Propaganda and Distortion in the Attack on Iraq*, ed. David Miller (London: Pluto, 2004), 220.

60. CNN.com, "Bush's Muslim Propaganda Chief Quits," 4 March 2003, http://www.cnn.com/2003/US/03/03/state.resignation/ (17 Jul. 2003).

61. CNN.com, "Bush's Muslim Propaganda Chief Quits," 2003.

62. Karen Matthews, "Report: Muslim World Largely Anti-American," *Associated Press*, 19 May 2005, http://www.truthout.org/cgi-bin/artman/exec/view.cgi/37/11214 (19 May 2005).

63. Editorial, "War Without Illusions," *New York Times*, 15 September 2001, 22(A).

64. Sebastian Mallaby, "Two Cheers for War," *Washington Post*, 17 September 2001, 27(A).

65. Editorial, "Afghanistan," *Washington Post*, 15 September 2001, 26(A).

66. Michael Kelly, "Pacifist Claptrap," *Washington Post*, 26 September 2001, 25(A).

67. Ronald Brownstein, "Clamping Down: Coalition Puts Unity to the Test," *Los Angeles Times*, 29 September 2001, 1(A).

68. Bill O'Reilly, *The O'Reilly Factor*, Fox News, 17 September 2001.

69. Elisabeth Bumiller, "President Rejects Offer by Taliban for Negotiations," *New York Times*, 15 October 2001, 1(A); Douglas Frantz, "Taliban Say They Want to Negotiate with the U.S. over bin Laden," *New York Times*, 3 October 2001, 1(B).

70. A review of the *Lexis Nexis* database in the above mentioned period shows that there were 40 headlines that focused on military preparation for the bombing of Afghanistan, as opposed to only 9 headlines focusing on negotiations with the Taliban, and only 6 headlines emphasizing Allied opposition to an attack on Afghanistan.

71. Michael Kelly, "With a Serious and Large Intent," *Washington Post*, 12 October 2001, 23(A).

72. Editorial, "Clearing the Way," *Washington Post*, 8 October 2001, 22(A).

73. David Rohde, "Anatomy of a Raid in the Afghan Mountains," *New York Times*, 3 June 2002, 9(A).

74. James Risen, "Taliban Chiefs Prove Elusive, Americans Say," *New York Times*, 20 December 2001, 1(B).

75. Paul Rogers, *A War on Terror: Afghanistan and After* (London: Pluto, 2004), 101.

76. Rogers, *A War on Terror*, 6, 14.

77. Human Rights Watch, "Cluster Bomblets Litter Afghanistan," 16 November 2001, http://hrw.org/english/docs/2001/11/16/afghan3365_txt.htm (23 Aug. 2005).

78. Human Rights Watch, "Cluster Bomblets Litter Afghanistan," 2001.

79. Human Rights Watch, "Afghanistan: New Civilian Deaths Due to U.S. Bombing," 30 October 2001, http://hrw.org/english/docs/2001/10/30/afghan3125_txt.htm (1 Jul. 2005).

80. Human Rights Watch, "Afghanistan: New Civilian Deaths Due to U.S. Bombing," 2001.

81. An analysis using *Lexis Nexis* of the period discussed reveals that there were 74 headlines focusing on military progress, as opposed to only 27 addressing humanitarian problems, and only 4 focusing on Afghan casualties.

82. Charles Krauthammer, "Bread and Bombs: The War is about Destroying the Taliban, not Feeding Afghanistan," *Washington Post*, 12 October 2001, 33(A).

83. Mohsen Makhmalbaf, "A Country Abandoned," *Z Magazine*, December 2001, 32.

84. Makhmalbaf, "A Country Abandoned," 2001.

85. Doyle McManus, "Warfare Given a New Face," *Los Angeles Times*, 8 October 2001, 1(A).

86. Mary McGrory, "The Afghan Famine Equation," *Washington Post*, 25 October 2001, 3(A).

87. Editorial, "Feeding Afghanistan," *Washington Post*, 17 October 2001, 34(A).

88. Editorial, "The American Offensive Begins," *New York Times*, 8 October 2001, 16(A).

89. James Dao, "U.S. Plane Crews Fight Hunger from the Sky," *New York Times*, 9 October 2001, 8(B); Dexter Filkins, "Food Falls from the Sky over Afghanistan, Strange but Welcome," *New York Times*, 13 October 2001, 7(B).

90. Anne Hull, "U.S. Planes Drop Food in Afghanistan," *Washington Post*, 17 October 2001, 14(A).

91. Barry Bearak, "Pakistan Readies Forbidding Moonscape of Rock for 10,000 Afghans," *New York Times*, 5 October 2001, 3(B); Barry Bearak, "Weary Afghans Flee Bombs, Hunger, and the Taliban Draft," *New York Times*, 15 October 2001, 7(B).

92. Nora Boustany, "Unfolding Catastrophe for Afghan Refugees," *Washington Post*, 21 September 2001, 26(A).

93. Chip Cummins, "U.S. Increases its Afghan Aid Efforts, Prepares more Airdrops of Food Supplies," *Wall Street Journal*, sec. 1, 9 October 2001, 8.

94. Damien Cave, "Too Quiet on the PR Front: U.S. Must Fight Image War," *Chicago Sun Times*, sec. 1, 4 November 2001, 8.

95. CNN.com, "Secretary of Defense Holds News Briefing," 18 October 2001, http://transcripts.cnn.com/TRANSCRIPTS/0110/08/se.21.html (23 Nov. 2005).

96. CNN.com, "Secretary of Defense Holds News Briefing," 2001.

97. Elizabeth Jensen and David Shaw, "Limited Access to Conflict Leaves Media Frustrated," *Los Angeles Times*, 10 October 2001, 3(A).

98. Jensen and Shaw, "Limited Access to Conflict Leaves Media Frustrated," 2001.

99. Editorial, "Finger on the Trigger," *Sunday Times*, sec. 1, 30 September 2001, 7.

100. Howard Zinn, *Terrorism and War* (New York: NY, Seven Stories, 2002).; Noam Chomsky, *9/11* (New York: Seven Stories, 2002).

101. James Dorsey and Carla A. Robbins, "On Day 2 of Bombing, U.S. Lays Groundwork for a Long Campaign," *Wall Street Journal*, sec. 1, 9 October 2001, 1.

102. Dan Balz, "U.S. Strikes Again at Afghan Targets," *Washington Post*, 10 October 2001, 1(A).

103. Balz, "U.S. Strikes Again at Afghan Targets," 2001.

104. Marc Herold, "Counting the Dead," *Guardian*, 8 August 2002, http://www.guardian.co.uk/afghanistan/comment/story/0,11447,770999,00.html (12 Jun. 2005).

105. Edward S. Herman, "Tragic Errors in U.S. Military Policy," *Z Magazine*, September 2002, 30.

106. Herman, "Tragic Errors in U.S. Military Policy," 29.

11

A Game Plan for Infinite War?

In early 2005, President Bush addressed reporters' questions regarding whether a U.S. attack on Iran would define the next stage in the "War on Terror." Although Bush explained that the "notion that the United States is getting ready to attack Iran is simply ridiculous," he conceded that "all options are on the table."[1] Bush's evasive answer was significant in that it represented a neglected opportunity for reporters to challenge the confusing messages the President was sharing about possible attacks against countries labeled as part of the "Axis of Evil." Important questions remain which should be asked by media institutions interested in informing the public about potential U.S. involvement in future military conflicts. Was the administration actually planning an imminent attack on Iran; and if so, what concrete and indisputable evidence, in light of the Iraq debacle, did the President possess to show that Iran posed an imminent threat to the American people? Most importantly, should the U.S. go to war with Iran over the alleged possession of weapons the United States itself already possesses? What are the implications of such a war when other nation-states continue to possess such weapons and retain U.S. support nonetheless?

Whether reporters and editors should take an explicit stand by answering these questions is up for debate, but it is vital nonetheless that these questions at least be posed to the political establishment, so that the public may be better informed over the possibility for, and soundness of, military action against Iran. These necessary questions have often been glossed over by media still intently focused on the war in Iraq. Reporters, outside of a few exceptions like Seymour Hersh of the *New Yorker*, have been reluctant to push the administration too hard to reveal further details on whether it is planning on going to war with Iran.

Media deference, in the face of the Bush administration's attempts to portray Iran as an emerging threat, continues unabated, and in light of the quandary of Iraq. An important example of the lack of skeptical coverage of the U.S. demonization of "enemy" states was seen in the release of the Nuclear Posture Review (NPR). The NPR, published in 2002, was a high-level military policy document that identified a number of potential targets as part of a military contingency plan in which the U.S. might use "low-yield, precision guided nuclear weapons."[2] The countries on the list considered for attack included: Libya, Syria, China, Russia, Iran, Iraq (pre-invasion), and North Korea, all of which were considered, to varying degrees, as risks to American power if left unchecked.[3] The possible targeting of these regimes was directly addressed in National Security Directive Seventeen, issued by the Bush administration in December of 2002, which indicated that the U.S. considered first-strike scenarios to "prevent any enemy from using WMD against the U.S."[4]

Although the Nuclear Posture Review only discussed the possible, not planned use, of nuclear weapons "in the event of surprising military developments" or in retaliation for nuclear, biological, or chemical weapons attacks against the U.S.,[5] one can only imagine the reaction of American policymakers and media pundits if an "enemy" state on the NPR list were to release a similar document indicating potential plans to bomb American targets with nuclear weapons. One would expect extensive coverage of such threats to U.S. national security in the American mass media, although such coverage did not materialize in relation to U.S. threats made in the NPR against other countries.

Major criticisms of, and challenges to, the NPR were lacking from mainstream media coverage. That the U.S. is moving to prohibit other countries' development of WMD, while simultaneously advocating the construction of a new generation of nuclear weapons for potential use on enemy targets, was not an issue singled out for media commentary, as discussion about the potential for a re-ignition of the nuclear arms race through development of a smaller generation of nuclear weapons was largely cast aside. The U.S. possession and use of WMD against civilian populations (whether through use of nuclear or chemical weapons or conventional bombing), all the while claiming that other countries must dismantle their WMD stockpiles, has also generally been an area of criticism considered out of bounds in media reporting and debate. Much of this relates to the ideological assumption—discernable throughout American elite culture—that the U.S. responsibly retains weapons of mass destruction, whereas enemy states irresponsibly possess or pursue them.

The American media establishment has generally declined to push the Bush administration on whether there is a specific timeframe in which they expect the "War on Terror" to be completed; rather, most reporters seem to have accepted the thesis that today's world is one in which global terror threats are constantly materializing, and prolonged engagement in foreign wars may be necessary for decades to come in order to fight terrorism. In light of this reluctance to push for a foreseeable end to the "War on Terror," media institutions have reaffirmed their subordinate status to the Bush administration, as non-adversarial standards of reporting prohibit journalists from actively playing a role in politics by putting forth critical analysis and questioning administration policy plans.

Media deference is apparent in a wide range of cases, as the examples of the verbal attacks on Syria, Iran, and North Korea demonstrate. The interests of these regimes are portrayed as inimical to the safety and way of life of the American people, as major print headlines discuss Iran and North Korea's having "Reignite[d] Fears" amongst Americans of "Atomic Programs"—with the leaders of "enemy" states long considered dead-set on holding the American people hostage with weapons of mass destruction.[6] The double standard is evident: U.S. possession of nuclear weapons and other weapons is considered necessary to promote stability and security throughout the world. Questioning the United States' "responsible" possession of WMD is usually considered a taboo topic altogether. American allies are accorded the same "right" to be trusted with WMD; conversely, enemy nations must heed administration warnings, as their possession of the same weapons incite fear, anger, and apprehension amongst Western leaders who "responsibly" possess, and "reluctantly" use, such weapons against both civilian and military forces.

The countries grouped together as part of the WMD-holding, "terrorist supporting" "Axis of Evil" are very similar in how they are treated in the American mainstream media. While these countries are rendered as a serious menace to the national security of the U.S. and its allies, in each case, there is mounting evidence questioning whether these countries really pose an immediate threat that would warrant a legally sanctioned pre-emptive attack. The highlighting of fabricated threats has not been a priority in American reporting and editorials.

It is not the case that evidence critical of the administration's WMD rhetoric has *never* materialized in mainstream reporting.[7] Such reporting, however, has not led major media sources to *actively* challenge the theory that "enemy" regimes pose a security threat to the U.S. This pattern of passivity and complicity was evident in WMD reporting in the lead-up to war in Iraq, when occasional evidence questioning whether Iraq was a threat did materialize, but did not cause most media outlets to systematically challenge the idea that Iraq was a danger to the United States.

The countries listed as part of the "Axis of Evil" are also similar in that the claims leveled against them have often been heavy on incendiary rhetoric, but light on substantive evidence. As with Iraq, vague conjecture about "emerging terrorist threats" is often considered enough for reporters and media outlets to group these countries together as a danger to U.S. citizens. Reporters and editors are encouraged not to "put their own views" into reporting by questioning such charges, as that would violate the professional standard prohibiting the challenge of the official reasons given war. As a result, official sources are considered adequate primary sources for reporters when they are filing news stories about WMD "threats."

Syria Graduates into the "Axis of Evil"

By classifying Syria as a "junior partner in the 'Axis of Evil,'" former Secretary of Defense Donald Rumsfeld has portrayed the government of Bashar Assad as intent on developing weapons of mass destruction (if he did not already possess them), and fomenting ties with Islamist groups like Al Qaeda, in order to disrupt American operations in occupied Iraq. These claims received a sympathetic ear in media reporting. American political leaders publicly indicate their preference for the overthrow of the Syrian regime, as Congress's authorization of the Syria

Accountability and Lebanese Sovereignty Restoration Act and political statements hostile to the Syrian government made in support of the bill make clear.
The "Syria Accountability" bill, while assailing Assad's government for "terrorist connections" and the possession of WMD, leveled sanctions against Syria by
prohibiting U.S. exports and barring any Syrian flights from entering areas of
U.S. jurisdiction in Iraq.[8]

A major part of the promotion of the Syrian threat is the argument that Assad's government is actively compromising U.S. military operations in Iraq.
Media sources have happily repeated such claims. Charges that "insurgents"
loyal to (now deceased) Abu Musab al-Zarqawi have "taken over at least five
key western Iraqi towns on the border with Syria" are reported alongside blame
placed on Syrian leaders for the estimated "300 to 400 insurgents operating in
the area," as Assad's government is said to "provide a safe transit route for foreign fighters" entering the country.[9] U.S. News and World Report ridiculed Syria
for its "support of terrorism and its refusal to prevent insurgents from crossing
into Iraq." The magazine cites Peter Rodman of the Defense Department, who
maintains that "elements in the Syrian" leadership "are actively colluding with
our enemies," and that "extremists in Iraq are using Syria as a place to organize
and to get support and to flow back and forth across the border. . . this means
they share responsibility for the killing of Americans, and this has to stop."[10]
Syrian complicity in providing "a major point of access" for fighters entering
Iraq is reported as a major problem for the U.S. in its occupation of Iraq.[11]

Reports that Syria has actually collaborated with the U.S. in the "War on
Terror" generally contradict the notion of a Syrian threat in that they indicate
that the government has indeed worked with the U.S. in regards to investigating
terror suspects. Syrian efforts to provide to the CIA intelligence that prevented
an Al Qaeda attack on the U.S. Fifth Fleet headquarters in Bahrain,[12] and the
State Department's own admission that Syria "has cooperated significantly with
the United States and other foreign governments against Al Qaeda, the Taliban,
and other terrorist organizations and individuals" are problematic for the Bush
administration and media's construction of Syrian complicity with terrorism
directed against the United States.[13]

Consumers of mainstream news need not look for substantive criticisms
within media commentary regarding whether the U.S. has a right to attack Syria.
Criticisms of potential U.S. plans to engage countries listed as part of the "Axis
of Evil" are generally restricted to points of procedural complaint and criticism
over the tactical dangers and drawbacks of going to war with Syria. For example, William Kristol of the Weekly Standard, admitting the drawbacks of a full-
scale invasion of Syria, asks: "Is our Air Force overextended right now? Are we
so weak that we can't deter or punish Syria?"[14] Spencer Ackerman of the New
Republic identifies other problems with an assault on Syria, not any that have to
do with the illegality of such an attack or the "imperialist" nature of such an
attack (as progressive critics have maintained), but more to do with logistical
goals. Attacking Syria, Ackerman admits, "won't mean 'winning' the Iraq
war...because the insurgency is overwhelmingly an Iraqi Sunni phenomenon."[15]

This revelation leads Ackerman to label a possible attack on Syria as "expressly counterproductive," rather than flatly illegal, aggressive, and imperial.[16]

Ackerman's argument about the homegrown nature of Iraqi resistance, however, is important in that it is reinforced by other reports on the growth of such forces. As discussed in chapter 5, the "foreign fighters" in which U.S. military leaders and many media reports complain are threatening American lives and entering through Syria only account for an estimated 5 to 10 percent of the total number of resistance fighters in Iraq. As the *Center for Strategic International Studies* states, most Iraqi fighters are not foreign terrorists, or "Saddam loyalists," but actually "members of Sunni Arab Iraqi tribes" who "do not want to see Mr. Hussein return to power," and are "wary of a Shiite-led government."[17]

The Iranian "Nuclear Challenge"

Iran has long been considered a major obstacle to American dominance in the Middle East, as many feel it is the most likely state to be targeted by the U.S. after Iraq. Media reporting has concentrated on this possibility, although to a limited degree. Long-time investigative journalist Seymour Hersh reported in the *New Yorker* that at least one high level intelligence official in the Bush administration verified Iran as the next country in which the U.S. military would like to attack. A number of possible military strategies were illustrated in Hersh's reporting, including the "possible authorization of secret commando groups and other Special Forces units to conduct covert operations against suspected terrorist targets" in Iran, as well as a number of other states.[18] Other preventive first strike options purportedly include reliance on Israel as a proxy force that may bomb Iranian nuclear facilities, as the *Jerusalem Post* reported in March of 2006. The *Jerusalem Post* summarized: "it is clear that Israel would have to coordinate with the US forces air control any attempt to fly over Iraq on the way to Iran, if Israel chooses to attack using the shortest route."[19] As mentioned earlier, President Bush has not ruled out the potential of a direct attack by the U.S. either.

Scholar and strategic analyst Michael Klare suggests that: "Given the immense stress now being placed on U.S. ground forces in Iraq, it is likely that the Pentagon's favored plan for military action in Iran involves some combination of air-strikes" and "the use of local Iranian opposition forces."[20] Iranian writer and activist Saman Sepehri believes that U.S. policy motives in regards to Iran are aimed at deterring the rise of a potential competitor with the U.S. and Israel in the region: "With a population of seventy million, nearly three times that of Iraq or Saudi Arabia, an educated and technically proficient population, and sizable armed forces, Iran is the dominant regional power in the Persian Gulf; a region which sits on top of two-thirds of the world's oil reserves."[21] Such a critical view of the administration's planned attack on Iran has been common enough in alternative media sources, but is not typically repeated in mainstream media reporting.

Iran's uranium enrichment, although advertised as necessary in domestic energy production, is often characterized in the American mass media as a ploy designed to mask the development of nuclear weapons. In its summary of Iran's "nuclear challenge," the editors of the *New York Times* claim that, "Despite its ritualistic denials, Iran gives every indication of building all the essential elements of a nuclear weapons program."[22] "Every indication" of a continued nuclear program, however, is not apparently taken to include the International Atomic Energy Agency's (the UN's international nuclear watchdog agency) assessments, which have "not uncovered evidence to support accusations that Iran has a secret nuclear weapons program," in fact citing "very good cooperation" by Iran in the inspections process and in allowing the IAEA access to suspected sites.[23] "Every indication" of a threat also seems to exclude available intelligence estimating that "Iran is about ten years from developing the key ingredients needed for a nuclear weapon,"[24] rather than on the brink of developing a weapon that will pose a threat to the West. This prompts the overlooked, but vital question: what exactly is the tangible threat of Iran, if any, to the U.S. and its allies? Equally important, is it the U.S. that is the major threat to Iran, rather than the other way around? Also, why has the Iraqi WMD scandal not led reporters, pundits and editors to more rigorously question official statements regarding Iran's alleged development of WMD? These questions are cast aside in U.S. mainstream political and media discourse, but are vital for consideration for any educated, democratic citizenry.

Despite a lack of substantive evidence demonstrating a clear and present danger from Iran, the Bush administration and mass media continue to push forward with the argument that Iran is of immediate or near-immediate danger to the U.S. William Beeman and Donald Weadon, writing in the *San Francisco Chronicle*, believe that the Iranian clergy serves a vital purpose in the search for new enemies after the end of the Cold War: "Iran is a perfect villain, just what America needs, and the nuclear issue is a perfect pretext for this hostile behavior—one that plays well to a nervous American public."[25]

Media and government statements reinforcing the idea that Iran is a serious threat to the U.S. have been effective, it seems, in convincing the American public that Iran may be an emerging threat to the West. One *CNN/USA Today* published Gallup Poll released in 2006 showed that Americans are concerned that "the [Bush] administration won't do enough to keep Iran from developing nuclear weapons," although they are also worried that the administration "will be too quick to use military force if diplomacy fails."[26] Public skepticism of an American attack might increase, however, if the administration begins to more actively push for military confrontation with Iran, assisted by media support for an aerial attack, or some other form of action.

Major media outlets have attempted to reconcile the contradictions between official rhetoric promoting the immediate or near-immediate threat of Iran with intelligence skeptical of any immediate danger. The *Los Angeles Times*, for example, actually invoked the IAEA as confirming the Iranian government's secret nuclear strategy, although the newspaper admits that there is an "absence of clear evidence" of an Iranian weapons program after "nearly two years of

[IAEA] inspections."[27] The dangers endemic in the "absence of evidence is evidence of an imminent threat" mode of thinking are ignored by those interested in promoting the Bush administration's notion that Iran is an emerging danger to U.S. national security. This tendency was also discernable in media reporting of the "threat" of Iraqi WMD, as chapter 3 discussed at great length.

Attacks on Iran alleging it is developing nuclear weapons have continued, despite IAEA objections to the thesis. In another editorial from the *New York Times*, the editors sought "to make it urgently and abundantly clear to Iran's President...that the West will brook no further delays, and that it is serious and united about imposing stern sanctions if Iran won't abandon its nuclear fuel enrichment efforts."[28] Kenneth Pollack of the *Los Angeles Times* spoke about the necessity "to hold Iran's feet to the fire," as he discussed the "imperative that the U.S. take a bigger leadership role" in the crisis by better addressing the "threat."

Condemnations of Iran have also taken a melodramatic, militaristic tone. Writing in *Time* magazine, Charles Krauthammer argued: "Ultimately, human survival" is "at stake in the dispute over Iranian nukes." Iran "is the most dangerous political entity on the planet. . . if we fail to prevent an Iranian regime run by apocalyptic fanatics from going nuclear, we will have reached a point of no return."[29] In a *Wall Street Journal* Op-Ed, Claudia Rossett deplored the "decayed, despot-infested collective that is the contemporary U.N.," prior to the Security Council's imposition of Sanctions in 2007, for its failure to prevent the Iranian regime from developing WMD. Rossett continued: "It is quite possible that—after years of delay and dithering by the U.N.'s International Atomic Energy Agency, the European Union, and the U.S. itself—there is no initiative that will by now stop Iran short of direct military force." As self-appointed world leader, Rossett assumes that "it is clearly the U.S. that will have to do the bulk of the cajoling, prodding and backroom bargaining to put together any coalition both able and willing. . . to get the job done."[30]

In generating the perception that Iran's "weapons of mass destruction menace"[31] constitutes a threat to the U.S., the mainstream media has largely relied on official allegations. A small sample of topically relevant headlines from news organizations like the *New York Times, Washington Post, Fox News*, and the *Associated Press* drives this point home in greater detail. The pattern that emerges is unambiguous in stories such as: "Rumsfeld Says Iran is Developing Nuclear Arms Under Guise of Civilian Program"; "Iran's Emerging Nuclear Plant Poses Test for U.S."; "Iran Ends Voluntary Cooperation with IAEA"; "Powell Says Iran is Pursuing Bomb"; "Bush: Iran Poses a Grave Threat"; and "U.S. has Photos of Secret Iran Nuclear Sites."[32] Such reporting does not have to explicitly state, beyond a shadow of a doubt, that Iran possesses weapons or constitutes an imminent threat. Headlines and articles merely need to cite official claims, without consistently incorporating the views of those who challenge such claims. The absence of counter-evidence implicitly conveys the impression that Iran poses a threat, while allowing journalists to maintain their status as "objectively" reporting the news.

The headlines listed above are comparable in that they imply that the claims of the Bush administration about a WMD "threat" are unworthy of serious question from corporate reporters, at least not within headline coverage. Balanced reporting, apparently, does not require that statements of the Bush administration be challenged by critical intelligence questioning whether Iran really constitutes an emerging threat.

"Professional" reporting clearly favors complimentary lines of questioning American political leaders, in which commentators ponder procedural points, such as whether the U.S. has the power, rather than the legal right, to conduct "surgical" strikes against suspected Iranian nuclear sites.[33] Challenges to official statements about Iran seem to come up mainly when other high level intelligence bodies and political leaders challenge them, further evidence of the indexing effect at work.

As with the case of Syria, the same charges of collusion with Al Qaeda and meddling in Iraq are re-applied against the Iranian theocracy. In one instance, Wolf Blitzer of *CNN* and Robin Wright of the *Washington Post* spoke of what is "believed to be a connection" between Iran and Al Qaeda.[34] The White House's warnings against Iran for "interfering with its efforts to organize a government" in Iraq fail to elicit much skepticism, as American leaders and the establishment media assume that their own presence in Iraq does not count as a foreign or unwanted meddling.[35] Only Iranian or Syrian intrusion, rather than American intrusion in Iraq, is of major concern.[36]

Media attention is also devoted to censuring "Iranian-trained agents" who "have crossed into southern Iraq since the fall of Saddam Hussein and are working in the cities of Najaf, Karbala, and Basra to promote friendly Shiite clerics and advance Iranian interests."[37] Media outlets uncritically report the administration's assumptions regarding what constitutes legitimate democracy in other countries: hence the failure to challenge the argument that "an Iranian model of government would not be consistent with the democratic and pluralistic principles the United States believes should be adopted by an emerging Iraqi government," regardless of whether the Iraqi people choose such a religiously-inspired government on their own.[38]

Establishment media sources speak of the Iran's stubbornness in the face of U.S. opposition to its nuclear enrichment, as if American leaders are entitled to grant the Iranian government various rights in the international arena. A case in point is a report from *CNN*, which explained that the Iranian government was "given" a "last chance to halt uranium enrichment." The unspoken assumption presented is that the U.S. and its European allies reserve the right to either authorize, or prevent other countries from developing and retaining nuclear weapons.[39] The power to intervene in another country's affairs is reserved for the U.S., even when media sources admit that evidence of an immediate threat is "scant" at best, and that there has been extraordinary difficulty in collecting evidence on the country's nuclear activities.[40] Outside the American establishment press, vigilant critiques of the media's reporting on the Iranian "threat" warn readers of the dangers of going to war with Iran. Scott Ritter argues in *Al Jazeera*: "The American media today is sleepwalking towards an American war with Iran with all of the incompetence and lack of integrity that is displayed during a similar path trodden during the buildup to our current war with Iraq."[41]

American Media and the British-Iranian Standoff:
An Application of the Propaganda Model

As those who were following news events unfolding in the Middle East in March 2007 certainly knew, there was no shortage of government propaganda on all sides of the British-Iranian detainment crisis. British and American leaders denounced Iran for intimidation, coercion, and arrogance, while Iranian leaders made similar charges against the Bush and Blair governments. The dispute between the three countries finally came to an end with the unconditional release of the British "hostages" (as they were labeled by Western leaders) two weeks after their initial detainment by Iran. It is worth seriously reflecting on American media coverage of the British-Iranian standoff, at least if one is interested in understanding the nature of American foreign policy news coverage of events in the Middle East.

In *Manufacturing Consent: The Political Economy of the Mass Media*, Edward Herman and Noam Chomsky lay the foundations for a "propaganda model," which postulates that American mass media reporting and editorializing strongly and uncritically privilege official perspectives. Official sources are treated with deference, and U.S. humanitarian rhetoric elaborating high-minded goals of American foreign policy is left largely unquestioned. The propaganda of U.S. allies and client regimes is accorded positive coverage (and certainly *not* referred to as propaganda), while dissidents and officially designated "enemies" of state are denigrated and denounced for coercive, terrorist, and/or aggressive behavior. Such claims against the American mass media are not meant to be taken lightly, as they should be made the subject of serious empirical testing and scrutiny. It so happens that the British-Iranian standoff represents an important opportunity to test the propaganda model in the real world.

On March 23, 2007, an Iranian gunship detained seven marines and eight sailors of the British Royal Navy near the Shatt al-Arab waterway off of the coast of Iran and Iraq. The British Navy personnel were inspecting vessels suspected of smuggling goods to and from Iraq when the Iranian Revolutionary Guard picked them up, claiming they had illegally entered Iranian national waters. American media reports soon referred to the situation as a major confrontation between Britain and Iran, as both governments placed blame squarely on the other, refusing to admit to any sort of wrongdoing.

American leaders, retaining a long history of antagonistic relations with Iran, predictably reacted by denouncing the detainment as a violation of international law and as an act of unprovoked aggression. Dan Bartlett, White House Counselor, described "a long history from the Iranian government of bad actions it's taken, further isolating themselves from the international community."[42] President Bush called the detainment "inexcusable," claiming about the Iranian personnel: "They're innocent, they did nothing wrong, and they were summarily plucked out of waters."[43]

Those hoping the American media would react more calmly than the U.S.

and British governments, carefully weighing evidence in favor of a fair portrayal of the conflict, were in for a disappointment. As the propaganda model predicts, the American mass media are quick to demonize the actions of official "enemies," while exonerating the U.S. or allied governments for any blame. In no uncertain terms, Max Hastings argued in the *New York Times* that "Iran represents a menace to the security of us all,"[44] while the *Washington Post* editors railed against the "illegal attacks against a major Western power," despite the fact that there was still uncertainty at the time over whether the British troops had been in Iranian waters or not. Of the four editorials initially run by the *Washington Post* and *Los Angeles Times* on the detainment incident, all condemned Iranian leaders for utilizing propaganda in pursuit of selfish motives. The *Los Angeles Times* editors labeled the sailors and marines "innocent" victims of Iranian "escalation."[45]

As with major editorials, American reporting on the conflict also tended to heavily promote official Western frames. Of the forty-nine major stories run by the *New York Times, Los Angeles Times*, and *Washington Post* (found through a comprehensive search of the *Lexis Nexis* database), 54 percent of all sources quoted were British, as opposed to 30 percent that were Iranian. Western sources (including British *and* American) dominated media narratives even more thoroughly, comprising on average 70 percent of all sources quoted by the three papers. Such sources tended more often to promote antagonistic views of Iranian leaders, while presenting heroic and resolute images of U.S. and British leaders, under siege as a result of Iranian aggression and coercion. Of course, there is nothing inevitable about the fact that most sources were pro-Western in nature. There were, after all, reporters in Iran from *Reuters* and the *Associated Press* amongst other reporting agencies and organizations operating in Tehran, who filed reports based upon the statements of Iranian leaders, military officials, media, dissidents, and specialists. If American media outlets really wanted to pursue a more balanced approach to reporting the standoff, equally citing British and Iranian sources, they could have done so. Pursuing a more balanced approach, however, would require that American reporters and editors not pursue (as one of their major objectives) the uncritical transmission of official propaganda at the expense of alternative views.

Table 11.1

Dominant Media Narratives
In British Detainment Crisis

Sources Quoted	*New York Times*	*Washington Post*	*Los Angeles Times*	Total
British	46 (51%)	45 (54%)	58 (57%)	149 (54%)
Iranian	26 (29%)	24 (24%)	32 (31%)	82 (30%)
U.S.	18 (20%)	15 (15%)	12 (12%)	45 (16%)
Total	72 (100%)	69 (100%)	102 (100%)	276 (100%)

Further evidence for claims of propagandistic news coverage is seen in the heavy reliance of the U.S. print media on American and British government officials, who were disproportionately quoted in reporting the British-Iranian standoff. Of all the British and American sources quoted in the major stories from the *New York Times*, *Los Angeles Times*, and *Washington Post* on the incident, 80 percent of British and 73 percent of American sources were either from government or former government officials, or from military sources. Conversely, only 20 percent of British and 27 percent of American sources came from non-government sources such as media, academics and specialists, activists and dissidents, or people on the street.

Aside from looking at source bias, there are other ways in which to test the propaganda model concerning American news coverage of the standoff. It so happens that the Iranian detainment of British personnel (in March 2007) was preceded by a detainment of Iranian government officials by the United States in Iraq (in January 2007). Both incidents are generally comparable in nature, although the U.S. detainment seems *more* extreme than the Iranian detainment, upon reflecting on the facts surrounding the cases.

Table 11.2

Source Breakdown of Media
Narratives in British Detainment Crisis

Total Number of Stories: 49

New York Times

Sources	British	Iranian	U.S.
Gov./Former Gov. Officials	29	16	15
Military	10	2	2
Media	5	3	1
Academics/Specialists	2	2	0
Activists/Dissidents	0	3	0

Washington Post

Sources	British Sources	Iranian	U.S.
Gov./Former Gov.	24	20	8
Military	11	1	1
Media	2	2	1
Academics/Specialists	3	0	5
Activists/Dissidents	1	1	0

Los Angeles Times

Sources	British	Iranian	U.S.
Gov./Former Gov.	34	22	6
Military	12	1	1
Media	5	4	0
Academics/Specialists	9	3	5
Activists/Dissidents	0	3	0

On January 11, U.S. armed forces conducted a raid on an Iraqi foreign liaison office in the Kurdish city of Irbil, detaining five Iranian intelligence officials who were a part of Iran's Revolutionary Guard. While the five were not officially diplomats, they were members of the Iranian Revolutionary Guard's al-Quds Brigade, on an official mission to Iraq, and representing the Iranian government. The officials were in the process of being awarded diplomatic status at the time of the U.S. detainment. The officials did not illegally enter the country on a covert mission; quite the contrary, Iraqi Foreign Minister Hoshyar Zebari explained that they were "not [on] a clandestine operation. . . they were known by us. . . they operated with the approval of the regional government and with the knowledge of the Iraqi government. We were in the process of formalizing that liaison office into a consulate."[46]

U.S. leaders claimed the raid was necessary in order to send a message to Iranian leaders to stop "meddling" in Iraqi affairs. Iran had been accused by U.S. leaders of providing improvised explosive devices to Iraqi "insurgents" to be used against American troops. Iran had also been accused of providing money, weapons, and training to Iranian militias and "insurgents," and in threatening U.S. attempts to "stabilize" a war-torn Iraq.[47] Iraqi leaders explicitly rejected U.S. charges of Iranian "meddling" in Iraqi affairs, filing numerous protests of the U.S. detainment operation. Kurdish officials labeled the attack as a violation of Iraqi sovereignty and a violation of international law.[48] Iraq's Foreign Minister explained that the detainment of one of the Iranian officials (who had been an accredited diplomat) was "embarrassing for my country."[49]

The U.S. and Iranian detainments represent a rare opportunity to conduct a natural experiment into the ways in which comparable military operations between the United States and "enemy" regimes are portrayed in the American media. The reasons for expecting comparable coverage between the two abduction stories are numerous. As the Iranian detainment of British sailors was protested as illegal by British and American leaders, so too was the U.S. detainment of Iranian officials protested by Iraqi and Iranian leaders as illegal. Both abductions represented major standoffs between powers attempting to exert their authority in the Middle East.

One could easily argue that the U.S. detainment of Iranian officials should have garnered even *more* attention than the Iranian detainment of British personnel. In the case of U.S. detainment operations, the Iranian officials were in Iraq legally, with the express permission of the Iraqi government. Conversely, the legal status of the British and American occupation of Iraq has been widely considered illegal under international law at the highest levels of organizations like the United Nations (hence any operations of British or American troops can also be deemed illegal). On another level, the U.S. detainment of the Iranian officials was explicitly authorized at the highest levels of the American government (a clear case of official U.S. provocation against Iran),[50] whereas it was unknown at the time of the reporting of the British-Iranian standoff whether the detainment of British Navy personnel was ordered at the highest levels of the Iranian government or not. Furthermore, Iran's detainment of British forces paled in comparison to the U.S. detainment of Iranians in terms of potential for

inciting a hostile reaction. This is most clearly evident in that the Bush administration explicitly authorized the kidnapping or *killing* of Iranian government
officials within Iraq, whereas the Iranian government made clear no such intentions in terms of its treatment of British detainees. The killing of foreign political officials has been expressly rejected as illegal under the 1963 Vienna Convention on Consular Relations and the 1973 Convention on the Prevention and
Punishment of Crimes Against Internationally Protected Persons, both of which
the United States and Iran have ratified. The assassination or killing of any Iranian official invited into Iraq, then, represents a violation of the aforementioned
international legal protections. Violation of such laws is a sufficient reason in-
and-of-itself for major coverage of the U.S. abduction of Iranian officials.

Despite expectations of comparable coverage, the propaganda model is once
again vindicated after one reviews the extreme imbalance of coverage of the two
detainment incidents. In the two-week period following the U.S. detainment of
Iranian officials, the *New York Times*, *Los Angeles Times*, and *Washington Post*
each reported only three major stories on the incident, for a total of nine stories.
Conversely, U.S. media coverage from these three newspapers totaled forty-nine
major stories in the two-week period following the Iranian detainment of British
personnel.

Table 11.3

**Number of Major Stories Reporting on U.S. and Iranian
Detainment Operations**

	Coverage of Iran's Detainment of British Sailors March 24-April 6, 2007	Coverage of U.S. Detain- ment of Iranian Intelligence Officials January 12-January 26, 2007
New York Times	18	3
Washington Post	16	3
Los Angeles Times	15	3
Total	49	9

In sum, the actions of an "enemy" regime were deemed far more salient and
worthy of attention than the potentially embarrassing actions of the United
States, which had been ardently condemned as a violation of international law

and Iraqi national sovereignty. While official narratives and frames largely dominated reporting on the British-Iranian standoff, the U.S. detainment operations were portrayed as essential in promoting American self-defense, protection of American troops, and in opposition to Iranian aggression and terrorism. Such points were perhaps most blatantly evident in a *Los Angeles Times* editorial insisting that the "U.S. has every *right* [emphasis added] to insist on the arrest, prosecution, or expulsion from Iraq of Iranians, officials or not, who abet terrorism."[51] Deference to U.S. justifications was also evident in light of overreliance on official statements, to the neglect of nonofficial ones.

In a final test of the propaganda model, one may examine the ways in the Iranian-British standoff was distinguished from the earlier U.S. detainment of Iranians in terms of discounting a possible cause and effect relationship. Did the U.S. abduction of Iranian officials incite Iranian leaders to respond against the U.S. or its allies in Iraq by abducting British military personnel? While a complete answer this question seems elusive, the posing of the question should have been a priority if the American media were committed to understanding possible root causes of the British-Iranian standoff.

In the case of British media coverage, one can see that the question of a causal link between the two incidents was focused on more intensively. In a number of potentially explosive stories reported during the March standoff, the *Independent* of London reported that the original targets in the U.S.-Iranian detainment in January had been government officials with far higher credentials than the low-level officials who were actually detained in U.S. operations. The United States, the *Independent* reported, had attempted to capture "two senior Iranian officers. . . Mohammed Jafari, the powerful deputy head of the Iranian National Security Council, and General Minojahar Frouzanda, the Chief of Intelligence of the Iranian Revolutionary Guard." The source of these charges came from Kurdish officials, who explained that Jafari and Frouzanda "were in Kurdistan on an official visit during which they met with Iraqi President Jalal Talabani and later saw Massoud Barzani, the President of the Kurdistan Regional Government (KRG)."

The significance of the failed capture of these officials was presented lucidly by Patrick Cockburn of the *Independent*: "The attempt by the U.S. to seize the two high-ranking Iranian security officers openly meeting with Iraqi leaders is somewhat as if Iran had tried to kidnap the heads of the CIA and MI6 while they were on an official visit to a country neighbouring Iran, such as Pakistan or Afghanistan. There is no doubt that Iran believes that Mr. Jafari and Mr. Frouzanda were targeted by the Americans."

In a number of reports, Cockburn suggested a direct cause-and-effect link between the original U.S. detainment and the following British-Iranian standoff ("The Botched U.S. Raid that Led to the Hostage Crisis," and "American Raid and Arrests Set Scene for Capture of Marines").[52] He argued that "Better understanding of the seriousness of the U.S. action in Irbil—and the angry Iranian response to it—should have led Downing Street and the Ministry of Defence to realize that Iran was likely to retaliate against American or British forces such as highly vulnerable Navy search parties in the Gulf. . . the attempt by the U.S. to seize the two high-ranking Iranian security officers" was "a far more serious and aggressive act. It was not carried out by proxies but by U.S. forces directly."[53]

While the *Independent's* reports were subsequently picked up by other mainstream British media sources,[54] neither the story, nor its charges, appear to have received any headline coverage in the major American print media. There was no coherent or systematic effort in the American press to report charges that the two abductions were directly related. This decontextualization is best seen in a breakdown of the nineteen stories (out of the total forty-nine major stories on the British-Iranian "standoff") in the *New York Times*, *Los Angeles Times*, and *Washington Post* that *did* mention the U.S. January abduction in their reporting. Out of those nineteen stories, only five (all from the *Washington Post*) suggested that there might be a causal relationship between the U.S. and Iranian detainments; fourteen stories either suggested no link or explicitly refuted suggestions of one. Only one story (from the *Los Angeles Times*) directly referenced the *Independent* story, although the reference was not in the headline, but buried deep within the article. Importantly, *none* of the forty-nine stories on the British-Iranian "standoff" discussed the charge that Iran's detainment of British personnel might have been motivated by the failed U.S. attempt to seize senior Iranian officials a few months earlier.

Whether it is in the over-reliance on British and American official sources over nonofficial ones, the systematic marginalization of comparable news coverage implicating both U.S. "enemies" *and* the U.S. in aggression or violation of international law, or the suppression of explosive charges against the United States for provoking a hostage crisis, the American press has revealed itself as subservient to the agendas of the American foreign policy elite. Official "enemies" are vilified (although at times for good reason), while the questionable actions of American leaders are largely left unchallenged, as professional norms of "objectivity" do not allow for the challenge of official statements. As the propaganda model suggests, American reporters have faithfully taken to the role of an unofficial propaganda arm for the state, most blatantly during times when the United States rules in favor of allies and client regimes against powers deemed antagonistic to U.S. interests.

North Korea: A Devil in the Making

The Bush administration and media have generally proceeded much more carefully with the North Korean regime of Kim Jong Il, than with Iraq, mainly as a result of the country's deterrents (military and nuclear) to attack. Despite Rumsfeld's calls for regime change in North Korea, he, along with other U.S. political leaders, has generally been hesitant to announce any specific plans for military action against the regime. Along with the Bush administration, the mainstream press has also taken to denouncing the North Korean regime, although mostly refraining from calls for a military attack.

Restraint in plans for war has not meant an absence of accusations and speculation concerning the North Korean debacle. Neil Cavuto of *Fox News*

described the authoritarian government of Kim Jong Il as "the world's #1 nuclear threat,"[55] ignoring evidence that it was the United States, not North Korea,
which put forth the idea of potential first-strike scenarios against an "enemy"
state (as seen in the Nuclear Posture Review). Also neglected in Cavuto's report
is the acknowledgement, as of yet, that North Korea, despite having testing a
nuclear device, is not known to have any sort of effective delivery mechanism
through which to deliver a weapon against Western targets. Regardless of a lack
of evidence, *CNN* has presented doomsday scenarios, where Kim Jong Il, the
"nuclear wildcard," might attempt to "help a terrorist group arm itself with a
nuclear weapon."[56]

Questioning exaggerations of a North Korean threat is not meant to imply
that there is no threat at all from the proliferation of nuclear weapons, but rather
to demonstrate the dangers inherent in assuming that such rogue regimes pose a
stronger threat than they really do. Such efforts to escalate the conflict between
the U.S. and North Korea are a major cause of concern for those who are intent
on defusing this nuclear crisis. Media pundits are typically more likely to blame
the North Korean regime for fueling tensions with the U.S., than they are to
level substantive criticisms against American political leaders for their share in
provoking a nuclear crisis.

The brutality of the North Korean communist regime makes it an easy target for attack in the American media. Take for instance, the statements of
Nicholas Kristof of the *New York Times*; in explaining the dangers of North Korea's development of WMD; he cites the threatening of American allies (China
and Japan), the risk of another Korean war, and increased proliferation throughout the region, although he is hesitant to place fault on the U.S. for exacerbating
the situation by further isolating the North Korean state and for refusing to fulfill
the agreements it made with Kim Jong Il's regime. Instead, Kristof argued: "In
fairness, all this is more Kim Jong Il's fault than Mr. Bush's. . . . North Korea is
the most odious country in the world today…while some two million North Koreans were starving to death in the late 1990's, Mr. Kim spent 2.6 million dollars
on Swiss watches. He's the kind of man who, when he didn't like a haircut once,
executed the barber."[57]

Attention is focused less, if at all, on the United States' well-documented
efforts to aggravate an already volatile situation by labeling North Korea as part
of an "Axis of Evil"—as well as other American actions that have provoked a
standoff, including the U.S. use of spy flights near North Korean air space (and
even over its sovereign air space),[58] the repositioning of U.S. bombers near
North Korea,[59] the initial reluctance to engage in bilateral peace talks and to
honor the requirements of those talks, and the continued presence of large U.S.
troop and military personnel concentrations in South Korea. Such escalation and
provocation of an already dangerous situation continued, as U.S. leaders demanded that other countries throughout the region punish North Korea as a
whole by cutting off food shipments and oil to a population already suffering
under Kim Jong Il's dictatorship.[60] In addition, the Bush administration escalated hostility with initiatives like "Operation Plan 5030," which calls for efforts

"to topple Kim's regime by destabilizing its military forces" so as to push for "regime change."[61]

What are considered acceptable or warranted responses to the North Korean predicament proposed throughout the media range from intimidation and isolation to a full out military strike, although the latter option is not seriously considered by a large number of pundits and analysts. Reflecting favorably on the extremist response, Stanley Kurtz of the conservative *National Review* argued in favor of regime change, claiming that: "we are on a course for war with North Korea. . . surely within the next six years. Nothing short of war will stop the North Koreans from developing and selling nuclear weapons and fuel. The question is whether we will go to war before, or after, North Korea spreads its nuclear material."[62]

Advocacy of a military response to North Korea's nuclear enrichment and testing of nuclear devices, however, has not been restricted to far-right venues like the *National Review*. The *Washington Post* has actively advocated a preventive attack on North Korea, as seen in Ashton Carter and William Perry's (formerly Assistant Secretary of Defense and Secretary of Defense respectively during the Clinton administration) Op-Ed, "If Necessary, Strike and Destroy." In that piece, the authors argued for a "precision" strike against a North Korean military installation they claimed, erroneously, was preparing for an attack against the United States. Carter and Perry contended that (in 2006) "North Korean technicians" were "reportedly in the final stages of fueling a long-range ballistic missile that some experts estimate can deliver a deadly payload to the United States." The authors continued: "Should the United States allow a country openly hostile to it and armed with nuclear weapons to perfect an intercontinental ballistic missile capable of delivering nuclear weapons to U.S. soil? We believe not...the United States should immediately make clear its intention to strike and destroy the North Korean Taepodong missile before it can be launched."[63] Carter and Perry's anxiety was later shown to be unfounded, as North Korea moved toward a negotiated settlement with the U.S. and its neighbors, rather than toward further escalation.

Justifications for military attacks on North Korea have sometimes relied on assertions—never accompanied by tangible evidence—that North Korea plans to provide nuclear technology or weapons to terrorist groups. Perry speculates in the *Washington Post* that "the greatest danger to the United States from [North Korea's nuclear program] is not that North Korea would be willing to commit suicide by firing a missile at the United States," but rather that "the North Koreans will sell one of the bombs or some of their plutonium to a terrorist group."[64] This statement, revealingly, contradicts the preceding argument made by Perry, that the primary threat is a North Korean first strike against the U.S.

The editors of the *Washington Times* argued that "North Korea's claim to have tested a nuclear weapon, specious or not, can only heighten concern that the regime might try to transfer nuclear weapons technology to a terrorist group...it is clear that the communist government, desperate for foreign exchange to prop up a collapsing economy, has little reluctance to sell destabilizing military items to anyone who can afford them."[65] The *Washington Post*'s editors also made vague references to the possibility that North Korea "may be looking beyond Libya for new customers for [nuclear] products," claiming that there may be "no way to neutralize this threat."[66]

In his piece in the *National Review*, Stanley Kurtz justified war by maintaining—without providing evidence—that, "the North Koreans will shortly be selling nuclear fuel manufactured in their clandestine plant(s) to Al Qaeda. We won't see it, but it's going to happen."[67] Kurtz's thesis is strikingly similar to the Bush administration's claim that war with Iraq was necessary to prevent an Al Qaeda attack on the U.S. with nuclear weapons. As with the Bush administration's claim of an unconfirmable threat in which the only proof may be found in the form of a "mushroom cloud," Kurtz also maintained that terrorists could strike at the U.S. with nuclear weapons without leaving fingerprints (hence his claim that "we won't see" North Korea supplying such a weapon). Such charges rely on heavily, again, on the "absence of evidence is evidence of an imminent threat" framework. The complete lack of demonstrated links between groups like Al Qaeda and North Korea is apparently inconsequential. Major attention to conspiracy theories, however, is deemed legitimate so long as those theories comport with administration propaganda and vilification of officially designated enemies.

Other assessments in the mass media are less intent on promoting military escalation, although they also pose primarily pragmatic assessments of the problems with going to war. A *CBS* news report cited below is well reflective of the dangers that accompany a direct military confrontation with the North Korean government: "The use of military force in North Korea. . . carries huge risks. North Korea is heavily militarized, with a million-person armed force and millions more in reserves, as well as powerful artillery that could kill tens of thousands of South Koreans in retaliation to any U.S. strike."[68] The regime's pursuit of nuclear weapons naturally makes the confrontation between the U.S., North Korea, and other regional nuclear powers even more capricious than before.

What are deemed proper responses to North Korean participation in nuclear proliferation include an increased American reliance on spaced based missile defense, and stronger efforts to isolate the regime and people of North Korea through imposition of comprehensive sanctions. As *Time* explains before the 2007 negotiations: "We should be grateful that Kim Jong Il wants to spare us more rounds of the pointless six-party talks on North Korea's nuclear program. They might otherwise have dragged on for years as Kim doggedly extracted all the aid and guarantees he wanted in exchange for more empty promises." Instead, [the country] "can be brought to the U.N. Security Council, which should impose sanctions for breaches of the Nuclear Nonproliferation Treaty that began some 20 years ago."[69]

Time's enthusiastic support for this policy path, however, negates the problem traditionally associated with comprehensive sanctions, namely that they are a rather blunt, imprecise instrument of foreign policy. Comprehensive sanctions fail, by design, to distinguish between repressive regimes and their citizens. Comprehensive punitive sanctions target the weakest of the weak, rather than focusing on the political regimes in which they are supposed to be concerned.

Humanitarian repercussions notwithstanding, such sanctions, coupled with belligerent rhetoric directed against the targeted nation, tend to create a rally around the flag effect by strengthening dictatorial regimes and hindering chances of grassroots, bottom-up democratization. Verbal denigration and proposed military attacks against the regime in question also hurt prospects for democracy in that they embolden national reactionaries to step up their repression under the guise of "protecting their country" from external and internal attack. This has certainly been the case in Syria, where national leaders have justified cracking down on protest and dissent under the rationale that the regime is under attack and pressure from the outside.

A final "desirable" path toward tackling the issue of North Korean nuclear weapons development was presented by *CNN* former *NewsNight* host Aaron Brown, who pondered whether weapons in space may be needed in order to deter the "rogue nation,"[70] despite numerous criticisms that reliance on a "missile shield" may reignite the nuclear arms race by encouraging another round of nuclear weapons proliferation.

Nukes, Negotiations, and Double Standards

North Korea's testing of a nuclear device in October of 2006 was correctly considered throughout the American mass media as a major turning point in the unfolding conflict between the Bush administration and Kim Jong Il. The incident served as a catalyst in highlighting past American failures in negotiations and in pushing for renewed dialogue with the North Korean regime. Media coverage heavily focused on criticisms of the North Korean regime for its role in proliferating weapons of mass destruction. A polarized framing of the heightened tensions between the United States and North Korea was constructed, as the U.S. was generally seen as working toward negotiated settlement—although making some serious mistakes along the way—while the Korean dictator was consistently seen as committed to derailing a peaceful resolution to the conflict.

The March 2007 six party talks between the United States, North Korea, South Korea, China, Japan, and Russia set a fairly comprehensive framework for peace, building upon the earlier 1994 and 2005 accords. North Korea was to close down its Yongbyon nuclear reactor within sixty days and readmit international inspectors, and in return receive 50,000 tons of fuel, food, or other aid, as well as another 950,000 tons of aid once it took further steps to dismantle its nuclear arsenal.[71] The United States committed to taking North Korea off its list of terrorist states and to lifting the sanctions leveled against Kim Jong Il's regime after he announced he was developing a nuclear weapons program in 2002.

Cautious optimism was in the air in most media editorials and reporting, as news editors celebrated the United States' self-proclaimed role as "the deal's lead enforcer,"[72] despite its long record of opposing a negotiated settlement. Optimism concerning the success of the talks, however, did not prevent North Korea from being widely ridiculed by American pundits. Blame was placed on Kim Jong Il following the preliminary September 2005 and Six Party March

2007 agreements which aimed at dismantling North Korea's nuclear weapons program. Little to no reference was made to American leaders' manipulation of the accords in pursuit of their own power politics objectives. Following the 2005 agreement, the editors of the *New York Times* remarked in light of a failed North Korean missile test that the nation "has again shown itself to be a dangerous rogue actor, ignoring the almost universal pleas from other countries to refrain from a [nuclear] test that can only add to regional tensions and multiply doubts about its trustworthiness and intentions."[73]

Critiques of the 2007 agreement focused on the alleged naiveté of the Bush administration and other parties to the talks, as well as on North Korea's deceptiveness. John O'Sullivan complained in the *Chicago Sun Times* that the 2007 deal was "very similar, if not identical to the bad old compromise that was agreed between Kim [Jong Il] and the Clinton administration." O'Sullivan continued: "there is some uncertainty about whether the North Koreans will actually get rid of all their nuclear facilities." The "U.S. government, eager to parade its sole diplomatic achievement, would be keen to turn a blind eye to any violations," and allow the regime to continue to develop weapons "with impunity." In the end, the deal "would prove to be a powerful incentive to nuclear proliferation worldwide," as "America and its partners. . . have told the rest of the world that one certain way to gouge aid out of the West and the United States is to start a nuclearization program for the express purpose of receiving bribes to close it down."[74] The editors of the *Boston Globe* criticized the Bush administration, this time for its "delusional belief that they could counter the nuclear proliferation threat [from North Korea] by forcing a regime change in Pyongyang."[75]

Unsurprisingly, media editorials spared the U.S. from ridicule for its longstanding opposition to a negotiated settlement. Rather than criticizing the United States, the *Washington Post*'s editors chose to denounce China's plans to participate in the 2007 agreement, specifically the Chinese government's "strategy [as part of the agreement] of preserving Kim Jong Il's totalitarian regime." While a critical observer of media coverage would probably expect American journalists and editors to exercise a strong level of skepticism toward an authoritarian regime with an extensive history of human rights violations, provocation, and deception, few substantive challenges were posed to American leaders with a similar record of intransigence. For example, the *Washington Post*'s editors asserted that: "If Mr. Kim is really prepared to give up his nukes, a path has been laid. A 'framework agreement' signed by the six parties more than a year ago (in 2005) called for North Korea to dismantle its program and receive aid and security guarantees. . . . Critics who harp on the need for the Bush administration to strike a deal with Mr. Kim tend to overlook the fact that this deal has already been struck. The question is whether North Korea is serious about it or whether it agreed to the plan merely to mollify China and South Korea and buy more time to develop missiles and nuclear warheads."[76]

The *Washington Post*'s portrayal of the actions of North Korean leaders, while partially accurate, also blatantly whitewashed U.S. responsibility for undermining the (2005) preliminary accord. Although the 2005 agreement *did* call on North Korea to destroy its nuclear weapons, it also required the Bush administration to guarantee North Korean national security concerns. It also stipulated that the U.S. provide support for the development of a new series of light water nuclear reactors, which were set to replace North Korea's old reactors (from which plutonium had been extracted and used for developing nuclear weapons). On both requirements, the United States consciously chose to undermine the agreement.

After the 2005 accord, U.S. leaders immediately cancelled plans for the light water reactors.[77] In addition, U.S. leaders refused to refrain from belligerent rhetoric directed against the regime, thereby reneging on their commitment to ensure North Korean national security. President Bush's 2006 State of the Union Address explicitly referenced the need for regime change in North Korea. Vice President Cheney also refused to dispel rumors of a possible military attack against North Korea, claiming publicly that: "if you are going to launch strikes," against North Korea, "you'd better be prepared to not fire just one shot."[78] In response to continued hostility from the United States, North Korean Vice Prime Minister Kim Kye Gwan announced that: "the nuclear issues [between the two countries] cannot be resolved until the United States takes a co-existence policy."[79]

The Bush administration's open contempt for a negotiated settlement did much to exacerbate the situation between the U.S., North Korea, and its neighbors in the region, although one would hardly know this by reading American mass media coverage. While at the beginning of the Bush presidency in 2001, North Korea was thought to have had only enough material for one or two nuclear weapons, it was believed to have in its possession nearly a half dozen weapons by early 2007. On this point, and concerning U.S. efforts to derail peace talks, American media outlets have been far less vociferous than news outlets throughout the Progressive-Left press and international media.

Alternative Modes of Framing
The North Korean Crisis

Media outlets outside the American mainstream were often substantively different in their criticisms of the United State's response to North Korea's nuclear weapons development. U.S. leaders were not mildly criticized for dragging their feet in negotiations, but were condemned for their contempt of any sort of negotiated settlement, and for hypocritical attempts to disarm other nuclear powers while maintaining their own nuclear arsenals. In the *Guardian* of London, Dan Plesch maintained: "North Korea's nuclear policy is not irrational at all. . . . Far from being crazy, the North Korean policy is quite rational. Faced with a U.S. government that believes the communist regime should be removed from the map, the North Koreans pressed ahead with building a deterrent." Plesch placed much of the blame for North Korea's weapons development at the hands of Western leaders, who "have tried to impose a double standard, hanging on to nuclear weapons for themselves and their friends while denying them to others. Like alcoholics condemning teenage drinking, the nuclear powers have made the spread of nuclear weapons the terror of our age, distracting attention from their own behaviour."[80]

Criticisms of U.S. leaders often targeted both political parties, rather than just the Bush administration. In *Z Magazine* and in the Asian Pacific Journal *Japan Focus*, Tim Beal portrayed the Clinton administration as "dilatory in implementing the [1994] agreement [with North Korea]. By the time it left office the Light Water Reactors were years behind schedule [from when they had been promised], and although Secretary of State Albright did visit Pyongyang in October 2000, little progress had been made on Pyongyang's key diplomatic goal, the normalization of relations with the U.S." Beal also attacked the Bush administration for failing to provide "compelling evidence" that North Korea was enriching uranium [in addition to plutonium], after the U.S. cut off aid to the regime in 2002. Neal suggested that the administration possessed ulterior motives in escalating the conflict: "Given the administration's record over Iraq, its attempts to 'mislead allies' over spurious claims of North Korean nuclear exports to Libya, and the recent report on Iran [claiming it was developing nuclear weapons] that was attacked by U.N. inspectors as 'outrageous and dishonest,' it seems much more likely that the American claim [about uranium enrichment] was bogus and designed to destroy Clinton's agreement rather than being based on any significant evidence that North Korea had a meaningful program."[81]

This chapter has demonstrated that mass media coverage of potential future targets in the "War on Terror" has been anything but critical, balanced, or "objective." Nationalist impulses push reporters, editors, and media owners to side with American political leaders against designated "enemy" states, and to give the Bush and Clinton administration the benefit of the doubt in their allegedly good intentions in negotiating with Syria, Iran, and North Korea. Again, the patterns of reporting in American mainstream media institutions are hardly inevitable or natural. Rather, such reporting reflects indirect and nationalistic pressures exerted on media outlets by government—at least if nationalism is interpreted as requiring support for U.S. geopolitical and power politics objectives, and a disregard for substantively critical views of the exercise of that power. Extraordinary uniformity of such nationalistic views are possible, as discussed throughout this work, due to extreme corporate concentration of media ownership, as media networks and newspapers are increasingly dominated by fewer and fewer conglomerates with close ties to those holding political power.

Notes

1. Michael A. Fletcher and Keith B. Richburg, "Bush Tries to Allay EU Worry over Iran," *Washington Post*, 23 February 2005, 1(A).

2. Michelle Ciarrocca, "The Nuclear Posture Review: Reading Between the Lines," *Common Dreams*, 17 January 2002, http://www.commondreams.org/views02/0117-10.htm (23 Jul. 2005).

3. CNN.com, "Report: Nuclear Weapons Policy Review Names Potential Targets," 10 March 2002, http://archives.cnn.com/2002/US/03/09/nuclear.weapons (22 Apr. 2005).

4. Ashraf Fahim, "Syria: the Next Domino?" *Z Magazine*, May 2003, http://zmagsite.zmag.org/may2003/fahimprint0503.html (14 Jul. 2005).

5. CNN.com, "Pentagon: Nuclear Review Not a Guide to US Plans," 10 March 2002, http://archives.cnn.com/2002/US/03/10/nuclear.weapons (27 Jul. 2005).

6. David E. Sanger, "Iran and North Korea Reignite Fears of Atomic Programs," *New York Times*, 25 June 2004, 8(A).

7. Dafna Linzer, "U.N. Inspectors Dispute Iran Report by House Panel," *Washington Post*, 14 September 2006, 17(A).

8. Saul Landau and Farrah Hansen, "Syria: Yet Another 'Enemy' to Muddle the Middle East Waters," *Z Magazine*, 16 September 2004, http://www.zmag.org/content/showarticle.cfm?ItemID=6240 (16 Sep. 2004).

9. Anna Badkhen, "Insurgents Seize 5 Towns Near Syria," *San Francisco Chronicle*, 27 September 2005, http://www.sfgate.com/cgi-bin/article.cgi?file/c/a/2005/09/27/MNG9 9EUI391.DTL (27 Sep. 2005).

10. U.S. News and World Report, "Trouble on Another Front," 22 November 2004, http://www.usnews.com/usnews/news/articles/041122/22iran.b.htm (22 Nov. 2004).

11. U.S. News and World Report, 2004.

12. Landau and Hansen, "Syria," 2004.

13. Farrah Hassen, "The Obsession with Syria," *Z Magazine*, 7 May 2005, http://www.zmag.org/content/showarticle.cfm?ItemID=7802 (9 May 2005).

14. William Kristol, "The War Presidency," *Weekly Standard*, 5 September 2005, http://www.weeklystandard.com/Content/Public/Articles/000/000/005/986uesrd.asp   (5 Sep. 2005).

15. Spencer Ackerman, "Roadblock to Damascus," *New Republic*, 22 September 2005, http://www.tnr.com/doc.mhtml?i=w050919&s=ackerman092205 (25 Sep. 2005).

16. Ackerman, "Roadblock to Damascus," 2005.

17. Tom Regan, "The 'Myth' of Iraq's Foreign Fighters," *Christian Science Monitor*, 23 September 2005, http://www.csmonitor.com/2005/0923/dailyUpdate.html (27 Sep. 2005).

18. Seymour M. Hersh, "The Coming Wars," *New Yorker*, 17 January 2005, http://www.newyorker.com/fact/content/?050124fa_fact (23 Jan. 2005).

19. Nathan Guttman, "U.S. Monitoring Israel's Iran Option," *Jerusalem Post*, 13 March 2006, http://www.truthout.org/docs_2006/031406K.shtml (13 Mar. 2006).

20. Michael T. Klare, "The Iran War Buildup," *Nation*, 21 July 2005, http://www.thenation.com/doc/20050801/klare (21 Jul. 2005).

21. Saman, Sepehri, "Intervention in Iran: Will the U.S. Attack?" *International Socialist Review*, July/August 2005, 52.

22. Editorial, "Iran's Nuclear Challenge," *New York Times*, 4 August 2004, 14(A).

23. Andrea Koppell, "IAEA: No Proof of Secret Iran Plan," 2 September 2004, http://www.cnn.com/2004/WORLD/meast/09/01/iran.nuclear/ (2 Sep. 2004).

24. Dafna Linzer, "Iran is Judged 10 Years from Nuclear Bomb," *Washington Post*, 2 August 2005, 1(A).

25. William O. Beeman and Donald A. Weadon, "Iran as Bush's Nuclear Bogeyman," *San Francisco Chronicle*, 30 September 2004, http://www.sfgate.com/cgi-bin/article.cgi?file=/chronicle/archive/2004/09/30/EDGB790KB01.DTL (3 Oct. 2004).

26. CNN.com, "Americans Nervous about Iran," 14 February 2006, http://www.cnn.com/2006/POLITICS/02/13/poll.iran/ (14 Feb. 2006).

27. Douglas Frantz, "Iran Moving Methodologically Toward Nuclear Capability," *Los Angeles Times*, 21 October 2004, http://www.latimes.com/news/nationworld/world/la-fg-iran21oct21,1,571740.story (25 Oct. 2004).

28. Editorial, "Iran's Nuclear Threat," *New York Times*, 22 October 2004, 22(A).

29. Charles Krauthammer, "Today Tehran, Tomorrow the World," *Time*, 3 April 2006, 96.

30. Claudia Rossett, "Excess Baggage," *Wall Street Journal*, 3 September 2006, http://www.opinionjournal.com/editorial/feature.html?id=110008891 (3 Sep. 2006).

31. David Ignatius, "Engage Iran," *Washington Post*, 26 November 2004, 39(A).

32. Richard Bernstein and Garmisch Partenkirchen, "Rumsfeld Says Iran is Developing Nuclear Arms Under Guise of Civilian Program," *New York Times*, 12 June 2003, 1(A); Dana Priest, "Iran's Emerging Nuclear Plant Poses Test for U.S.," *Washington Post*, 29 July 2002, 1(A); Associated Press, "Iran Ends Voluntary Cooperation with IAEA," *MSNBC.com*, 5 February 2006, http://www.msnbc.msn.com/id/11105378/ (5 Feb. 2006); Keith B. Richburg and Robin Wright, "Powell Says Iran is Pursuing Bomb," *Washington Post*, 18 November 2004, 1(A); Fox News.com, "Bush: Iran Poses a Grave Threat," 15 January 2006, http://www.foxnews.com/story/0,2933,181556,00.html (15 Jan. 2006); CNN.com, "US has Photos of Secret Iran Nuclear Sites," December 13, 2002, http://archives.cnn.com/2002/WORLD/meast/12/12/iran.nuclear/ (2003, Nov. 4).

33. Wolf Blitzer, *News from CNN with Wolf Blitzer*, CNN, 9 February 2005.

34. Blitzer, *News from CNN with Wolf Blitzer*, CNN, 13 December 2004.

35. Douglas Jehl and David E. Sanger, "U.S. Tells Iran Not to Interfere in Iraq Efforts," *New York Times*, 24 April 2003, 1(A).

36. Edward Wong, "Iran is in Strong Position to Steer Iraq's Political Future," *New York Times*, 3 July 2004, 6(A).

37. Douglas Jehl, "Iran Said to Send Agents into Iraq," *New York Times*, 23 April 2003, 1(A).

38. Jehl, "Iran Said to Send Agents into Iraq," 2003.

39. CNN.com, "World Gives Iran 'Final Chance,'" 1 February 2006, http://edition.cnn-.com/2006/WORLD/meast/02/01/iran.wrap.1300/ (1 Feb. 2006).

40. Reuters, "Data on Iran Scant, U.S. Official Says," *Los Angeles Times*, 14 March 2005, 4(A).

41. Scott Ritter, "Sleepwalking to Disaster in Iran," *Al Jazeera*, 1 April 2005, http://english.aljazeera.net/NR/exeres/1B5FCF4A-FBF6-443A-93A9-5E37C43FDE0B.htm (1 Apr. 2005).

42. Jim Rutenberg, "U.S. Keeping Pressure on Iran over Seizure of 15 Britons at Sea," *New York Times*, 2 April 2007, 9(A).

43. Borzou Daragahi and Ramin Mostaghim, "Iranian Leader Accuses Britain of Arrogance," *Los Angeles Times*, 1 April 2007, 4(A).

44. Max Hastings, "Iran, the Vicious Victim," *New York Times*, 27(A); Editorial, "End of a Standoff," *Washington Post*, 30 March 2007, 20(A).

45. Editorial, "End of a Standoff," *Washington Post*, 6 April 2007, 20(A); Editorial, "The Results of Diplomacy," *Washington Post*, 29 March 2007, 18(A); Editorial, "Iran the Inscrutable," *Los Angeles Times*, 2 April 2007, 12(A); Editorial, "Valuable Lessons," *Los Angeles Times*, 6 April 2006, 24(A).

46. Edward Wong, "U.S. is Reviewing Request by Iran to let its Envoy Visit 5 Iranians Seized in a Raid in Iraq," *New York Times*, 5 April 2007, 8(A).

47. Robin Wright and Nancy Trejos, "U.S. Troops Raid 2 Iranian Targets in Iraq," *Washington Post*, 12 January 2007, 16(A).

48. James Glanz, "G.I.s in Iraq Raid Iranian's Offices," *New York Times*, 12 January 2007, 1(A).

49. Alissa J. Rubin, "Captors Release Kidnapped Iranian Diplomat in Baghdad," *New York Times*, 4 April 2007, 7(A).

50. Reuters, "U.S. Military Says it Captured 5 Iranians Linked to Group that Arms Insurgents in Iraq," *Washington Post*, 14 January 2007, 16(A); David E. Sanger and Michael R. Gordon, "Bush Authorized Iranians' Arrest in Iraq, Rice Says," *New York Times*, 13 January 2007, 1(A).

51. Editorial, "Valuable Lessons," *Los Angeles* Times, 6 April 2006, 24(A).

52. Patrick Cockburn, "The Botched US Raid that Led to the Hostage Crisis," *Independent*, 3 April 2007, http://news.independent.co.uk/world/middle_east/article2414760.-ece (5 Apr. 2007).; Patrick Cockburn, "American Raid and Arrests Set Scene for Capture of Marines," *Independent*, 26 March 2007, http://news.independent.co.uk/world/middle_-east/article2393336.ece (5 Apr. 2007).

53. Cockburn, "The Botched US Raid that Led to the Hostage Crisis," 2007.

54. Times, "Britons Seized in 'Revenge' Mission," *Times*, 3 April 2007, Sec. 1, 2; Guardian, "Provocation," *Guardian*, 3 April 2007.

55. Neil Cavuto, *Your World with Neil Cavuto*, Fox News, 6 December 2004.

56. Aaron Brown, *CNN Presents*, CNN, 11 December 2004.

57. Nicholas D. Kristof, "N. Korea, 6, and Bush, 0," *New York Times*, 26 April 2006, 19(A).

58. Associated Press, "North Korea: Washington Flew 1,200 Spy Flights Over Country," *Fox News*, 25 July 2004, http://www.foxnews.com/story/0,2933,126940,00.html (3 Aug. 2005).

59. Associated Press, "U.S. Repositioning Bombers Near North Korea," *USA Today*, 4 March 2003, http://www.usatoday.com/news/world/2003-03-04-us-nkorea_x.htm (15 Jun. 2005).

60. Joseph Kahn, "China Says U.S. Impeded North Korea Arms Talks," *New York Times*, 13 May 2005, http://www.nytimes.com/2005/05/13/international/asia/13korea.ht ml?ex=1273636800&en=d682b8ecb7abc176&ei=5088&partner=rssnyt&emc=rss (13 May 2005).

61. Bruce Cummings, "Decoupled from History: North Korea in the "Axis of Evil," in *Inventing the Axis of Evil: The Truth about North Korea*, eds. Bruce Cummings, Ervand Abrahamian, and Moshe Ma'oz (New York: New Press, 2004), 62.

62. Stanley Kurtz, "An Ominous Cloud," *National Review*, 21 March 2003, http://www.nationalreview.com/kurtz/kurtz032103.asp (14 May 2005).

63. Ashton B. Carter and William J. Perry, "If Necessary, Strike and Destroy," *Washington Post*, 22 June 2006, 29(A).

64. William J. Perry, "In Search of a North Korea Policy," *Washington Post*, 11 October 2006, 19(A).

65. Editorial, "North Korea and Iran," *Washington Times*, 11 October 2006, http://www.washingtontimes.com/op-ed/20061010-090342-4850r.htm (20 Mar. 2007).

66. Editorial, "North Korea's Threat," *Washington* Post, 12 February 2005, 18(A).

67. Kurtz, "An Ominous Cloud," 2003.

68. CBS News, "N. Korea, Iran: Twin Nuke Troubles," 28 September 2004, http://www.cbsnews.com/stories/2004/09/28/politics/main645949.shtml (8 Dec. 2005).

69. Jasper Becker, "It's Time to Disengage with Kim Jong Il," *Time*, 14 February 2005, http://www.time.com/time/asia/covers/501050221/nk_vpt.html (18 Jul. 2005).

70. Aaron Brown, *CNN NewsNight*, CNN, 14 July 2004.

71. Jim Yardley and David E. Sanger, "In Shift, A Deal is Being Weighed by North Korea," *New York Times*, 13 February 2007, 1(A).

72. Editorial, "The Lesson of North Korea," *New York Times*, 14 February 2007, http://www.nytimes.com/2007/02/14/opinion/14wed1.html?ex=1329109200&en=970339 af3c46e985&ei=5088&partner=rssnyt&emc=rss (26 Feb. 2007).

73. Editorial, "North Korea's Folly," *New York Times*, 5 July 2006, http://www.nytimes.com/2006/07/05/opinion/05wed2.html?ex=1309752000&en=0142d1 0205e5b473&ei=5090&partner=rssuserland&emc=rss (26 Feb. 2007).

74. John O'Sullivan, "'Success' in N. Korea will Fail in Long Run," *Chicago Sun Times*, 20 February 2007, http://www.suntimes.com/news/osullivan/263597,CST-EDT-osul20.article (20 Feb. 2007).

75. Editorial, "Ignoring Hawks, Changing Tack," *Boston Globe*, 24 March 2007, http://www.boston.com/news/globe/editorial_opinion/editorials/articles/2007/03/24/ignoring_hawks_changing_tack?mode=PF (24 Mar. 2007).

76. Editorial, "North Korea Talks," *Washington Post*, 1 November 2006, 20(A).

77. Associated Press, "North Korean Reactors Canceled," *International Herald Tribune*, 23 November 2005, http://www.iht.com/articles/2005/11/23/news/reactor.php (26 Nov. 2005).

78. CNN.com, "Cheney Plays Down N. Korea Strike Calls," 23 June 2006, http://www.cnn.com/2006/WORLD/asiapcf/06/22/nkorea.missile/index.html (23 Jun. 2006.

79. Le Tian, "Nuclear Talks Reach 'Fork in the Road,'" *China Daily*, 18 December 2006, http://www.chinadaily.com.cn/china/2006-12/18/content_760984.htm (20 Mar. 2007).

80. Dan Plesch, "North Korea's Nuclear Policy is not Irrational at all," *Guardian*, 10 October 2006, http://www.guardian.co.uk/comment/story/0,,1891454,00.html (10 Oct. 2006).

81. Tim Beal, "North Korea's Nuclear Test—Bush's Godchild?," Z Magazine, 6 November 2006, http://www.zmag.org/content/showarticle.cfm?ItemID=11358 (6 Nov. 2006).

Conclusion

Progressive Media Reform:
A Movement for the 21st Century

While corporate consolidation and conglomeration increasingly define American media ownership, these trends are relatively recent, and hardly inevitable. Furthermore, the extreme monopolization of American media documented by media critics like Ben Bagdikian is even more recent, spanning over only the last few decades. Gerald Baldasty, author of *The Commercialization of the News in the Nineteenth Century*, recounts that the trend toward mass advertising and conglomeration in media did not begin to materialize until the late nineteenth and early twentieth centuries: "Advertising in the American press grew dramatically in the late nineteenth century. Advertising was virtually nonexistent at the time of the Civil War; by World War I, advertising expenditures had passed a billion dollars annually. . . advertisers had arrived as the key constituent of the American press. Their vision of the press was fundamentally commercial in nature. They cared little about the news function of the press and sought, instead, to assure that newspapers served their own marketing needs. They provided much of the newspapers' revenues and profits, and, in turn, expected a grateful press to help them when possible."[1]

Today, critiques of corporate media ownership and monopolization are not merely restricted to dissidents operating outside of the system. Consensus has materialized amongst a number of prominent people in the media, in opposition to prioritizing profits over quality reporting of the news.

The Problem of Media Monopoly

In highlighting the dangers of the monopolization of media, veteran reporters and editors from within the mainstream media have laid out the vital first step in a mass movement toward media transformation. Gene Robert's edited work, *Leaving Readers Behind: The Age of Corporate Newspapering*, incorporates the perspectives of a number of insider journalists who draw attention to the detrimental effects of conglomeration on media competition. Cost cutting has resulted in a "diminishing amount of real news available," as newspapers and news reports become "thinner and blander," and "some stories simply never get covered" at all due to the pressures of ever increasing profits.[2] Bonnie Anderson, a long-time reporter for *CNN* and *MSNBC*, comments: "For the corporations that own the major television news organizations, journalism has become exclusively a bottom-line business." Anderson cites a number of grievances pertaining to the current path of bottom-line reporting, including "repeated cutbacks in staff"; "trimmed international bureaus as well as domestic news offices"; and the "adding of entertainment to news, and getting rid of older correspondents in favor of younger, more attractive ones."[3]

While growing dissent at middle and lower ranks in corporate media is becoming increasingly common, executives are also beginning to join the fray in their concern over the consequences of monopolization. Ted Turner, founder of *CNN* and former Vice Chairman at *AOL-Time Warner*, is among the most vociferous about the perils of monopoly domination, lambasting a media climate where "independent broadcasters simply don't survive for long" and "media companies are more concentrated than at any time over the past forty years, thanks to a continual loosening of ownership rules by Washington."[4] Turners' warnings are based in large part on his own experiences at *CNN* and *TBS* before they were absorbed by *AOL-Time Warner*:

> When *CNN* reported to me, if we needed more money for Kosovo or Baghdad, we'd find it. If we had to bust the budget, we busted the budget. We put journalism first, and that's how we built *CNN* into something the world wanted to watch. I had the power to make these budget decisions because they were my companies. I was an independent entrepreneur who controlled the majority of the votes and could run my company for the long term. Top managers in these huge media conglomerates run their companies for the short term. After we sold *Turner Broadcasting* to *Time Warner*, we came under such earnings pressure that we had to cut our promotion budget every year at *CNN* to make our numbers. Media mega-mergers inevitably lead to an overemphasis on short-term earnings.[5]

Former *CBS* lead anchor Walter Cronkite has also spoken up against the corporate obsession with profits to the neglect of professional journalism. In a keynote address to graduate students at Columbia University's School of Journalism, Cronkite chastised media corporations for cutting resources needed "to expose truths that powerful politicians and special interests often [do] not want exposed." Journalists "face rounds and rounds of job cuts and cost cuts that require them to do ever more with ever less." Although "consolidation and cost cutting may be good for the bottom line in the short-term," Cronkite warned, "that isn't necessarily good for the country or the healthy of the news business in the long-term."[6] Tom Rosentiel, a former *Los Angeles* reporter, complains about the current state of corporate reporting: "the problem is most [papers] are not engaged in a lot of serious news gathering. They are largely engaged in repackaging material that other people have produced."[7]

When "Huge Profits" Are Not Enough

It has become modus operandi for media executives to claim that reductions in profits and circulations justify further vertical and horizontal integration. As newspapers continue to lose revenue to Internet advertising, and since fewer and fewer Americans are following print media—so the argument goes—media firms are forced to look for new ways to adapt. While declines in circulation are hardly of a major magnitude, they are significant enough for corporate managers to take notice. The *Chicago Tribune* reports, as of late 2006, that "Eighteen of the top twenty U.S. newspapers showed slippage in average weekday circulation."[8] While technological innovations like the Internet have transformed the advertising industry, to the detriment of other media sources, print media is in no danger of extinction. While the *Chicago Tribune* reports: "the industry still generates huge profits," the paper defends cuts in budgets and layoffs, citing the "pressure [placed on firms] to become more efficient."[9] Major newspapers have acted accordingly, forcing large numbers of employees out of work and filtering out those who stand in the way. In one instance, Dean Baquet, an editor for the *Los Angeles Times*, was fired after refusing another round of job cuts, as over 200 people were laid off at a time when the paper's circulation had dropped by 8 percent to over 750,000 readers per issue.[10]

Although the relative declines in readership and advertising revenue are clearly significant, it would be a mistake to overestimate their impact on the power of corporate media. Although Internet news sites and advertisers are now competing with more traditional news mediums, older news sources still generate immense profits, more so than they did in previous decades. This has not stopped reporters from exaggerating the threats prominent newspapers face from other advertising mediums. The *Tribune Co.*, for example, along with its "struggling properties," was framed as "under an unprecedented state of siege from [advertising on] the Internet."[11]

Thomas Williams, former state and federal court reporter for the *Hartford Courant* questions the claim that big media is in the midst of financial crisis today:

> In spite of the Internet's allure, and a variety of news sites like *Salon* and *Slate*, many competing newspapers are still making 20 percent profits. That is five percent more than used to be acceptable in the decades when publishers understood the costly but essential responsibility of being part of the Fourth Estate, while scrutinizing and reporting on government and corporate corruption.[12]

As expectations of major increases in profits have been met with disappointment in recent years, journalism continues to suffer due to cost cutting and downsizing. The fixation with ever-increasing profits is the inevitable consequence of further corporate conglomeration; and although media companies remain extraordinarily lucrative, this is simply not seen as enough in the minds of business elites expecting each quarter's profits to significantly exceed its predecessor.

The Ideology of Monopolization

Although it may be difficult to find many defenders of media consolidation amongst the general public, ideological justifications for loosening ownership rules remain commonplace amongst media elites. It should come as no shock that the media conglomerates standing to make the most from the relaxation of media regulations are the most vehemently supportive of such initiatives. Corporations such as *News Corporation, Viacom, AOL-Time Warner, Disney,* and others stand at the forefront of the lobbying movement aimed at convincing political leaders and government regulators about the virtues of "deregulation." Initiatives aimed at removing hurdles to consolidation are vital, as far as media executives are concerned, for their companies to become much larger, more profitable, and less competitive. While media firms do "compete" with each other on some level, a true forum for competition amongst these companies is actually quite undesirable for media executives and owners, who view the high-stakes that come along with cut-throat competition as a serious danger to their companies' dominance and pursuit of profit.

While many intellectuals, media personalities, and political leaders are hesitant to publicly defend unpopular "deregulatory" efforts directed at big media ownership, a small group of affluent and determined government officials and regulators, corporate elites, and intellectuals have stepped forward to pursue such a goal. Stephen Hayes of the neoconservative *Weekly Standard* defends corporate monopoly domination and increased media consolidation under the assumption that it has *increased* diversity of programming and views: "Is there any question that news consumers today have more options—and more high-quality options—today than ever before? Include news websites and, more recently, smart and informative weblogs, and the 'media consolidation' arguments crumble."[13] FCC commissioner Kathleen Abernathy has dismissed warnings about the dangers of a "mythical media monopoly."[14] Similarly, Jack Shafer of *Slate* magazine points to a significant number of media institutions, such as the *New York Times, Los Angeles Times, Washington Post, Wall Street Journal,* which exist outside of the "Big Five" media firms that critics like Ben Bagdikian address when they discuss media monopoly.

More than any other public figure, Michael Powell, former Chairman of the Federal Communications Commission and son of former Secretary of State Colin Powell, has served as the poster boy for the media consolidation movement.[15] Powell has long been a staunch supporter of the "market" approach to regulating media, expounded upon by a number of academics. Elliot Cohen, in his work *Corporate Media Ownership and its Threat to Democracy*, speaks of this "corporate theology"—"the faith that somehow, by letting these corporate monolithic giants pursue their bottom line, the common good will be served in the end...by deregulating the corporate media, letting its bottom line freely expand, it will more efficiently deliver what viewers need and want."[16] Powell's stance clearly fits the "free market" description provided by Cohen. At the forefront of the media consolidation movement—at least before the 2003 public backlash—Powell was described by *Business Week* as a "brilliant visionary" for his efforts "to liberate the media from ownership caps."[17] But Powell has not been deemed a visionary because of any deep understanding of how media regulation can further the public good, for he himself has admitted that he has "no idea" what even constitutes the public interest.[18] Rather, his positions have been celebrated by corporate America because of his staunch commitment to furthering corporate profits, regardless of any negative effects on media diversity and the quality of journalism.

As the former head of one of the United States' most prominent regulatory bodies, Powell has paradoxically advocated an approach that "let(s) markets pick winners and losers," and where "the oppressor is regulation."[19] Powell systematically refused to consider the argument that consolidation might be detrimental to the common good, claiming that: "monopoly is not illegal by itself in the United States." He expressed befuddlement toward warnings regarding the dangers of plutocratic domination of the media, since such warnings have "been so thoroughly discredited in this nation and in countries around the world."[20] Powell is not beyond distorting reality in framing the importance of "deregulation." In defending rollbacks on FCC regulations on media ownership, Powell cited "a real worry about the long-term survivability of free, over-the-air television," postulating that "I think there is a very easy way for it to collapse" under current legal restrictions.[21]

Powell's ardently pro-business position set the stage for the public battle against the FCC as it ruled in a 2003 decision to relax media ownership restrictions. By mid-year, the stage had been set for FCC commissioners to throw out a number of regulations spanning back decades, prohibiting media companies from owning multiple venues in the same market. The commission, citing a need to update allegedly outdated media rules, threw out rules preventing one corporation from owning both a newspaper and television or radio station within the same market, as well as allowing a single media firm to own networks and stations that reach up to 45 percent of the nation, rather than the old 35 percent maximum. Agency staffers also recommended revising another rule prohibiting a single company from owning more than two television stations within larger markets. The *Washington Post* reported that effects of the ruling "are likely to unleash a wave of buying," similar to that of the 1996 Telecommunications Act, which rescinded national limits on how many radio stations a corporation could own.[22] One such merger was pursued shortly after the ruling, between *DirecTV* and *News Corporation*, which added an audience of over ten million to the *News Corp.* conglomerate.

The campaign to downplay the negative consequences of media monopoly extends beyond Michael Powell. One could implicate the FCC itself in deception as well, as evidence has surfaced of its complicity in concealing reports highlighting the negative effects of media conglomeration. Two reports were "shelved" by agency officials, although later leaked to Democratic political leaders. One of the reports suggested that locally owned stations operating outside media conglomerates actually produce *more* news than local stations owned by large media firms. The other report highlighted the harmful effects of the 1996 Telecommunications Act on the radio industry, summarizing that between 1996 and 2003, while the number of commercial radio stations increased nationally by almost 6 percent, the number of station owners actually decreased by 35 percent, as fewer and fewer companies bought up more outlets.[23]

Public Rebellion and the Government Response

Few may have expected the mass public uprising following the ill-publicized 2003 FCC decision. The diversity of the groups that rose up to protest the FCC ruling demonstrated that the issue of media reform is not merely one of "Left" vs. "Right," but one concerning the strength and viability of American democracy. Will Americans tune in and read from news sources owned and dominated by fewer and fewer vested business interests, or will there be some diversity amongst their choices?

At the forefront of the public rebellion, surprisingly, were commissioners of the FCC itself, specifically Michael Copps and Jonathan Adelstein. In a passionate attack on the FCC's three Republican commissioners, Adelstein remarked:

> The public stands little to gain and everything to lose by slashing the protections that have served them for decades. This plan is likely to damage the media landscape for generations to come. It threatens to degrade civil discourse and the quality of our society's intellectual, cultural and political life. I dissent, finding today's Order poor public policy, indefensible under the law, and inimical to the public interest and the health of our democracy.[24]

Copps cited grassroots public opposition as his main reason for opposing the ruling: "During the more than a dozen hearings and forums on media concentration that I attended from coast to coast, I saw and heard first-hand stories of hundreds of citizens about the detrimental impact that consolidation has already had on their local media and their fears about where still more concentration will lead."[25] Copps' experiences with public opinion are reinforced by national polls revealing similar feelings amongst the general public. One poll taken around the time of the FCC ruling indicated that about 50 percent of those questioned felt that increased media consolidation was a "negative development," whereas the number increased dramatically to 70 percent amongst those who followed the issue more closely. Conversely, just 10 percent of those questioned viewed more consolidation as a good thing.[26] Public activism also reached an impressive magnitude, as over two million letters, faxes, and e-mails of complaint were sent into the FCC in opposition to the new ruling.[27] Activists from diverse groups, including *Code Pink*, the *NRA*, *MoveOn.org*, *Free Press*, *NOW*, and the *Parents Television Council*, joined together to challenge the FCC ruling.

Powell's Intransigence

As mentioned earlier, Powell was generally hesitant to take into account public protests of the FCC ruling. Commissioner Copps' suggestions that the FCC organize hearings around the country about media consolidation were met with animosity by Powell, who refused to attend any of the nine scheduled events. In regards to public opinion, Powell displayed his lack of concern by explaining that, while opposition to deregulation may be opposed by most Americans, "The [FCC] does not have the luxury of always doing what is popular."[28] In addition, Powell provided little more than generic justifications for his stance, claiming that Congress required that the organization undertake a full review of the older regulations in question. That may have been the case, but this did not mean that Congress *required* the elimination of ownership limits placed upon media conglomerates.

Powell chose to ignore the ways in which increased monopolization would hurt media diversity. Contrary to the Powell's claims about deregulation and media freedom, the Supreme Court ruled in 1978 that: "diversification of mass media ownership serves the public interest by promoting diversity of program and service viewpoints, as well as by preventing undue concentration of economic power."[29] As the court's ruling suggests, when a small number of corporations dominate what most Americans see and read, the citizenry is restricted to choosing between the viewpoints of a small number of elites. And while there may be more television channels and radio stations today than at any other time in recent history, the narrow ownership of those outlets ensures a strong uniformity of news and views. This book has been dedicated to exposing the extreme imbalance that already exists in the corporate media when it comes to open debate, and a full discussion of controversial issues. It is difficult to see how *further* consolidation will do anything but exacerbate this problem.

Congress and the Courts Take Action

As swiftly as the FCC ruled to relax media ownership rules, American political leaders stepped in to roll back the agency's unpopular measures. Democratic Senator Byron Dorgan attacked the commission's actions as "wrongheaded and destructive." Dorgan worried that the ruling would set the stage for "an orgy of mergers and acquisitions," and blamed the FCC for not having "the strength to stand up against corporate interests."[30] Presidential candidate Howard Dean promised that: "I certainly would reverse media deregulation. . . . I would go back to the limitations on how many stations you can own in a given market."[31]

By September of 2003, a panel from the Philadelphia Third Circuit U.S. Court of Appeals ruled in favor of the *Prometheus Radio Project*, prohibiting the FCC's ruling from being implemented; by June of 2004, the court had thrown out the FCC's decision entirely, sending the issue back to the FCC for consideration. By 2004, Congress had also voted to repeal the 45 percent ownership cap set by the FCC, setting the new restrictions so that a single media firm could only reach up to 39 percent of the nation's total audience.[32] Political rebukes of the FCC were so strong that they appear to have pressured the Bush administration to reconsider its plans to appeal the Circuit Court's ruling to the Supreme Court.

Despite the public's "victory" against the FCC ruling, the movement for media reform remains largely reactive, rather than proactive, in terms of challenging corporate media monopolization. A small number of corporations continue to dominate the American mainstream media, and serious dissent questioning government propaganda is still sorely lacking in most media coverage. Clearly then, a more proactive approach is sorely needed if activists and citizens groups are ever to realize their vision of mass media transformation.

Proposals for Media Reform

For media reform to succeed, citizen groups must pursue a dynamic, multi-faceted campaign aimed at the American public, as well as political leaders and media institutions. Media critics have made a number of proposals for change, some which may be achieved from within the current political system, and some of which will require pressure and action from the outside. Journalist Steve Rendall of *Fairness and Accuracy in Reporting* supports a renewed application of the Fairness Doctrine as a means of better balancing political debate in the mainstream press. The Fairness Doctrine, although repealed during the Reagan administration, was designed in order to promote diversity of viewpoints in media by requiring outlets to allow the expression of multiple points of view on important issues. Rendall summarizes about the Fairness Doctrine that:

> As a guarantor of balance and inclusion, the Fairness Doctrine was no panacea. It was somewhat vague, and depended on the vigilance of listeners and viewers to notice imbalance. But its value, beyond the occasional remedies it provided, was in its codification of the principle that broadcasters had a responsibility to present a range of views on controversial issues.[33]

While reinstitution of the Fairness Doctrine is surely no end-all solution to the problem of corporate media bias, it is an important step in terms of reaffirming media responsibility in fulfilling public interest obligations for more balanced debate. One area in particular where the doctrine might be most effective is in regards to news and talk radio, which have long been dominated by conservative and reactionary commentators. Clearly, the Fairness Doctrine would not prohibit conservative views from being expressed, but it would prevent them from being the *only* views expressed in radio news outlets.

While the growth of technology and the increasing popularity of the Internet have been touted as a remedy for increased media consolidation, scholars have expressed major reservations. Robert McChesney disputes the assumption that the Internet will rectify the problem of media conglomeration: "Those who believe that all they need is a website and protection from government censorship to leapfrog the commercial media are dreaming. . . . The Internet has not spawned a new group of commercially viable media companies with existing firms...the leading media content websites are primarily associated with media giants."[34] As with more traditional news mediums, the Internet is dominated by a small number of corporations that blackball substantive dissenters who challenge status quo political ideas.

An "answer" to the problem of media uniformity, then, rests in large part with a further diversification of ownership and control of media, rather than further conglomeration. In his book, *The Problem of the Media: U.S. Communication Politics in the 21st Century*, McChesney theorizes: "The bias in free societies must be toward diverse and decentralized ownership whenever possible...we need a strong nonprofit and noncommercial media sector. Such a sector is necessary for high-quality children's programming, experimental entertainment, and high-quality material frowned upon by the market."[35] Corporate owners have demonstrated that they lack the willingness to pursue critical news programming independent of corporate profit motivations. As *Clear Channel* CEO Lowry Mays explains: "We're not in the business of providing news and information...we're simply in the business of selling our customers' products."[36] A major structural solution to this problem, then, seems to entail support for a viable public media sector that can exist alongside corporate media.

But what exactly would such a "public" media look like? The U.S. government and taxpayers already subsidize the *Public Broadcasting Service*. Is this outlet an adequate alternative to corporate media, as far as critics of media monopoly are concerned? In short, most critics would likely answer a resounding no, considering that *PBS* has increasingly been dominated by corporate donors and business-oriented content as its budget is slashed further and further. One study conducted by media professor William Hoynes of a two week period of *PBS* broadcasting analyzed seventy-five different programs, only to find a strong bias in favor of business officials. Over one-third of all guests in those two weeks were corporate officials, while 75 percent of the stories dealing with economic issues were directly corporate or investment-related.[37]

Along similar lines to McChesney and other critics, consumer activist Ralph Nader endorses the creation of a vastly larger public media sector, funded by taxpayer dollars. Rather than controlled directly by the government, Nader supports funding for a media system which is run by "government-chartered, citizen membership organizations."[38] Danny Schechter supports the creation of a "Media Democracy Act," whereby political leaders and citizens groups might "package proposals for an anti-trust program to break up media monopolies," in addition to supporting "free broadcasts for political debate across the spectrum;

limits on advertising and monitoring for honesty and accuracy," and "guarantees for media freedom in the public interest."[39]

Although there has been much speculation on particularly *what* a new public media would look like, it should also be noted that a number of participatory media outlets already exist. The *New Standard*, for example, is a nonprofit media outlet, which is supported entirely by reader donations, rather than through advertising. The paper provides critical news reports on domestic and global news, questioning economic and political elites who hold major power. Other examples of grassroots media that provide critical, independent news include *Alternet, Z Magazine, Truthout, In These Times,* the *Progressive,* and *Common Dreams,* all of which are known for their adversarial editorials and reporting. While these outlets, in-and-of themselves are not the "answer" to the problem of corporate media monopolization, they do demonstrate that public media alternatives do exist, should citizens and political leaders desire to forge a new route and create a vibrant national public media system.

With the onset of the National Conference for Media Reform, citizen activism has transitioned from the initial discussion phase of media reform into active planning. The first conference, held in 2003, was attended by a coalition of hundreds of activist groups, including *MoveOn.org, Media Channel, FAIR, Common Cause, Reclaim the Media, Free Press,* and *Free Speech TV,* amongst other organizations. Similarly, thousands of activists attended the 2005 follow-up conference, as was also the case with the 2007 conference, held in Memphis. One of the most promising prospects to come out of the 2007 conference was House Representative Dennis Kucinich's commitment to place media reform at the forefront of federal policy debates in the future. In supporting the creation of a new House subcommittee specifically for the purpose of exploring possibilities for structural media change, Kucinich demonstrated that leaders at the highest levels of government are addressing the problem of media monopoly.

It should be noted that opposition to media consolidation draws its legitimacy primarily from the activities and demands of citizens and activist groups committed to media reforms. Activist groups have provided the brunt of public pressure needed to roll back the FCC's efforts at media "deregulation." Just as citizen groups have been at the center of the campaign to roll back the FCC's 2003 ruling, so too will such groups need to stand at the forefront of a movement to create a reinvigorated public media system. Such a system needs to be independent of corporate funding, influence, and control, as well as from government censorship and manipulation.

Those participating in the creation of an independent public media need to be drawn from a wider range of the American public than the current group running corporate media in favor of government and business interests. Any truly independent public media system would also need to incorporate a far wider spectrum of opinion in its reporting and editorializing, as contrasted with the current standard in corporate media of relying disproportionately on government and business officials to the exclusion of dissident voices. Citizen groups would also be needed to ensure a critical standard of reporting, perhaps through an oversight role or one involving more direct participation in creating the news.

Clearly, the exact role of such groups would obviously need to be determined through extensive public deliberation. The question of how to create democratic media in the U.S. is far too important to be left to one individual, or to be addressed in just one book. This book's goal has been far more modest than laying out a comprehensive plan for revolutionary media reform, as I have sought to thoroughly dissect corporate media bias, while also providing a glimpse into future prospects for media transformation. Aside from promoting substantive change in the American media, I encourage newsreaders and viewers to follow mass media reporting with a more critical eye. Understanding the major problems and biases associated with media reporting and editorializing is the first step in understanding how to bring about positive change within that system.

Notes

1. Gerald J. Baldasty, *The Commercialization of the News in the Nineteenth Century* (Madison, Wi.: University of Wisconsin, 1992), 59-60.

2. Gene Roberts, ed., "Leaving Readers Behind," *Leaving Readers Behind: The Age of Corporate Newspapering* (Fayetteville, Ak.: University of Arkansas, 2001), 2, 3, 15.

3. Bonnie Anderson, *News Flash: Journalism, Infotainment, and the Bottom-Line Business of Broadcast News* (San Francisco: Wiley & Sons, 2004), 9-10.

4. Ted Turner, "My Beef with Big Media," *Washington Monthly*, July/August 2004, http://www.washingtonmonthly.com/features/2004/0407.turner.html

5. Turner, "My Beef with Big Media," 2004.

6. Anick Jesdanun, "Cronkite Warns Drive for Media Profits Poses Threat to Democracy," *Associated Press*, 9 February 2007, http://www.commondreams.org/headlines07/-0209-11.htm (15 Apr. 2007).

7. Jesdanun, 2007.

8. Phil Rosenthal, "Circulation for Biggest Papers Shows Few Signs of Turnaround," *Chicago Tribune*, sec. 3, 31 October 2006, 1.

9. Michael Oneal, "A Tidal Shift for Newspapers," *Chicago Tribune*, sec. 3, 2 November 2006, 1.

10. Mary Wisniewski, "Trib Forces out L.A. editor," *Chicago Sun Times*, 8 November 2006, 69.

11. Frank Ahrens and David Cho, "New Tune for the 'Grave Dancer,'" *Washington Post*, 3 April 2007, 1(D); Michael Oneal and David Greising, "Entrepreneur Faces Daunting Challenge," *Chicago Tribune*, 2 April 2007, http://www.chicagotribune.com/business-chi-070402zell-profile,1,6531843.story (15 Apr. 2007).

12. Thomas D. Williams, "The Decline of Journalism," *Truthout*, 20 November 2006, http://www.truthout.org/docs_2006/printer_112006Z.shtml (13 Jan. 2007).

13. Stephen Hayes, "Beware Corporate Domination," *Weekly Standard*, 31 May 2002, http://www.weeklystandard.com/content/public/articles/000/000/001/302cgoxv.asp?pg=2 (13 Jan. 2007).

14. Jim Lehrer, *Online Newshour*, PBS, 2 June 2003, http://www.pbs.org/newshour/bb/media/jan-june03/powell_6-2.html (14 Jan. 2007).

15. Jack Shafer, "The Media Monotony," *Slate*, 4 August 2004, http://www.slate.com/-id/2104777/ (14 Jan. 2007).

16. Elliot D. Cohen, "Corporate Media's Betrayal of America," in *News Incorporated: Corporate Media Ownership and its Threat to Democracy*, ed. Elliot D. Cohen (Amherst, NY: Prometheus, 2005), 20.

17. Jane Black, "Michael Powell's Communication Failure," *Business Week*, 23 July 2003, http://www.businessweek.com/technology/content/jul2003/tc20030723_5352_tc0-24.htm (13 Jan. 2007).

18. Janine Jackson, "Their Man in Washington," *Extra!* September/October 2001, http://www.fair.org/extra/0109/powell.html (13 Jan. 2007).

19. Robert McChesney, "The Escalating War Against Corporate Media," *Monthly Review*, March 2004, http://www.monthlyreview.org/0304mcchesney.htm (13 Jan. 2007).

20. Jackson, "Their Man in Washington," 2001.

21. Eric Boehlert, "Last Stop Before the Media Monopoly," Salon, 23 May 2003, http://dir.salon.com/story/news/feature/2003/05/23/powells_fight/index.html (13 Jan. 2007).

22. Frank Ahrens, "A New Era for Media Firms?" *Washington Post*, 13 May 2003, 1(E).

23. John Dunbar, "Senator Says Media Study Suppressed," *Boston Globe*, 18 September 2006, http://www.boston.com/news/nation/washington/articles/2006/09/18/senator_says_media_study_suppressed/ (14 Jan. 2007).

24. Jonathan Adelstein, "A Dark Storm Cloud is Looming over the Future of the American Media," *Common Dreams*, 2 June 2003, http://www.commondreams.org/views03/0602-13.htm (13 Jan. 2007).

25. Michael Copps, "Where is the Public Interest in Media Consolidation?" in *The Future of Media: Resistance and Reform in the 21st* Century, Ed. Robert McChesney, Russell Newman, and Ben Scott (New York: Seven Stories, 2005), 120.

26. Eric Boehlert, "Congress to Big Media: Not so Fast," *Salon*, 23 June 2003, http://dir.salon.com/story/news/feature/2003/07/23/fcc/index_np.html (13 Jan. 2007); Pew Research Center, "Strong Opposition to Media Cross-Ownership Emerges," 14 July 2003, http://people-press.org/reports/display.php3?ReportID=188 (13 Jan. 2007).

27. Amy Goodman, "In Surprise Decision, Federal Judges Block FCC Media Ownership Rules," *Democracy Now!*, 4 September 2003.

28. Stephen Labaton, "Senators Move to Restore FCC Limits on the Media," *Truthout*, 5 June 2003, http://www.truthout.org/cgi-bin/artman/exec/view.cgi/19/939 (13 Jan. 2007).

29. Elliot D. Cohen, "Corporate Media's Betrayal of America," in *News Incorporated: Corporate Media Ownership and its Threat to Democracy*, ed. Elliot D. Cohen (Amherst, NY: Prometheus, 2005), 160.

30. Labaton, 2003.

31. Jim VandeHei, "Dean Calls for New Controls on Business," *Washington Post*, 19 November 2003, 9(A).

32. Andrew Jay Schwartzman, Cheryl A. Leanza, and Harold Feld, "The Legal Case for Diversity in Broadcast Ownership," in *The Future of Media: Resistance and Reform in the 21st* Century, Ed. Robert McChesney, Russell Newman, and Ben Scott (New York, NY: Seven Stories, 2005), 151; Amy Goodman, "In a Stunning 400-21 Vote, House Howls Foul Over Powell & FCC Media Regulations," *Democracy Now!*, 24 July 2003, http://www.democracynow.org/article.pl?sid=03/07/24/1510216 (13 Jan. 2007).

33. Steven Rendall, "The Fairness Doctrine," *Extra!* January/February 2005, http://www.fair.org/index.php?page=2053 (13 Jan. 2007).

34. Robert McChesney, *The Problem of the Media: U.S. Communication Politics in the 21st Century* (New York: Monthly Review, 2004), p. 220-21.

35. McChesney, *The Problem of the Media*, 226, 248.

36. Hightower, Jim, "The People's Media Reaches More People Than Fox Does," *Common Dreams*, 15 June 2004, http://www.commondreams.org/views04/0615-14.htm (15 Apr. 2007).

37. FAIR, "New Study: Public TV More Corporate, Less Public Than Ever," 28 June 1999, http://www.fair.org/index.php?page=1905 (14 Jan. 2007).

38. Ralph Nader, "Bold Proposals," *Boston Review*, 2007, http://www.bostonreview.net/BR23.3/nader.html (12 Jan. 2007).

39. Danny Schechter, "Why We Need a Media Democracy Act," *Common Dreams*, 22 May 2005, http://www.commondreams.org/views05/0522-25.htm (15 Jan. 2007).

Bibliography

Achcar, Gilbert. *The Clash of the Barbarisms: September 11 and the Making of the New World Order*. New York: Monthly Review, 2002.

Alger, Dean. *Megamedia: How Giant Corporations Dominate Mass Media, Distort Competition, and Endanger Democracy*. Lanham, Md.: Rowman & Littlefield, 1998.

Ali, Tariq, and David Barsamian. *Speaking of Empire and Resistance: Conversations with Tariq Ali*. London: New Press, 2005.

Anderson, Bonnie. *News Flash: Journalism, Infotainment, and the Bottom-Line Business of Broadcast News*. San Francisco: Wiley & Sons, 2004.

Bagdikian, Ben H. *The New Media Monopoly*. Boston: Beacon, 2004.

Baker, C. Edwin. *Advertising and a Democratic Press*. Princeton, NJ.: Princeton, 1994.

Baldasty, Gerald J. *The Commercialization of the News in the Nineteenth Century*. Madison, Wi.: University of Wisconsin, 1992. Bennett, W. Lance, and David L. Paletz. *Taken By Storm: The Media, Public Opinion, and U.S. Foreign Policy in the Gulf War*. Chicago: University of Chicago, 1994.

Barsamian, David., ed. *Stenographers to Power: Media & Propaganda*. Monroe, Me.: Common Courage, 1992.

Bennett, W. Lance, and David L. Paletz., eds. *Taken by Storm: The Media, Public Opinion, and U.S. Foreign Policy in the Gulf War*. Chicago: University of Chicago, 1994.

Bernays, Edward. *Propaganda*. New York: IG, 2005.

Blum, William. *Killing Hope: U.S. Military and CIA Interventions Since World War II*. Monroe, Me.: Common Courage, 1995.

Boggs, Carl., ed. *Masters of War: Militarism and Blowback in the Era of American Empire*. New York: Routledge, 2003.

Borjesson, Kristina., ed. *Feet to the Fire: The Media After 9/11*. New York: Prometheus, 2005.

Bozell, Brent L. *Weapons of Mass Distortion: The Coming Meltdown of the Liberal Media*. New York: Crown, 2004.

Burke, Jason. *Al Qaeda: The True Story of Radical Islam*. London: I.B. Tauris, 2004.

Chebab, Zaki. *Inside the Resistance: The Iraqi Insurgency and the Future of the Middle East*. New York: Nation, 2005.

Chomsky, Noam. *Necessary Illusions: Thought Control in Democratic Societies*. Boston: South End, 1989.

———. *9/11*. New York: Seven Stories, 2002.

———. *Failed States: The Abuse of Power and the Assault on Democracy*. New York: Metropolitan, 2006.

Chomsky, Noam, and David Barsamian. *Imperial Ambitions: Conversations on the Post 9/11 World*. New York: Metropolitan, 2005.

Clarke, Richard. *Against All Enemies*. New York: Free Press, 2004.

Cohen, Bernard C. *The Press and Foreign Policy*. Berkley, Ca.: University of California, 1993.

Cohen, Elliot D. *News Incorporated: Corporate Media Ownership and its Threat to Democracy*. Amherst, NY: Prometheus, 2005.

Cohen, Jeff. *Cable News Confidential: My Misadventures in Corporate Media*. Sausalito, Ca.: PoliPoint, 2006.

Coulter, Anne. *Slander: Liberal Lies About the American Right*. New York: Crown, 2002.

———. *Treason: Liberal Treachery From the Cold War to the War on Terrorism*. New York: Crown, 2003.

Crick, Bernard. *George Orwell: A Life*. London: Secker and Warburg, 1980.

Cromwell, David, and David Edwards. *Guardians of Power: The Myth of the Liberal Media*. London: Pluto, 2006.

Crothers, Lane, and Charles Lockhart., eds. *Culture and Politics: A Reader*. New York: St. Martins, 2000.

Crouteau, David, and William Hoynes. *By Invitation Only: How the Media Limit Political Debate*. Monroe, Me.: Common Courage, 1994.

Cummings, Bruce, Ervand Abrahamian, and Moshe Ma'oz. *Inventing the Axis of Evil: The Truth About North Korea, Iran, and Syria*. New York: New Press, 2004.

De Jong, Wilma, Martin Shaw, and Neil Stammers., eds. *Global Activism, Global Media*. Ann Arbor, Mi: Pluto, 2005.

Dearing, James W., and Everett M. Rogers. *Agenda Setting*. London: Sage, 1996.

El-Nawawy, Mohammed, and Adel Iskandar. *Al Jazeera: The Story of the Network That is Rattling Governments and Redefining Modern Journalism*. Cambridge: Westview, 2003.

Enders, David. *Baghdad Bulletin: Dispatches on the American Occupation*. Ann Arbor: Mi.: University of Michigan, 2005.

Entman, Robert. *Projections of Power: Framing News, Public Opinion, and U.S. Foreign Policy*. Chicago: University of Chicago, 2004.

Foerstel, Lenora., ed. *War Lies, & Videotape: How Media Monopoly Stifles Truth*. New York: IAC, 2000.

Glantz, Aaron. *How America Lost Iraq*. New York: Penguin, 2005.

Glasgow Media Group. *Really Bad News*. New York: Writers and Readers, 1982.

Goldberg, Bernard. *Arrogance: Rescuing America from the Media Elite*. New York: Warner, 2003.

Goodman, Amy. *Exception to the Rulers: Exposing Oil Politicians, War Profiteers, and the Media That Love Them*. New York: Hyperion, 2004.

Hannity, Sean. *Let Freedom Ring: Winning the War of Liberty Over Liberalism*. New York: Regan, 2002.

Herman, Edward, and Noam Chomsky. *Manufacturing Consent: The Political Economy of the Mass Media*. New York: Pantheon, 1988.

Herman, Edward. *The Myth of the Liberal Media: An Edward Herman Reader*. New York: Peter Lang, 1999.

Hersh, Seymour. *Chain of Command: The Road from 9/11 to Abu Ghraib*. New York: Harper Perennial, 2005.

Hitchens, Christopher. *Why Orwell Matters*. New York: Basic, 2002.

Hoynes, William. *Public Television for Sale: Media, the Market, and the Public Sphere*. Boulder, Co.: Westview, 1994.

Iyengar, Shanto, and Donald R. Kinder. *News That Matters: Television and American Opinion*. Chicago: University of Chicago, 1987.

Iyengar, Shanto. *Is Anyone Responsible? How Television Frames Political Issues*. Chicago: University of Chicago, 1991.

Johnson, Chalmers. *The Sorrows of Empire: Militarism, Secrecy, and the End of the Republic*. New York: Henry Holt, 2004.

Johnson, Chris, and Jolyon Leslie. *Afghanistan: The Mirage of Peace*. London: Zed, 2004.

Khalidi, Rashid. *Resurrecting Empire: Western Footprints and America's Perilous Path in the Middle East*. Boston: Beacon, 2003.

Lindblom, Charles. *Politics and Markets: The World's Political Economic Systems*. New York: Basic, 1977.

Lippmann, Walter. *Public Opinion*. New York: Free Press, 1997.

Lutz, William., ed. *Beyond Nineteen Eighty-Four: Doublespeak in a Post-Orwellian Age*. Urbana, Il.: National Council of Teachers of English, 1989.

Macarthur, John R. *Second Front: Censorship and Propaganda in the Gulf War*. Berkley, Ca.: University of California, 1993.

McChesney, Robert. *Rich Media, Poor Democracy: Communication Politics in Dubious Times*. New York: New Press, 1999.

———. *The Problem of the Media: U.S. Communication Politics in the 21st Century*. New York: Monthly Review, 2004.

McChesney, Robert, Russell Newman, and Ben Scott., eds. *The Future of Media: Resistance and Reform in the 21st Century*. New York: Seven Stories, 2005.

McCombs, Maxwell, and David L. Protess., eds. *Agenda Setting: Readings on Media, Public Opinion, and Policymaking*. Mahway, NJ: Lawrence Erlbaum, 1991.

McManus, John H. *Market-Driven Journalism: Let the Citizen Beware?* Thousand Oaks, Ca.: Sage, 1994.

Mermin, Jonathon. *Debating War and Peace: Media Coverage of U.S. Intervention in the Post-Vietnam Era*. Princeton, NJ: Princeton, 1999.

Meyers, Jeffrey. *Orwell: A Wintry Conscience of a Generation*. New York: W. W. Norton, 2000.

Miles, Hugh. *Al Jazeera: The Inside Story of the Arab News Channel That is Challenging the West*. New York: Grove, 2005.

Miller, David., ed. *Tell Me Lies: Propaganda and Media Distortion in the Attack on Iraq*. London: Pluto, 2004.

Nassar, Jamal. *Globalization and Terrorism: The Migration of Dreams and Nightmares*. Lanham, Md.: Rowman and Littlefield, 2004

Nichols, John, and Robert W. McChesney. *Tragedy & Farce: How the American Media Sell Wars, Spin Elections, and Destroy Democracy*. New York: New Press, 2006.

Orwell, George. *A Collection of Essays by George Orwell*. New York: Doubleday, 1954.

———. *Animal Farm: A Fairy Story*. New York: Harcourt Brace, 1995.

Orwell, Sonia, and Ian Angus. *The Collected Essays, Journalism, and Letters of George Orwell: 1945-1950, Vol. 4*. New York: Hancourt, Brace, & World, 1968.

Page, Benjamin I. *Who Deliberates? Mass Media in Modern Democracy*. Chicago: University of Chicago, 1996.

Parenti, Christian. *The Freedom: Shadows and Hallucinations in Occupied Iraq*. New York: Free Press, 2004.

Parenti, Michael. *Inventing Reality: The Politics of News Media*. New York: St. Martins, 1993.

———. *Against Empire*. San Francisco: City Lights, 1995.

———. *America Besieged*. San Francisco: City Lights, 1998.

Perse, Elizabeth M. *Media Effects and Society*. Mahway, NJ: Lawrence Erlbaum, 2001.

Pitt, William Rivers, and Scott Ritter. *War on Iraq: What Team Bush Doesn't Want You to Know*. New York: Context, 2002.

Rampton, Sheldon, and John Stauber. *The Best War Ever: Lies, Damned Lies, and the Mess in Iraq*. New York: Jeremy Tarcher, 2006.

Risen, James. *State of War: The Secret History of the CIA and the Bush Administration*. New York: Free Press, 2006.

Ritter, Scott. *Frontier Justice: Weapons of Mass Destruction and the Bushwhacking of America*. New York: Context, 2003.

Roberts, Gene., ed. *Leaving Readers Behind: The Age of Corporate Newspapering*. Fayetteville, Ak.: University of Arkansas, 2001.

Rogers, Paul. *A War on Terror: Afghanistan and After*. London: Pluto, 2004.

Soley, Lawrence. *Censorship Inc. The Corporate Threat to Free Speech in the United States*. New York: Monthly Review, 2002.

Solomon, Norman. *War Made Easy: How Presidents and Pundits Keep Spinning us to Death*. Hoboken, NJ: Wiley & Sons, 2005.

Sparrow, Bartholomew H. *Uncertain Guardians: The News Media as a Political Institution*. Baltimore: Johns Hopkins, 1999.

Squires, James D. *Read All About It! The Corporate Takeover of America's Newspapers*. New York: Times, 1993.

Z, Mickey. *The Seven Deadly Spins: Exposing the Lies Behind War Propaganda*. Monroe, Me.: Common Courage, 2004.

Zayani, Mohamed., ed. *The Al Jazeera Phenomenon: Critical Perspectives on New Arab Media*. Boulder, Co.: Paradigm, 2005.

Zinn, Howard. *Declarations of Independence: Cross-Examining American Ideology*. New York: Harper Perennial, 1990.

———. *Terrorism and War*. New York: Seven Stories, 2002.

Index

149-151, 166, 196, 201, 237, 239,
297
censorship, 45-47, 152-153, 159-160,
232, 235, 236, 245-246
Chalabi, Ahmed, 67
Chebab, Zaki, 111, 121, 199
Cheney, Dick, 62, 198, 300
Chicago American, 51
Chicago Sun Times, 51, 139, 204, 270-
271, 299
Chicago Tribune, 3, 15, 51, 58, 61, 64,
93, 101-102, 110-111, 121, 135,
197, 204, 309
Chomsky, Noam, 16, 18, 44, 63, 164,
224, 272, 287-294
civil war (Iraq), 120-127
CNN, 3, 10, 13-14, 17, 28-29, 44, 48-
50, 60, 64, 77, 79, 83-84, 86-87,
91, 116, 136, 142-143, 146, 166,
181, 189, 194, 197, 239, 242-243,
254, 263, 266, 286, 295 298, 308
CNN International, 42, 143, 181, 183
Coalition Provisional Authority, 85,
105, 113, 221, 227
Cockburn, Patrick, 5, 111, 116-117,
126, 218, 229, 293
Cohen, Bernard, 8
Cohen, Elliot, 311
Cohen, Jeff, 22, 147
Colbert, Stephen, 138-139
collateral damage, 187-195
Colmes, Alan, 44, 91
Common Dreams, 3, 112, 124, 229
Cooper, Anderson, 79
Copps, Michael, 312-313
corporations (media), 1-3, 14-16, 18-
20, 24-25, 49-53, 307-317
Coulter, Anne, 46, 87
Counter Punch, 102
Couric, Katie, 11
Covert Action Quarterly, 110
Coyer, Kate, 1-2
Cromwell, David, 51, 53
Cronkite, Walter, 40, 308-309
Crossfire, 136
Crouteau, David, 32

Daily Mirror (UK), 226, 244
Daily Show, 138
Dana, Mazen, 218-219
Dearing, James, 8, 16
DeJong, Wilma, 1

Democracy Now!, 26, 223-224, 229
Detroit Free Press, 15
Deyong, Karen, 73
Disney, 152-153
dissent, 135-153
Dobbs, Lou, 83, 85, 145
Donahue, Phil, 143, 147, 162
doublethink, 159-174
Dowd, Maureen, 90
Downing Street Memo, 57-61
Duelfer Report, 72
Dunphy, Jack, 44

Edwards, David, 51, 53
Ehrenreich, Barbara, 44
Ekeus, Rolf, 71
ElBaradei, Mohammad, 65, 71
El-Nawawy, Mohammed, 240
Ellsberg, Daniel, 225
embedding, 219, 231, 236-238, 272
Enders, David, 6, 218, 221, 245
Entman, Robert, 23
Erlich, Reese, 23
Extra!, 25, 229

Fahrenheit 9/11, 152-153
Falluja, 101-105, 112-113, 118,
167, 185, 189, 194-195, 220, 223,
226, 230-231, 239, 242
Fairness and Accuracy in Reporting
(FAIR), 22, 48, 60-61, 142, 147, 198,
314, 316
fairness doctrine, 314
Federal Communications Commission
(FCC), 6, 310-314, 317
filtering, 42
Fisk, Robert, 5, 218, 222, 227-229,
232, 265
fluff news, 49-50
Fox News, 3, 14, 17, 28-29, 40, 44,
48-49, 60, 77, 84-87, 91, 93, 115,
140, 142, 144-145, 148, 151, 164,
183, 194, 233, 236, 239, 243, 269,
285, 294
framing, 2, 21-24, 40-45, 83, 201
Friedman, Thomas, 82, 88-89, 141

Gannett, 15
Gerbner, George, 9
Getler, Michael, 60, 139-140
Gibson, Charles, 11
Glantz, Aaron, 6, 218, 220, 222

Bibliography

Achcar, Gilbert. *The Clash of the Barbarisms: September 11 and the Making of the New World Order*. New York: Monthly Review, 2002.

Alger, Dean. *Megamedia: How Giant Corporations Dominate Mass Media, Distort Competition, and Endanger Democracy*. Lanham, Md.: Rowman & Littlefield, 1998.

Ali, Tariq, and David Barsamian. *Speaking of Empire and Resistance: Conversations with Tariq Ali*. London: New Press, 2005.

Anderson, Bonnie. *News Flash: Journalism, Infotainment, and the Bottom-Line Business of Broadcast News*. San Francisco: Wiley & Sons, 2004.

Bagdikian, Ben H. *The New Media Monopoly*. Boston: Beacon, 2004.

Baker, C. Edwin. *Advertising and a Democratic Press*. Princeton, NJ.: Princeton, 1994.

Baldasty, Gerald J. *The Commercialization of the News in the Nineteenth Century*. Madison, Wi.: University of Wisconsin, 1992. Bennett, W. Lance, and David L. Paletz. *Taken By Storm: The Media, Public Opinion, and U.S. Foreign Policy in the Gulf War*. Chicago: University of Chicago, 1994.

Barsamian, David., ed. *Stenographers to Power: Media & Propaganda*. Monroe, Me.: Common Courage, 1992.

Bennett, W. Lance, and David L. Paletz., eds. *Taken by Storm: The Media, Public Opinion, and U.S. Foreign Policy in the Gulf War*. Chicago: University of Chicago, 1994.

Bernays, Edward. *Propaganda*. New York: IG, 2005.

Blum, William. *Killing Hope: U.S. Military and CIA Interventions Since World War II*. Monroe, Me.: Common Courage, 1995.

Boggs, Carl., ed. *Masters of War: Militarism and Blowback in the Era of American Empire*. New York: Routledge, 2003.

Borjesson, Kristina., ed. *Feet to the Fire: The Media After 9/11*. New York: Prometheus, 2005.

Bozell, Brent L. *Weapons of Mass Distortion: The Coming Meltdown of the Liberal Media*. New York: Crown, 2004.

Burke, Jason. *Al Qaeda: The True Story of Radical Islam*. London: I.B. Tauris, 2004.

Chebab, Zaki. *Inside the Resistance: The Iraqi Insurgency and the Future of the Middle East*. New York: Nation, 2005.

Chomsky, Noam. *Necessary Illusions: Thought Control in Democratic Societies*. Boston: South End, 1989.

———. *9/11*. New York: Seven Stories, 2002.

———. *Failed States: The Abuse of Power and the Assault on Democracy*. New York: Metropolitan, 2006.

Chomsky, Noam, and David Barsamian. *Imperial Ambitions: Conversations on the Post 9/11 World*. New York: Metropolitan, 2005.

Clarke, Richard. *Against All Enemies*. New York: Free Press, 2004.

Cohen, Bernard C. *The Press and Foreign Policy*. Berkley, Ca.: University of California, 1993.

Cohen, Elliot D. *News Incorporated: Corporate Media Ownership and its Threat to Democracy*. Amherst, NY: Prometheus, 2005.

Cohen, Jeff. *Cable News Confidential: My Misadventures in Corporate Media*. Sausalito, Ca.: PoliPoint, 2006.

Coulter, Anne. *Slander: Liberal Lies About the American Right*. New York: Crown, 2002.

———. *Treason: Liberal Treachery From the Cold War to the War on Terrorism*. New York: Crown, 2003.

Crick, Bernard. *George Orwell: A Life*. London: Secker and Warburg, 1980.

Cromwell, David, and David Edwards. *Guardians of Power: The Myth of the Liberal Media*. London: Pluto, 2006.

Crothers, Lane, and Charles Lockhart., eds. *Culture and Politics: A Reader*. New York: St. Martins, 2000.

Crouteau, David, and William Hoynes. *By Invitation Only: How the Media Limit Political Debate*. Monroe, Me.: Common Courage, 1994.

Cummings, Bruce, Ervand Abrahamian, and Moshe Ma'oz. *Inventing the Axis of Evil: The Truth About North Korea, Iran, and Syria*. New York: New Press, 2004.

De Jong, Wilma, Martin Shaw, and Neil Stammers., eds. *Global Activism, Global Media*. Ann Arbor, Mi: Pluto, 2005.

Dearing, James W., and Everett M. Rogers. *Agenda Setting*. London: Sage, 1996.

El-Nawawy, Mohammed, and Adel Iskandar. *Al Jazeera: The Story of the Network That is Rattling Governments and Redefining Modern Journalism*. Cambridge: Westview, 2003.

Enders, David. *Baghdad Bulletin: Dispatches on the American Occupation*. Ann Arbor: Mi.: University of Michigan, 2005.

Entman, Robert. *Projections of Power: Framing News, Public Opinion, and U.S. Foreign Policy*. Chicago: University of Chicago, 2004.

Foerstel, Lenora., ed. *War Lies, & Videotape: How Media Monopoly Stifles Truth*. New York: IAC, 2000.

Glantz, Aaron. *How America Lost Iraq*. New York: Penguin, 2005.

Glasgow Media Group. *Really Bad News*. New York: Writers and Readers, 1982.

Goldberg, Bernard. *Arrogance: Rescuing America from the Media Elite*. New York: Warner, 2003.

Goodman, Amy. *Exception to the Rulers: Exposing Oil Politicians, War Profiteers, and the Media That Love Them*. New York: Hyperion, 2004.

Hannity, Sean. *Let Freedom Ring: Winning the War of Liberty Over Liberalism*. New York: Regan, 2002.

Herman, Edward, and Noam Chomsky. *Manufacturing Consent: The Political Economy of the Mass Media*. New York: Pantheon, 1988.

Herman, Edward. *The Myth of the Liberal Media: An Edward Herman Reader*. New York: Peter Lang, 1999.

Hersh, Seymour. *Chain of Command: The Road from 9/11 to Abu Ghraib*. New York: Harper Perennial, 2005.

Hitchens, Christopher. *Why Orwell Matters*. New York: Basic, 2002.

Hoynes, William. *Public Television for Sale: Media, the Market, and the Public Sphere*. Boulder, Co.: Westview, 1994.

Iyengar, Shanto, and Donald R. Kinder. *News That Matters: Television and American Opinion.* Chicago: University of Chicago, 1987.

Iyengar, Shanto. *Is Anyone Responsible? How Television Frames Political Issues.* Chicago: University of Chicago, 1991.

Johnson, Chalmers. *The Sorrows of Empire: Militarism, Secrecy, and the End of the Republic.* New York: Henry Holt, 2004.

Johnson, Chris, and Jolyon Leslie. *Afghanistan: The Mirage of Peace.* London: Zed, 2004.

Khalidi, Rashid. *Resurrecting Empire: Western Footprints and America's Perilous Path in the Middle East.* Boston: Beacon, 2003.

Lindblom, Charles. *Politics and Markets: The World's Political Economic Systems.* New York: Basic, 1977.

Lippmann, Walter. *Public Opinion.* New York: Free Press, 1997.

Lutz, William., ed. *Beyond Nineteen Eighty-Four: Doublespeak in a Post-Orwellian Age.* Urbana, Il.: National Council of Teachers of English, 1989.

Macarthur, John R. *Second Front: Censorship and Propaganda in the Gulf War.* Berkley, Ca.: University of California, 1993.

McChesney, Robert. *Rich Media, Poor Democracy: Communication Politics in Dubious Times.* New York: New Press, 1999.

———. *The Problem of the Media: U.S. Communication Politics in the 21st Century.* New York: Monthly Review, 2004.

McChesney, Robert, Russell Newman, and Ben Scott., eds. *The Future of Media: Resistance and Reform in the 21st Century.* New York: Seven Stories, 2005.

McCombs, Maxwell, and David L. Protess., eds. *Agenda Setting: Readings on Media, Public Opinion, and Policymaking.* Mahway, NJ: Lawrence Erlbaum, 1991.

McManus, John H. *Market-Driven Journalism: Let the Citizen Beware?* Thousand Oaks, Ca.: Sage, 1994.

Mermin, Jonathon. *Debating War and Peace: Media Coverage of U.S. Intervention in the Post-Vietnam Era.* Princeton, NJ: Princeton, 1999.

Meyers, Jeffrey. *Orwell: A Wintry Conscience of a Generation.* New York: W. W. Norton, 2000.

Miles, Hugh. *Al Jazeera: The Inside Story of the Arab News Channel That is Challenging the West.* New York: Grove, 2005.

Miller, David., ed. *Tell Me Lies: Propaganda and Media Distortion in the Attack on Iraq.* London: Pluto, 2004.

Nassar, Jamal. *Globalization and Terrorism: The Migration of Dreams and Nightmares.* Lanham, Md.: Rowman and Littlefield, 2004

Nichols, John, and Robert W. McChesney. *Tragedy & Farce: How the American Media Sell Wars, Spin Elections, and Destroy Democracy.* New York: New Press, 2006.

Orwell, George. *A Collection of Essays by George Orwell.* New York: Doubleday, 1954.

———. *Animal Farm: A Fairy Story.* New York: Harcourt Brace, 1995.

Orwell, Sonia, and Ian Angus. *The Collected Essays, Journalism, and Letters of George Orwell: 1945-1950, Vol. 4.* New York: Hancourt, Brace, & World, 1968.

Page, Benjamin I. *Who Deliberates? Mass Media in Modern Democracy.* Chicago: University of Chicago, 1996.

Parenti, Christian. *The Freedom: Shadows and Hallucinations in Occupied Iraq.* New York: Free Press, 2004.

Parenti, Michael. *Inventing Reality: The Politics of News Media.* New York: St. Martins, 1993.

———. *Against Empire.* San Francisco: City Lights, 1995.

———. *America Besieged.* San Francisco: City Lights, 1998.

Perse, Elizabeth M. *Media Effects and Society*. Mahway, NJ: Lawrence Erlbaum, 2001.

Pitt, William Rivers, and Scott Ritter. *War on Iraq: What Team Bush Doesn't Want You to Know*. New York: Context, 2002.

Rampton, Sheldon, and John Stauber. *The Best War Ever: Lies, Damned Lies, and the Mess in Iraq*. New York: Jeremy Tarcher, 2006.

Risen, James. *State of War: The Secret History of the CIA and the Bush Administration*. New York: Free Press, 2006.

Ritter, Scott. *Frontier Justice: Weapons of Mass Destruction and the Bushwhacking of America*. New York: Context, 2003.

Roberts, Gene., ed. *Leaving Readers Behind: The Age of Corporate Newspapering*. Fayetteville, Ak.: University of Arkansas, 2001.

Rogers, Paul. *A War on Terror: Afghanistan and After*. London: Pluto, 2004.

Soley, Lawrence. *Censorship Inc. The Corporate Threat to Free Speech in the United States*. New York: Monthly Review, 2002.

Solomon, Norman. *War Made Easy: How Presidents and Pundits Keep Spinning us to Death*. Hoboken, NJ: Wiley & Sons, 2005.

Sparrow, Bartholomew H. *Uncertain Guardians: The News Media as a Political Institution*. Baltimore: Johns Hopkins, 1999.

Squires, James D. *Read All About It! The Corporate Takeover of America's Newspapers*. New York: Times, 1993.

Z, Mickey. *The Seven Deadly Spins: Exposing the Lies Behind War Propaganda*. Monroe, Me.: Common Courage, 2004.

Zayani, Mohamed., ed. *The Al Jazeera Phenomenon: Critical Perspectives on New Arab Media*. Boulder, Co.: Paradigm, 2005.

Zinn, Howard. *Declarations of Independence: Cross-Examining American Ideology*. New York: Harper Perennial, 1990.

———. *Terrorism and War*. New York: Seven Stories, 2002.

Index

Glasgow University Media Group, 42
globalization, 1, 19, 88
Goldberg, Bernard, 86
Goodman, Amy, 6, 26, 44, 223-224
Gross, Larry, 9
Guardian (UK), 5, 45, 52, 85, 126, 186,
  218, 221-222, 226-227,229, 232,
  273, 300
Gulf War (1991), 41, 108, 192, 225,
  236, 272
Gupta, AK, 124

Hannity, Sean, 44, 86
Hanson, Victor Davis, 108
Hayden, Tom, 124
Hearst, Randolph, 40
Hedges, Chris, 77, 190, 236
Herbert, Bob, 59, 89-90
Herman, Edward, 18, 44, 48, 126-127,
  204, 273, 287-294
Herold, Marc, 193, 273
Hersh, Seymour, 197, 279, 283
Hitchens, Christopher, 145, 160-161
Hoagland, Jim, 110
Horowitz, David, 142
Houston Chronicle, 15, 204
Hoynes, William, 32
Human Rights (Iraq), 179-208
Human Rights Watch, 196, 199, 260,
  268
Hume, Brit, 44, 142

Ignatius, David, 91, 172
Il, Kim Jong, 294-297, 299
imperialism, 84, 89-91, 93, 141, 159-
  174
Independent (UK), 5, 45, 52, 60, 111,
  117, 135, 182, 186, 204, 217, 219,
  221, 226-228, 232, 265, 293-294
indexing, 19, 24, 93-94, 217
indoctrination, 32
Indymedia, 1-2
Insurgents (Iraqi), 101-120, 179-180,
  188, 191, 193, 197, 204, 220-221
International Atomic Energy Agency,
  63, 284-285
internet news, 17-18
In These Times (magazine), 3, 25, 224,
  229, 264, 316
International Herald Tribune, 246
international law, 45, 57, 62-63, 85,
  137-138, 146, 292

International Socialist Review, 25
invasion (Iraq), 78-82, 120, 193, 241
Iran, 283-294
Iraq, 26-33, 57-74, 77-94, 101-127,
  179-208
Iraq Body Count, 184-195, 227
Iraqi Media Network, 42
Iraqi National Congress, 67
Iskandar, Adel, 240
Islamism, 106-107, 115-118, 147, 188,
  198, 222, 258-260, 263
Iyengar, Shanto, 9, 42-43

Jaafari, Ibrahim al-, 181
Jamail, Dahr, 6, 218, 223
Jennings, Peter, 85
Johnson, Chalmers, 84

Kagan, Daryn, 136, 242
Karzai, Hamid, 254, 258
Kelley, Jack, 13, 253
Kevin, Tony, 231-232
Khader, Samir, 232, 233
Kinder, Donald, 9, 43
Kindy, Kliff, 183, 195-196, 206-207
Kinsley, Michael, 60
Klare, Michael, 79
Knight Ridder, 16, 65, 74
Koppel, Ted, 46-47
Krauthammer, Charles, 105, 144, 255,
  269, 285
Kristof, Nicholas, 81, 90, 295
Krugman, Paul, 59, 90

Lancet reports, 184-187
Landay, Jonathan, 65
Lehrer, Jim, 142
Left Hook, 116
Limbaugh, Rush, 87, 144
Lindblom, Charles, 32
Los Angeles Times, 3, 15, 52, 66, 71,
  79, 85-86, 101, 104, 108, 117, 142,
  167, 185, 189, 194, 197, 204, 263,
  268-269, 284-285, 288-290, 292-
  294, 309-310
Lynch, Jessica, 182-183

MacArthur, John, 41
Mahajan, Rahul, 6, 219, 223
Mahdi Army, 126
Maliki, Nouri al-, 181
mass media, 20-21

Massing, Michael, 65
McBride, Allen, 9-10
McCain, 60, 151
McChesney, Robert, 43, 49, 151, 189, 315
McClellan, Scott, 135-136, 244
McCombs, Maxwell, 8
McGeough, Paul, 6, 230-231
media effects, 7-33, 39-42
Mermin, Jonathon, 23
Miles, Hugh, 235-236, 239
Miller, Judith, 66-68
Moore, Michael, 145, 152-153, 162
MSNBC, 14, 22, 49, 60, 77, 106, 117, 140, 143, 147-148, 308
Multinational Monitor, 25, 229
Murdoch, Rupert, 40, 44

Nader, Ralph, 45
Nation (magazine), 3, 25, 192, 223, 229
National Guard (scandal), 149-150
National Review, 44, 111, 144, 240, 296-297
nationalism (and media), 135-153
New Republic, 3, 79, 82, 92, 108, 141, 170, 188, 282
Newsday, 125, 183, 204
Newsweek, 8, 22, 25, 83, 110, 115, 122-123, 135-138, 167, 182, 230, 272
Newsweek Koran (scandal), 135-138, 162
New Standard, 225, 229, 316
New York Daily News, 15, 266
New York Post, 15
New York Times, 3-4, 10, 13-16, 22, 39-40, 45, 47-48, 52, 58-59, 62, 65-74, 77-92, 94, 101-103, 105-106, 108, 110, 115, 121, 125, 135, 140, 142, 149, 153, 167 169, 172-173, 181, 183, 185, 188, 190, 193-194, 196-201, 204, 226, 236, 242, 254, 263, 268-270, 284-285, 288-290, 292, 294-295, 299, 310
New Yorker, 196, 279, 283
NBC, 3, 11, 14, 20, 28-29, 48, 60, 64, 85, 121, 142, 147, 151, 239, 242
Natioanl Public Radio, 143
North Korea, 294-301
Northern Alliance, 261
Novak, Robert, 44, 88
Nuclear Posture Review, 279-280, 295

objectivity, 22, 47, 50, 53, 78
Observer (UK), 226
occupation (Iraq), 78-86, 106, 206
oil (Middle Eastern), 47, 79, 170-172, 202, 228, 230
Operation Enduring Freedom, 192
Operation Iraqi Freedom, 29, 86, 148
O Reilly, Bill, 44, 46, 86-87, 140, 147, 197, 233, 267
Orwell, George, 4, 159-174

Pacifica, 191, 220, 222, 229
pacifism, 142-143
Page, Benjamin, 32-33
Parenti, Christian, 203, 218, 222
Parenti, Michael, 9, 18, 44, 84
Public Broadcasting Service (PBS), 29, 48, 60, 142, 315
Peshmerga, 122
Phillips, Peter, 19
Program on International Policy Attitudes (PIPA), 28
Plame, Valerie, 66
political economy, 19, 41-42
Powell, Michael, 310-313
priming, 42
Progressive (magazine), 3, 25, 108, 223, 229, 316
Project for Excellence in Journalism, 14
Prometheus Radio Project, 314
propaganda, 2-3, 23-32, 47-49, 89
public opinion, 7-32, 39, 113-114, 205-208

Rather, Dan, 43, 46, 82, 141, 148-150, 265
reconstruction (Iraq), 201-204
Red Cross, 137, 194, 199
resistance (Iraq), 83-85, 101-120, 167, 195
Reuters, 16, 196, 204, 218, 231, 288
Rice, Condoleeza, 136, 146
Ricks, Thomas, 73, 80, 84
Ritter, Scott, 62, 64-65, 68, 71, 118, 194
Rivers, William, 42
Roberts, Gene, 308
Rogers, Everett, 8, 16
Rumsfeld, Donald, 71, 122, 125, 169-170, 202, 235, 240-241, 267, 271, 281, 285

About the Author

Anthony DiMaggio has taught Middle East Politics and American Government at Illinois State University. As an independent journalist, he has written over one hundred news stories and editorials on a variety of domestic and international issues, and regularly contributes to publications such as *Z Magazine* and *Counterpunch* . He has also appeared on national and local radio programs discussing Middle East Politics, Arabic language and culture, and mass media. His current research is focused on comparative news coverage in American and British media, as well as on American media coverage of social welfare issues such as public housing, education, and the minimum wage.